Plumbing Estimating Methods

Second Edition

Includes:
- ***Standard Plumbing & Fire Protection Systems***
- ***Special Systems Such As Medical Gas & Glass Piping***

Joseph J. Galeno and Sheldon T. Greene

RSMeans®

Plumbing Estimating Methods

Second Edition

Includes:

- *Standard Plumbing & Fire Protection Systems*
- *Special Systems Such As Medical Gas & Glass Piping*

Joseph J. Galeno and Sheldon T. Greene

R.S. Means Company, Inc.
Construction Publishers & Consultants
Construction Plaza
63 Smiths Lane
Kingston, MA 02364-0800
(781) 585-7880

The editors for this book were Mary Greene, manager, Reference Books; Marla Marek and Melville Mossman. The production manager was Michael Kokernak. The production coordinators were Marion Schofield and Wayne Anderson. The electronic publishing specialist was Michael Kokernak. The book and cover were designed by Norm Forgit.

Printed in the United States of America

10 9 8 7 6 5 4 3 2 1

Library of Congress Cataloging in Publication Data

ISBN 0-87629-536-7

ABOUT THE AUTHORS

Authors

Joseph J. Galeno, MBA, is Chief Executive Officer of Projex, Inc., a construction management firm in New York City. He has more than 30 years' experience in construction management, claims, cost engineering, and scheduling. His work has covered virtually all types of commercial, industrial, utility, institutional, and medical facilities in the public and private sectors. Mr. Galeno is the author of the *Plumbing Estimating Handbook* (Van Nostrand Reinhold, 1976) and of numerous articles on claims and other construction topics. He is a member of the American Association of Cost Engineers, the American Society of Sanitary Engineers, and the Building Contractors Association, and has served as a construction arbitrator for the American Arbitration Association.

Sheldon Greene, Senior Construction Consultant on plumbing/ mechanical estimating, construction management, and value engineering for Projex, Inc., has over 40 years' experience as a construction professional. His work has focused on managing projects in the areas of cost control, contract negotiations, and field supervision. He is a co-author of the *National Plumbing Estimator* (O.T.S., Inc. 1983), and of the *Building Cost File* (Construction Publishing Co., Inc., 1974). Mr. Greene serves as an arbitrator for the American Arbitration Association, is an Assistant Adjunct Professor at New York University, and is on the board of directors of the American Society of Sanitary Engineering. He is a member of the American Society of Plumbing Engineers, the American Society of Professional Estimators, the American Association of Cost Engineers, and the American Arbitration Association.

TABLE OF CONTENTS

PREFACE

The *Plumbing Estimating Handbook* was written to help readers become competent plumbing estimators. It should also serve as a valuable reference in fulfilling the everyday assignments of the job.

Unfortunately, an individual wishing to make estimating his career will find it difficult to locate colleges or technical schools that offer practical, comprehensive estimating programs. The courses that are offered usually lack depth and are intended only to show the future architect or engineer the role that estimating plays in the construction industry. There are many excellent reference manuals published today, but these books are, for the most part, written for the seasoned plumbing estimator rather than the beginner.

The obvious question then is: "How does one become a plumbing estimator?" The usual procedure consists of on-the-job training with a plumbing contractor or construction consultant. The estimator trainee is placed under the guidance of a senior estimator and taught the fundamentals of taking off and pricing a job. The problem with this method is that the training process is constantly interrupted by the everyday business of the firm. The education of an estimator trainee can become a long, tedious, and often costly effort for all concerned.

The book explains and illustrates plumbing estimating procedures on a step-by-step basis. It assumes a basic knowledge of plumbing systems and the ability to read architectural/engineering drawings. By the time the reader completes the last chapter, he will have the basic knowledge required to function as a competent plumbing estimator.

INTRODUCTION

The Second Edition of *Means Plumbing Estimating Methods* contains the same essential information on plumbing systems and estimating as the earlier edition, but now includes the authors' updated prices for square foot estimates, and Means latest union and non-union wage rates, and city and historical cost indexes. Also included is a greatly expanded Chapter 8, which provides a thorough explanation of how to utilize *Means Plumbing Cost Data* together with numerous sample pages from the latest edition. Sources of code information and price guides has also been completely updated.

Part I of the book, "The Plumbing System," provides an in-depth view of the materials, components, and subsystems that together form a plumbing system. The text, charts, and illustrations cover plumbing fixtures, piping systems, valves, pipe fittings, and equipment. This section also includes discussions on "thin wall" steel sprinkler piping, combination hubless DWV systems, Halon fire suppression systems, grooved pipe mechanical joint systems, and an expanded section on medical gases. Charts of standard symbols used by engineers on design drawings have been included in the Appendix.

Part II, "Plumbing Estimating," consists of Chapters 3 through 8, which deal exclusively with estimating, from the initial preparation stage to the completion of a final contract bid estimate. Included is a discussion of the estimating tools and reference manuals that are necessary and helpful. Sample takeoff and estimate forms are provided, along with step-by-step instructions on how to take off a plumbing job. There is also a sample takeoff, job specification, drawings, and an estimate. The estimate is based on comprehensive man-hour production tables for fixtures, devices, equipment and piping found in the Appendix, along with a chart showing the average prevailing hourly wage rates for plumbers in 30 major U.S. and Canadian cities.

It should be noted that all costs included in the sample takeoff and estimate in Chapters 5 and 6 are included only for use in illustrating plumbing estimating methods. They are not intended as a pricing reference for creating estimates. Regardless of the year or the project location, the procedures will be identical, the material and labor costs will vary geographically and productivity will vary according to the crew, supervision, and the plumbing contractor's efficient use of tools, manpower, and scheduling.

Chapter 6 discusses the various markups necessary to complete the estimate, along with the summary sheet for the sample job takeoff. Chapter 7 covers different methods and types of estimating, such as change order analysis, estimating for additions and alterations, budget estimating, and a systems approach to plumbing costs, as well as a section on computerized estimating systems. In Chapter 8, the proper use of *Means Plumbing Cost Data* is explained along with sample pages from the book.

Part 1

THE PLUMBING SYSTEM

Part 1

INTRODUCTION

The word *plumbing* is derived from the Latin word *plumbum*, meaning lead, which was the basic metal plumbers worked with until about sixty years ago. History tells us that plumbing was seen as a necessity by the earliest known ancient civilizations. However, plumbing as a complete system providing water for various needs such as bathing, drinking and waste removal, is a relatively new idea developed in the United States in the early part of the nineteenth century. One can define plumbing today as the system of piping and other apparatus for conveying water, liquid wastes, sewage, storm water, and certain special gases or liquids within or adjacent to any building. A complete plumbing system, much like a complete electrical system, consists of smaller subsystems and components.

The authors believe that before one can successfully estimate plumbing costs, one must have at least a working knowledge of what a plumbing system is and how it functions. Part I of this book is designed to convey that knowledge to less experienced plumbing estimators, and to serve as a review for those who are well versed in plumbing installations.

Part I consists of Chapter 1, which describes the basic materials and methods used in various subsystems, and Chapter 2, which covers individual subsystems and components that together form a complete plumbing system. Part II follows with six chapters detailing plumbing estimating procedures.

Chapter 1
BASIC MATERIALS AND METHODS

A plumbing system is composed of a number of smaller subsystems. Many of the same materials and methods are used to construct various subsystems. For example, copper tubing may be used in both a domestic water system and in medical gas systems. Excavation and backfill is used on both sanitary and storm systems, as well as water or gas systems. Familiarity with the basic systems and materials is essential to the plumbing estimator. Therefore, we begin with an in-depth discussion of this subject.

Pipe and Pipe Fittings for Interior Plumbing

Pipe is available in a wide variety of sizes and materials; the size depends on the characteristics and quantity of the substance to be conveyed, and the service requirements. We shall learn in Chapter 2 that service factors include the materials to be conveyed, hot or cold water, sanitary waste, storm water, natural gas, or acid waste. Pipe materials are also selected based on whether they will be used above or below grade, system pressure, external loads and problems of corrosion. Costs, too, are an important consideration.

Pipe is classified by its nominal size. Pipe materials are ferrous (containing iron), non-ferrous, and non-metallic. Examples of ferrous pipe are cast iron and black or galvanized steel. Brass and copper are commonly used non-ferrous materials. Non-metallic pipe materials include plastics and glass for use in building plumbing systems. For site work, pipe is also made of such other non-metallic materials as concrete and vitrified clay. The different types of pipe are categorized further into certain classes or schedules.

Pipe materials and sizes used for each type of plumbing subsystem will be described in Chapter 2. The next section will begin with piping terms, how pipes are joined, and pipe fittings.

Steel Pipe (Ferrous)

Steel pipe is manufactured as either black or galvanized (zinc-coated) with plain, threaded, or grooved ends, and can be purchased in random lengths up to 21′. The following grades of steel pipe are the most commonly used for plumbing and process systems.

1. Schedule 5 (Thin Wall)
2. Schedule 10 (Thin Wall)

3. Schedule 40 (Standard Weight)
4. Schedule 80 (Extra Strong)
5. Schedule 160 (Double Extra Strong)

These schedules are based on wall-thickness. Of the schedules mentioned, Schedule 40 threaded pipe is the one most commonly found in plumbing work. Although rather susceptible to corrosion, steel pipe is strong, comes in a wide range of sizes, and is less expensive in comparison to other metals used for similar applications.

Joints and Fittings

Although steel pipe may be welded using carbon steel weld fittings, this method is rarely used for plumbing installations other than large diameter gas lines. Tapered threads and grooved mechanical joints are the most common forms of joining steel pipe for plumbing and gas work.

A recent steel piping innovation that has gained industry-wide acceptance is **thin wall steel pipe** for use on sprinkler systems. Thin wall pipe provides the industry with a properly engineered lower cost alternative for use in fire protection applications. Further discussion on thin wall pipe can be found in Chapter 2 under Fire Protection Systems.

Pipe threading is done by manual or power-operated threading devices equipped with hard tempered steel dies. Dies are available in all size ranges necessary to produce tapered pipe threads. Threads are gauged according to standards set forth by the American Standards Association. Figure 1.1 illustrates a threaded joint.

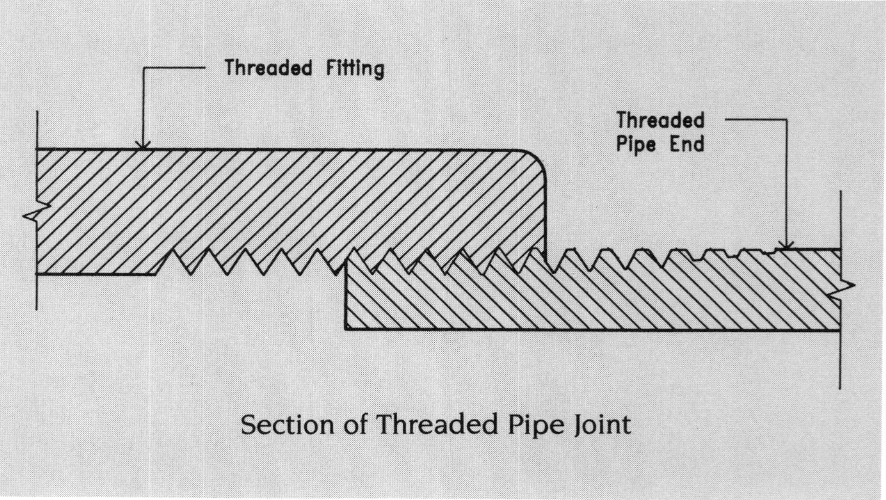

Section of Threaded Pipe Joint

Figure 1.1

In joining threaded pipe, the plumber first cleans the male threads of the pipe and the female threads of the fitting with a hard wire brush, then applies pipe joint compound to the male end. The pipe and fitting are then aligned and tightened by hand. Finally, the plumber completes the joint by tightening with a pipe wrench. In some systems Teflon tape is used in lieu of pipe joint compound.

Grooved mechanical joint piping systems have steadily gained in popularity in recent years. The system eliminates many of the time-consuming installation requirements used in welding, threading, and flanging pipe, thereby resulting in labor savings. Grooved mechanical joints combine the advantages of low cost installation, complete design integrity and simple, economic maintenance. This system and its associated fittings are used in the fire protection field, building service systems (i.e., storm and sanitary drains), potable, heating, cooling, and condenser water systems (not available for steam or gas piping). The fittings are designed for use with plain end, cut grooved, roll grooved or bevel end steel pipe (see Figure 1.2), and are available plain or galvanized finish. This kind of fitting is produced for use with lighter schedules of piping, as well as with standard weight (Schedule 40). The wide variety of sizes and configurations of grooved mechanical joint fittings allows a complete system to be assembled using only these fittings. Special tools are required for field or shop cutting, rolling of grooves, and drilling outlets in the pipe wall where hook-type or other mechanically joined outlets are substituted for tees or welded nozzles.

Depending on the particular service, fittings used to join steel pipe may be cast iron, malleable iron, and cast iron drainage pattern, all of which are available in black or galvanized. Pressure ratings indicate the recommended maximum basic pressure under which the fitting will properly function.

Where short pieces (1″ to 6″ long) of threaded pipe are required to connect fixtures and equipment, pipe nipples are used. Pipe nipples are manufactured in sizes ranging from 1/2″ to 12″. Pipe nipples longer than 12″ can be obtained on special order. Figure 1.3 illustrates typical threaded iron pipe fittings and nipples. See Figure 1.4 for a complete list of fittings in this category.

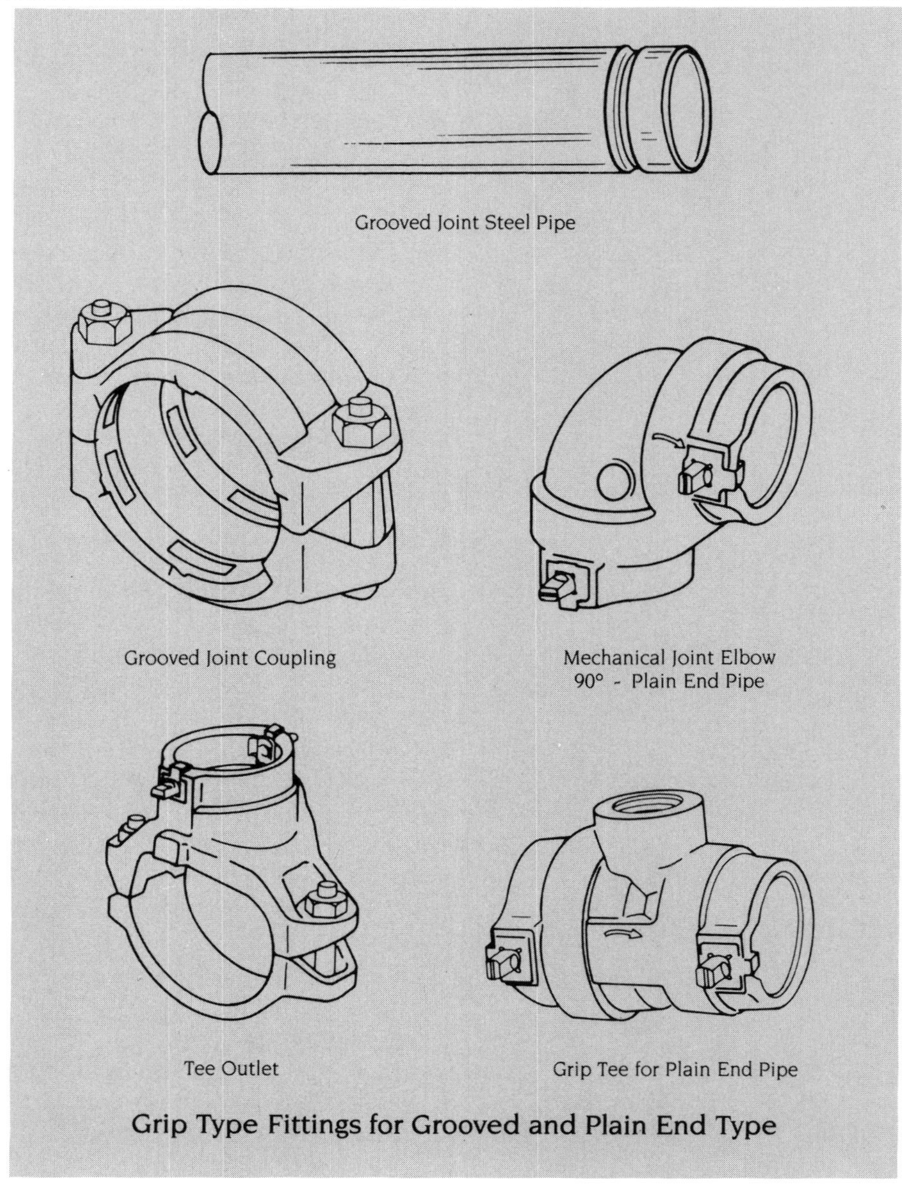
Grooved Joint Steel Pipe
Grooved Joint Coupling
Mechanical Joint Elbow
90° - Plain End Pipe
Tee Outlet
Grip Tee for Plain End Pipe
Grip Type Fittings for Grooved and Plain End Type

Figure 1.2

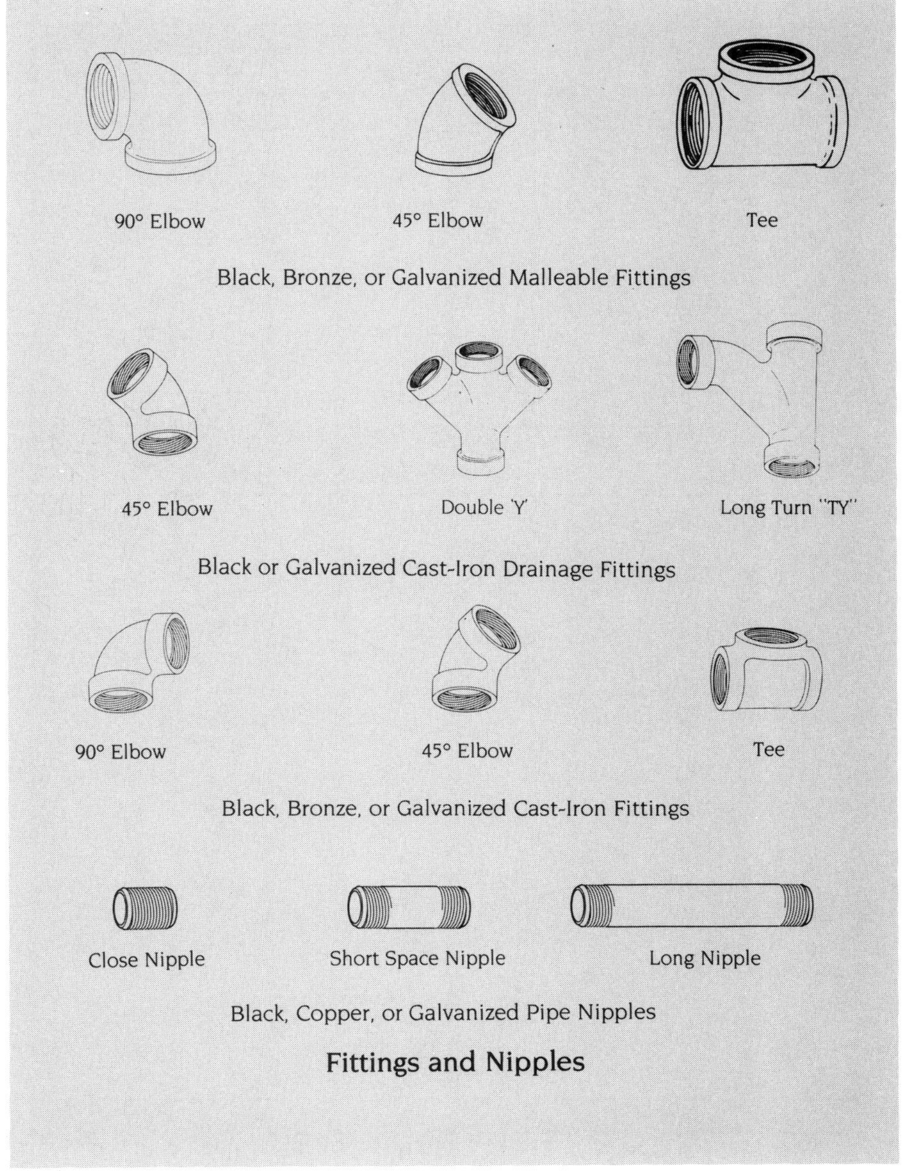
90° Elbow
45° Elbow
Tee
Black, Bronze, or Galvanized Malleable Fittings
45° Elbow
Double 'Y'
Long Turn "TY"
Black or Galvanized Cast-Iron Drainage Fittings
90° Elbow
45° Elbow
Tee
Black, Bronze, or Galvanized Cast-Iron Fittings
Close Nipple
Short Space Nipple
Long Nipple
Black, Copper, or Galvanized Pipe Nipples
Fittings and Nipples

Figure 1.3

MANUFACTURED BLACK OR GALVANIZED MALLEABLE IRON FITTINGS (THREADED) (1/8″ TO 12″ PIPE DIAMETER)	
90° Elbows	Return Bends
90° Reducing Elbows	Side Outlet Elbows
90° Street Elbows	Female Drop Elbows
90° Reducing Street Elbows	Side Outlet T
45° Elbows	Couplings
45° Street Elbows	Caps, Plugs
T's	Street T's
Reducing T's	Reducing Street T's
Crosses	'Y' Branches
Unions	

MANUFACTURED BLACK OR GALVANIZED CAST-IRON DRAINAGE FITTINGS (THREADED) (1½″ TO 12″ PIPE DIAMETER)	
90° Short Turn Elbows	Short Turn 'TY's
90° Short Turn Reducing Elbows	Long Turn 'TY's
90° Long Turn Elbows	Reducing Short Turn 'TY's
45° Long Turn Elbows	Reducing Long Turn 'TY's
45° Short Turn Elbows	Short Turn Double 'TY's
90° Extra Long Turn Elbows	Long Turn Double 'TY's
60° Elbows	Reducing Short Turn Double 'TY's
Three-Way Elbows	Reducing Long Turn Double 'TY's
22½° Elbows	45° 'Y' Branches
Three-Way Reducing Elbows	45° Reducing 'Y' Branches
11¼° Elbows	45° Reducing Double 'Y' Branches
90° Elbows w/2″ Side Outlet	60° 'Y' Branches
90° Elbows w/2″ Heel Outlet	'P' Traps
90° Street Elbows	60° Reducing 'Y' Branches
45° Degree Street Elbows	Running Traps
Basin T's	Bath 'P' Traps
Hub Roof Connections	'S' Traps
T's	Half 'S' Traps
Increasers	Tucker Connections
Couplings	
Reducing T's	

MANUFACTURED BRONZE THREADED, CAST-IRON THREADED, PLASTIC, SOLDER JOINT AND BRAZED FITTINGS (1/8″ TO 12″ PIPE DIAMETER)	
90° Elbows	Couplings
90° Elbows (Reducing)	Couplings (Reducing)
90° Elbows (Long Turn)	45° 'Y' Branches
45° Elbows	45° 'Y' Branches (Reducing)
90° Elbows (Street)	Return Bends
T's	Adapters
T's (Reducing)	Caps
Crosses	Plugs
Crosses (Reducing)	Bushings
Unions	

Figure 1.4

Ductile Iron Water Pipe (Ferrous)

Ductile iron water pipe is a steel-iron alloy, manufactured with flanged, mechanical or push-on joints, and can be purchased in 18' lengths. The class of pipe can be specified by pressure or by wall thickness. Pressure classes are 50, 100, 150, 200, 250, 300, and 350 psi, the pressure under which the particular class of pipe is designed to operate.

Pipe wall thickness classes for ductile iron pipe are 50, 51, 52, 53, 54, and 56. A cement lining for the inside walls of the pipe is available for use in locations where soft water could cause an encrusting condition called *tuberculation*. Ductile iron offers excellent resistance to corrosion, and resists physical damage during backfill operations or other stressful occurrences.

Joints and Fittings

Flanged joints on ductile iron water pipe are made by threading flanges onto threaded pipe ends. A rubber or special application face gasket is placed between the two flanges to be joined, which are then bolted together (see Figures 1.5 and 1.6).

Push-on joints are compression-type joints with rubber or neoprene gaskets which are inserted into the hub or bell end of the pipe (see Figure 1.5). A special joining tool is used to slip the spigot or plain end of the pipe into the bell end. Push-on joints allow speedy, low-cost installation. Push-on fittings are manufactured with bell ends.

A mechanical joint is actually a cross between a flanged and a push-on joint. The bell end of the pipe is cast with a flange facing; the spigot end of the pipe section to be joined is inserted into the bell end with a rubber ring gasket and an outer ductile iron retainer gland. When this operation is complete, the two sections are bolted together. (See Figure 1.5) Bell-end mechanical joint fittings are available in a variety of patterns. See Figure 1.6 for a complete list of fittings in this category.

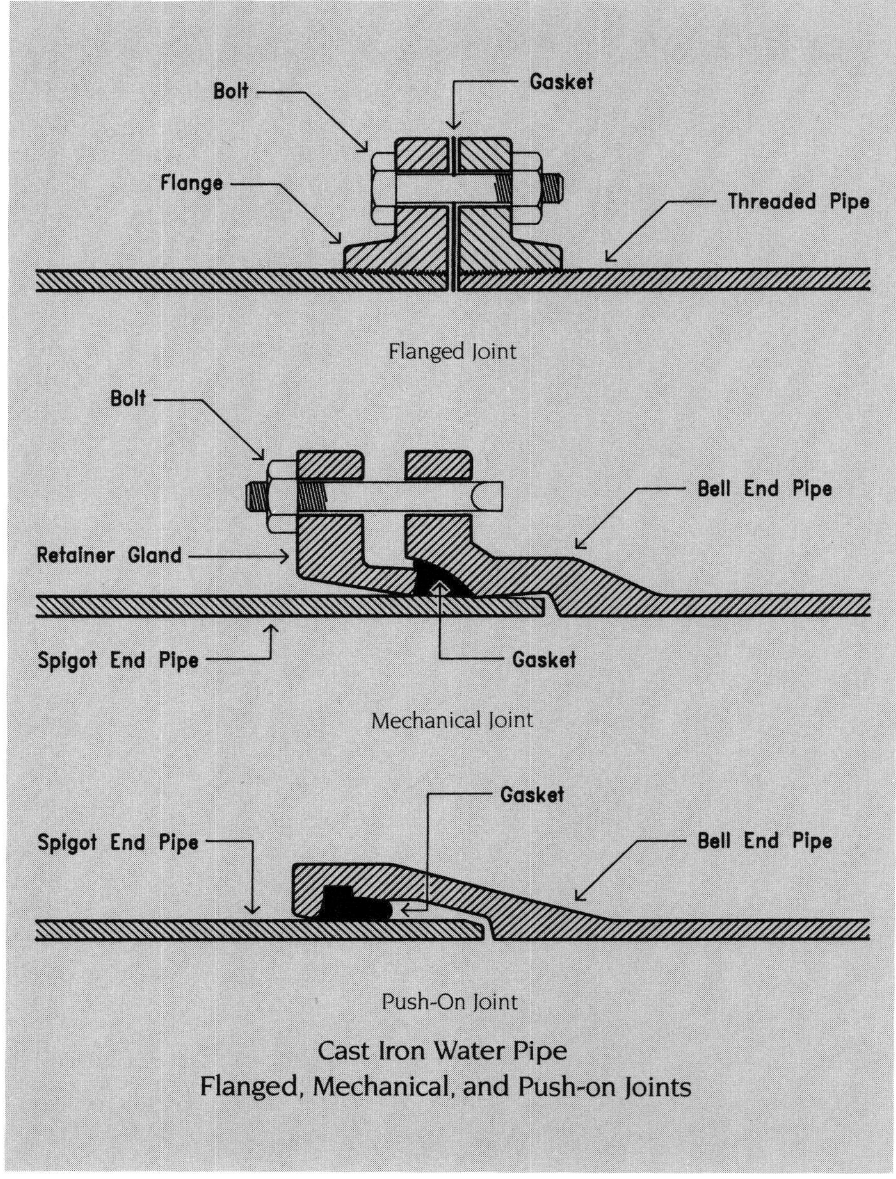

Cast Iron Water Pipe
Flanged, Mechanical, and Push-on Joints

Figure 1.5

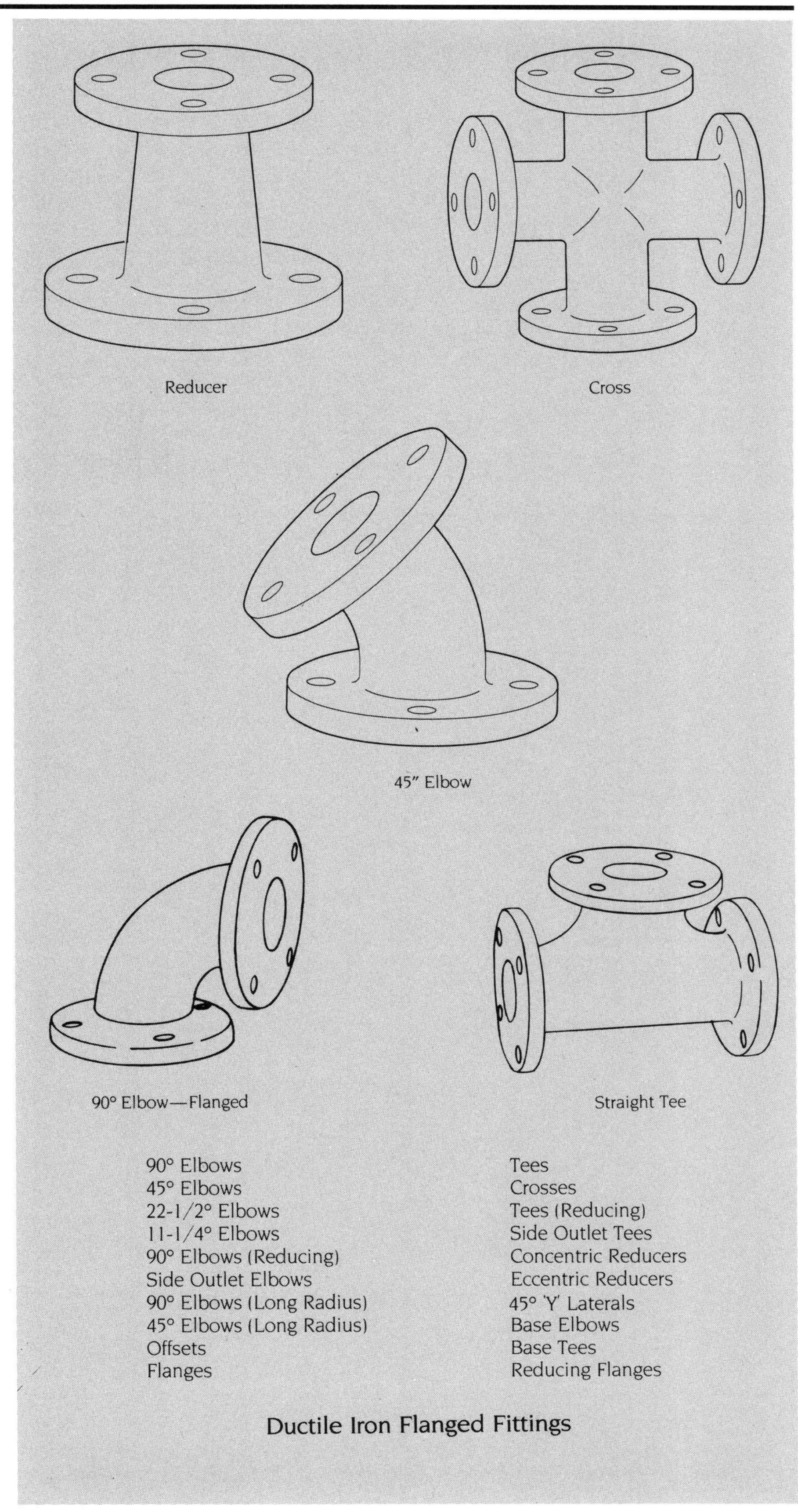

Ductile Iron Flanged Fittings

Figure 1.6

Cast Iron Soil Pipe (Ferrous)

Cast iron soil pipe is manufactured in 5′ and 10′ lengths and is available as either *service*, or *extra-heavy weight*, depending on the pipe-wall thickness. Joints are either lead and oakum (caulked), push-on, or clamp joint (hubless). Cast iron soil pipe offers excellent resistance to corrosion, to hydrogen sulphide gas action (an oxidation process creating sulphuric acid which can damage piping), and to abrasion from sand and gravel particles. (See Figure 1.7 for a list of soil pipe fittings.)

Joints and Fittings

The lead and oakum or caulked joint is made with molten lead and oakum packing. (See Figure 1.8.) The spigot end of the pipe or fitting is inserted into the bell end of the pipe or fitting to be joined. The oakum packing is then inserted in the bell with a caulking tool, followed by molten lead poured over the oakum. After the lead has cooled, it is driven into the joint with a caulking tool, and a tight, leakproof joint is formed.

MANUFACTURED C.I. SOIL PIPE FITTINGS
(BELL & SPIGOT LEAD OR PUSH-ON JOINTS) (2″ TO 15″ PIPE DIAMETER)

Increasers
Quarter Bends
Fifth Bends
Sixth Bends
Eighth Bends
Sixteenth Bends
Quarter Bend w/Heel Inlet
Quarter Bend w/Inlet
Long Quarter Bend
Long Eighth Bend
Short Sweep
Long Sweep
Long Sweep (Reducing)
Long Sweep (Increasing)
Double Quarter Bend
Double Hub Quarter Bend
Double Hub Eighth Bend
Double Spigot Quarter Bend
Long Double Spigot Quarter Bend
T
Sanitary T
Inverted 'Y'
T w/Inlet
Sanitary Tee w/Inlet
'Y' w/Inlet
Sleeves
Traps
T w/Brass Cleanout
Fresh Air Inlet
Reducing 'Y'
Combination 'Y' & Eighth Bend
Sanitary Cross
Long Sanitary Cross
Double 'Y'
'Y'
Cross w/Brass Cleanout
Upright 'Y'
Tapped T
Tapped Sanitary T
Tapped 'Y'
Long Tapped T
Reducing Sanitary Cross
Double Comb. 'Y' & Eighth Bend
Closet Fittings
Tapped Cross
Sanitary T w/Brass Cleanout
'Y' w/Brass Cleanout
'Y' & ⅛ Bend w/Brass Cleanout
Offsets
Plugs
Reducers
Iron Body Cleanouts

MANUFACTURED HUBLESS C.I. SOIL PIPE FITTINGS
(CLAMP JOINT) (1½″ TO 6″ PIPE DIAMETER)

Quarter Bends
Fifth Bends
Sixth Bends
Eighth Bends
Sixteenth Bends
Quarter Bends w/2″ Heel Outlet
Quarter Bends w/2″ Side Outlet
Double Quarter Bend
Tapped Quarter Bends
Short Sweeps
Long Sweeps
Long Quarter Bends
Long Eighth Bends
Sanitary T's
Sanitary T's w/2″ Side Outlet
San. Tees w/2″ Inlet Both Sides
Sanitary T's w/2″ 90° Inlet R&L Above Center
Sanitary T's w/2″ 45° Inlet Above Center
Sanitary Tap T's
Double Vertical San. Tap T's
Sanitary Tap T's w/90° Side Tap
'Y's
Upright 'Y's
Double 'Y's
Tapped 'Y's
Comb. 'Y' & Eighth Bend
Double Comb. 'Y' & Eighth Bends
Sanitary Crosses
Sanitary Tapped Crosses
'P' Traps
Reducers
Increasers
Plugs
Hub Adapters
Test T's
Ferrules

Figure 1.7

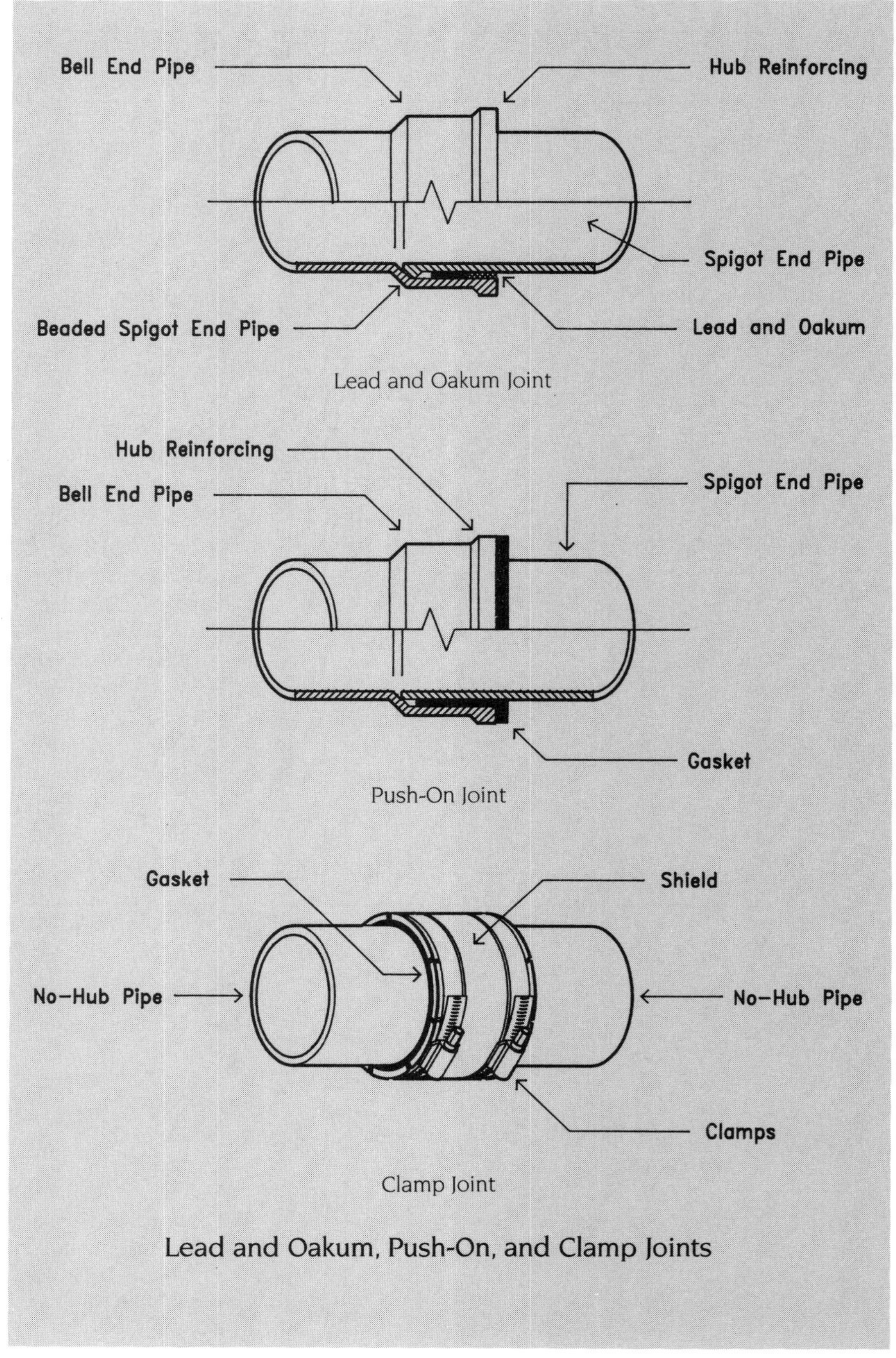

Lead and Oakum, Push-On, and Clamp Joints

Figure 1.8

The push-on joint is a compression joint similar in principle to that previously described for ductile iron water pipe (See Figure 1.5).

The clamp or hubless joint is a relatively new innovation for cast iron soil pipe and fittings (See Figure 1.8). The clamp joint is made by inserting a neoprene gasket around the hubless pipe and fitting joint, after which a stainless steel shield is placed around the gasket and tightened with two stainless steel bands.

Cast iron soil pipe fittings (Figure 1.9) are manufactured in a wide variety of design patterns for all three types of joints mentioned above (See Figure 1.8). See Figure 1.7 for a list of fittings in this category.

A recent innovation in hubless soil pipe systems is the combination hubless DWV system. The system, as designed, utilizes ordinary hubless pipe, fittings, and couplings along with multi-outlet and other special purpose fittings (see Figure 1.10). Various roughing combinations can be fabricated off-site or at the point of installation, with no wasted joints or space. Since the system is mainly designed to be fabricated off-site, the plumbing contractor can expect a better installation with few delays (such as those caused by inclement weather).

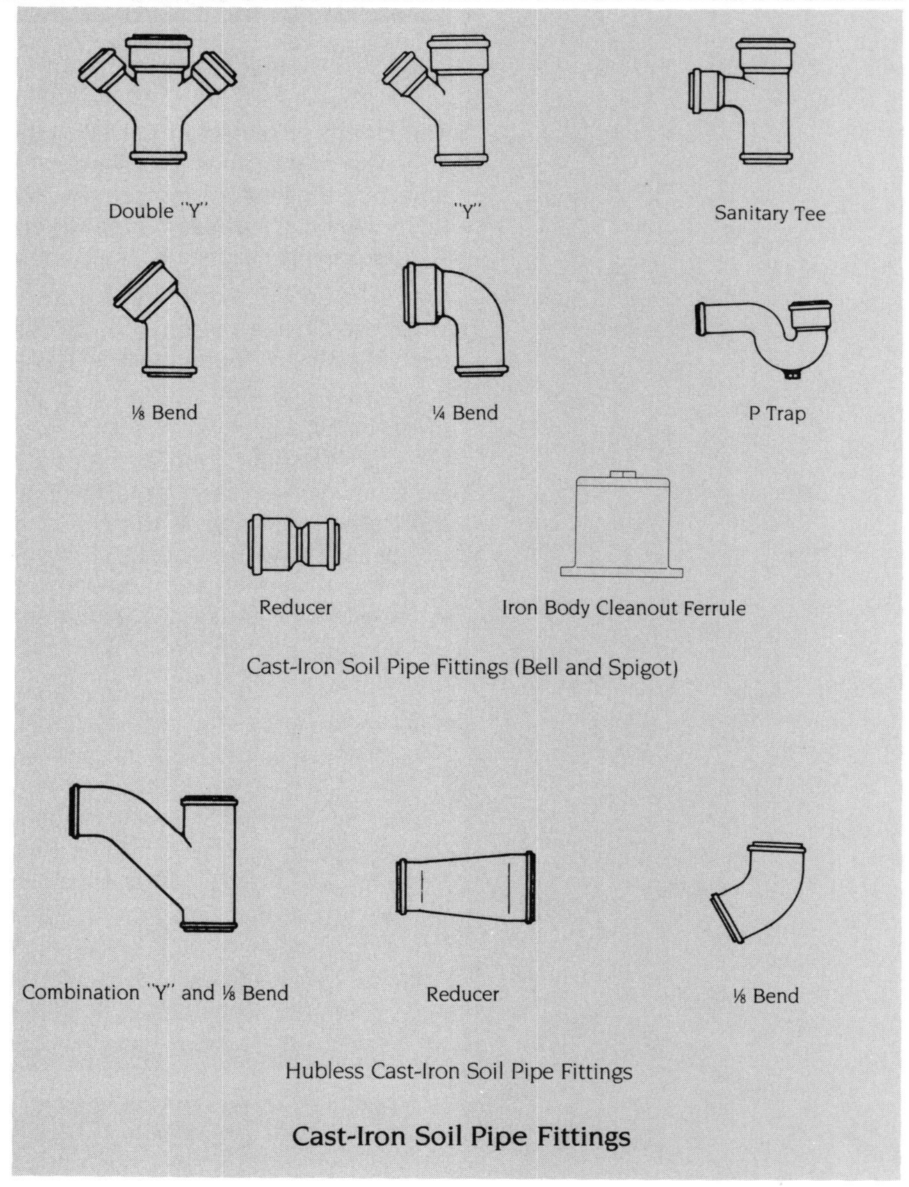
Double "Y"
"Y"
Sanitary Tee
⅛ Bend
¼ Bend
P Trap
Reducer
Iron Body Cleanout Ferrule
Cast-Iron Soil Pipe Fittings (Bell and Spigot)
Combination "Y" and ⅛ Bend
Reducer
⅛ Bend
Hubless Cast-Iron Soil Pipe Fittings
Cast-Iron Soil Pipe Fittings

Figure 1.9

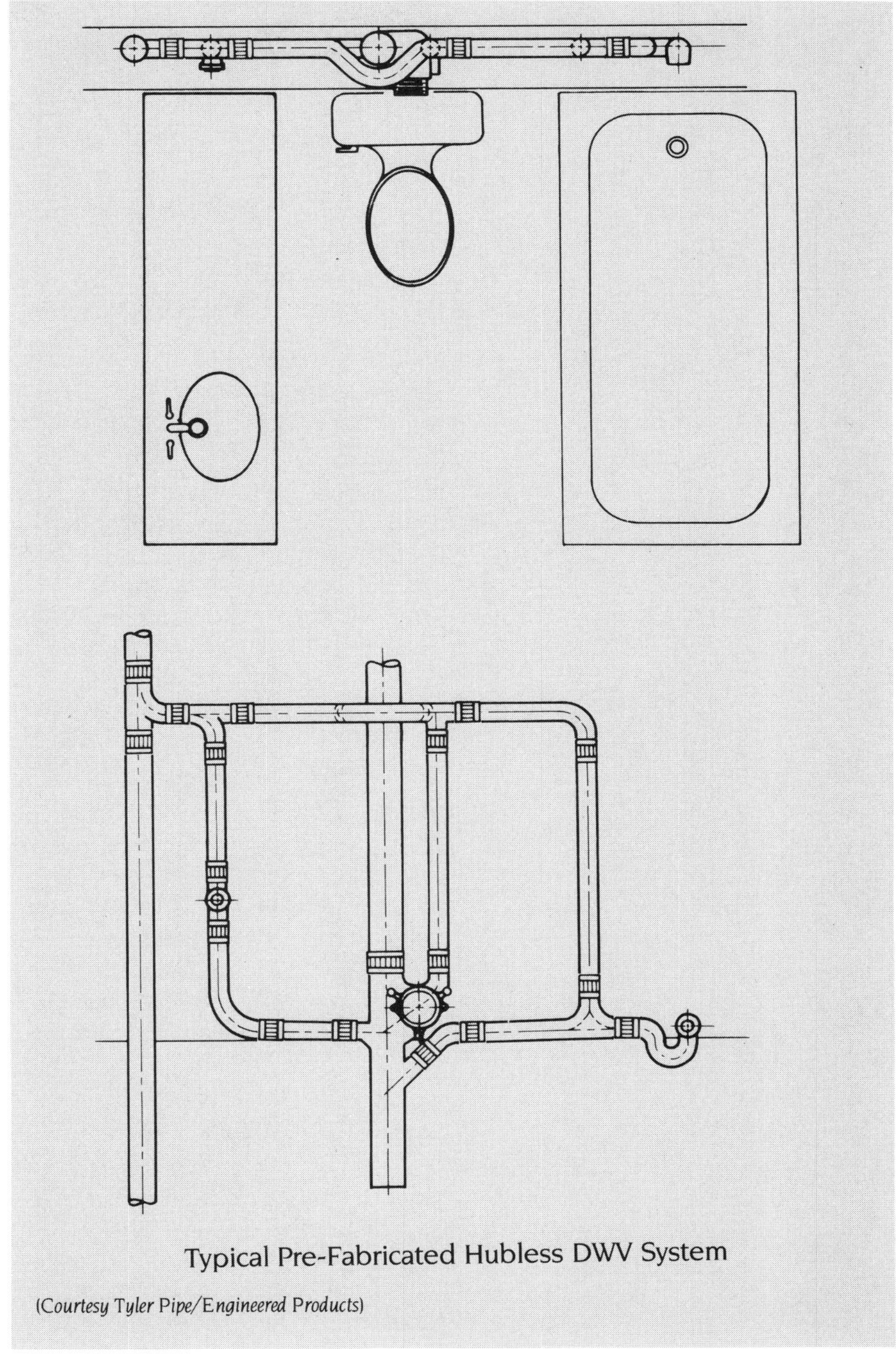

Typical Pre-Fabricated Hubless DWV System

(Courtesy Tyler Pipe/Engineered Products)

Figure 1.10

It should be noted that the plumbing contractor must investigate local union regulations to determine whether it is permissible to prefabricate units off site. In addition, it is important to state that the optimal benefit realized by using this system is on multiple/typical roughing installations.

Red Brass Pipe (Non-Ferrous)

Red brass pipe is made from an alloy of 85% copper and 15% zinc. Brass pipe can be purchased in lengths of 12' to 16' and is produced with threaded ends. Brass offers excellent resistance to corrosion.

Joints and Fittings

Threaded cast-bronze fittings or flanged cast-bronze fittings may be used to join brass pipe. The threading operation is similar to that for steel pipe.

For special requirements, threadless fittings are produced for brazing to pipe. Brazing is a joining method using brazing filler metals which melt at temperatures ranging from 1100°F to 1500°F. The filler metals are alloys containing silver or copper and phosphorous. In making a brazed joint, burrs on pipe must be removed and the pipe thoroughly cleaned. Brazing flux is applied to remove any traces of oxides. Heat is then applied to the pipes being joined, using an oxyacetylene flame. Once the proper temperature is achieved, the brazing filler rod or wire is placed at the joint and will enter the socket of the fitting, completing the joint. (Figure 1.4 lists a complete line of fittings in this category.)

Plastic Pipe (Non-Ferrous)

Plastic is a material that has been growing in popularity in recent years. *Plastic pipe* is actually a broad title for many different types of pipe of plastic composition. Some of the most popular plastic piping materials manufactured today are:

PVC–Polyvinyl chloride
CPVC–Chlorinated polyvinyl chloride
PE–Polyethylene
PB–Polybutylene
PP–Polypropylene
FRP–Fiberglass reinforced plastic
ABS–Acrylonitrile-butadiene-styrene

Most of the above pipe is manufactured in 20' lengths, and each has its own distinctive applications and characteristics. PVC is stronger than most thermoplastics and has excellent chemical resistance to corrosive fluids, but it may be damaged by certain hydrocarbons. CPVC has the capacity to handle corrosive fluids at a temperature 40°F to 60°F above other plastics. CPVC also will not sustain combustion. PE offers excellent chemical resistance and can be used at temperatures below 130°F, but its bending strength is less than most other thermoplastics. PP is the lightest plastic piping material, yet is stronger and has greater corrosion and chemical resistance than PE. Unlike other plastic materials, FRP is reinforced with fiberglass, which gives it very high strength. ABS is light and easy to handle, yet strong and corrosion-resistant.

With respect to systems applications, PVC pipe is the most commonly used material on drain, waste, and vent (DWV) and cold water systems. PVC competes with acrylonitrile butadiene styrene (ABS) piping, especially in DWV applications. Polypropylene is another competitor in DWV applications. Chlorinated PVC (CPVC) pipe has been developed for use in hot water systems; polyethylene in cold water systems; and polybutylene in both hot and cold water applications. CPVC and polybutylene are approved for use in wet type fire protection systems, while polyethylene is commonly used in gas and water services.

Plastics, on the whole, are non-toxic, lightweight, corrosion-resistant, low in cost, and easily installed.

Joints and Fittings

There are at least three different methods of joining plastic pipe, depending on the particular application. The most popular methods are threading, solvent cement, and heat fusion. Threading is usually restricted to schedule 80 or heavier walled pipe. The threading operation is the same as for steel pipe.

A cement joint is made by applying solvent cement to both the pipe end and fitting socket. Prior to the setting of the cement, the two pieces are joined and rotated. Heat fusion is a method in which the joint surfaces of both the pipe and the fitting are heated at the same time. An electrical 120 volt, 4 ampere fusion power unit is used. A prefabricated fusion coil is placed on the pipe, then both the coil and pipe are inserted into the fitting. A compression clamp is placed over the fitting shoulder and the power unit attached to the clamp. The wire tail piece of the fusion coil is attached to a terminal post on the clamp, and the power unit is then turned on for approximately 90 seconds to create the fused joint.

Additional fitting types are compression, socket weld, butt weld, brass insert, plastic insert, clamp, grip, flared, and flanged.

Plastic fittings for both pressure and drainage applications are manufactured in a wide variety of sizes and patterns. (See Figure 1.11 for illustrations of pressure type fittings. Drainage fittings generally conform to the same shape as copper drainage fittings.) (See Figure 1.13 for a complete list of fittings in this category.)

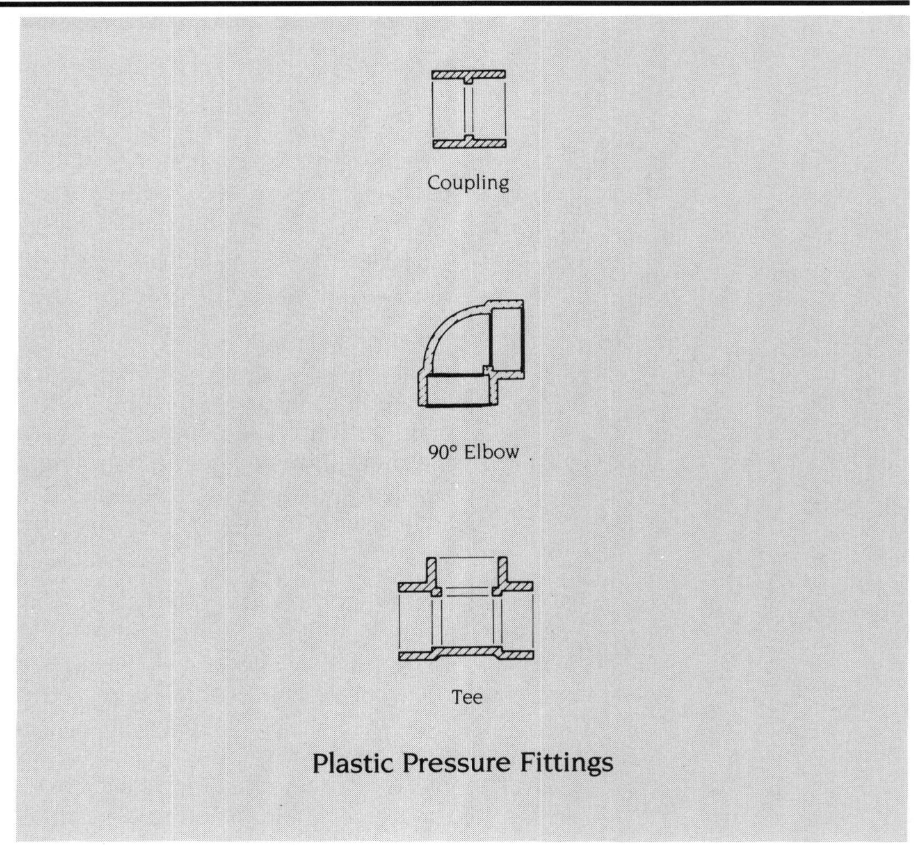

Figure 1.11

Glass Pipe (Non-Ferrous)

Glass pipe is used in plumbing work to convey acid or acid-bearing wastes. Glass pipe is manufactured in regular or heavy schedule, and may also be wrapped with fiberglass and polyester resin for underground installations. Glass pipe is manufactured in either 5′ or 10′ lengths. This is one of the best materials for resisting corrosion. Glass pipe is also used for high purity water systems.

Joints and Fittings

Beaded-end glass pipe and fittings are the most common joint method used in plumbing work. A metal compression coupling with a corrosion-resistant Teflon gasket is designed to receive one beaded end and one plain cut end. The coupling is tightened with two bolts which are part of the metal housing of the coupling. Couplings designed to receive two beaded ends are also available. A complete line of drainage fittings such as elbows, 45's, tees, wyes, and other shapes are manufactured. See Figure 1.12 for a complete list of fittings in this category.

Conical joint glass piping is coupled via flanged, gasketed joints.

MANUFACTURED GLASS DRAINAGE FITTINGS 1½″ TO 6″ PIPE DIAMETER	
Quarter Bends	Offsets
Sixth Bends	Return Bends
Eighth Bends	Cleanout and Test T's
Sixteenth Bends	Cleanout Plugs
Quarter Bend Reducers	P Traps
Sanitary T's	Swivel 'P' Traps
Compact Sanitary T	Swivel 'S' Traps
Drainline 'Y's	Running Traps
Compact Drainline 'Y's	Swivel 'P' Drum Traps
Combination 'Y's/Eighth Bends	Swivel 'S' Drum Traps
Compact Combination'Y's/Eighth Bends	Drum Traps
Upright 'Y's	Universal Traps
Vent Stack Increaser	Trap Cleanouts
Reducers	Cup Sinks
Double Quarter Bend	Couplings

Figure 1.12

Pipe and Pipe Fittings — Site (Outside)

In addition to ductile iron pipe discussed earlier in this chapter, there are certain types of pipe used exclusively for outside or buried applications. In sewer and site drainage, the most common types of pipe found are concrete, vitrified clay and galvanized corrugated metal.

Concrete Pipe

Concrete pipe is manufactured in two classes: *reinforced* and *non-reinforced*. The reinforced class is broken down further into five separate classes: I, II, III, IV, and V. These are based on the D-load (test load expressed in pounds per linear foot per foot of diameter) necessary to produce a crack in the pipe. The two joining methods used for concrete pipe are the single rubber ring gasket joint and the cement mortar joint. Concrete fittings are stock manufactured or can be custom made; however, where large diameters are involved, manholes are often used at the junction point instead of fittings.

Vitrified Clay Pipe

Vitrified clay pipe is manufactured in both standard and extra-heavy strengths. The pipe is molded of clay and glazed to make it more impervious to contamination. Clay pipe is manufactured in 2-1/2' and 3' lengths. The most popular joining method used today is "O" ring gasket joints. Fittings are manufactured for all size ranges.

Galvanized Corrugated Metal Pipe

Galvanized corrugated metal pipe is classified according to metal gauge, (16, 14, 12, 10, and 8 gauge). Corrugated metal pipe is heavily galvanized. A bituminous coating can be applied for added protection. The corrugated design increases the beam strength of the pipe. The pipe walls are joined by a number of methods: riveted seams, spot welded seams, helical lock seams, or bolted seams. Fittings are available and can also be custom fabricated.

Tube and Tube Fittings

Any student of plumbing estimating should understand the basic differences between *pipe* and *tubing*. Tubing generally has a thinner wall than pipe and is never threaded. Tubing is manufactured in both coils and lengths; coils are possible because of its greater bending flexibility.

Copper water tubing is manufactured in three classes according to wall thickness; the heaviest, Type K; medium-grade, type L; and lightest-grade, Type M. Types K and L are available in soft or hard temper (hard temper tubing resists freezing very well). Soft temper copper is available in longer coils. The manufactured length of hard drawn copper tubing is 20'. Copper tubing is popular because it is lightweight, corrosion-resistant, requires no threading, and the soft temper bends easily

Another type of copper tubing is DWV, designed exclusively for soil and waste drainage systems. The advantages of type DWV copper tubing over cast iron soil pipe are that it is manufactured in 20' lengths, thus requiring fewer joints; is easily cut; and when joined, is lightweight and space-saving due to its smaller outside diameter compared to bell end soil pipe.

Joints and Fittings

Copper tube is joined by either *brazing*, *soldering*, or *roll groove couplings*. Brazed joints are completed using the same method for threadless brass pipe described earlier in this chapter. Soldering is used for copper tubing where temperatures do not exceed 250°F. Solder joints create a capillary action which draws the molten solder into the fitting. Flux is used as a wetting agent to assure a uniform spreading of the solder over the joint. Two types of solder are used to join copper tubing: 50-50 tin-lead solder for drainage and vent systems and 95-5 tin-antimony (or other lead-free materials) for potable water systems. The use of lead in solder for potable water systems, has been banned in most areas of the country. 95-5 tin-antimony solder can be used on moderate to high pressure temperature services and offers greater joint strength. In making up a solder joint, all burrs should be removed from the tubing and all surfaces to be joined should be cleaned. Flux is applied to the tube end and to the socket of the fitting. They are then joined. Using a propane torch, heat is then applied to the joint. When the metal is hot enough, the flame should be removed and the solder applied and melted at the joint. When cooled, the solder joint is completed.

Fittings used for copper water tube are wrought copper or cast bronze solder joint. Cast bronze solder joint drainage fittings and wrought copper joint drainage fittings are used for DWV copper. See Figure 1.14. (Figures 1.4 and 1.13 show complete lists of fittings.)

MANUFACTURED D.W.V. COPPER & PLASTIC FITTINGS (1¼″ TO 8″ PIPE DIAMETER)	
Adapters Slip Joint	Elbows 11¼°
Adapters Soil Pipe	Elbows 60°
Adapters Threaded Female	Plugs
Adapters Threaded Male	Sanitary T's
Bushings	T's
Closet Flanges	'Y's
Couplings	Test Caps
Elbows 90° Short Radius	Vent Increasers
Elbows 90° Long Radius	Long Turn 'T's
Elbows 45°	Short Turn 'TY's
Elbows 22½°	Double Long Turn 'TY's

Figure 1.13

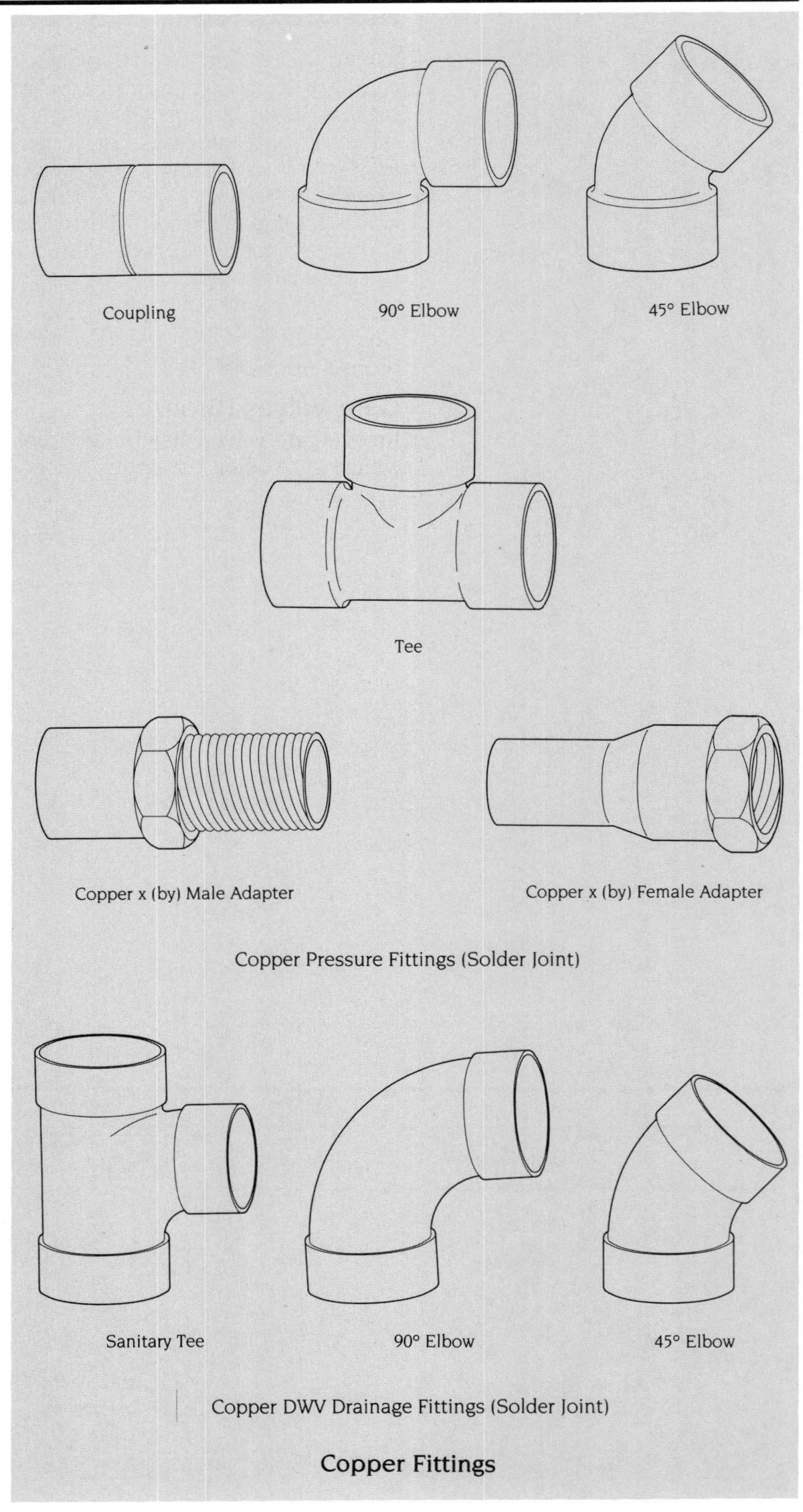
Coupling
90° Elbow
45° Elbow
Tee
Copper x (by) Male Adapter
Copper x (by) Female Adapter
Copper Pressure Fittings (Solder Joint)
Sanitary Tee
90° Elbow
45° Elbow
Copper DWV Drainage Fittings (Solder Joint)
Copper Fittings

Figure 1.14

Valves and Control Devices

The contents of every piping subsystem must be controlled to ensure the proper system operation. The flow of liquids and gases, system pressures and overall system operations are controlled with valves and devices. Valves are available in a wide variety of styles, materials, and sizes, with the style and material determined by the application and the size and on its capacity to control the liquid, gas, or pressure. Chapter 2 covers the valves and control devices found on various plumbing subsystems. This section introduces various valve and device categories, materials used, and terminology.

The major types of valves found in plumbing work are *gate*, *globe*, *check*, *butterfly*, and *ball*. These valves are manufactured for plumbing use in bronze, iron, and plastic.

Gate Valves (Bronze)

Bronze gate valves may be of either a split or solid wedge design, the wedge gate being the control piece regulating the flow (see Figure 1.15). Gate valves are required where full and unobstructed flow is required. Gate valves come equipped with rising stems or, where headroom is a factor, non-rising stems. Rising stems are particularly useful in determining the position of the wedge (open or closed). Another gate valve design is the outside screw and yoke type, desirable where frequent maintenance and lubrication is required. OS & Y valves also indicate by stem position whether the valve is opened or closed. Working pressures range from 125 psi to 300 psi steam, and 200 psi to 600 psi water, oil, and gas. Gate valves are manufactured with flanged, threaded, soldered, socket, or grooved ends.

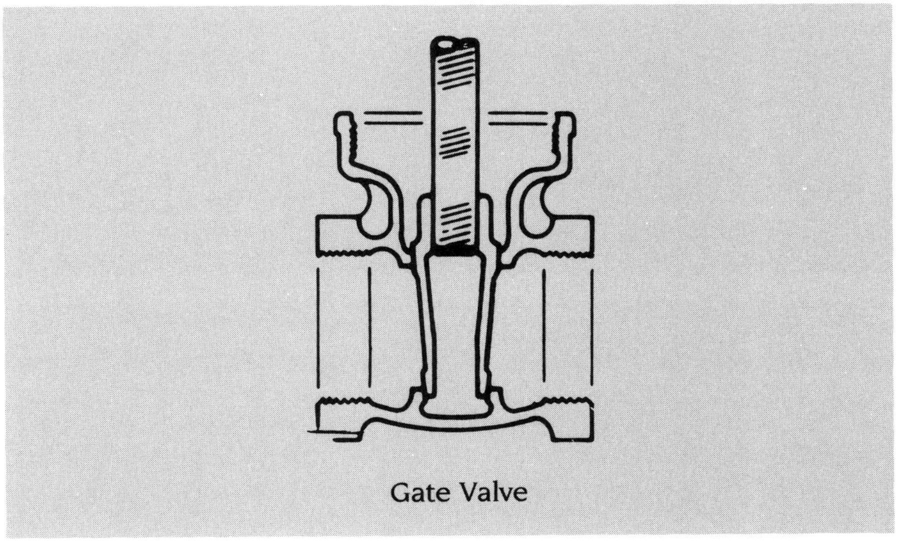

Figure 1.15

Gate Valves (Iron-Body)

Like bronze valves, iron-body gate valves are of the wedge design. Their iron body construction keeps costs down to a minimum, making them desirable where large sizes are required. Outside screw and yoke designs are available in iron-body gate valves. Iron-body gate valves that are to be used for fire protection systems must be made to Underwriter and Factory Mutual specifications. Most iron-body valves start at 2″ I.P.S.; however, there are one or two designs available in smaller pipe sizes. Valve ends are either threaded or flanged.

Gate Valves (Plastic)

Polyvinyl chloride gate valves are available from 1/2″ to 6″ I.P.S. with socket, threaded, or flanged ends. They are manufactured with a working pressure rating of 125 psi. Plastic gate valves are normally limited in use to plastic piping systems only.

Globe Valves (Bronze)

Bronze globe valves are of the composition or plug disc design (See Figure 1.16). Globe valves are desirable where close flow control is important. Outside screw and yoke, angle and hose end designs are also available. Working pressures range from 150 to 300 psi for steam service, and 150 to 600 psi for water, oil, and gas. Globe valves are manufactured with flanged, threaded, soldered, or socket ends.

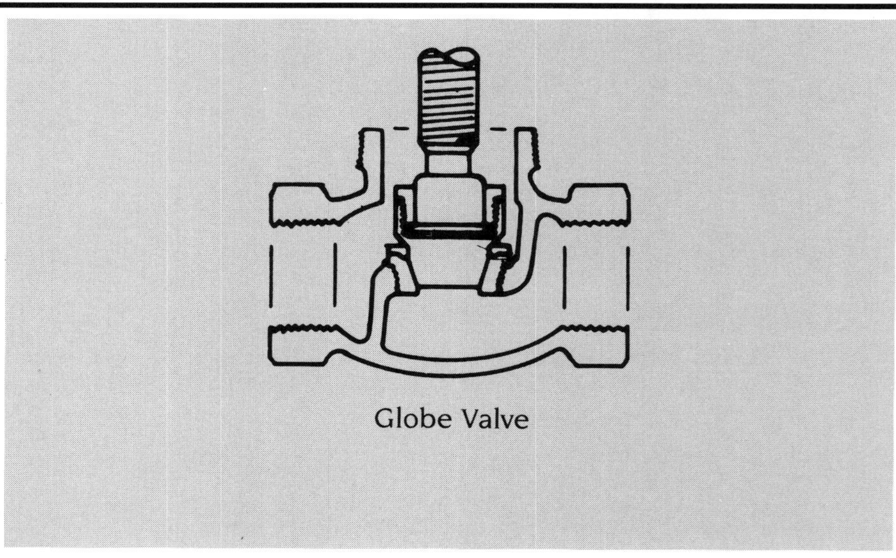

Figure 1.16

Globe Valves (Iron-Body)

Iron-body globe valves, like bronze globe valves, are desirable where close flow control is important. However, like iron-body gate valves, their iron-body construction keeps costs down and is desirable where large sizes are required. Valve ends are either threaded or flanged. Most sizes begin at 2″ I.P.S., with a few designs available starting at 1/2″ I.P.S.

Check Valves (Bronze)

Bronze check valves are of the lift or swing check design (see Figure 1.17). Check valves are required to prevent reverse flow in a pipeline. They are opened by pipeline pressure and closed by back pressure or the weight of the swing check mechanism. Working pressures range from 125 to 300 psi for steam, and 175 to 300 psi for water, oil, and gas. Check valves are manufactured with threaded, flanged, soldered, or socket ends.

Check Valves (Iron-Body)

Iron-body check valves are similar to bronze check valves in that they are either of the lift, swing check, or non-slam spring-loaded design. As with iron-body gate and globe valves, the iron-body construction is less costly than bronze, making them desirable for use in large size installations. The operating principle is the same as that for bronze check valves. Iron-body check valves are manufactured with either threaded or flanged ends.

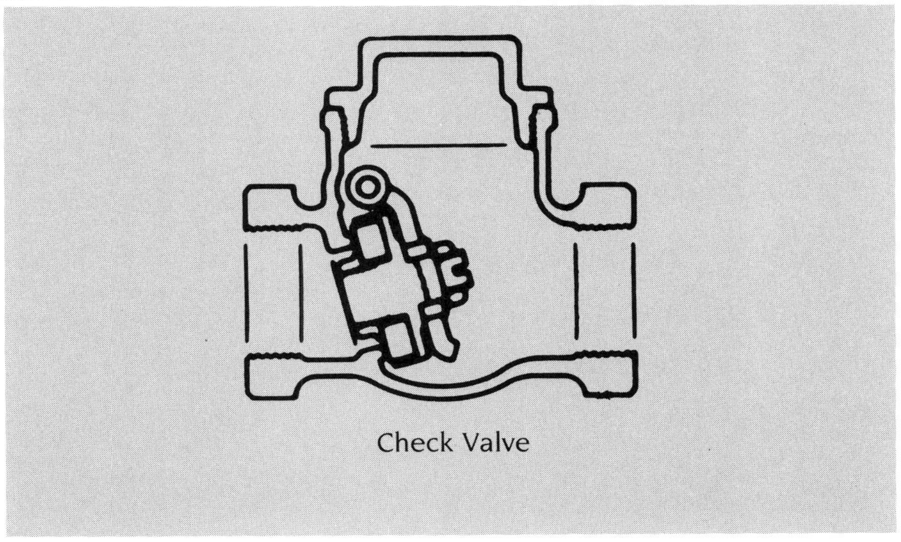

Check Valve

Figure 1.17

Ball Valves (Bronze)

Ball valves are popularly used, especially for control of medical gases. Ball valves are compact, have little flow restriction, and are relatively low in cost. Working pressures are 150 psi for steam and 400 psi for water, oil, and gas. Sizes range from 1/4" to 2" I.P.S. Figure 1.18 illustrates a typical ball valve.

Ball Valves (Plastic)

Plastic ball valves are manufactured in polyvinyl chloride (PVC), chlorinated polyvinyl chloride (CPVC) and polypropylene (PP). Working pressure is 150 psi, and sizes range from 1/4" to 4" I.P.S. Plastic ball valves are available with socket or threaded ends and should only be used on plastic piping systems.

Butterfly Valves (Iron-Body, Carbon Steel, Bronze)

Butterfly valves are a low cost, lightweight, and compact piping component. The valves are quickly and easily installed, utilizing flanged or grooved ends. Butterfly valves are designed to ensure bubble tight shut-off and to provide low pressure drop through the valve. Figure 1.19 illustrates a typical butterfly valve.

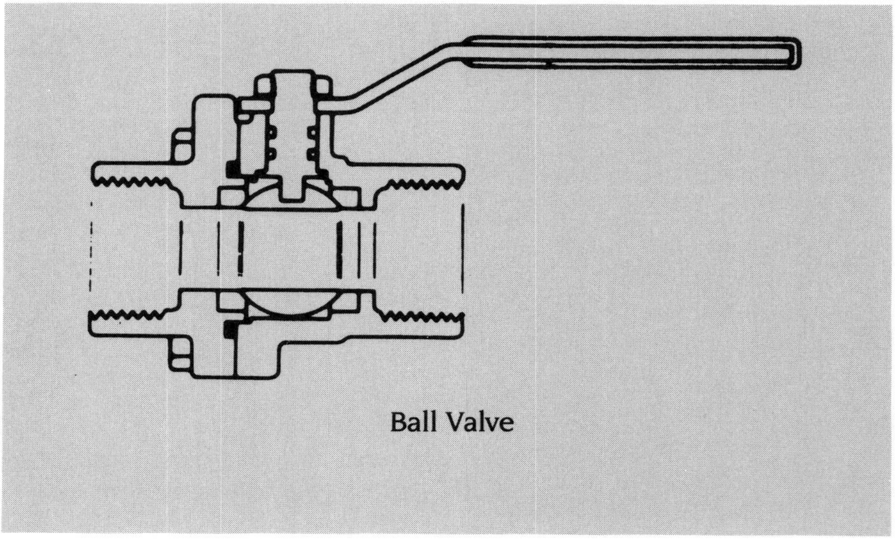

Figure 1.18

Control Devices

Control devices include any devices on a piping subsystem (other than standard valves) which aid the control of one or more subsystem functions. Examples of control devices are pressure reducing valves, temperature and pressure relief valves, backflow preventers, strainers, vacuum breakers, shock absorbers, expansion joints, and hose bibbs (see Figure 1.20). The next chapter covers in greater detail their functions and applications.

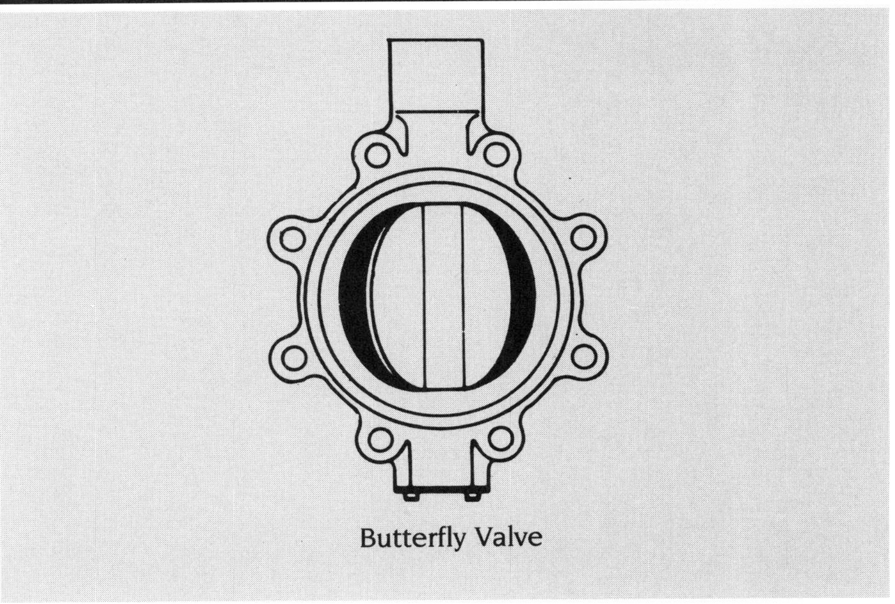

Figure 1.19

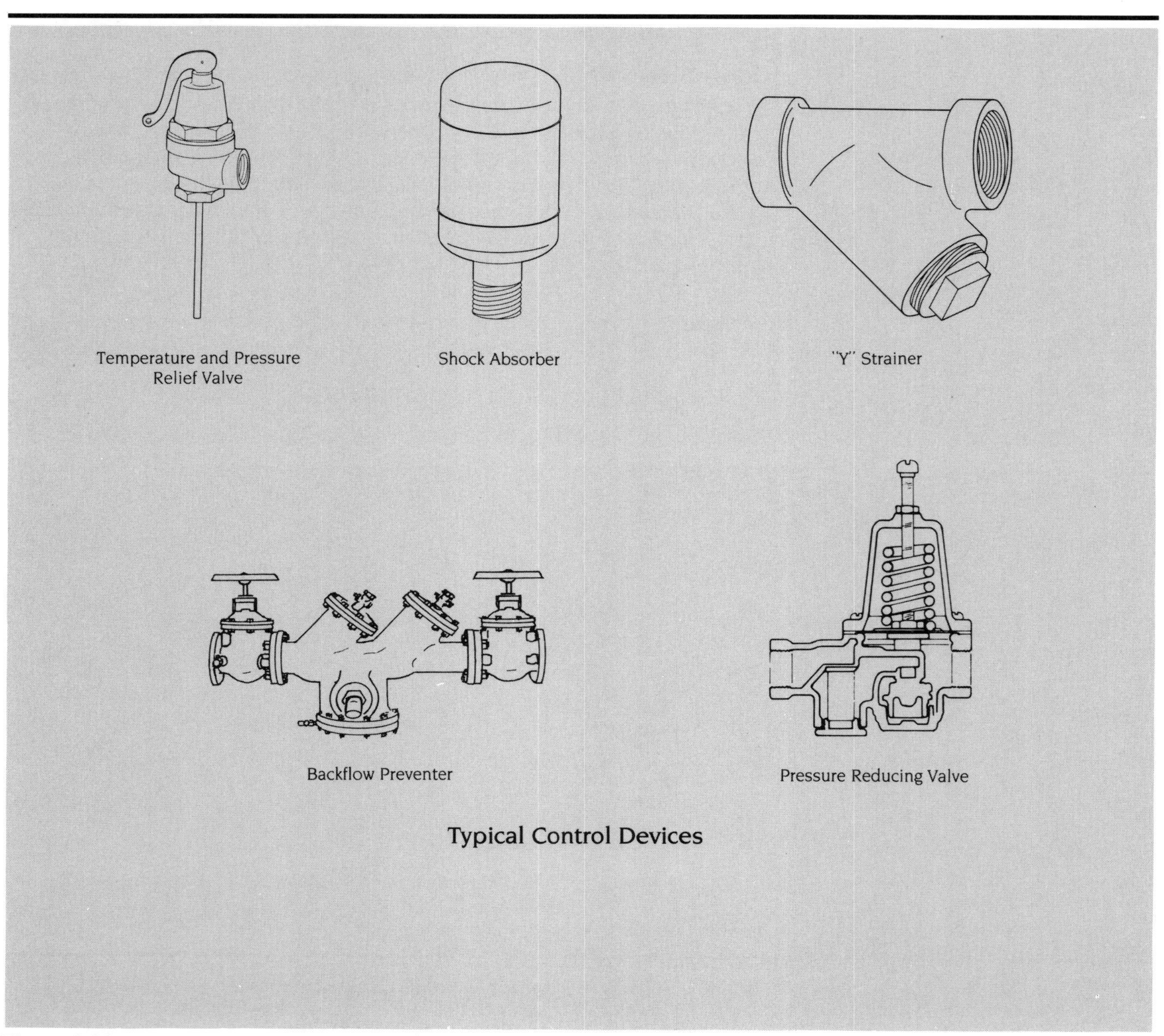
Temperature and Pressure
Relief Valve
Shock Absorber
"Y" Strainer
Backflow Preventer
Pressure Reducing Valve
Typical Control Devices

Figure 1.20

Pipe Support Systems

Pipe supports fasten and support piping systems to walls, ceilings, floor slabs, or structural members within a building (see Figures 1.21a, b, c, and d). Some supports carry single pipelines, such as *band hangers, clevis hangers, single or double rod roll hangers*, and *riser clamps*. Other supports carry multiple pipe runs, such as *trapeze hangers* and *pipe racks*. Hanger or support assemblies used in plumbing are usually of the band, clevis, roll, or trapeze design. Clevis hanger assemblies consist of a clevis hanger, insert and threaded rods with nuts. Depending on the type of floor construction used in a building, various methods are used to anchor hangers. For a metal deck with concrete fill, all inserts are set before concrete is poured. After the pour is complete and the inserts imbedded in the cured slab, the plumber installs the hanger rods and clevis hangers to make a complete installation.

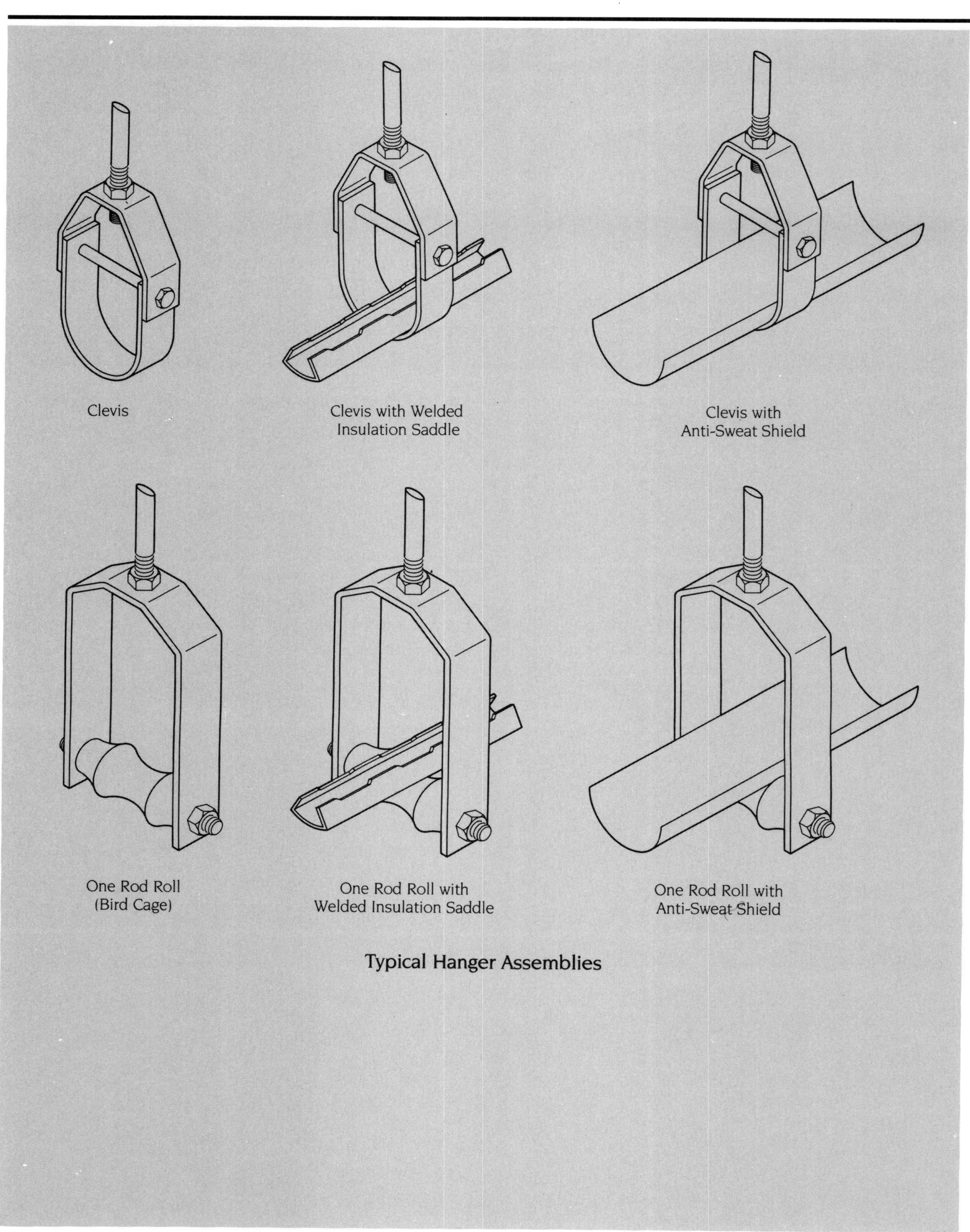

Typical Hanger Assemblies

Figure 1.21*a*

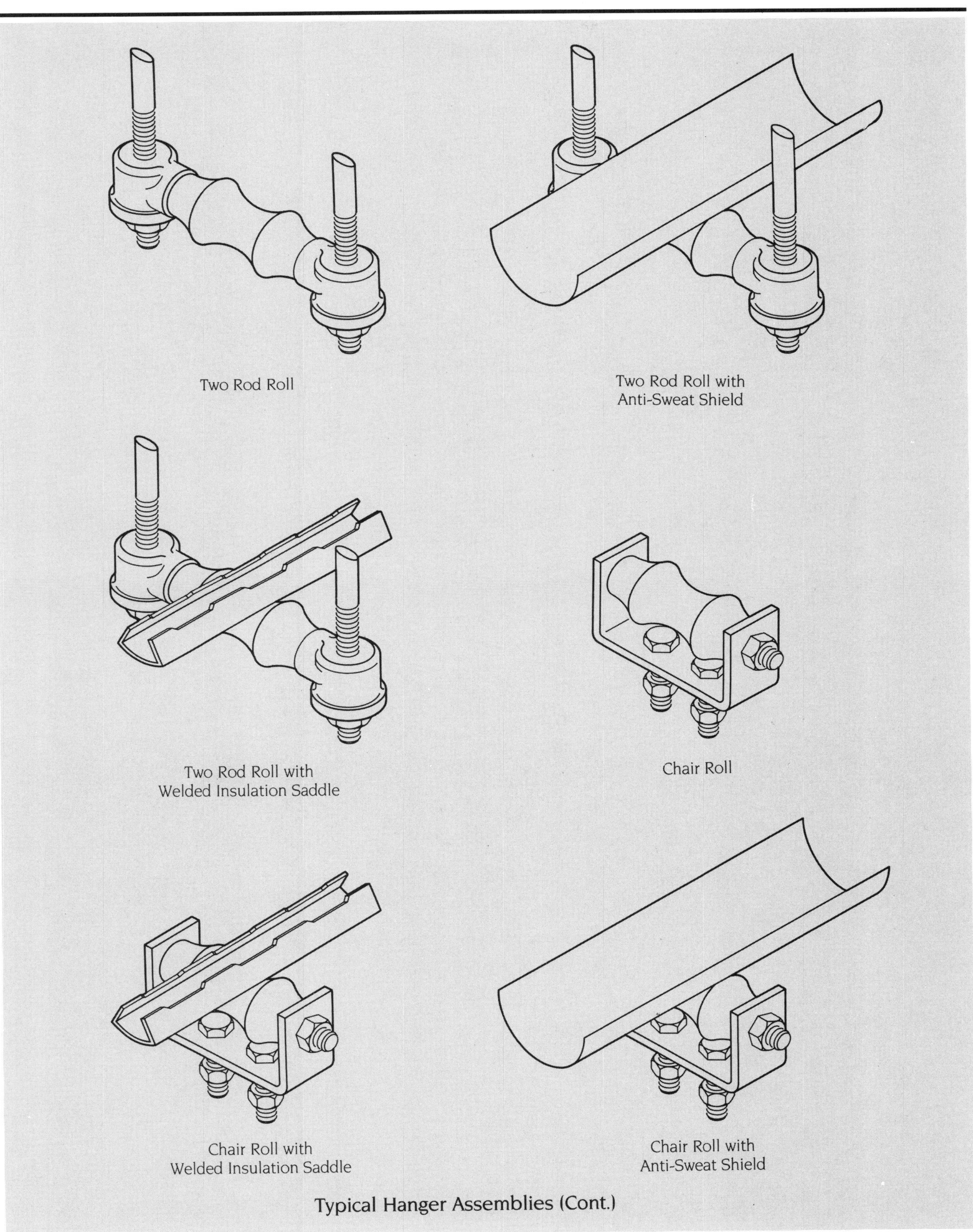

Typical Hanger Assemblies (Cont.)

Figure 1.21b

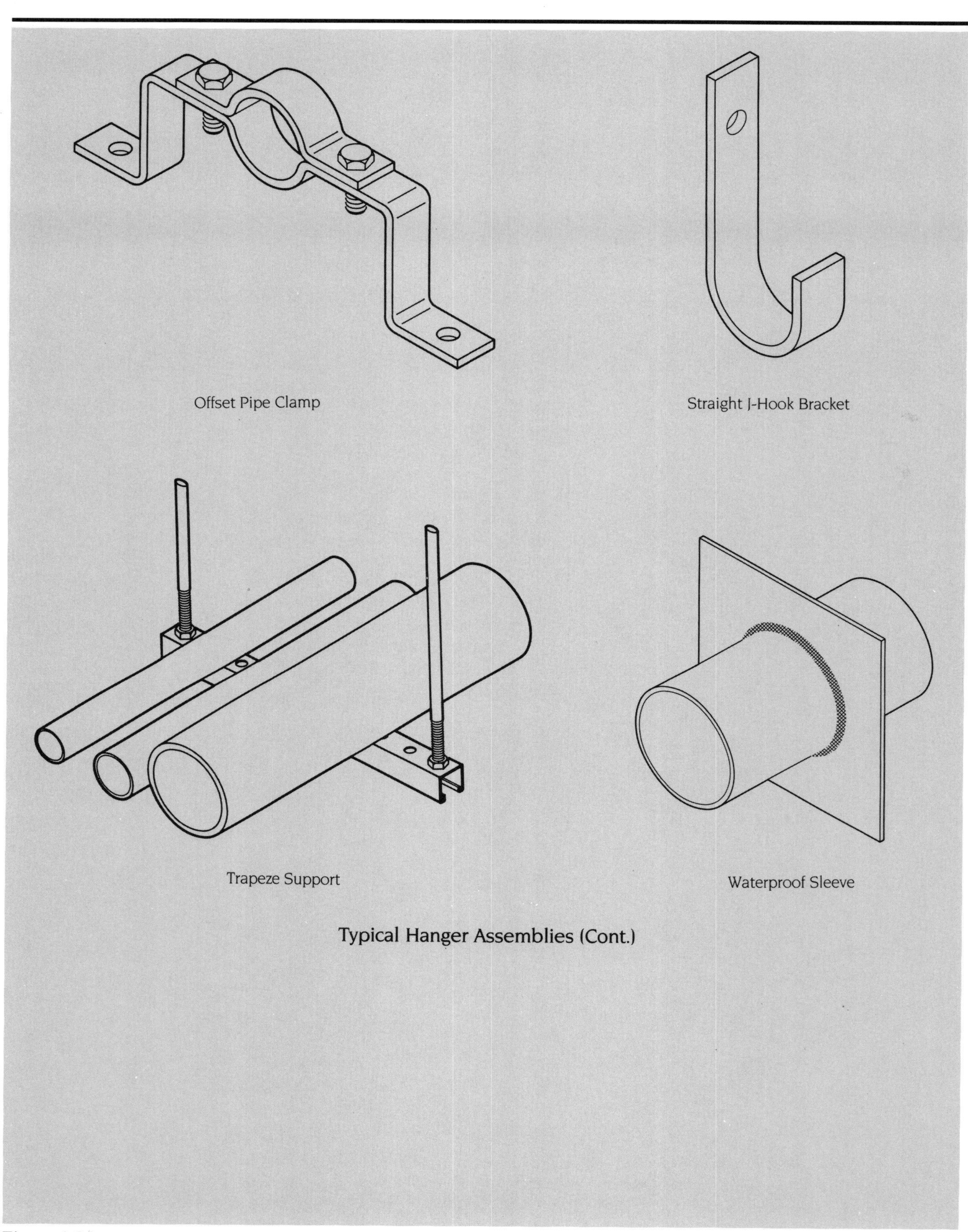
Offset Pipe Clamp
Straight J-Hook Bracket
Trapeze Support
Waterproof Sleeve
Typical Hanger Assemblies (Cont.)

Figure 1.21*c*

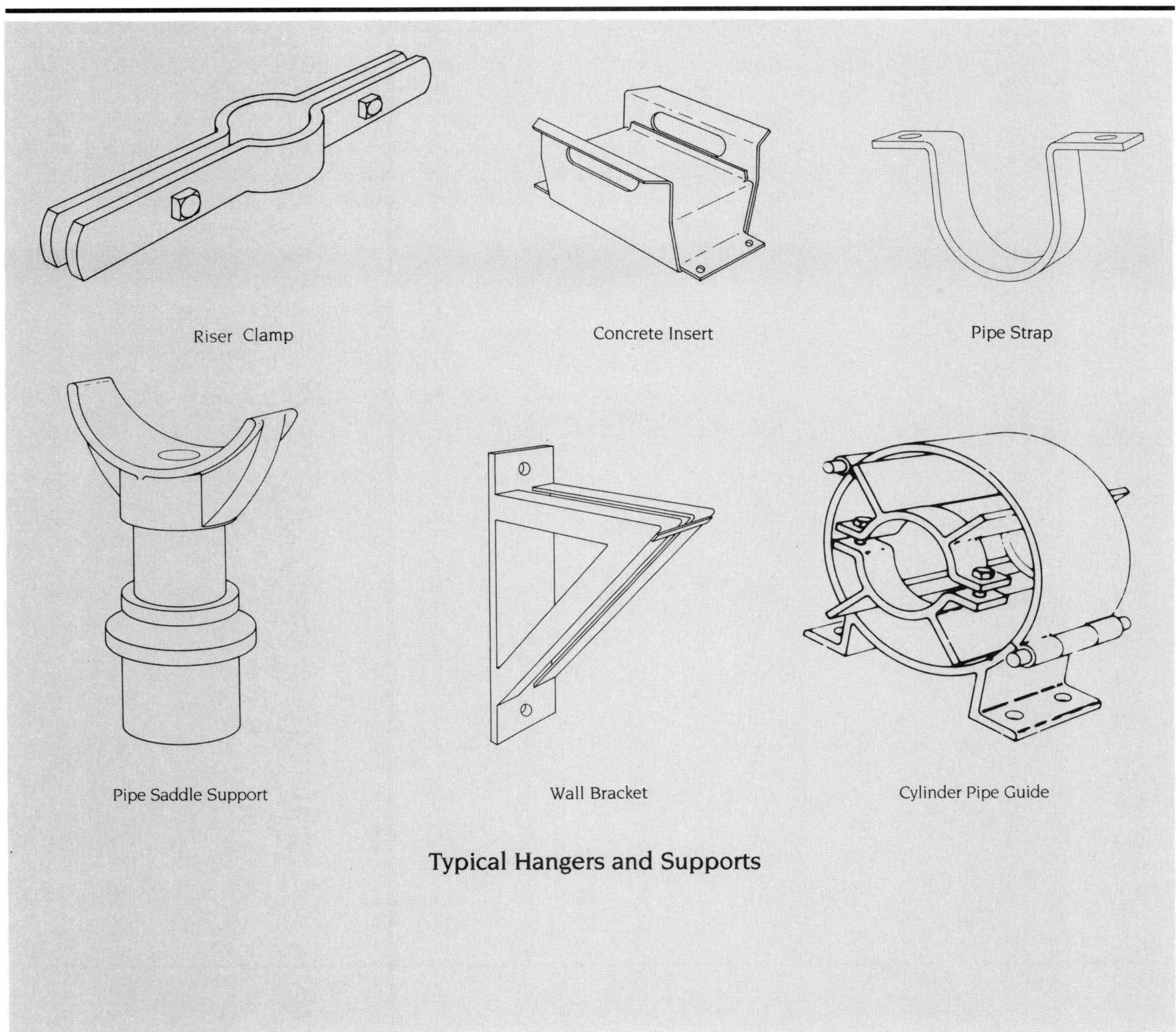
Riser Clamp
Concrete Insert
Pipe Strap
Pipe Saddle Support
Wall Bracket
Cylinder Pipe Guide
Typical Hangers and Supports

Figure 1.21*d*

Pipe clamps are used as supports for vertical risers and are usually installed at every other floor. Pipe clamps are manufactured in two pieces. The clamp is secured around the pipe with two bolts and rests on the floor slab. Trapeze hangers are anchored much like clevis hangers, except that two threaded rods are required for each assembly. Sleeves are used within a building for individual piping lines passing through walls and floors. Fire-rated sleeves are designed to prevent the penetration of flames during fire. Watertight sleeves are used for piping lines passing through walls and floors exposed to outside elements, such as foundation walls and floor slabs on grade. A pipe sleeve is made of steel or plastic and is usually two sizes larger than the pipe passing through it (or the outside diameter of the pipe insulation).

If the estimator does not have recommended intervals for pipe supports indicated in his job specifications or on the drawings, Figure 1.22 can be used as a guide.

MINIMUM RECOMMENDED INTERVALS FOR PIPE SUPPORTS	
Vertical Piping	
Cast-Iron Soil Pipe	At base and at each story height, but in no case at intervals greater than 20'.
Threaded Pipe	At every other story height but in no case at intervals greater than 25'
Copper Tubing (Hard Temper)	At each story height.
Horizontal Piping	
Cast-Iron Soil Pipe	At 5' intervals and behind every hub.
Threaded Pipe (1" or less)	At 8' intervals
Threaded Pipe (1¼" or more)	At 12' intervals
Copper Tubing (1¼" or less)	At 6' intervals
Copper Tubing (1½" or more)	At 10' intervals

Additional support must be considered where large valves, strainers, meters, etc. contribute added weight to the piping system.

Figure 1.22

Pipe Insulation

Pipe insulation or covering is installed on piping systems to retard heat loss and prevent condensation. In plumbing, all concealed hot, cold, and recirculating water piping should be insulated. It is also good engineering practice to insulate all horizontal offsets or storm drainage piping in hung ceilings to prevent condensation.

Insulation is available in rigid or flexible form and is manufactured from fiberglass, cellular glass, rock wool, polyurethane foam, closed cell polyethylene, flexible elastomeric, rigid calcium silicate, phenolic foam or rigid urethane. However, fiberglass is by far the most common material used to insulate plumbing lines. Insulation thickness for hot, cold, recirculation, and storm lines is usually 1/2" and 1-1/2" for piping lines exposed to freezing conditions. Pipe insulation comes with a vapor barrier jacket made of aluminum foil between layers of kraft paper. Fiberglass insulation should not have a thermal conductivity exceeding .22 BTU per square inch per hour at a mean temperature of 75°F. Fittings and valves should be insulated with hydraulic setting cement insulation of the same thickness specified for piping. Jacketing is also required for fittings and valves and should be coated with white vapor barrier lap cement.

The plumbing contractor usually subcontracts the pipe insulation to an insulation contractor. The insulation contractor will, in turn, submit his marked-up price to the plumbing contractor to be included in the plumbing estimate.

Painting and Identification

Painting of piping may or may not be part of the plumbing contract, although it is very often a part of the plumbing estimate and is usually a subcontracted item. Exposed piping systems are painted according to color codes set forth by the architect or engineer in the job specifications. The types of primer, paint, and number of coats required will also be stated in the specifications. Painting of pipe is generally estimated per lineal foot.

Pipe system identification is usually accomplished by one of two methods:

1. Spray-on stenciling
2. Manufactured pipe markers

Location and type of pipe markers are outlined in the job specifications. Valve tags are a manufactured item and are usually attached to valves with metal "S" hooks. In addition to tags, the contractor must turn over to the owner a valve chart clearly showing the location and function of all strategic valves. Markers and tags are taken off according to the specified number of required locations.

Clearly marked piping systems and valves are essential to an owner so that his maintenance crews can readily identify a system or valve in case of emergency.

Rigging

Rigging is the labor and equipment needed to hoist or place heavy items. The rigging work plumbers generally encounter on a project is the hoisting of heaters, pumps, and heavy fixtures such as bathtubs onto various floors of multi-story buildings. On small projects up to eight stories high, the plumbing contractor may decide to rent his own hoist with a qualified engineer present, if required by local union regulations.

On high-rise projects, it might be beneficial for the plumbing contractor to hire a union rigger if the general contractor's hoist is not available. Average costs for both methods are usually similar, differing only by a few dollars. If rigging is required on projects, an estimator should obtain a quote from a licensed rigger during the bidding stage.

Concrete Pads and Vibration Isolation

Concrete pads and vibration isolators are usually required for all large, motorized pieces of plumbing equipment such as circulating/pressure pumps, fire pumps, and air compressors. Concrete pads and vibration isolators ensure proper structural load distribution and noise abatement. Depending on the job specifications, the responsibility to furnish and install these pads may or may not be part of the plumbing contract. The size of the concrete pad is usually governed by the equipment manufacturer's recommendations. If the concrete pad is furnished by others, it is still the plumbing contractor's responsibility to provide manufactured vibration isolators to the installing contractor. If the concrete pad is the responsibility of the plumbing contractor, he will usually subcontract this work to a concrete contractor, who furnishes a price for inclusion in the plumbing estimate. Since pad sizes vary according to the piece of equipment, the plumbing estimator should request a quote for the particular job from a concrete contractor. However, if it is not possible to get a quote, some rule-of-thumb costs for concrete pads–including all formwork, bolts and vibration isolators, based on selected weights of equipment–are furnished in Appendix D or can be obtained using *Means Plumbing Cost Data* book.

Excavation and Backfill

Excavation for pipelines should be treated on an individual job basis. Due to the variety of soil conditions on different projects, soil classifications are generally broken into four classes:

Class 1 (Good): Soft clay, loose medium sand, stiff clay, loose coarse sand, sand-gravel mixtures, loose gravel, compact fine sand, compact coarse sand, and gravel.

Class 2 (Fair): Soft broken bedrock, compact partially cemented gravels and sand, and hardpan.

Class 3 (Difficult): Foliated rock such as schist and slate, and sedimentary rock such as shale and sandstone.

Class 4 (Poor): Massive bedrocks such as granite, diorite, and gneiss.

Class 3 may require blasting and Class 4 almost surely will. Blasting should be treated as a separate contract by the plumbing contractor.

Most excavation for plumbing work is accomplished with a trencher or backhoe and backfilled with a bulldozer. In tight areas or existing structures, hand excavation may be necessary.

Regardless of the class of soil or method employed, all excavation is estimated by the cubic yard. Figure 1.23 is a guide for calculating the total cubic yards of excavation required to install piping. It should be noted, however, that the table does not take into consideration sheeting, shoring, extreme depths, or multiple pipelines.

Figure 1.23

Condition	WIDTH IN FEET	DEPTH IN FEET 2	3	4	5	6	7	8	9	10	11	12	13	14	15	16	17	18
Condition 'A'	1	.07	.11	.15	.19	.22	.26	.30	.33	.37	.41	.44	.48	.52	.56	.59	.63	.67
	2	.15	.22	.30	.37	.44	.52	.59	.67	.74	.81	.89	.96	1.04	1.11	1.18	1.26	1.33
	3	.22	.33	.44	.56	.67	.78	.89	1.00	1.11	1.22	1.33	1.44	1.56	1.67	1.78	1.89	2.00
	4	.30	.44	.59	.74	.89	1.04	1.18	1.33	1.48	1.63	1.78	1.92	2.07	2.22	2.37	2.52	2.67
	5	.37	.56	.74	.93	1.11	1.30	1.48	1.67	1.85	2.04	2.22	2.41	2.59	2.78	2.96	3.15	3.33
	6	.44	.67	.89	1.11	1.33	1.55	1.78	2.00	2.22	2.44	2.66	2.89	3.11	3.33	3.55	3.77	4.00
	7	.52	.78	1.04	1.30	1.55	1.81	2.07	2.33	2.59	2.85	3.11	3.37	3.63	3.89	4.14	4.40	4.67
Condition 'B'	1	.14	.28	.45	.65	.89	1.17	1.48	1.83	2.22	2.65	3.10	3.61	4.15	4.72	5.33	5.98	6.67
	2	.22	.39	.60	.83	1.11	1.43	1.77	2.17	2.59	3.05	3.55	4.09	4.67	5.27	5.92	6.61	7.33
	3	.29	.50	.74	1.02	1.34	1.69	2.07	2.50	2.96	3.46	3.99	4.57	5.19	5.83	6.52	7.24	8.00
	4	.37	.61	.89	1.20	1.56	1.95	2.36	2.83	3.33	3.87	4.44	5.05	5.70	6.38	7.11	7.87	8.67
	5	.44	.73	1.04	1.39	1.78	2.21	2.66	3.17	3.70	4.28	4.88	5.54	6.22	6.94	7.70	8.50	9.33
	6	.51	.84	1.19	1.57	2.00	2.46	2.96	3.50	4.07	4.68	5.32	6.02	6.74	7.49	8.29	9.12	10.00
	7	.59	.95	1.34	1.76	2.22	2.72	3.25	3.83	4.44	5.09	5.77	6.50	7.26	8.05	8.88	9.75	10.67
Condition 'C'	1	.22	.44	.74	1.11	1.55	2.07	2.67	3.33	4.07	4.89	5.77	6.73	7.77	8.89	10.06	11.32	12.67
	2	.30	.55	.89	1.29	1.77	2.33	2.96	3.67	4.44	5.29	6.22	7.21	8.29	9.44	10.65	11.95	13.33
	3	.37	.66	1.03	1.48	2.00	2.59	3.26	4.00	4.81	5.70	6.66	7.69	8.81	10.00	11.25	12.58	14.00
	4	.45	.77	1.18	1.66	2.22	2.85	3.55	4.33	5.18	6.11	7.11	8.17	9.32	10.55	11.84	13.21	14.67
	5	.52	.89	1.33	1.85	2.44	3.11	3.85	4.67	5.55	6.52	7.55	8.66	9.84	11.11	12.43	13.84	15.33
	6	.59	1.00	1.48	2.03	2.66	3.36	4.15	5.00	5.92	6.92	7.99	9.14	10.36	11.66	13.02	14.46	16.00
	7	.67	1.11	1.63	2.22	2.88	3.62	4.44	5.33	6.29	7.33	8.44	9.62	10.88	12.22	13.61	15.09	16.67

Guide for Calculating the Total Cubic Yards of Excavation Required to Install Piping

Sheeting and shoring should be included in excavation costs where piping is deeper than 6′ or where unstable soil conditions exist. The cost per cubic yard of excavation and backfill will have to be determined by soil conditions, depths, and the particular method used. The recommended bottom trench width for various pipe diameters is shown in Figure 1.24.

Tests and Adjustments

All piping systems in a plumbing installation, whether in the building or on the site, must be tested to uncover any material defects, improper connections, and poor workmanship. There are many methods used to test piping systems: soil, waste, vent, drain, water, and gas piping systems are tested using either *water, smoke, air,* or *oil of peppermint*. There are generally two construction periods during which tests are performed. The first takes place after all roughing has been completed: The plumber caps all lines, with the exception of the opening from which the test material will enter the system. The second test is performed after the installation of all fixtures.

In the air test, compressed air is forced into the system until a pressure of 3 psi is attained. If any leaks occur, there will be a pressure drop.

The oil of peppermint test is done by mixing an oil of peppermint solution with hot water and pouring it into the vent terminals on the roof. If any leaks are present, an odor of peppermint will be detected. The water test is done in a similar fashion, and if leaks are present, water will appear at the defective joint.

The estimator should include testing costs (labor) and a percentage for possible material replacement. Testing costs are generally estimated as a percentage of the total direct job cost. The plumbing estimator can generally assume a range of 2 to 4% of the direct cost. This percentage includes all material, labor, and test equipment.

RECOMMENDED BOTTOM TRENCH WIDTH FOR VARIOUS PIPE DIAMETERS

DIAMETER OF PIPE	BOTTOM TRENCH WIDTH
2″ to 12″	2 feet
14″ to 18″	3 feet
20″ to 24″	4 feet
27″ to 36″	5 feet
42″ to 48″	6 feet
54″ to 60″	7 feet

Figure 1.24

Chapter 2

PLUMBING SUBSYSTEMS AND COMPONENTS

Conversant with the various materials and methods used on a plumbing system, we next shall study the various subsystems and components that together form the complete plumbing system. Depending on the type of building or facility, a *complete* plumbing system must be designed to meet the needs of the project. For example, a medical gas system would most certainly be required in a hospital, while it may or may not be a consideration in a nursing home.

Plumbing Fixtures and Trim

A plumbing fixture (sink, water closet, shower) is probably the most basic plumbing component within a plumbing system. A plumbing fixture is any receptacle, device, or appliance that is supplied with water, or receives or discharges liquids or liquid-borne wastes. Each fixture performs an individual function, such as a shower, lavatory, washing machine, etc. Depending on the type of building, different types of fixtures will be encountered by the plumbing estimator, such as clinical service sinks, flushing rim sinks in hospitals and nursing homes, or wash fountains in schools and factories. There are also different styles of fixtures performing the same function, like wall-hung water closets with flush valves, as compared to water closets with floor-mounted tank and bowl combinations.

Plumbing fixtures are manufactured of various types of materials, most commonly *vitreous china, cast iron, enameled steel, stainless steel,* and *fiberglass.* Vitreous china possesses certain desirable qualities, such as resistance to chipping, scratching, and household acids. Cast iron offers the same benefits and is also exceptionally durable. Enameled steel, though not as durable as cast iron, is an excellent choice where budget-priced, attractive fixtures are desired. Stainless steel is very durable and, with no plating or coating, it is virtually chip-proof. However, the use of stainless steel is generally limited to sinks, drinking fountains, and certain special prison fixtures. Fiberglass is a material that has gained in popularity in recent years. Fixtures such as toilets, lavatories, bathtubs, shower stalls, and combination bath/shower/wall "surround" systems are now commonplace. The light weight of fiberglass reduces installation time considerably. Fiberglass tub and shower walls and bathtub eliminate the need for tiled walls.

Floor, roof, and area drains are generally constructed of cast iron, which is resistant to corrosion and exceptionally strong.

Figures 2.1 through 2.4 illustrate examples of typical fixtures installed by plumbing contractors.

Every fixture needs trim, which consist of devices that control the flow of water between the piping system and the fixture. Trim is normally exposed and chrome-plated. (See Figure 2.5.)

Examples of trim (some are supplied with the plumbing fixture; others are purchased separately) are flush valves, faucets, vacuum breakers, cup strainers, traps, supply fittings, and stop valves. Certain trim items may be rough brass, or, where exposed to the eye, chrome-finish.

Figure 2.6 shows a representative plumbing fixture and trim schedule. The fixtures correspond to those shown in Figures 2.1 to 2.3. Some of the listed trim is shown in the fixture illustrations.

This schedule is by no means complete, since there are hundreds of different types of plumbing fixtures on the market today. However, the schedule gives the estimator a cross-section of common fixtures. In an actual project, the estimator would consult the engineer's specifications (discussed in Chapter 4) for the specific manufacturers and types of fixtures and trim required.

Figure 2.1

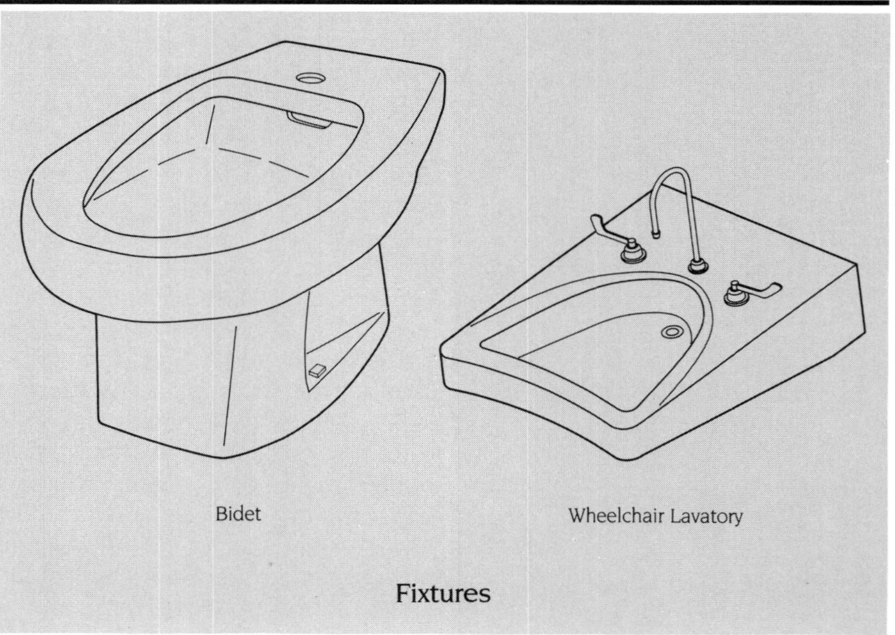

Fixtures

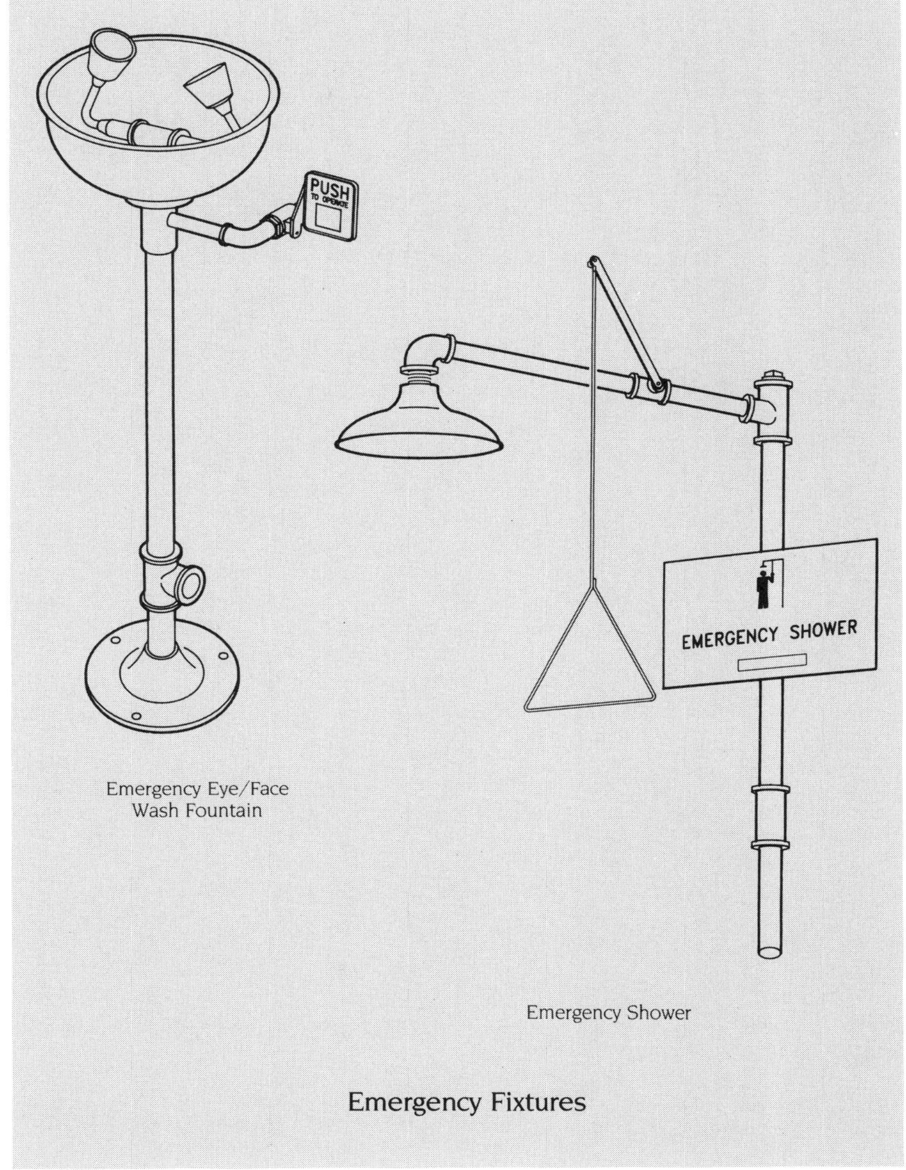
PUSH
TO OPERATE
EMERGENCY SHOWER
Emergency Eye/Face
Wash Fountain
Emergency Shower
Emergency Fixtures

Figure 2.2

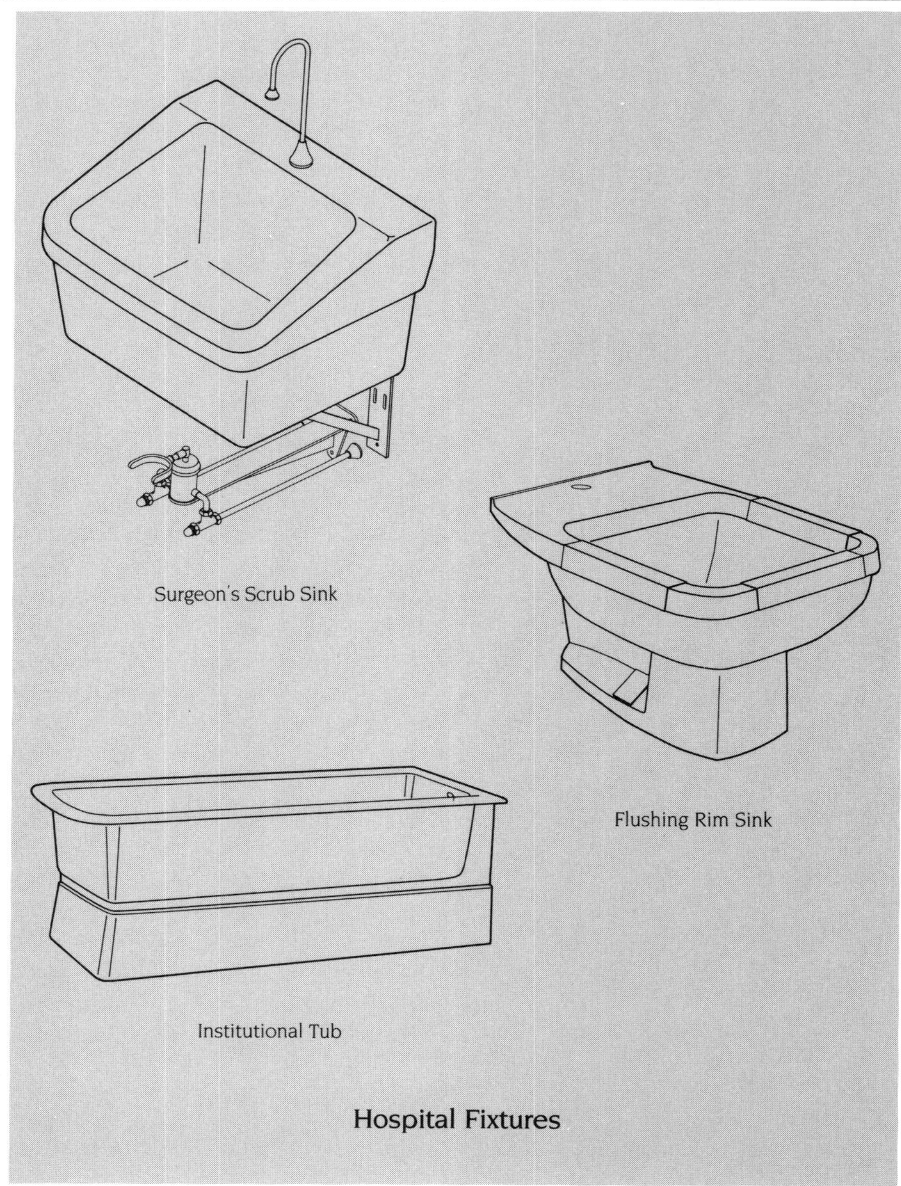
Surgeon's Scrub Sink
Flushing Rim Sink
Institutional Tub
Hospital Fixtures

Figure 2.3

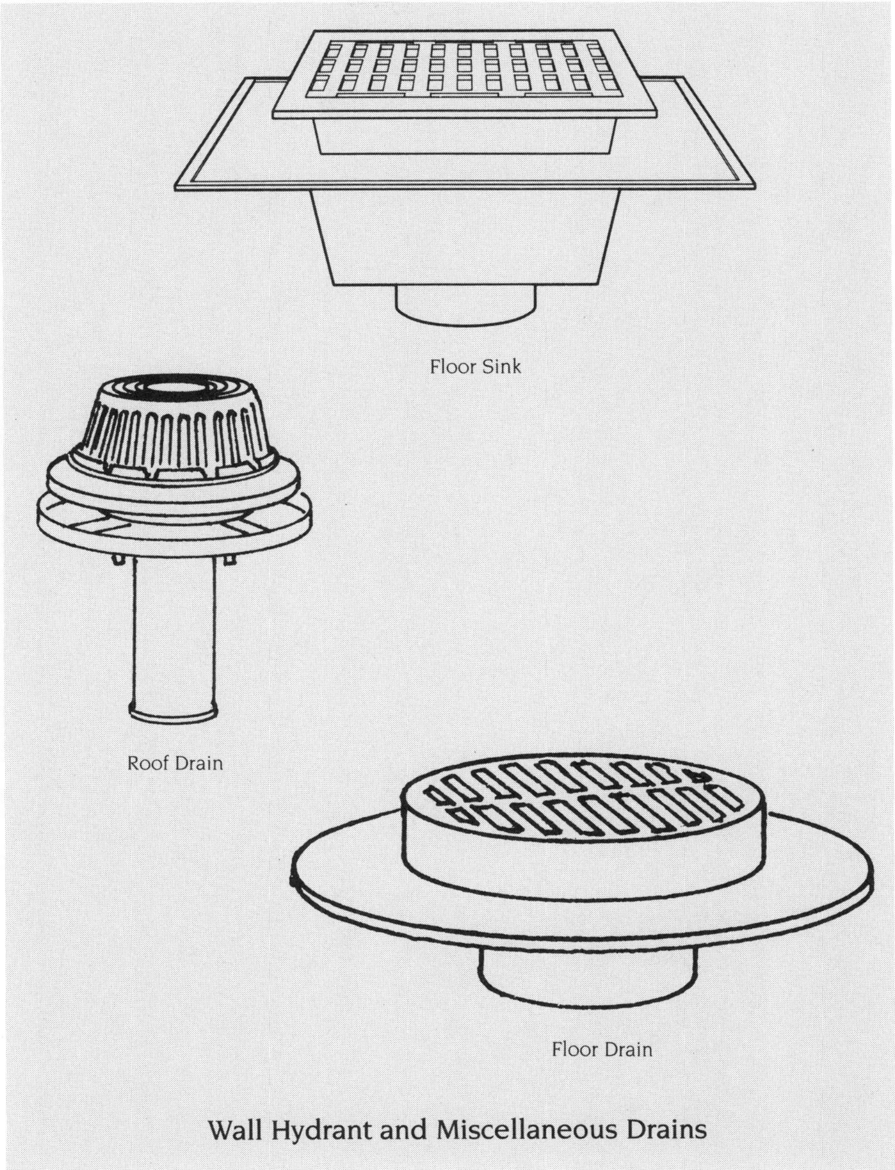
Floor Sink
Roof Drain
Floor Drain
Wall Hydrant and Miscellaneous Drains

Figure 2.4

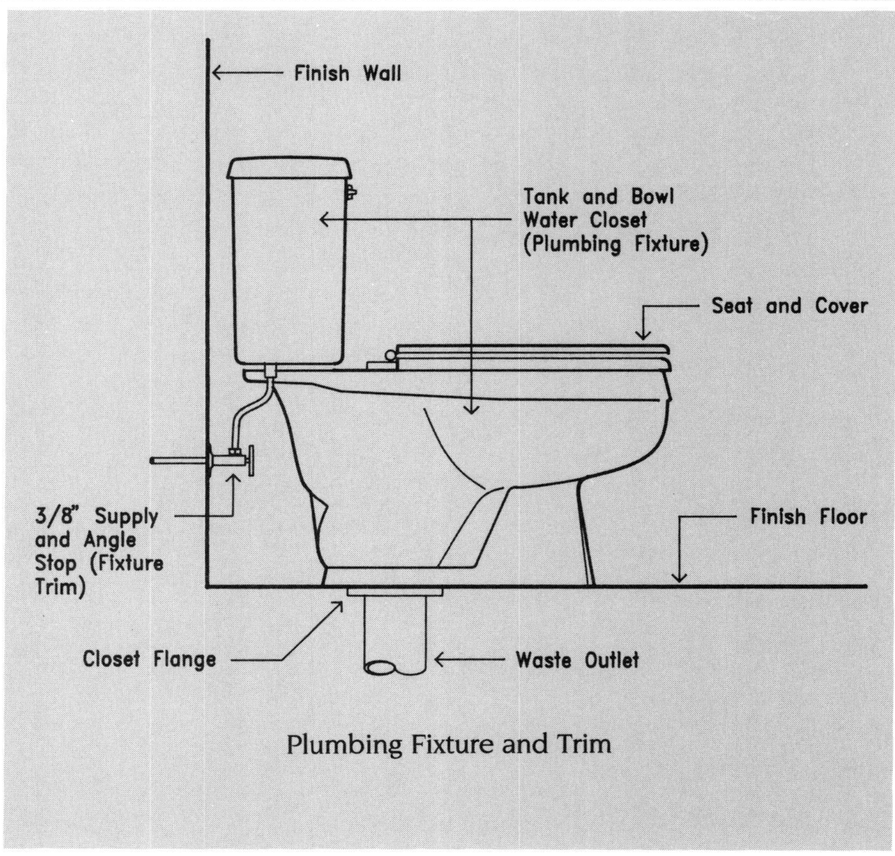

Plumbing Fixture and Trim

Figure 2.5

TYPICAL PLUMBING FIXTURE AND TRIM SCHEDULE			
FIXTURE	TRIM	TRIM SUPPLIED WITH FIXTURE	
		Yes	No
Water Closet (Flush Valve Type, Wall-Hung) (Vitreous China) *Note*: Carrier fitting included with rough piping.	Toilet seat	*X	
	Flush valve		X
Water Closet (Tank Type, Floor-Mounted) (Vitreous China)	3/8″ supply/angle stop and escutcheon		X
	Wax gasket/closet or lead bend		X
	Toilet seat	*X	
	Bolt caps/closet flange	X	
	Water control/flush/trip lever	X	
Lavatory (Vitreous China)	3/8″ faucet/1 1/4″ pop-up drain		X
	1 pair 3/8″ supplies/angle stops and escutcheons		X
	1 1/2″ "P" trap/tailpiece		X
Service Sink (Vitreous China)	1/2″ service sink faucet		X
	Rim guard, vacuum breaker, bucket hook, integral stops (all optional)		X
	3″ trap with strainer		X
Sink (Kitchen) (In-counter Type) (Enameled Cast Iron) *Note*: Stainless Steel Counter Frame not Provided by Plumber.	3/8″ faucet with spray		X
	1 1/2″ crumb cup strainer/tailpiece		X
	1 1/2″ cast brass "P" trap		X
	1 pair 3/8″ straight stops		X
Bathtub (with Shower) (Enameled Cast Iron)	Shower head, arm and escutcheon		X
	Bath spout		X
	Bath/shower diverter valve with handles		X
	1 1/2″ remote pop-up bath drain with tailpiece and outlet tee		X
Electric Water Cooler	Drain strainer and bubbler	X	
	3/8″ self-closing valve	X	
	1 1/2″ x 1 1/4″ cast brass "P" trap/ tailpiece and 3/8″ supply		X
Dishwasher	3/8″ angle stop and supply		X
	Special 1 1/4″ x 1/2″ "Y" tailpiece cast brass		X
Clothes Washer	(1) Drain hose (2) Fill hoses with female threaded connections and vacuum breakers	X	
	1 pair 1/2″ hose end control valves		X

*Seat not always supplied with fixture, check model number

Figure 2.6

TYPICAL PLUMBING FIXTURE AND TRIM SCHEDULE			
FIXTURE	TRIM	TRIM SUPPLIED WITH FIXTURE	
		Yes	No
Wash Fountain (54″ Diameter) (Granite, Stainless Steel)	Spray head, supporting tube, strainer, foot valve, operating mechanism, foot levers, rail, mixing and volume control valves, combination stop, check valves, and soap dispenser	X	
	2″ cast brass "P" trap		X
Drinking Fountain (Wall-Hung, Semi-Recessed) (Vitreous China)	Cross handle supply valve, brass strainer plate, 3/8″ service shut-off valve, 1 1/4″ tailpiece waste-outlet	X	
	Mounting frame		X
	1 1/2″ x 1 1/4″ cast brass "P" trap		X
Shower (Stall) 36″ x 34″ (Terrazzo) Receptor In lieu of tile walls, metal wall panels may be specified (Check specification)	4″ grid drain with 2″ caulked outlet	X	
	Shower head, arm and escutcheon		X
	1 pair angle valves or (1) mixing valve		X
	2″ cast brass "P" trap		X
Shower (Column Type) (Wall Pack)	Units are supplied with necessary trim. Piping for water supplies, vents, and drain are connected directly to units.	–	–
Urinal (Flush Valve Type, Wall-Hung) (Vitreous China) *Note*: Carrier, if required, is included in rough piping.	Flush valve		X
Flushing Rim Sink (Wall-Hung, Integral Trap) (Vitreous China)	Flush valve with vacuum breaker		X
	Rim guard		X
	1/2″ supply fitting with screwdriver stops, 6″ elbow control handles, spout with bucket. Hook and fork brace		X
Institutional Tub (Cast Iron) *Note*: Thermostatic Mixing Valve necessary unless tempered water system used.	Cast iron enamel base. Built-in over-rim bath filler with compression		X
	Bypass valves, four-arm handles, and escutcheons. Built-in spray fitting with compression valves		X
	Elevated vacuum breaker, nozzle with hook, 3′ rubber hose with spray four-arm handles and escutcheons		X
	Lever-operated pop-up drain with 2″ tailpiece		X

Figure 2.6 (*cont'd.*)

TYPICAL PLUMBING FIXTURE AND TRIM SCHEDULE			
FIXTURE	TRIM	TRIM SUPPLIED WITH FIXTURE	
		Yes	No
Bidet (Floor-Mounted) (Vitreous China)	Supply fittings, vacuum breakers, bolt caps 1¼″ cast brass 'P' trap	X	X
Scrub Sink (Wall-Hung) (Vitreous China)	½″ supply fitting with 2″ spray screwdriver stops, 6″ elbow control handles		X
	Drain plug with metal grid and 1½″ tailpiece		X
	1½″ cast brass 'P' trap		X
	1½″ trap nipple with cast escutcheon		X
Floor Drains (Integral Trap) (Cast Iron)	Clamping device		X
	Strainer	X	
Roof Drain (Cast Iron)	Dome strainer	X	
	Deck clamp, drain receiver		X
Wall Hydrant (Box Type)	Wall clamp, nikaloy finish, cylinder lock, extra deep box, nozzle type vacuum breaker, elbow union assembly		X
Emergency Shower	1″ self-closing valve, deluge head, 32″ chain and pull-ring	X	
Eye Wash Fountain	½″ supply w/ball valve, 1½″ drain pipe, 1½″ drain tee, stainless steel bowl and aerators, floor stand, 1½″ cast brass 'P' trap	X	
Area Drain (Cast Iron)	Strainer, hinged top	X	
Trench Drain (Cast Iron)	Strainer	X	
	Additional sections		X
Floor Sink	Strainer (vitreous enameled)	X	
	Sediment bucket, flashing ring, trap primer		X

Figure 2.6 (*cont'd.*)

Bathroom Accessories

Accessories are actually neither plumbing fixtures nor trim. However, since some accessories are functionally related to certain types of fixtures or areas requiring fixtures, we have included them in this section of the book. Unless specified or because of a local union regulation, lavatory accessories are not usually the responsibility of the plumbing contractor, but this is not always the case. For some projects, these accessories are specified to be supplied and installed by the plumbing contractor. In others, accessories are supplied by the general contractor and installed by the plumbing contractor.

Therefore, the plumbing estimator should be aware if these items are to be included in the price.

A list of toilet and bath accessories would include:

- Toilet paper holders
- Soap dispensers
- Towel dispensers
- Waste receptacles
- Sanitary napkin dispensers
- Sanitary napkin disposers
- Facial tissue dispensers
- Mirrors
- Medicine cabinets
- Grab bars (handicapped)
- Soap dishes
- Tumbler and toothbrush holders
- Towel bars
- Pail and ladder hooks
- Shower curtain rods
- Broom and mop holders
- Shelving
- Robe hooks

Toilet and bath accessories are generally constructed of stainless steel, chrome, or anodized aluminum. If the accessories are part of the plumbing contract, the estimator, before attempting a quantity takeoff, should obtain a set of drawings showing exact locations of the specified accessories, and should verify these locations with the architect.

Hook-Up of Fixtures and Trim Supplied by Others

Depending on the engineer's specification, certain plumbing fixtures or equipment may be owner- or general contractor-supplied. However, the rough-in and installation of these items are usually the responsibility of the plumbing contractor. The estimator should consult the architect and/or specifications to learn exactly which items, supplied by others, the plumbing contractor must install.

Owner- or general contractor-furnished fixtures are usually found in, but not limited to, the following areas:

Kitchens and Cafeterias

- Sinks
- Steam kettles
- Ranges
- Griddles
- Coffee urns
- Dishwashers

- Ice makers
- Refrigerators

Laboratories and Hospitals

- Lab sinks
- Fume hoods
- Cup sinks
- Hydro-therapy baths
- Autopsy tables
- Laboratory tables
- Sterilizers
- Bedpan sterilizers

There are generally accepted standards of pipe sizes for connecting fixtures to hot and cold water, vent, and waste lines, as shown in Figure 2.7. While this table can be used as a guide, the estimator should refer to local plumbing codes for exact requirements.

Domestic Hot and Cold Water System

The domestic hot and cold water system is a common piping system found on virtually every plumbing job. The domestic hot and cold water system in a building consists of:

–Water distribution piping (mains, risers, branches, runouts)

–Fittings

–Control valves and devices

–Hot water generators

–Pumps

–All appurtenances used for conveying water to the plumbing fixtures

The cold water supply in a building begins once it enters the building wall. It is usually connected to a *water meter* (see Figure 2.8a) at this point of entry, and from the meter begins its distribution to the necessary fixtures and equipment. (Note: Water meters can also be located outside the building in concrete vaults.) The hot water supply starts from the hot water generation equipment and from there begins its distribution to the fixtures. In some buildings, a hot water circulation main is desired to provide continuous hot water circulation throughout the entire system.

The domestic water system in a building is the potable water system which means it is suitable and used for human consumption, being sufficiently free of impurities that could cause disease. However, there is increasing concern that the water we drink is not pure enough. As a result, more sophisticated filtration systems are becoming popular, as is the use of backflow preventers. Backflow preventers provide greater protection from cross connections in industrial, commercial, and institutional buildings. A typical example of a backflow preventer is shown in Figure 2.8b.

PLUMBING FIXTURE AND MINIMUM PIPING CONNECTION SCHEDULE				
FIXTURE	WASTE	VENT	HOT WATER	COLD WATER
Water Closet (Flush Valve)	4″	2″	–	1″
Water Closet (Tank Top, Low Flush)	4″	2″	–	½″
Lavatory	1½″	1½″	½″	½″
Service Sink	3″	2″	¾″	¾″
Sink (All-purpose)	1½″	1½″	½″	½″
Bathtub	1½″	1½″	½″	½″
Electric Water Cooler	1½″	1½″	–	½″
Kitchen Sink	1½″-2″	1½″	½″	½″
Dishwasher	1½″	1½″	½″	–
Clothes Washer	1½″	1½″	½″	½″
Wash Fountain 54″ Dia.	2″	1½″	¾″	¾″
Drinking Fountain	1½″	1½″	–	½″
Shower (Stall)	2″	1½″	½″	½″
Shower (Column Type)	3″	1½″	1″	1″
Shower (Wall-Pack)	3″	1½″	¾″	¾″
Urinal (Flush Valve)	2″	1½″	–	¾″
Flushing Rim Sink	3″	2″	½″	(1)1″ (1)½″
Clinical Sink	3″	2″	½″	1″
Institutional Tub	2″	1½″	(2)½″	(2)½″
Scrub Sink	1½″	1½″	½″	½″
Bidet	1½″	1½″	½″	½″
Floor Drain	2″-3″-4″	1½″	–	–
Roof Drain	2″-3″-4″-5″-6″	–	–	–
Wall Hydrant	–	–	–	¾″
Emergency Shower	–	–	–	1″
Eye Wash Fountain	2″	1½″	–	¾″
Area Drain	3″-4″-5″-6″	–	–	–
Trench Drain	3″-4″-5″-6″	–	–	–
Floor Sink	2″-3″-4″	1½″	¾″	¾″

Figure 2.7

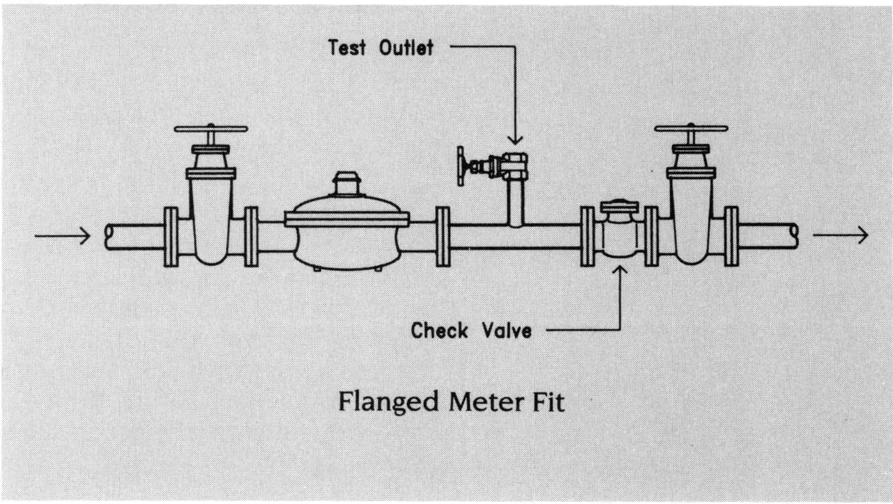

Figure 2.8a

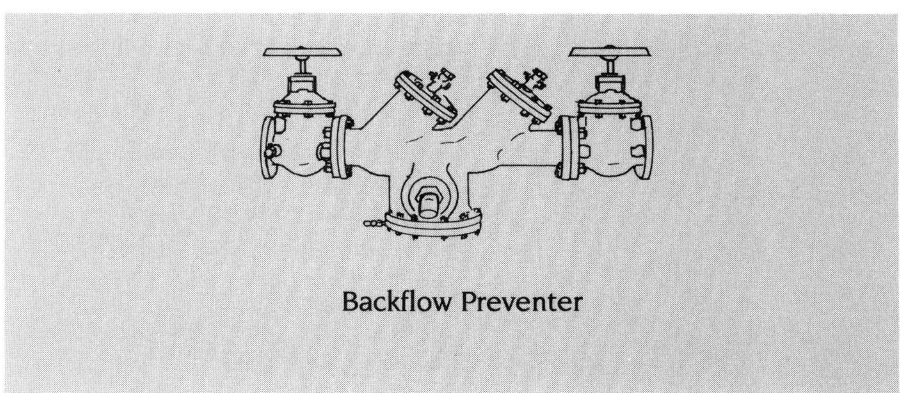

Figure 2.8b

The standard piping materials used in domestic water systems are type L and K copper tubing, and in limited applications, brass and galvanized steel pipe. On cold water, polyvinyl chloride (PVC) plastic pipe is gaining a wider acceptance in certain areas of the country.

All of these are used for aboveground installations. In cases where large diameter pipe is called for, especially around pumps and equipment, flanged ductile iron or cast iron water pipe may be used. Ductile and cast iron are especially desirable for these applications because of their relatively low cost in comparison to copper or steel (which become very expensive for sizes 4" in diameter and larger). Type K soft or hard copper tubing is generally used inside the building or for below-grade or buried installations. Of the five types of materials mentioned for aboveground use, type L copper tubing is the most commonly used material today.

The types of fittings and joining methods used for hot and cold water systems are solder-joint, or roll grooved pressure fittings for copper tubing; threaded, or flanged cast brass fittings for brass pipe; and threaded galvanized cast iron fittings for steel pipe; and threaded- or cement-joint fittings for PVC pipe. They are available in many sizes and a wide variety of types, as shown in Figures 1.4 and 1.7.

Figure 2.9 is a concise guide to the various types of pipe, fittings, recommended service, and sizes generally used on domestic hot and cold water systems. The flow and operation of a hot and cold water system is controlled through various valves and other devices. (See Figures 1.5, 1.6, 1.7, 1.8 and 1.9.) Gate valves are the standard method of controlling water in a system, and are used where full and unobstructed flow is required. Globe valves become more desirable when operation is frequent and close, and more critical flow control is essential. Check valves are designed to prevent reverse flow in the piping system.

Valves are located in critical areas: around equipment, at fixture branches, and at runouts to risers to ensure isolation, if necessary. The various types of valves and control devices encountered by the estimator on a hot and cold water system are described later in this chapter, in Figure 2.10.

DOMESTIC WATER PIPING AND FITTING SCHEDULE			
PIPE	SERVICE	SIZE	FITTINGS
Type L Copper Hard-Drawn	Hot and Cold Water Above Grade	4″ and Under	Cast Bronze—Solder Joint Wrought Copper—Solder Joint
Brass Pipe Threaded	Hot and Cold Water Above Grade	4″ and Under	Cast Bronze—Threaded Joint
Galvanized Steel Pipe Threaded Schedule 40	Hot and Cold Water Above Grade	2½″ and Above	Galvanized C.I. Threaded Fittings 125 lb.
Type K Copper Hard-Drawn	Hot and Cold Water Below Grade	3″ and Under	Wrought Copper—Solder Joint
PVC Plastic Pipe Schedule 40 Threaded or Cement Joint	Cold Water Above and Below Grade	4″ and Under	PVC Cement Joint Fittings Schedules 40 and 80
Ductile-Iron Water Pipe (Flanged, Mechanical or Neoprene Joint) Class 150 or 250	Cold Water Above and Below Grade	4″ and Above	D.I. Fittings Flanged, Mechanical or Neoprene Joint

Figure 2.9

DOMESTIC WATER SYSTEM VALVE AND CONTROL DEVICE CHART		
VALVE OR DEVICE	DESCRIPTION	APPLICATION
Globe Valve (Straight Pattern)	Bronze Construction, Threaded ⅛"-3", Flanged 1"-3", 150 p.s.i. Pressure Rating, Composition Disc, Screw-Over Bonnet. 125 lb. Working Pressure.	General purpose globe for water system, beneficial where close flow control is essential.
Globe Valve (Angle Type)	Bronze Construction, Threaded ⅛"-3", 150 p.s.i. Pressure Rating, Composition Disc, Screw-Over Bonnet. 125 lb. Working Pressure.	Same as above except used where angle connection is desired.
Globe Valve (Solder End)	Bronze Construction, Solder Joint ¼"-3", 300 p.s.i. Pressure Rating (Water), Composition Disc. 125 lb. Working Pressure.	Standard globe valve used on domestic water lines. Solder ends for joining to type K, L, and M copper.
Gate Valve (Straight Pattern)	Bronze Construction, Threaded ¼"-3", Flanged ½"-3", 150-300 p.s.i. Pressure Rating, Inside Screw Non-Rising Stem, Solid Wedge. Screw-In Bonnet. 125 lb. Working Pressure	General purpose gate for shut-off control, is particularly useful where headroom is limited.
Gate Valve (Solder End)	Bronze Construction, Solder Joint ⅜"-3", 200 p.s.i. Pressure Rating (Water), Inside Screw Non-Rising Stem, Solid Wedge. 125 lb. Working Pressure.	Standard gate valve used on domestic water lines. Solder ends for joining to type K, L, and M copper.
Gate Valve (Solder End)	Bronze Construction, Solder Joint ⅜"-3" 200 p.s.i. Pressure Rating (Water), Traveling Stem, Solid or Split Wedge. 125 lb. Working Pressure.	Similar to valve above except equipped with traveling stem which indicates wedge position.
Check Valve (Swing Type)	Bronze Construction, Threaded ¼"-3". Bronze Disc. Screw-In Cap. 300 p.s.i. Pressure Rating. 125 lb. Working Pressure.	General purpose check valve, for prevention of backflow on water lines.
Check Valve (Swing Type Solder End)	Bronze Construction, Solder Joint ⅜"-3". Bronze Disc. Screw-In Cap. 300 p.s.i. Pressure Rating. 125 lb. Working Pressure.	Ideal check valve for water lines, providing non-return control service. Solder ends for joining to type K, L, and M copper.
Globe Valve (Iron Body Straight Pattern)	Iron Body Construction, Threaded 2"-4", Flanged 2"-8", 125 p.s.i. Pressure Rating, Composition Disc, Outside Stem and Yoke, Renewable Bronze Seat Ring. 125 lb. Working Pressure.	Utilized where large pipe sizes occur, iron body construction keeps cost at a minimum. Globe valve ideal where close flow control is desired.
Gate Valve (Iron Body Straight Pattern)	Iron Body Construction, Threaded 2"-4", Flanged 2"-20", 150 p.s.i. Pressure Rating, Inside Screw, Non-Rising Stem, Bronze Trim, Solid Wedge. 125 lb. Working Pressure.	General purpose gate for large pipe sizes, low-cost iron body construction. Ideal where full and unobstructed flow is essential.
Ball Valves (Bronze, Plastic)	Bronze or Plastic Construction Threaded, Solder Cement Joint. 150 lb. Working Pressure.	General purpose valve for water system, few flow restrictions.
Butterfly Valves (Iron Body, Carbon Steel, Bronze)	Iron Body, Bronze and Carbon Steel Construction. Flanged or Grooved Joints. 125-200 lb. Working Pressure.	General purpose, low cost. Ideal for equipment hook-up, due to size and serviceability.

Figure 2.10

DOMESTIC WATER SYSTEM VALVE AND CONTROL DEVICE CHART		
VALVE OR DEVICE	DESCRIPTION	APPLICATION
Check Valve (Iron Body Swing Type)	Iron Body Construction, Threaded 2"-4", Flanged 2"-12". 125 p.s.i. Pressure Rating, Bronze Seat Ring and Disc, Bolted Cover. 125 lb. Working Pressure.	Low-cost iron body construction. Used to prevent reverse flow in piping system.
Pressure and Temperature Relief Valves	Bronze Construction, Temperature Relief 210°F., Pressure Ranges 75 to 175 lbs. ½" to 2" Pipe Size.	Used to prevent high water temperature and pressure on a hot water tank or heater, which can cause flashing of steam at faucets and tank damage.
Pressure Reducing Valves	Bronze Body and Trim or Iron Body with Bronze Trim. Threaded ⅜"-2", Flanged 1"-12". Reduced Pressure Ratings 2-150 p.s.i.	Used to regulate downstream pressures on water system.
Backflow Preventers	Bronze Body and Trim or Iron Body with Bronze Trim ¾"-10" Screwed or Flanged.	Used on direct water connections where the possibility of non-toxic contamination from backflow exists.
Expansion Joints	Piston or Bellows Type, Threaded, Flanged or Solder Joint. ½"-20". 150-250 p.s.i.	Used to control expansion and contraction of pipe lines due to temperature changes.
Strainers (Y-Type)	Bronze Construction, Threaded ¼"-4", Iron Body, Flanged ½"-14". 150-600 p.s.i. Pressure Ratings.	Used to strain foreign matter from pipe lines.
Shock Absorbers	Precharged Nitrogen Water Hammer Arresters, Stainless Steel Construction. Plumbing and Drainage Institute Sizes A through F. Fixture Ratings from 1 through 330.	Used to prevent water hammer caused by quick closing valves or lever faucets at fixtures.
Vacuum Breakers	Bronze Construction, Threaded ¼"-3"	Used to prevent back-syphonage of polluted water into potable water lines.
Hose Bibbs	Bronze Construction, ½"-3" Threaded or Solder Joint. 125 lb. Working Pressure. Threaded Hose Outlet Connection.	Used as hose connection for washdown or garden hose attachment.

Figure 2.10 (*cont'd.*)

Hot water in a building is obtained through the use of hot water/steam heaters or generators (see Figures 2.11 and 2.12.) There are five basic water heater classifications:

- Storage
- Instantaneous
- Semi-instantaneous
- Steam and water-mixing valve
- Water blending valve (hot/cold)

The heat sources for these generators can be steam, hot water supply (boiler), electric, and gas- or oil-fired. The tanks are constructed of steel and are ASME-rated pressure vessels. (The American Society of Mechanical Engineers founded this committee–Boiler and Pressure Vessels–to develop standards for construction of steam boilers and other pressure vessels.) Linings for the tanks can be cement, copper silicone, or glass. Capacity, size, and type of heater vary depending on the hot water demand for the particular building, and are usually specified by the mechanical engineer.

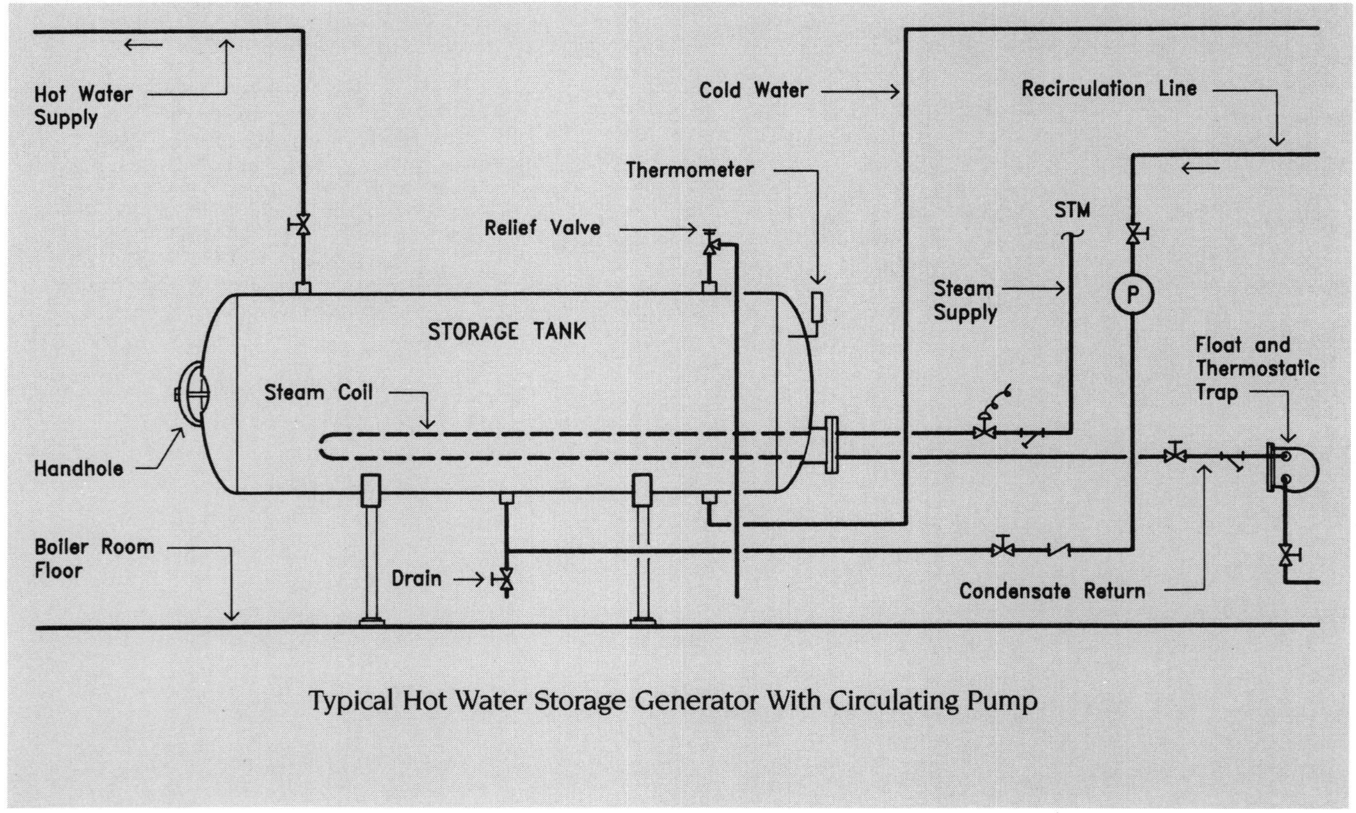

Typical Hot Water Storage Generator With Circulating Pump

Figure 2.11

In buildings where a hot water circulation line has been designed, it becomes necessary to furnish a hot water circulating pump. These pumps are usually small, in-line fractional horsepower pumps of bronze or iron-body construction.

In high-rise buildings or buildings where outside street water pressure is inadequate, it becomes necessary to furnish a cold water booster or constant pressure pumps (see Figure 2.13). Booster pumps are usually duplex or triplex in design and are sized according to the required water demand. These are rather large pumps ranging from 5 to 25 horsepower and are of the vertical turbine or centrifugal design. Some engineers may specify a roof tank system for buildings requiring a large water demand. The water is pumped up to the roof tank, which serves a dual purpose as a domestic water reservoir and fire system reservoir. In case of a pump breakdown, the building's water supply needs can still be met for a short period through means of gravity. Roof tanks are usually constructed of wood (fir, cypress, or redwood), and are subcontracted to contractors specializing in their construction.

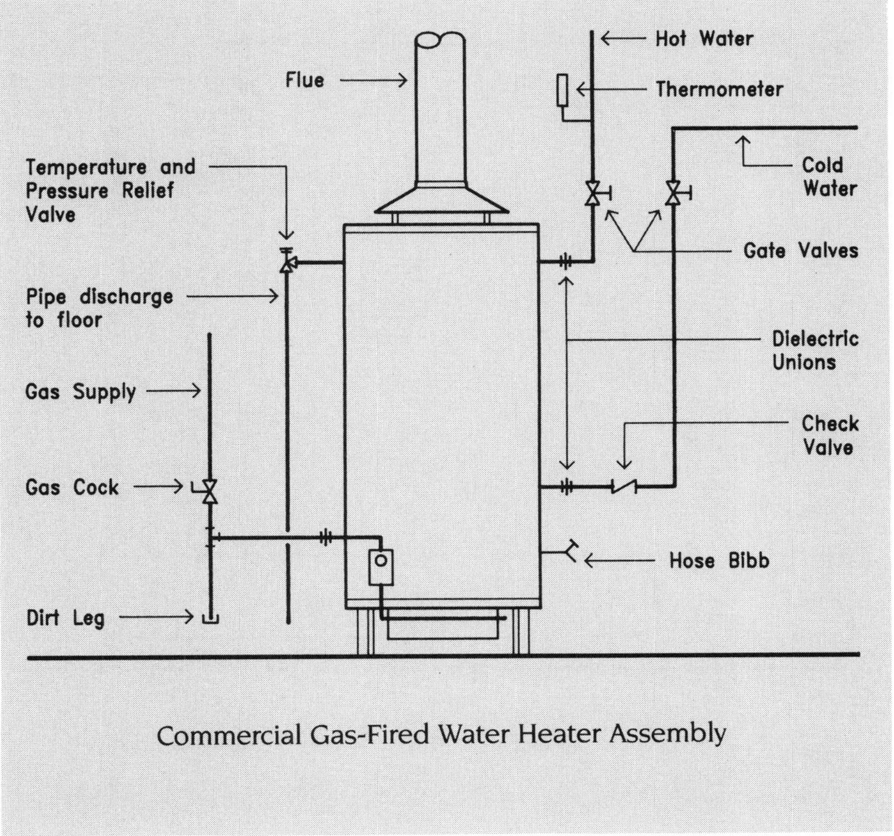

Commercial Gas-Fired Water Heater Assembly

Figure 2.12

Local municipalities usually require water meters in most buildings to accurately determine water consumption. Meters generally range in size from 3/4" to 8" but, unlike gas meters, are furnished and installed by the plumber (see Figure 2.8a).

Sanitary Waste and Vent Systems

The sanitary waste and vent system in a building carries sewage only and excludes storm, surface, and ground water. The system consists of three areas:

1. Building house drain (sanitary)
2. Soil/waste piping and stacks
3. Vent piping and stacks

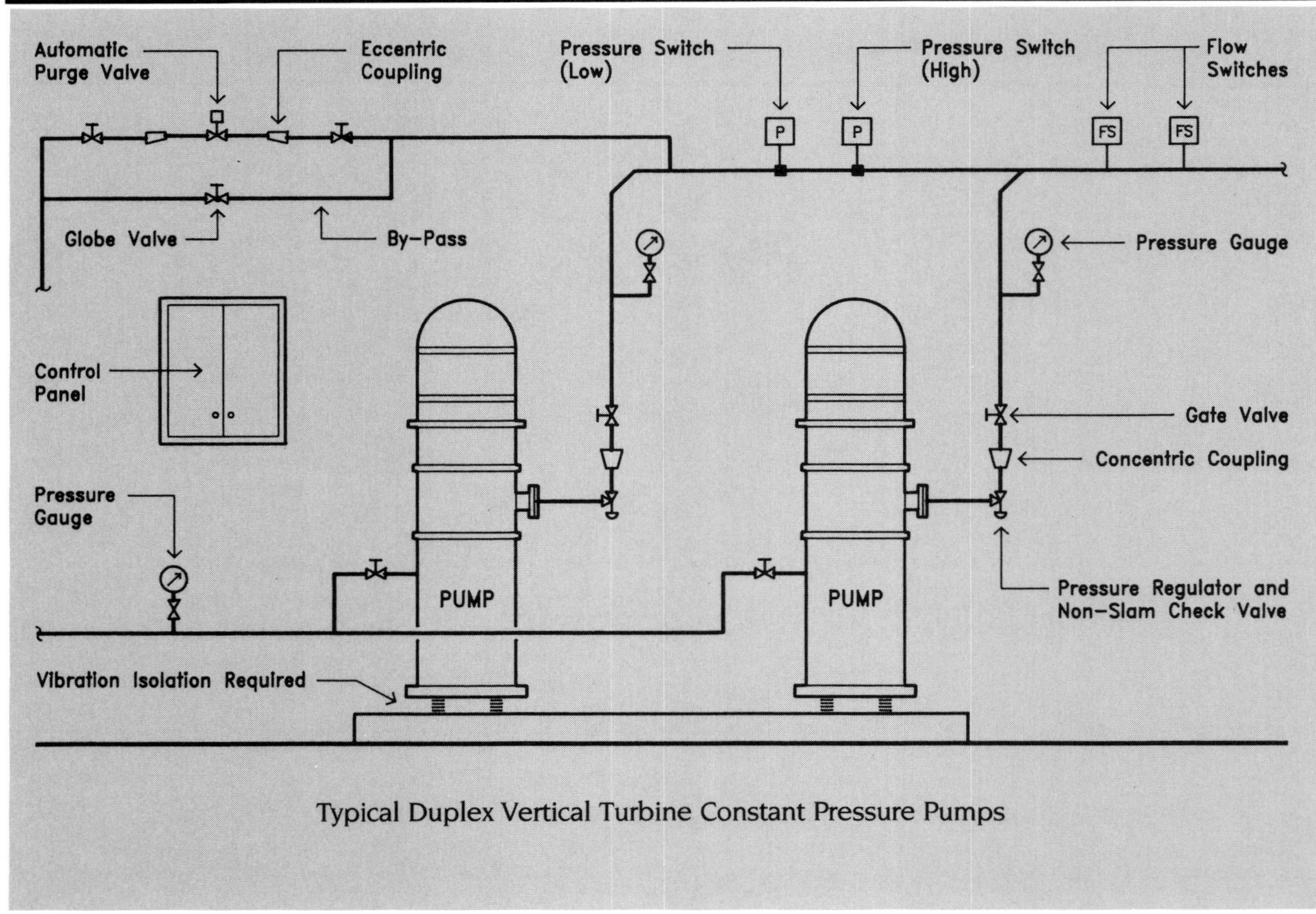

Typical Duplex Vertical Turbine Constant Pressure Pumps

Figure 2.13

Building House Drain

The building house drain is that part of the lowest piping of a drainage system that receives the discharge from the soil, waste and other drainage pipes of the building and conveys it to the building house sewer by gravity.

The building house drain must have a house trap and fresh air inlet. The house trap should be located near the foundation wall of the structure and should be the same size as the building house drain. The purpose of the house trap is to prevent circulation of air between the house drainage system and the building house sewer. The fresh air inlet is connected to the building house drain immediately upstream from, and within four feet of, the house trap.

Soil/Waste Piping and Stacks

Soil piping is that part of the sanitary waste and vent system that conveys sewage which contains fecal (animal or vegetable wastes) matter to the building house drain. Waste piping, like soil piping, discharges into the building house drain; however, it conveys only liquid waste, free of fecal matter. Both soil and waste piping are shown in Figure 2.14.

Also shown is a soil stack which is any vertical soil pipe riser extending floor to floor. Soil and waste lines from the plumbing fixtures are connected to the main soil stack.

Cleanouts (see Figure 2.15) should be installed on all soil and waste lines at every change in direction greater than 45° on all horizontal pipes of the drainage system. In addition, a cleanout should be provided at or near each vertical waste or soil stack.

In some cases, it may be necessary to install *grease* or *oil interceptors*. These devices are designed to separate and retain grease, oil, or any undesirable matter from normal wastes and permit normal sewage or liquid wastes to discharge into the disposal terminal by gravity. A grease trap can be seen in Figure 2.15.

If fixtures or floor drains are installed below the sewer level outside and cannot drain into the gravity system, a *sewage ejector* is necessary (see Figure 2.16). Ejectors are usually duplex in design and are installed in concrete or cast iron basins. The ejector has the capability to force the sewage up to the gravity system through a pump discharge line.

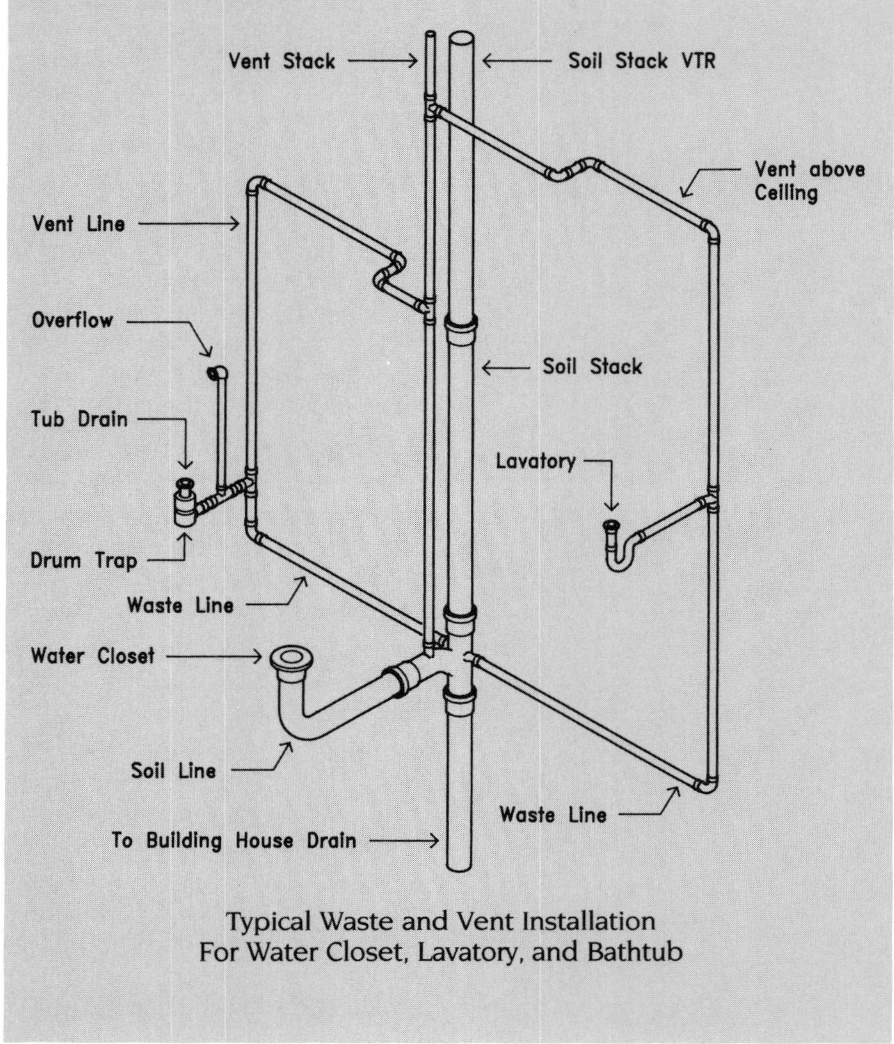
Vent Stack
Soil Stack VTR
Vent above Ceiling
Vent Line
Overflow
Soil Stack
Tub Drain
Lavatory
Drum Trap
Waste Line
Water Closet
Soil Line
Waste Line
To Building House Drain
Typical Waste and Vent Installation
For Water Closet, Lavatory, and Bathtub

Figure 2.14

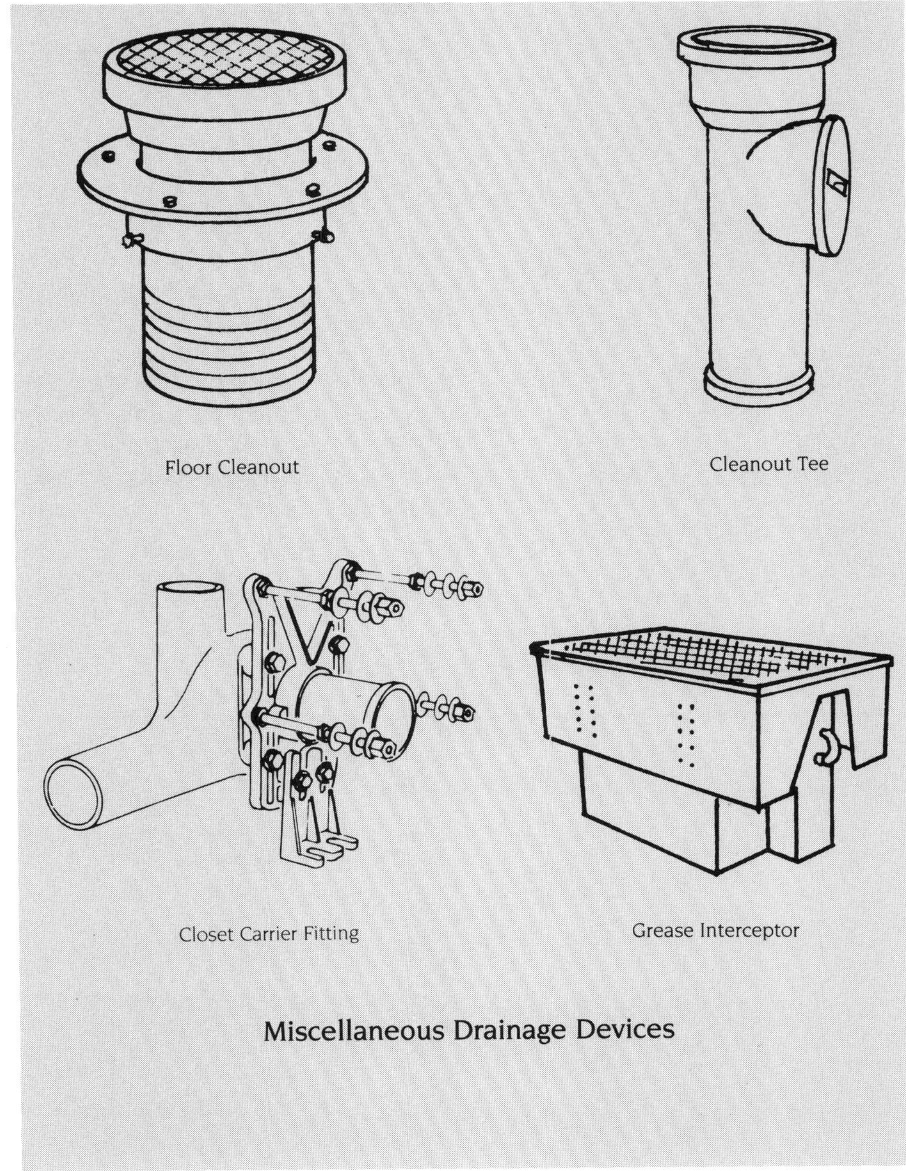

Miscellaneous Drainage Devices

Figure 2.15

Vent Piping and Stacks

The vent piping shown in Figure 2.14 is installed as part of the sanitary system, primarily to provide:

- A flow of air to or from a drainage system.
- A circulation of air within such a system to protect trap seals from siphonage and back pressure.

The vent stack, also shown on Figure 2.14, is any vertical vent pipe extending floor to floor, connected to the vent system to provide circulation of air to and from any part of the drainage system. The vent stack ends at a minimum of two feet above the roof. This is called the *vent terminal* or *extension*. The vent terminal is flashed with lead or copper sheet flashing to make it weather-tight. In areas of the country where freezing poses a problem, vent terminals should be at least four inches in diameter to prevent frost or snow from clogging the vent opening.

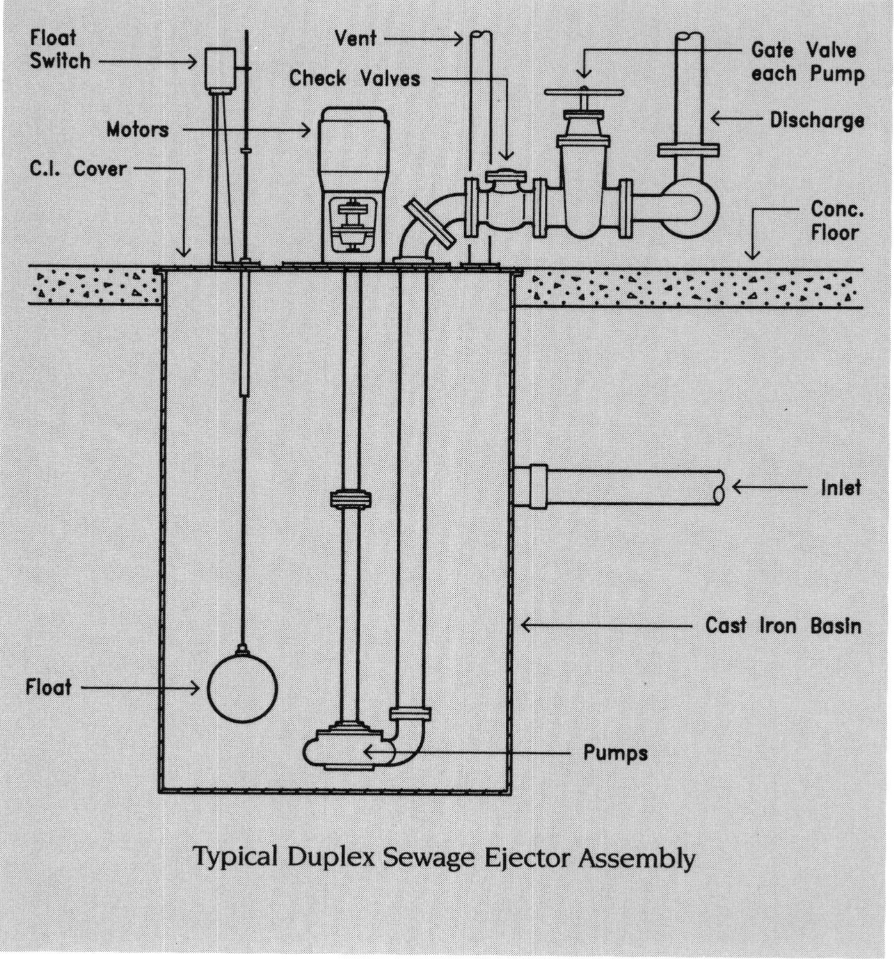

Typical Duplex Sewage Ejector Assembly

Figure 2.16

In some cases, vent lines may be connected to the soil stack at a point above the highest fixture. This is called *stack venting*.

There are a number of different methods used to vent fixtures and drains on a sanitary system, some of which are listed below. The choice will depend on prevailing codes.

- Common vent and vent header
- Circuit vent
- Back vent
- Sovent

Definitions of these venting methods appear in the Glossary.

There are a number of different piping materials suitable for installation on a sanitary waste and vent system:

- Cast iron soil pipe
- Galvanized steel pipe
- DWV copper
- DWV plastic (PVC, ABS)

Compatible fittings are available for all of the above pipe, as shown in Figures 1.4, 1.7, and 1.8. Gaining wider acceptance and popularity over bell and spigot lead joint pipe and fittings are the neoprene and hubless joint design, as described in Chapter 1. Both of these designs can be used throughout the whole system, with the exception that hubless joints cannot be used for underground installations. Combination hubless DWV fittings, as described in Chapter 1, may be used if appropriate to the design. Galvanized steel pipe with galvanized drainage fittings are also specified quite often on aboveground installations and almost always on vent lines 2-1/2" in diameter and below.

DWV copper and plastic are very popular because of the relative speed with which they can be installed due to light weights and ease of handling. However, these materials can only be installed in aboveground installations.

The above mentioned piping materials and associated fittings, which are found on sanitary waste and vent systems, are outlined further in Figure 2.17. Wall-mounted plumbing fixtures such as urinals and water closets are supported by carrier fittings (shown in Figure 2.15), which are an integral part of the sanitary system roughing. Carrier fittings are made of cast iron or steel. The carrier fittings are completely concealed in the wall and support the fixture by a face and base plate, which is anchored to the floor. Fixture supports are manufactured in various combinations and are readily adaptable to virtually any roughing layout.

Storm Drainage System

A storm drainage system is required on virtually all buildings whose design includes a flat roof. The storm system components are:

1. Building house storm drain
2. Storm branch lines
3. Leaders

The building house storm drain is that part of the lowest piping of a storm drainage system that receives clear water drainage from leaders, surface run-off, ground water, subsurface water, condensate, cooling water, or other similar storm or clear water drainage pipes inside the walls of the building. This system conveys the drainage to the building house storm sewer by gravity.

The storm branch lines are all the horizontal drainage lines located above and connected to the building storm drain, the only exception being any horizontal pipe connected to a *single* roof or gutter drain which is considered part of the leader.

A leader is the vertical drainage pipe for conveying storm water from roof or gutter drains to the building storm drain, building house drain (combined), or other means of disposal.

The storm drainage system is similar to the sanitary system in a number of ways.

- House trap required
- Cleanouts required
- Types of pipe and fittings

These devices were fully explained in the previous section. All roof drains should be flashed with lead or copper sheet flashing for weatherproofing. Storm drainage that cannot drain into the gravity system because it is below the outside sewer invert will require a sump pump (see Figure 2.18). Sump pumps are simple or duplex in design and are installed in either cast iron or concrete basins.

SANITARY WASTE AND VENT PIPING AND FITTING SCHEDULE			
PIPE	SERVICE	SIZE	FITTINGS
Cast-Iron Soil Pipe Lead, Neoprene Joint	Soil, Waste, Vent lines above and below grade	2″-15″	Cast-Iron Soil Fittings Lead, Neoprene Joint
Cast-Iron Soil Pipe Hubless-Clamp Joint	Soil and Waste lines above grade	1½″-10″	Cast-Iron Soil Fittings Hubless-Clamp Joint
Galvanized Steel Pipe Threaded Schedule 40	Soil, Waste, Vent lines above grade	1¼″-12″	Galvanized C.I. Drainage Fittings for Soil and Waste Galvanized Malleable Iron Fittings for Vent
D.W.V. Copper Solder Joint	Soil, Waste, Vent lines above grade	1¼″-8″	D.W.V. Copper Solder Joint Fittings (Wrought or Cast Drainage)
D.W.V. PVC, ABS Cement Joint	Soil, Waste, Vent lines above grade	1½″-8″	D.W.V. Plastic PVC Cement Joint

Figure 2.17

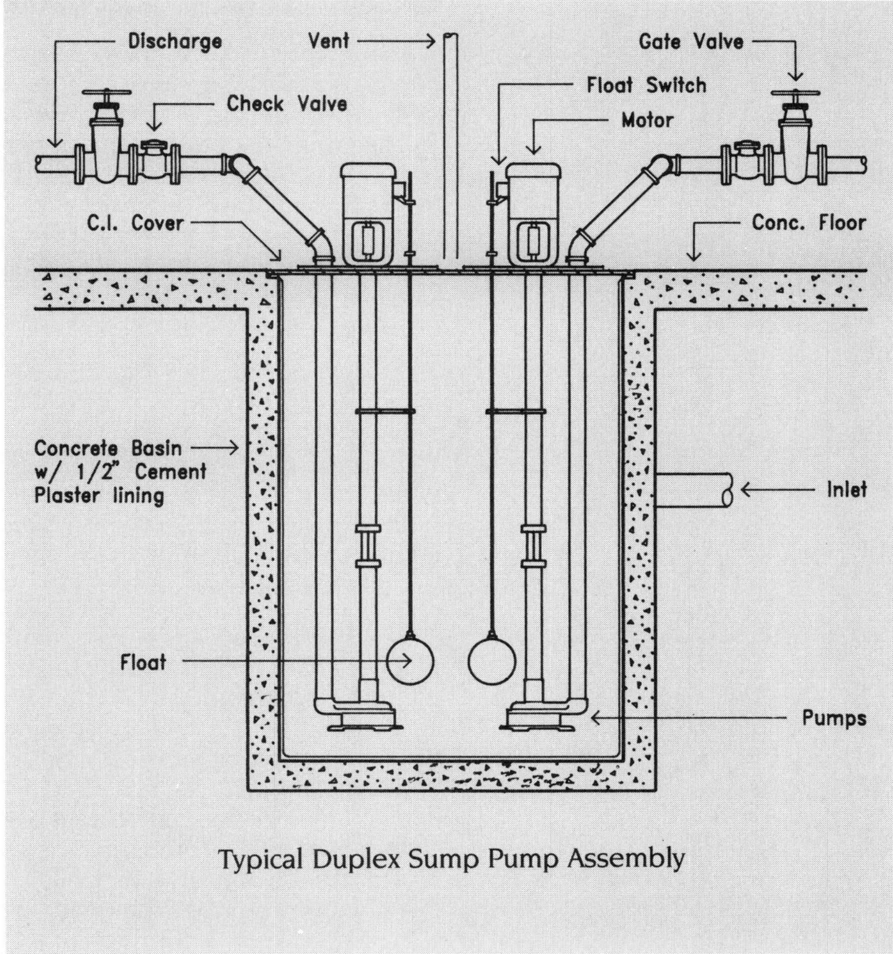

Typical Duplex Sump Pump Assembly

Figure 2.18

Fire Protection Systems

The three fire protection systems that will be discussed in this section are fire standpipe systems, automatic sprinkler systems, and halon systems. While fire, as a source of damage and destruction will never be totally eliminated, the efforts of professionals should mitigate the tragedy it causes. Recently, major fires have resulted in multi-billion dollar lawsuits involving not only owner and owner agencies, but materials specifiers, architects, engineers, and even code writing certification groups. With all of these parties becoming involved, fire safety has become a major issue and a war is being waged against destructive fires.

Fire safety begins with the proper design and construction of fire-safe structures. Incorporated into that design should be a total systems approach to fire protection. There are three basic components of an engineered fire protection system: detection, alarm, and suppression. When integrated with architectural considerations such as separation walls, fireproof or fire-resistant materials, and a comprehensive fire education/evacuation program, the highest degree of reliability and life safety can be achieved.

Fire Standpipe Systems

In most areas of the country, the fire standpipe system is part of the plumbing contractor's work, when not connected to or part of the sprinkler system. On the other hand, sprinkler systems are not always in the scope of plumbing work. For example, all sprinkler work in New York City is done by sprinkler contractors belonging to the *steamfitters union*. In many other municipalities across the country, however, sprinkler systems are part of the plumbing contract, even if the plumbing contractor subcontracts his work to a separate sprinkler contractor. In many areas fire protection contractors employ sprinkler fitters.

A fire standpipe is a system of piping for fire-fighting purposes (see Figure 2.19), consisting of a water supply that serves one or more hose outlets. Standpipe systems and their locations are governed by the various local codes. However, a standpipe system is usually required in buildings exceeding three stories in height, or two or more stories in height that have a net floor area of 10,000 square feet or more on any floor.

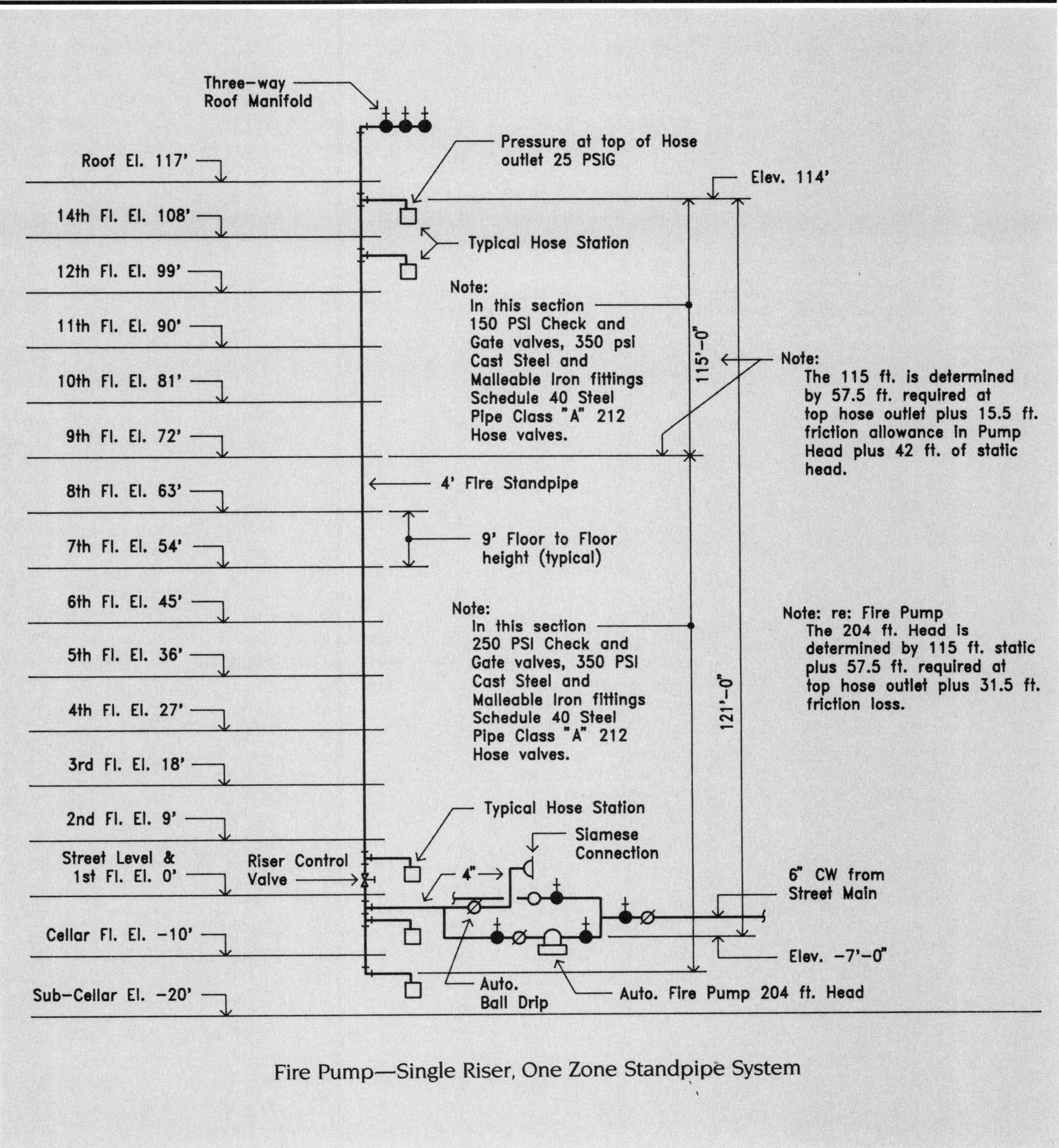

Three-way Roof Manifold
Roof El. 117'
Pressure at top of Hose outlet 25 PSIG
Elev. 114'
14th Fl. El. 108'
Typical Hose Station
12th Fl. El. 99'
Note:
In this section 150 PSI Check and Gate valves, 350 psi Cast Steel and Malleable Iron fittings Schedule 40 Steel Pipe Class "A" 212 Hose valves.
11th Fl. El. 90'
115'-0"
Note:
The 115 ft. is determined by 57.5 ft. required at top hose outlet plus 15.5 ft. friction allowance in Pump Head plus 42 ft. of static head.
10th Fl. El. 81'
9th Fl. El. 72'
8th Fl. El. 63'
4' Fire Standpipe
7th Fl. El. 54'
9' Floor to Floor height (typical)
6th Fl. El. 45'
Note:
In this section 250 PSI Check and Gate valves, 350 PSI Cast Steel and Malleable Iron fittings Schedule 40 Steel Pipe Class "A" 212 Hose valves.
Note: re: Fire Pump
The 204 ft. Head is determined by 115 ft. static plus 57.5 ft. required at top hose outlet plus 31.5 ft. friction loss.
5th Fl. El. 36'
4th Fl. El. 27'
121'-0"
3rd Fl. El. 18'
2nd Fl. El. 9'
Typical Hose Station
Siamese Connection
Street Level & 1st Fl. El. 0'
Riser Control Valve
4"
6" CW from Street Main
Cellar Fl. El. -10'
Elev. -7'-0"
Sub-Cellar El. -20'
Auto. Ball Drip
Auto. Fire Pump 204 ft. Head

Fire Pump—Single Riser, One Zone Standpipe System

Figure 2.19

There are two types of standpipe systems: *wet* and *dry*. A wet standpipe system is one in which all piping is filled with water under pressure that is immediately discharged upon the opening of any hose valve. A dry standpipe system is one in which all piping is *filled with air* (whether compressed or at atmospheric pressure) to prevent winter freezeup. Water enters the system through a control valve actuated either automatically by the reduction of air pressure within the system or by the manual activation of a remote control located at each hose station. The hose stations are usually located within each stair enclosure or adjacent to the entrance of such enclosure. Fire hose stations consist of a 2-1/2" fire department valve with 75', 100', or 125' of hose on racks or in cabinets. Certain municipalities require a fire reserve roof tank capable of delivering 3,500 gallons of water to each standpipe zone. In buildings where outside water main pressure is inadequate to handle the prescribed water demand, a fire pump is required. Siamese connections are fittings connected to a fire standpipe system, and are installed on the outside of a building with two hose inlets for use by the fire department, to furnish or supplement the water supply to the system. Siamese connections are required on all standpipe systems. One Siamese connection should be installed for every 300' of exterior building wall.

The standard piping materials for a standpipe system are black steel Schedule 40 or 80 pipe with 350 lb. malleable iron fittings and 150 to 500 lb.-rated fire underwriter gate and check valves. The joining methods used are usually threaded or grooved. In addition to steel, and where code permits, chlorinated PVC piping is used on fire standpipe installations.

Sprinkler Systems

The sprinkler system is the system of piping, valves, and sprinkler heads for fire-fighting purposes, connected to one or more sources of water. According to the National Fire Protection Association (NFPA), "sprinklers are the most effective means of automatically controlling fire in buildings." Sprinkler systems are versatile since they trigger the alarm, react immediately, and concentrate directly on the fire with continuous operation until the fire is completely extinguished.

The NFPA also states that sprinklers are 96.2% effective. The 3.8% that might be considered "failures" were due to improper water supply or failure by the facility to modify the system to account for an increased fire hazard.

No other fire extinguishing agent functions as thoroughly as water. It cools and smothers the fire, while diluting and emulsifying the combustibles. Water damage is kept to a minimum by sprinkler systems for two reasons. First, only sprinkler heads directly over the blaze open up and discharge water. Second, when compared to a standard 2-1/2" diameter firefighting hose, the sprinkler at 75 psi delivers approximately 50 gallons of water per minute, as compared to the hose's 400 gallons per minute. Water consumption by sprinklers is minimal. For example, 37.4% of all reported sprinkler fires were controlled by one head; 73.4% were controlled by five or fewer heads; and 85% were controlled by 10 or fewer heads.

Lastly, and perhaps more important, records show that there have been only a dozen or so instances in which occupants have been killed by fire in a fully sprinklered building. The victims were killed by the fire itself, and were not "drowned" by the sprinkler system.

There are basically five types of automatic sprinkler systems: wet pipe, dry pipe, pre-action, deluge, and firecycle. A sprinkler design engineer normally selects the proper system for the facility he or she is designing, based on its hazard classifications. Buildings are evaluated and given a hazard classification based on two criteria: building construction, and building occupancy.

While there are numerous municipal building and fire codes, the most widely used and recognized minimum standards are the 16 volumes of the National Fire Code published annually by the National Fire Protection Association. In the NFPA Code, hazard classifications (light, ordinary, extra) are given to various types of buildings based on their occupancy. See Figure 2.20 for NFPA listings.

The five types of sprinkler systems mentioned above are designed for specific applications.

1. **The Wet Pipe System:** This system is the most common sprinkler used. The wet pipe system employs automatic sprinklers attached to piping containing water under pressure at all times. When the heat from a fire exceeds the temperature rating of the sprinkler head, it melts a fusible link, and water contained within the piping is discharged immediately onto the fire. This system is generally used wherever there is no danger of the pipes freezing. See Figure 2.21a for a typical wet pipe system.
2. **The Dry Pipe System:** Dry pipe sprinkler systems are used in unheated areas, such as parking garages. The system has automatic sprinklers attached to piping containing air under pressure. When a sprinkler head opens, pressurized air is exhausted or reduced through the heat until water begins to flow. Dry systems cost more than wet systems because of the necessary larger pipe sizes, additional equipment (accelerator, air compressor, etc.), and they require additional maintenance. See Figure 2.21b for a typical dry pipe system.
3. **The Pre-Action System:** Pre-action systems prevent accidental water discharge from defective sprinkler heads and/or fittings. The dry system is normally used in areas that contain costly equipment, such as computer rooms. Pre-action sprinklers operate faster and reduce both fire and water damage in comparison with conventional dry pipe systems. Because piping is dry, it is non-freezing and therefore applicable to conventional dry pipe service. The system piping supervision is provided by low pressure air, leakage of which sounds an alarm without tripping the main valve. The water supply valve is actuated independently of the opening of sprinklers, i.e., the valve is opened by the operation of an automatic fire detection system and not by the fusing of the sprinklers. Pre-action systems are limited to 1,000 sprinklers.

FIRE HAZARD CLASSIFICATION BY OCCUPANCY

LIGHT HAZARD

- AUDITORIUMS
- CHURCHES
- CLUBS
- EDUCATIONAL
- HOSPITALS
- INSTITUTIONAL
- LIBRARIES (EXCEPT LARGE STACK ROOMS)
- MUSEUMS
- NURSING HOMES
- OFFICES
- RESIDENTIAL
- RESTAURANTS
- SCHOOLS
- THEATERS

ORDINARY HAZARD

- AUTOMOTIVE GARAGES
- BAKERIES
- BEVERAGE MANUFACTURING
- BLEACHERIES
- BOILER HOUSES
- CANNERIES
- CEMENT PLANTS
- CLOTHING FACTORIES
- COLD STORAGE WAREHOUSES
- DAIRY PRODUCTS MANUFACTURING
- DISTILLERIES
- DRY CLEANING
- ELECTRIC GENERATING STATIONS
- FEED MILLS
- GRAIN ELEVATORS
- ICE MANUFACTURING
- LAUNDRIES
- MACHINE STOPS
- MERCANTILES
- PAPER MILLS
- PRINTING & PUBLISHING
- SHOE FACTORIES
- WAREHOUSES
- WOOD PRODUCT ASSEMBLY

EXTRA HAZARD

- AIRCRAFT HANGARS
- CHEMICAL WORKS
- EXPLOSIVES MANUFACTURING
- LINOLEUM MANUFACTURING
- LINSEED OIL MILLS
- PAINT SHOPS
- SHADE CLOTH MANUFACTURING
- SOLVENT EXTRACTING
- VARNISH WORKS
- OIL REFINERIES
- VOLATILE OR FLAMMABLE LIQUID MANUFACTURING AND USE

Figure 2.20

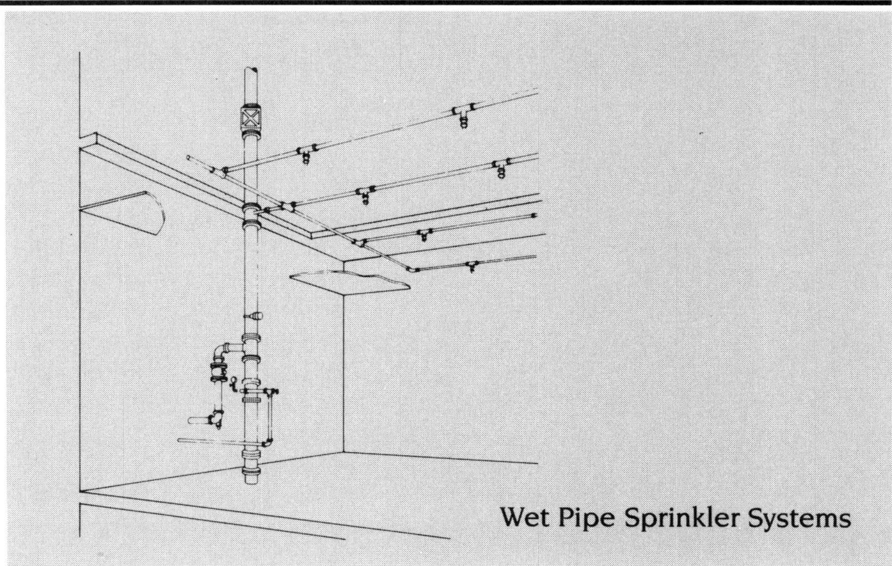

Figure 2.21a

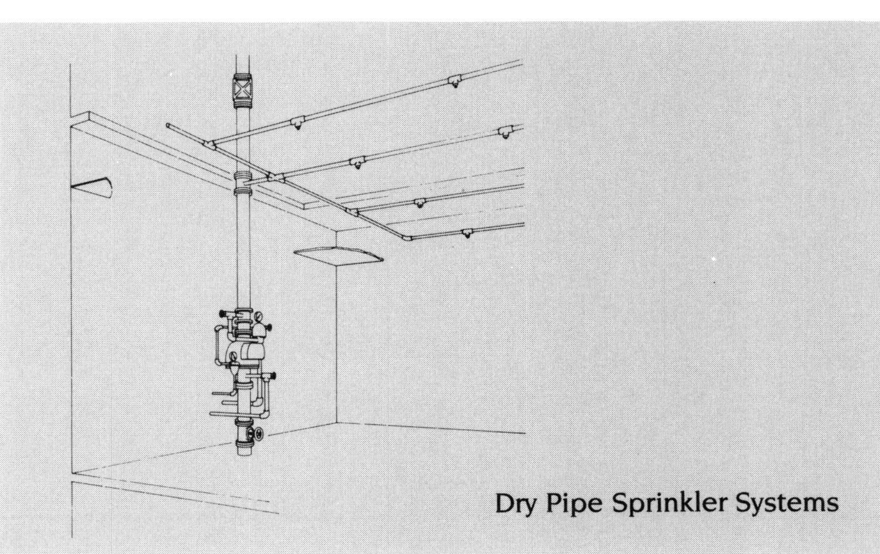

Figure 2.21b

4. **Deluge System:** Although different in application, deluge and pre-action sprinkler systems are very similar in design. Both use automatic fire detection systems, and both use the same main valve. The primary difference is that deluge systems use open sprinklers, while pre-action systems use closed sprinklers. A deluge system is designed to discharge water simultaneously from every sprinkler head in the system. Unlike the other three systems, the sprinkler head has no fusible link and, therefore, remains open. When a detection system is activated, the deluge valve opens and water floods the area. Deluge systems are used where flammable liquids or other materials can spread quickly and endanger life safety. Deluge systems are limited in size to 225 sprinklers. See Figure 2.22 for typical pre-action and deluge systems.
5. **Firecycle System:** Technically speaking, firecycle is an on-and-off cycling pre-action sprinkler system. Through the use of heat detectors and an electrical control panel, firecycle systems have the capability of continued on-and-off cycling while controlling fire, and shutting off the flow of water when the fire is extinguished. The system has been widely used in areas where water damage must be minimized. Because water cannot flow unless initiated by signal from the heat detection system, firecycle also eliminates the possibility of water damage stemming from accidents to sprinklers or piping. See Figure 2.23 for a typical firecycle system.

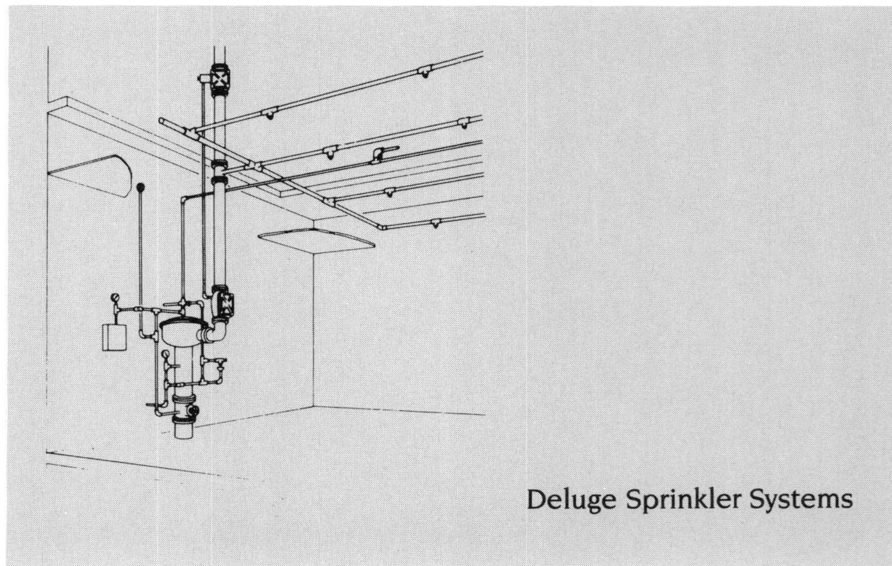
Deluge Sprinkler Systems

Figure 2.22

Sprinkler booster pumps may also be required if outside street pressure is inadequate. Depending on local jurisdiction, fire lines may be required to have fire detector meters. Piping materials, valves, and fittings for sprinkler systems are similar to those specified for fire standpipe systems.

No discussion of sprinkler systems is complete without a detailed look at the various types of sprinkler heads offered by manufacturers for specific applications. All automatic sprinkler heads are engineered to spread a blanket of finely divided water over an immediate fire area. They act quickly, before the fire gets out of control. They perform positively without fail.

Sprinkler heads are produced to operate at a variety of temperature ranges. The heads have their water opening securely capped. The cap is held in place with lever arms or rods which, in turn, are held by a fusible link. In case of fire, the solder in the link fuses. Instantly the lever arms or rods are thrown clear by the spring pressure of the frame. The water cap is thrown out by water pressure. Through the orifice, water strikes the deflector, then distributes the water in a uniform pattern. See Figure 2.24 for various types of sprinkler heads.

Fire extinguishers are another of the fire-fighting devices which may fall under the plumbing, sprinkler, or general contract. They are mentioned here simply to note that they may have to be included in the estimate costs for fire protection.

Halon and Chemical Replacement Fire Suppression

Halon and replacement fire suppression systems are used because they are fast, effective, and clean (shown in Figure 2.25). These systems are called "clean" because they leave no residue that must be cleaned up or that could contaminate valuable items (i.e., records or electronic equipment). Because halon gas is a non-conductor of electricity and is several times heavier than air, it permeates the working area and penetrates cabinets or other electric or electronic enclosures where chemical powders cannot.

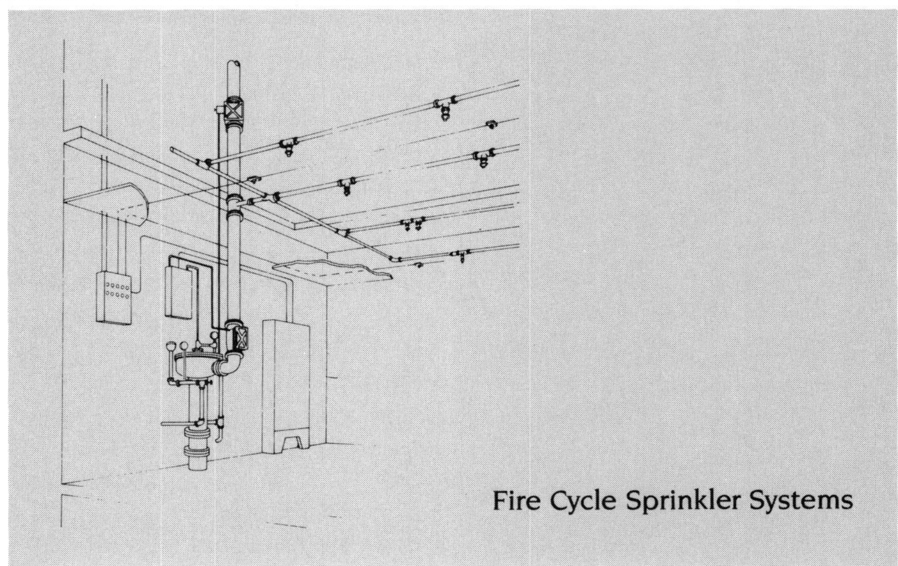

Figure 2.23

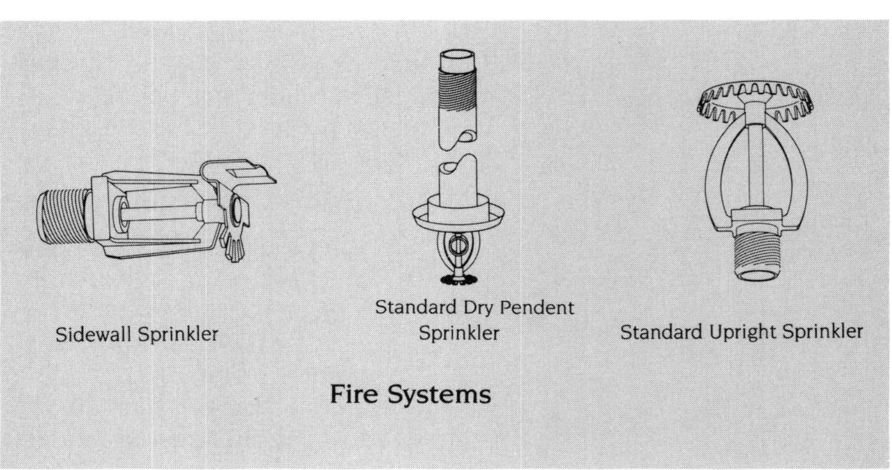

Figure 2.24

Depending on its concentration, halon gas ranges from non-toxic to low toxity. Halon 1301 is normally used in a concentration of 5-7%. This concentration has no effect on personnel in the area.

Seven to ten percent concentration requires evacuation within one minute of exposure; concentrations above 10% require evacuation prior to discharge. Halon 1301 and its replacements are also colorless and produces minimal visual interference to hamper evacuation.

Chemicals may be applied to fires by portable extinguishers, local application of strategically placed cylinders (or prepackaged systems), or by a centrally located cylinder or battery of storage cylinders connected to a piping distribution system and discharge nozzles. The local application or modular system is the most effective type of system because it eliminates the piping installation costs encountered in a centrally located system.

Detection and actuation are critical requirements for fast extinguishing, to eliminate not only fire damage but also the accompanying risks of smoke, heat, carbon monoxide, and oxygen depletion. Fire and smoke detectors are wired to a control panel that activates the alarm systems, verifies or proves the existence of combustion, and releases the extinguishing agent, all in a matter of seconds.

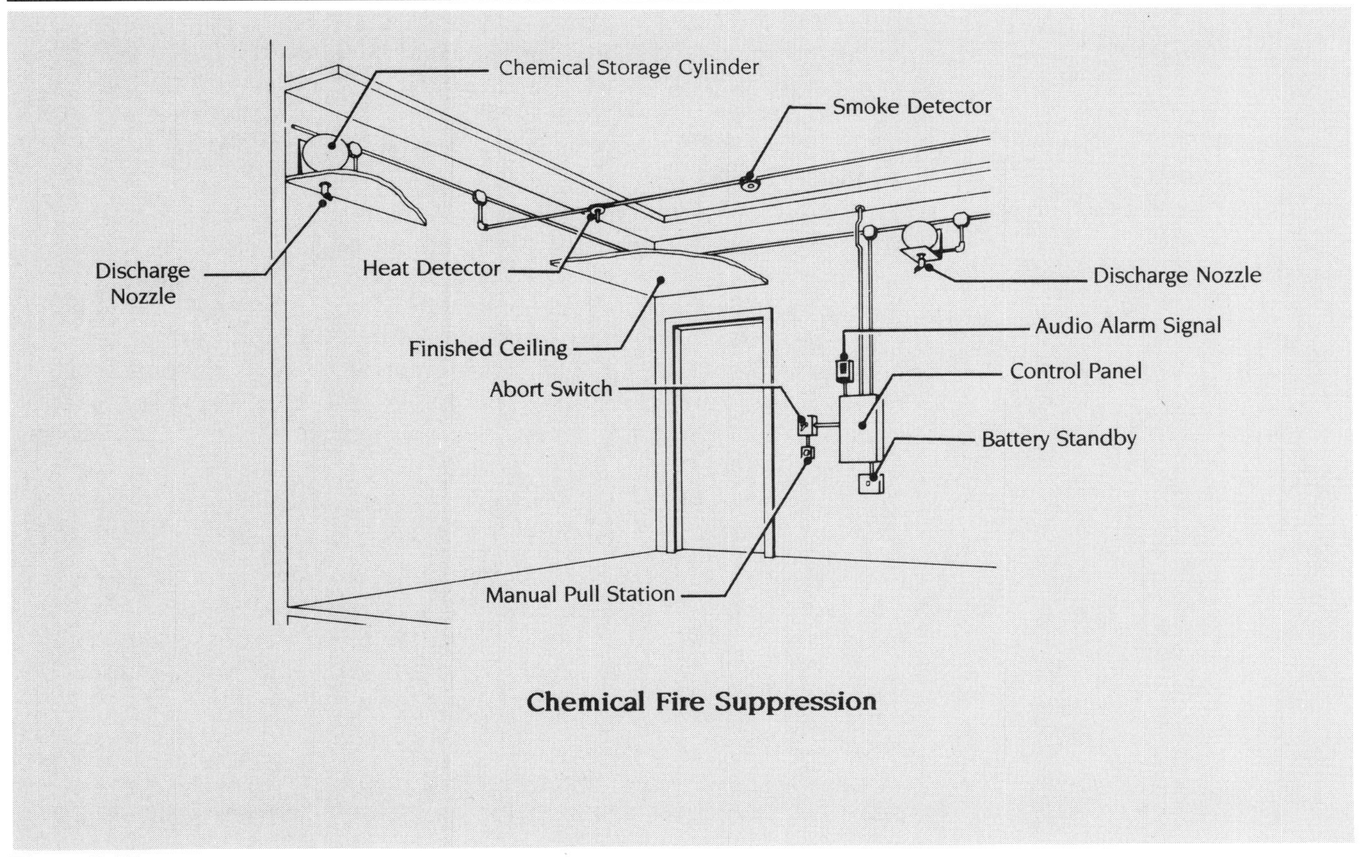

Chemical Fire Suppression

Figure 2.25

The halon fire suppression system is most effective in an enclosed area. The control system may also have the capability of closing doors and shutting off exhaust fans. These systems are in popular use in the following places:

- Aircraft (both cargo and passenger)
- Libraries and museums
- Bank and security vaults
- Electronic data processing
- Transformer and switchgear rooms
- Tape and data storage vaults (rooms)
- Telephone exchanges
- Laboratories
- Radio and television studios
- Flammable liquid storage areas

Special Piping Systems

Plumbing estimators are apt to encounter a variety of specialized piping systems in the course of a career. A book could be written about these special systems alone, so we will cover only the more common specialized systems in this section. They include:

- Natural gas systems
- Medical gas systems
- Acid waste systems
- Swimming pool and filtration systems

Natural Gas System

Natural gas serves as an energy source for items such as boilers, burners, hot water generators, unit heaters, etc. Gas is generally supplied to customers via gas mains supplied and maintained by local gas companies. In most cities, the gas service and meter to individual buildings is also provided by the gas company. However, the estimator should check with the local utility for a listing of the regulations for each particular project.

The gas system within a building is all the piping, valves, and devices starting from the gas meter. The plumber begins the distribution of piping within the building after the gas meter, supplying a gas regulator if required. Gas regulators are usually required if the gas supply is at a pressure in excess of 1/2 psi. Pressures of up to 3 psi are permitted upon approval in certain cases, such as commercial or industrial buildings. Depending on the type of building, gas is used as a fuel for gas-fired equipment, or as in the case of laboratories, as a fuel for laboratory tables and equipment.

The most common piping material for a gas system within the building is Schedule 40 black steel pipe with 150 lb. black malleable iron fittings.

The flow of gas is controlled through the use of approved brass or iron-body gas cocks for pipe sizes 1/2" to 2", and through the use of lubricated plug valves for sizes 2-1/2" and up. All pieces of equipment, such as boilers, gas ranges, unit heaters, and laboratory equipment should be individually controlled using these valves.

Medical Gas Systems

The medical gas system in a hospital is made up of five medical gas subsystems: oxygen, nitrogen, compressed air, nitrous oxide, and a vacuum subsystem. (See Figure 2.26.)

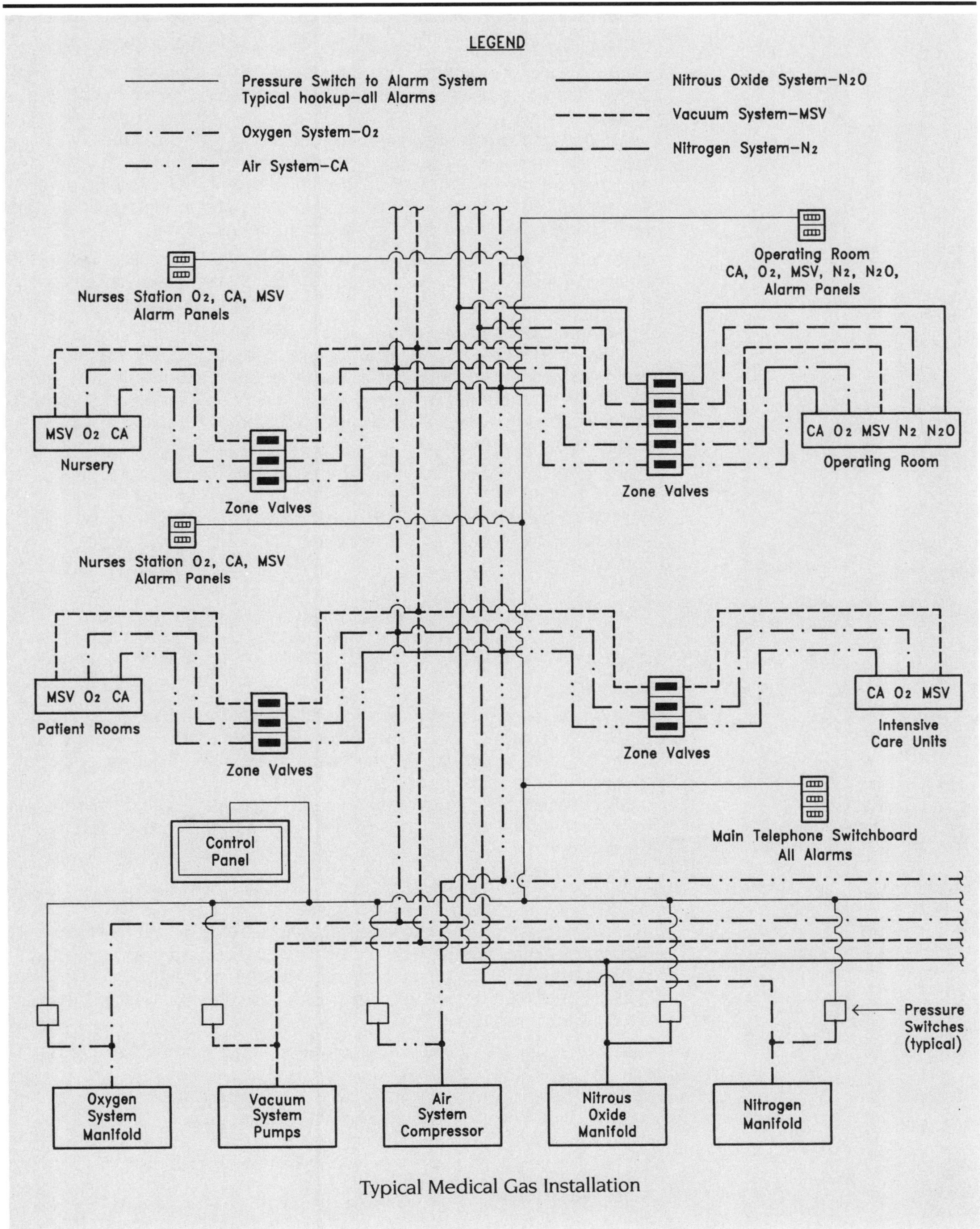

Typical Medical Gas Installation

Figure 2.26

Oxygen is used for respiratory therapy. Oxygen supply in a hospital should always be plentiful, with outlets located in strategic and convenient areas. Oxygen is supplied to the system by one of two methods–either through a bulk oxygen storage tank on the site (furnished by a medical gas supplier) or through a gas manifold with individual cylinders of oxygen connected to it. Manifolds are either automatic or semi-automatic in design, but automatic manifolds are suggested for large installations since they require no maintenance other than changing depleted cylinders and routine inspection.

Nitrogen is a gas used to drive surgical tools, and its location within the hospital is usually limited to surgical suites. Nitrogen is supplied to the system by a manifold similar to the one used for oxygen.

A vacuum subsystem serves a variety of functions throughout the hospital. In the area of patient treatment, it is used to remove fluids during surgery and post-operative drainage. In the laboratory, it is used for transferring liquids from one container to another and for filtering and cleaning apparatus. The vacuum is created by rotary-oil and water-sealed vacuum pumps.

Compressed air is used for respiratory therapy. Compressed air is usually specified for intensive care units, nurseries, emergency rooms, out-patient clinics, surgical suites, and laboratories. Compressed air is supplied to the system by reciprocating air-cooled or oil-free air compressors.

Nitrous oxide, the analgesic gas that produces a loss of sensitivity to pain, is supplied to the system by manifolds similar to the types used for oxygen and nitrogen. Oxygen and nitrous oxide are two gases that support combustion and should be adequately controlled in all areas.

System Control

All medical gas systems are controlled by zone control valves that are capable of isolating each of the medical gases in individual areas. For example, there would be separate zone valve assemblies for operating rooms, patient rooms, nurseries, etc. (See Figure 2.26.) Access to medical gases is obtained through medical gas outlets. Outlets are manufactured for various applications, such as individual outlets in patient rooms, hose-reel ceiling outlets for overhead services, and surgical ceiling columns in surgical suites.

Alarms

All medical gas systems have audio-visual monitoring alarm systems. Sudden pressure drops are picked up by pressure switches which relay the signal to an alarm panel located at strategic points, such as nurses' stations. Local alarms are used in areas where the supply of gas may be critical to life support.

Type L or K copper tubing is the common piping material used for all medical gases. The fittings used on medical gas systems are wrought or cast bronze solder joint. Control valves are either globe or ball valves (solder joint). The copper tubing used for medical gases is washed with either a hot solution of sodium carbonate or trisodium phosphate. Tubing can be purchased prewashed or can be washed after installation.

Acid Waste and Vent System

The acid waste system is a special drainage system of pipe and fittings used to convey, from laboratory sinks or other receptacles, acid-bearing wastes prior to their dilution and discharge into the sanitary house drain (see Figure 2.27). Acid waste systems are generally located in laboratory areas of hospitals, schools, research laboratories, and colleges. Acid wastes cannot drain directly into the house sanitary system because of potentially dangerous or noxious fumes being released into that system. Damage to standard cast iron, copper, or steel drain lines is also likely to occur if acid wastes are allowed to drain into the sanitary system undiluted.

Acid wastes are diluted in individual or central acid neutralizing sumps filled with limestone chips. Individual sumps are usually located adjacent to or beneath each acid sink or fixture. If a central acid sump is used for several fixtures, it should be located at the lowest story above the sanitary house drain.

Consulting engineers usually specify one of three types of piping materials for use on acid waste systems:

- Glass pipe and fittings
- Polypropylene pipe and fittings
- Cast iron high-silicone pipe and fittings

Glass pipe is the most popular of the three materials. Although mainly used for above grade applications, glass can be buried below grade if heavy schedule pipe is encased with a special covering to give it greater loadbearing strength.

Polypropylene pipe is gaining wider acceptance because of its light weight and ease of handling during installations, but its use is limited to above and below ground installations.

Cast iron high-silicone pipe has been around for some time and is excellent for use on both above and below ground installations.

Swimming Pool and Filtration Systems

On a project where a swimming pool is to be installed, it is usually the responsibility of the plumbing contractor to furnish and install all the piping and filtration equipment. The plan of a typical swimming pool is shown in Figure 2.28, and the pool filter system is illustrated in Figure 2.29. The following is a list of components which are generally found in every pool system and should be included in the plumbing estimate, unless otherwise noted in the engineer's specifications.

- Filter
- Circulating pump
- Pool heater (if required)
- Soda ash and hypochlorinator
- Alum feed
- Filtration pipe, fittings and valves
- Vacuum piping and fitting
- Gutter drain piping and fittings
- Main drain piping and fittings
- Pool supply piping and fittings

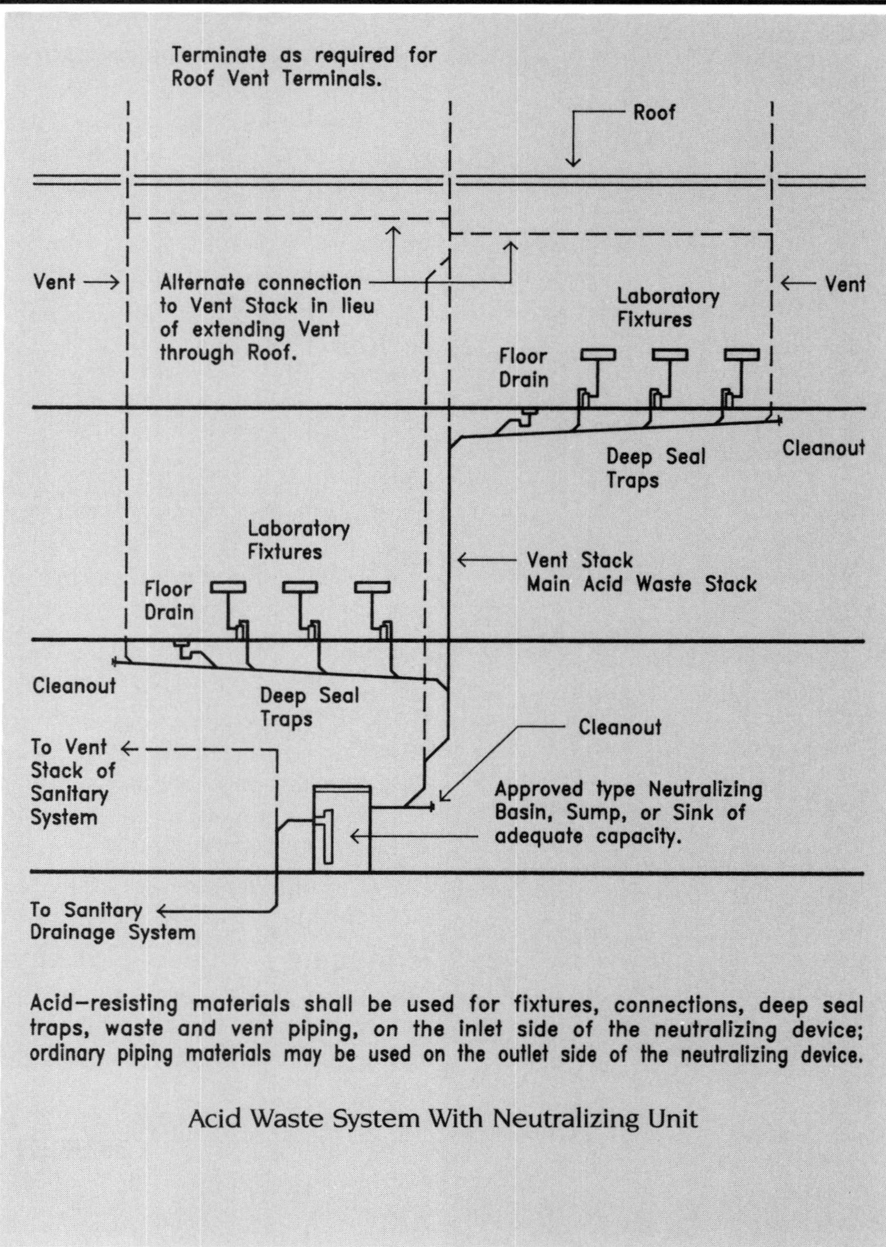
Terminate as required for
Roof Vent Terminals.
Roof
Vent
Alternate connection
to Vent Stack in lieu
of extending Vent
through Roof.
Vent
Laboratory
Fixtures
Floor
Drain
Cleanout
Deep Seal
Traps
Laboratory
Fixtures
Vent Stack
Main Acid Waste Stack
Floor
Drain
Cleanout
Deep Seal
Traps
Cleanout
To Vent
Stack of
Sanitary
System
Approved type Neutralizing
Basin, Sump, or Sink of
adequate capacity.
To Sanitary
Drainage System
Acid–resisting materials shall be used for fixtures, connections, deep seal traps, waste and vent piping, on the inlet side of the neutralizing device; ordinary piping materials may be used on the outlet side of the neutralizing device.

Acid Waste System With Neutralizing Unit

Figure 2.27

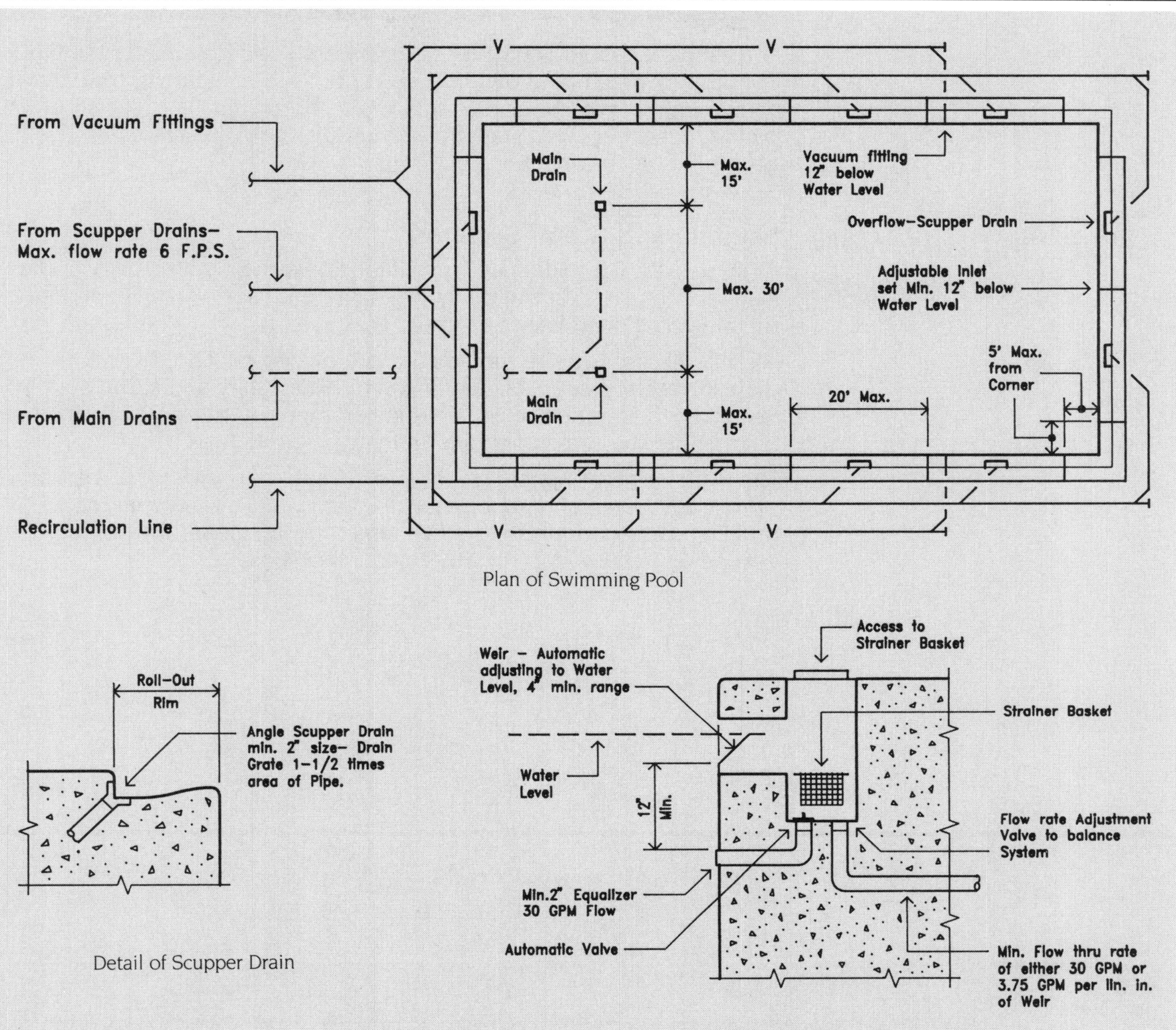

Plan of Swimming Pool

Detail of Scupper Drain

Detail of Skimmer Recirculating System

NOTES:

1. Main Drain Grate shall have open area equal to 4 times the area of Main Drain Pipe, or maximum velocity through the Grate of 1-1/2 F.P.S.
2. If Skimmers are used Handholds must be provided.
3. One Skimmer for every 500 SF of Pool surface area or fraction thereof shall be provided.
4. If Skimmers are used, omit Scupper Drains and Surge Tank. Some Skimmers also have Built-in Vacuum fittings thereby eliminating the need for Vacuum Piping.

Typical Swimming Pool Plan

Figure 2.28

The estimator should consult the engineer's specifications for the type of filtration system and obtain a quote for such equipment from a pool equipment manufacturer. Depending on the system and specifications, piping found in pool installations is usually polyvinyl chloride, galvanized steel, copper, or cast iron.

Plumbing Site Work Systems

Sanitary and Storm Systems

At some sites, large drainage installations are the responsibility of the general contractor, but in many cases site drainage work will fall under the plumbing contractor's scope of work.

We will discuss the site sanitary and storm systems together because the estimator often encounters a combined sanitary and storm system. Secondly, the method of installation and types of materials specified are often either the same or similar in many respects.

The sanitary sewer system on the project site is considered to be all the piping, manholes, and appurtenances conveying sewage from the building sanitary drain to a public sewer, private sewer, individual sewage disposal system, or other point of disposal.

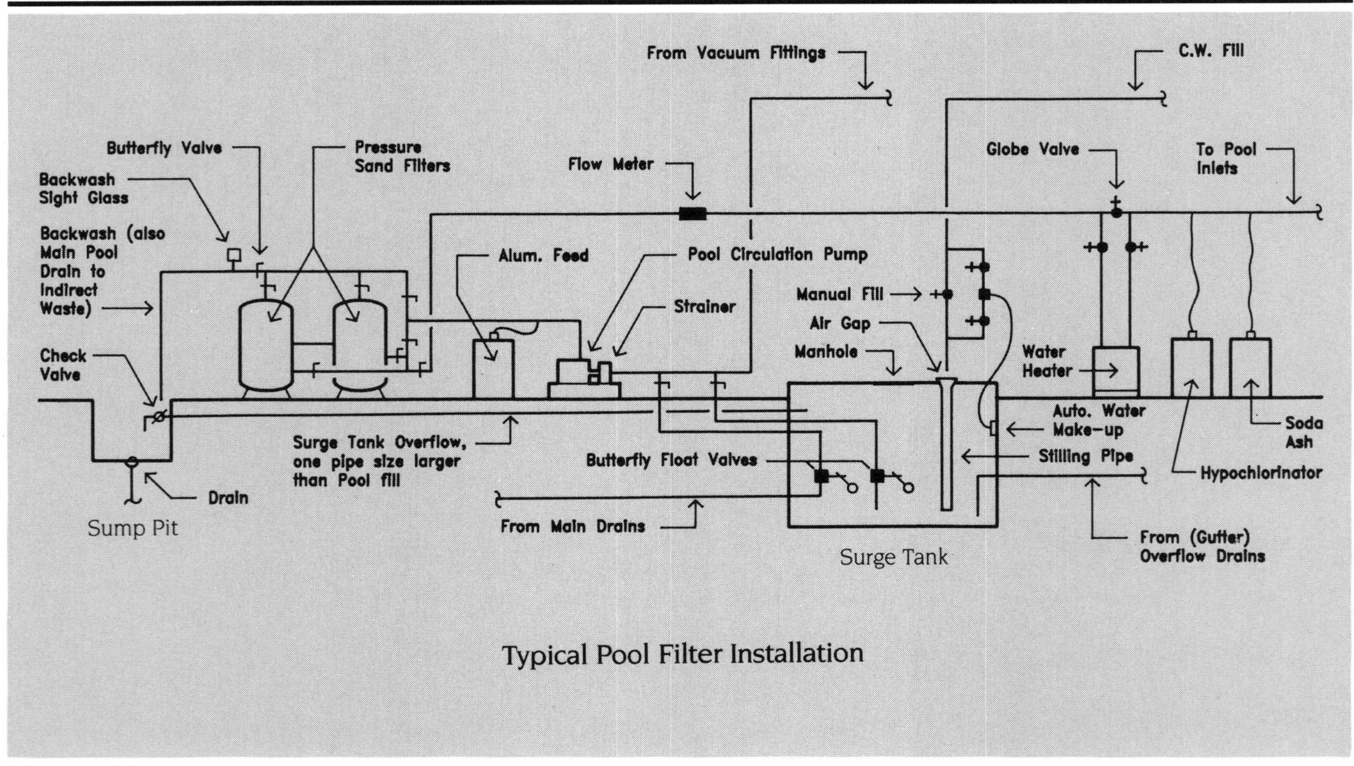

Figure 2.29

The site storm drainage is the system of piping, manholes, catch basins, yard drains, dry wells, and all other appurtenances that convey clear storm water drainage from the building storm drain and from all other site areas requiring drainage, such as roads, parking lots, and plazas, to a public storm sewer, combined sewer, or drainage basin. A combined sewer is any sewer conveying sewage, storm water, and other clear water wastes. Sanitary, storm, and combined site sewer systems begin at a point five feet beyond the building wall.

All sewer lines must be installed very carefully on the site for various reasons. Pipelines should be laid with the proper pitch (1/8″ per foot or more) to ensure that the lines will meet the invert of the existing public sewer or manhole. The sewer lines should enter the public sewer above the center to prevent the sewer backing up into the house sanitary drain as shown in Figure 2.30.

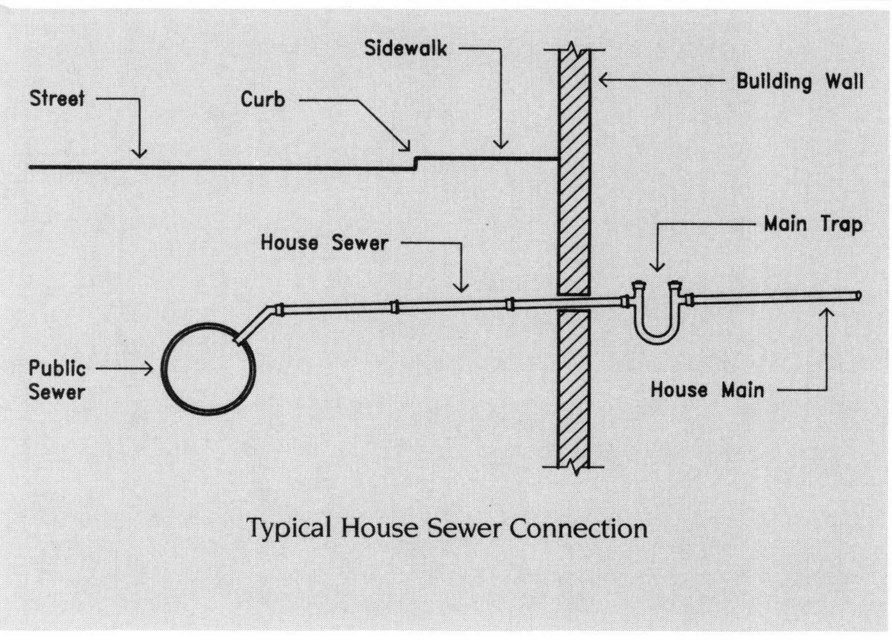

Figure 2.30

If soil conditions on the site are unstable, the plumbing contractor should take the steps necessary to prevent sagging of the lines, which could break and restrict the flow of wastes. Two methods of correcting sagging are wood piling supports placed at every hub or connection, or a crushed stone bed installed beneath the pipe.

Manholes are a very important part of any sewer system. In addition to their use for inspection and cleaning services, they are used as connection points where two or more sewer lines join together. Manholes are usually constructed of brick or are purchased in precast concrete sections. A pre-cast manhole is illustrated in Figure 2.31.

Figure 2.31

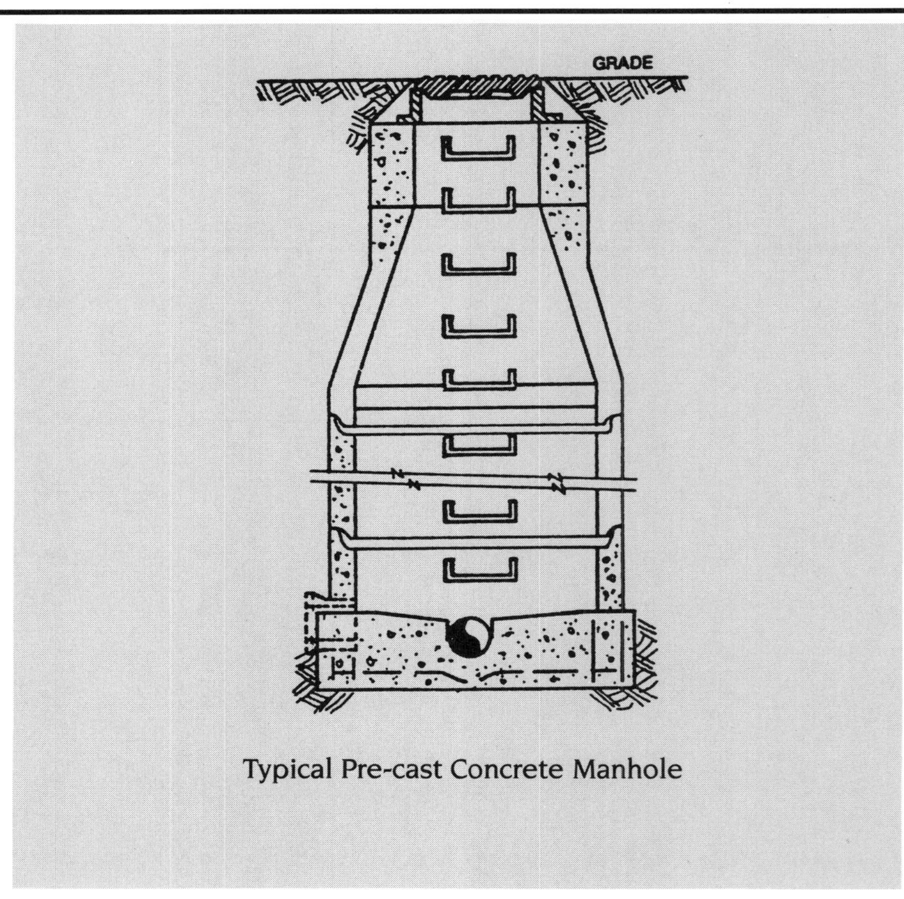

Typical Pre-cast Concrete Manhole

Proper drainage of areas such as parking lots and roads is essential to prevent flooding conditions. In many cases, surface drainage is sufficient to handle any site drainage problems. Surface drainage is simply the system of allowing rainwater to run off a properly graded site and seep back into the earth. However, surface drainage is usually inadequate where paved areas (such as parking lots or roads) are located on low or depressed areas of the site. Parking lots and roads are usually drained through a system of catch basins or yard drains which are connected to the storm drainage sewer or independent dry wells.

It should be noted here that the connection of the new sewer system to the existing public sewer is performed by the plumbing contractor. Permits for the sewer connection and for any street breaking have to be obtained and paid for by the plumbing contractor, who should include these costs in his estimate.

There are many different types of piping materials used for site drainage systems. The kind of piping material used by the contractor on a sewer project is usually governed by local codes or highway departments. Figure 2.32 gives the reader an excellent cross-section of commonly used drainage system piping materials used on the site.

Water Service Piping

The site water service piping is that portion of the water supply system extending from the street water main to the house control valve or meter. The procedure for installing any water main begins at the existing live main in the street. The street main is tapped by a special procedure performed by the local utility company. This procedure is called a *wet connection* for buildings requiring services of 3″ or larger, or *wet taps* for services under 3″. They are so called because the connection to the street main is made while water under pressure is present in the main. Wet taps and connections avoid shutdown of the main and probable interruption of service.

STANDARD SITE DRAINAGE PIPING MATERIALS		
PIPE	RECOMMENDED SERVICE	SIZE RANGES
Reinforced Concrete Pipe Classes 1, 2, 3, 4 and 5 Ring Joint	Storm and Sanitary Sewers requiring large diameter pipe and exposed to heavy traffic or buried to extreme depths.	12″-96″
Unreinforced Concrete Pipe Ring Joint	Storm and Sanitary Sewers requiring small to medium diameter pipe and not exposed to heavy traffic or extreme depth pressure	6″-24″
Galvanized Corrugated Metal Pipe 16, 14, 12 and 8 Gage Bolted Joints	Storm Sewers requiring large diameter pipe where resistance to external loads is important.	8″-72″
Vitrified Clay Pipe Standard and Extra-Strength Ring Joint	Sanitary and Storm Sewers requiring small to medium size pipe.	4″-36″
Extra Heavy Cast Iron Soil Pipe Lead or Neoprene Joint	Sanitary and Storm Sewers requiring small to medium size pipe but requiring maximum durability.	2″-15″

Figure 2.32

The utility companies leave a street valve in the closed position for the plumber to begin his portion of the installation, for which the plumbing contractor must secure a permit. A water main is usually buried at least 4' from the top elevation of the pipe. This is usually the frost line in most areas of the country. The plumbing contractor then runs the main to the building, providing a sidewalk valve in a service box for easy access. Similar to sewer regulations, a permit for street cutting must be secured by the plumbing contractor. Depending on local regulations, the plumbing contractor may be charged to restore the street to its previous condition, and almost all municipalities require the plumbing contractor to install at least temporary or bagged pavement. The materials used for installing water mains on the site are outlined further in Figure 2.33.

Site Fire Protection System

Very often the plumbing estimator will encounter designs with extensive fire mains throughout the site. Buildings are often erected on large sites, and the nearest fire hydrant may be thousands of feet away from the structure. This makes it necessary for the engineer to design a complete fire loop system with fire hydrants strategically located throughout the site.

Fire hydrants are usually of the compression type design with various nozzle arrangements, as shown in Figure 2.34. Each fire hydrant is valved separately, with the valve located in a valve box. For site fire protection systems, it is always of the utmost importance for fire crews to see if certain valves are opened or closed. The use of indicator posts, as shown in Figure 2.34 remedies this situation. Indicator posts are placed over the buried valve, with windows indicating if the valve is open or shut. A wrench supplied with the indicator post is used to open or close the valve when and if necessary.

STANDARD SITE WATER PIPING MATERIALS		
PIPE	RECOMMENDED SERVICE	SIZE RANGES
Cement-lined Ductile Iron Pipe Classes 150 and 250 Lead, Neoprene or Mechanical Joint	Services requiring water mains larger than 3" in diameter.	4"-48"
Type 'K' Copper Tubing Solder Joint	Services requiring water mains 3" in diameter or less.	½"-3"

Figure 2.33

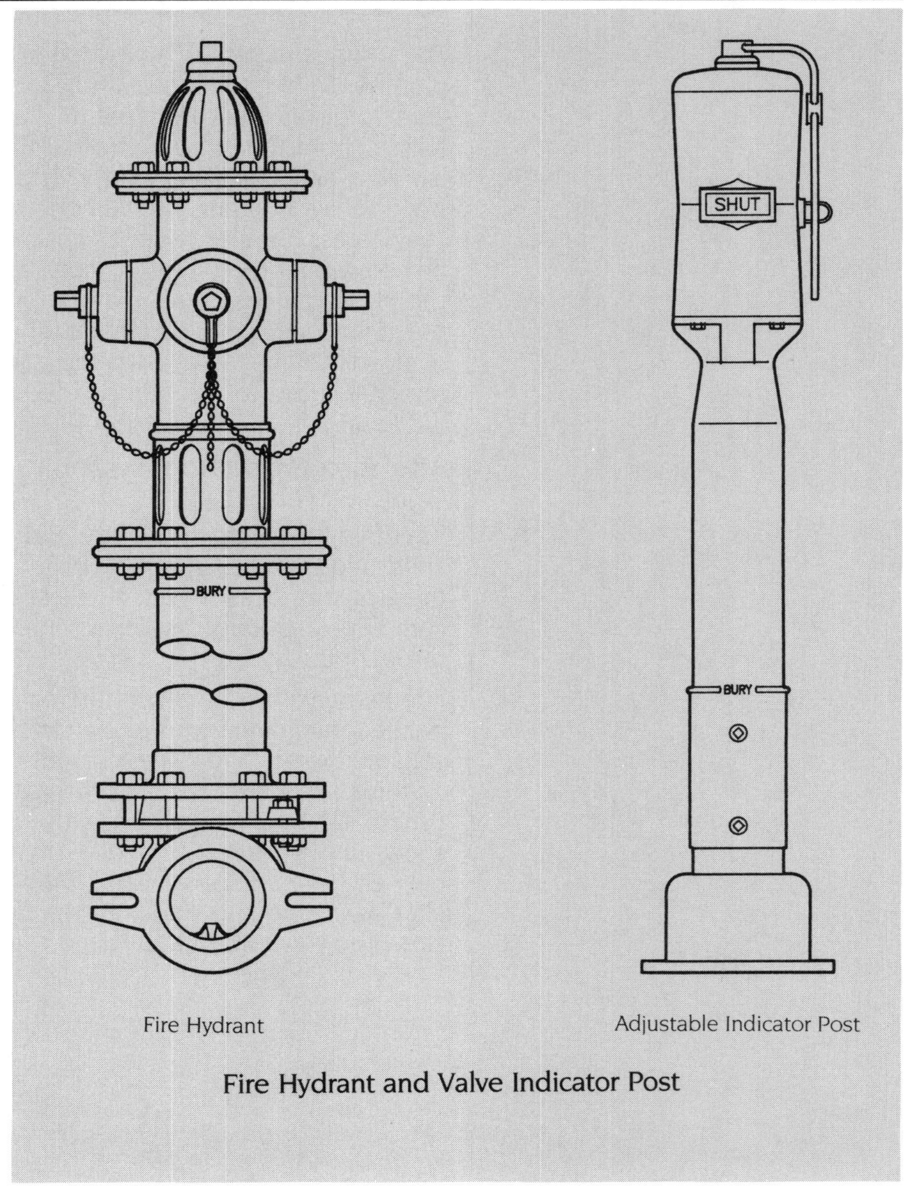
SHUT
BURY
BURY
Fire Hydrant
Adjustable Indicator Post
Fire Hydrant and Valve Indicator Post

Figure 2.34

Septic Tank System

In areas where no public sewer facilities are available, human wastes must be disposed of in some other fashion. The septic tank system of disposal has long been the accepted practice for dealing with this problem. The septic tank system is basically a three-step operation. Wastes from the building enter the septic tank, which is designed to separate solids from liquids. The solid wastes settle to the bottom of the septic tank, while the liquid effluent is discharged to a distribution box and then into a leaching area of perforated, split-tile pipe, or seepage pits (see Figure 2.35). Both the solid and liquid wastes decompose through bacterial action and other natural processes. Septic tanks and distribution boxes are usually constructed of precast concrete and can be purchased in varying capacities. It is essential that septic tanks be of sufficient capacity to handle the incoming sewage. Septic tanks must be cleaned periodically, but there are chemicals which help decomposition, thus making the cleaning intervals less frequent.

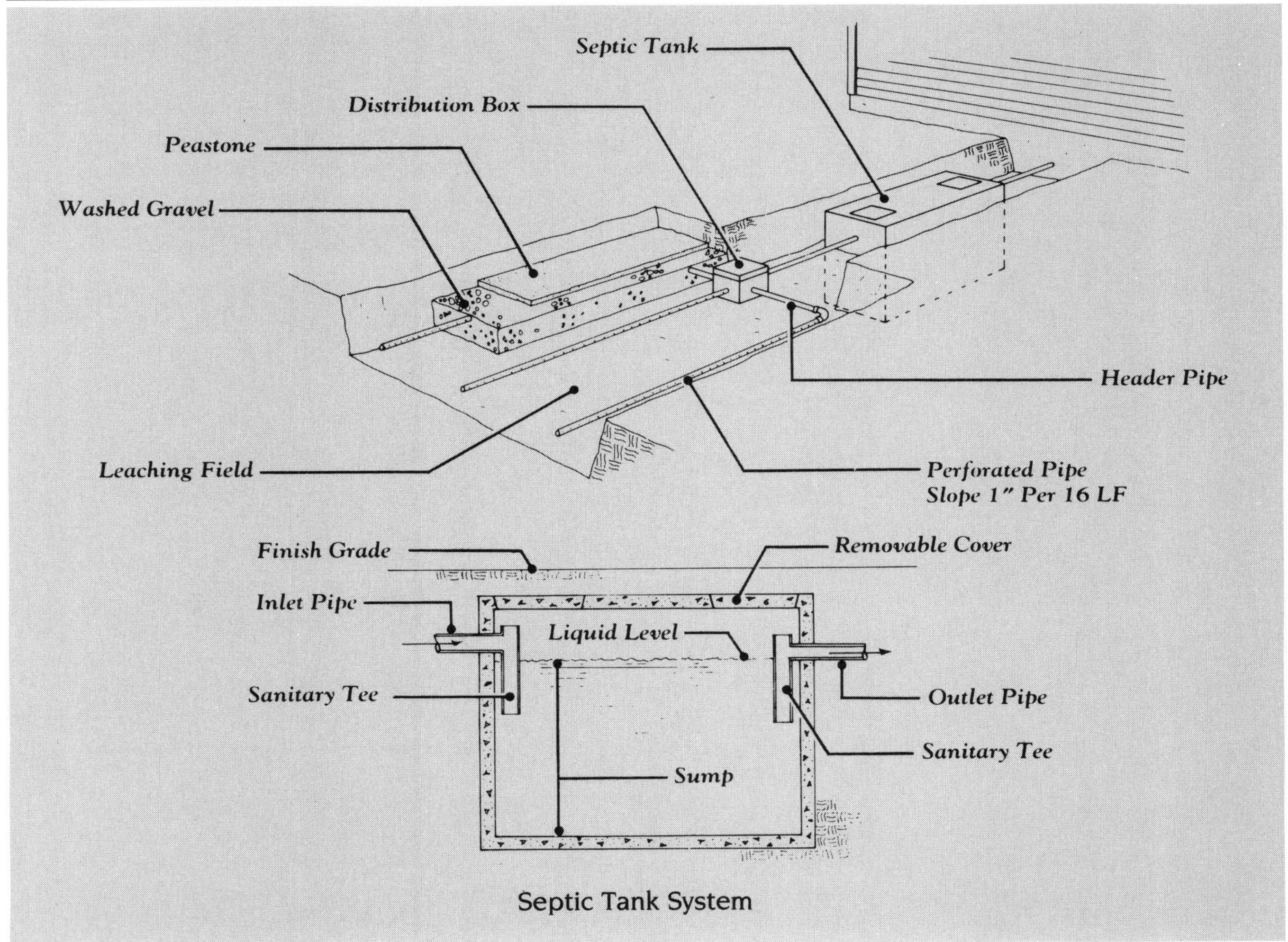

Figure 2.35

Lawn Sprinkler System

Lawn sprinkler systems have gained steadily in popularity and are being included more frequently in the design criteria of a project. This popularity stems from the efficiency with which lawn sprinklers can perform their function. Buildings with large lawn areas such as schools, colleges, and industrial parks cannot depend on maintenance men with garden hoses to water lawns, which tends to be a more costly and less efficient method of operation.

Lawn sprinkler systems can function both manually and automatically and, if properly maintained, require little maintenance. Lawn sprinklers are designed to give an even distribution of water with complete lawn coverage. Sprinkler heads are placed in patterns so that the spray from each head will slightly overlap. This also compensates for some loss in water pressure, which is bound to happen from time to time. The sprinkler system is zone-designed, and each zone is controlled by a manifold of valves (either manually or automatically) with timer devices. Sprinkler heads are usually of the pop-up design, which lift up into the spray position by water pressure. The piping, usually Schedule 80 PVC plastic pipe, is buried in the ground 6" to 12" inches deep. The piping should have a slight pitch so that the system can be drained in the winter months. This is achieved by installing a drain valve at the end of each zone.

Part 2
PLUMBING ESTIMATING

Part 2
INTRODUCTION

An estimate is defined as an approximate judgment of the dollar value of a project. However, if one looks beyond the strict definition of the word, he will find a procedure that is neither all art nor all science, but perhaps a little of each; an art, in that it takes skill and talent to perform, and a science, in that it deals with facts, laws, and systems.

Chapter 3 discusses the preparation required to perform a plumbing estimate. Taking off, writing up, pricing, and completing the estimate are covered in Chapters 4 through 6.

Chapters 7 and 8 present other forms of plumbing estimating and provide information useful throughout an estimating career.

Chapter 3

PREPARING FOR THE ESTIMATE

This chapter describes some basic preparation necessary before one can put pen to paper to begin taking off and pricing an estimate. The estimator must gather the proper tools, forms, and reference materials, and might want to use a checklist of these items to get organized. We will begin with a list of basic tools.

Estimating Tools

Like other craftsmen, an estimator needs the right tools to achieve professional results. The three basic tools an estimator should have on the work table before beginning any estimate are measuring devices, a calculator, and pencils.

Plumbing drawings, like architectural drawings, give all dimensions in feet and inches. These dimensions are reduced in size by use of an appropriate scale. The most commonly used scale on drawings is 1/8″ equals 1′. Other scales used are 1/4″ = 1′, 1/2″ = 1′, 1″ = 1′, 3/8″ = 1′, and 3/4″ = 1′. The larger scales are usually used for details and equipment rooms, or other areas requiring greater clarity on the drawings. There are a number of measuring devices manufactured for reading the above scales.

An architectural scale rule resembles an ordinary ruler, but it has fractional scale divisions embossed on it. There are four edges to a flat architectural scale rule, with two scales embossed on each edge, making a total of eight scales. The scales run in opposite directions on each edge. For example, the 1/8″ scale is read from left to right, while the 1/4″ scale is read from right to left. Triangular rules with six scales are also in current usage. Various types of scales appear in Figure 3.1.

A tape measure is a retractable steel tape, equipped with only two fractional scale divisions, 1/8″ on one side and 1/4″ on the other side (see Figure 3.1). This device is especially desirable for piping takeoff because large measures can be accumulated at one time, as the 1/8″ scale has the capacity to measure up to 480′, and the 1/4″ scale can measure up to 240′

The rotometer, or wheel, is the measuring device best suited to a large piping takeoff (see Figure 3.1). The rotometer is a precision instrument for measuring curved or straight distances in feet. It has three scale markings: 1/8″, 1/4″, and 1/2″, but most important, it has a cumulative register dial which enables the plumbing estimator to take off a maximum of 2,400′ on the 1/8″ scale, 1200′ on the 1/4″ scale, and 600′ on the 1/2″ scale. As with any tools, these function only as well as the person using them. The estimator must take great care in reading the scales properly. Many mistakes are made because of carelessness, and contractors can lose a great deal of time and money as a result.

A calculator is an essential item to the estimator. Of the many types on the market today, the electronic desk calculator and the pocket calculator are among the most popular. The authors recommend that estimators use a model with a printed tape, rather than rely solely on calculators with lighted numerical displays. Estimators can ill afford to reach a final cost estimate without being able to recheck figures. A calculator (or adding machine) with a printed tape enables the user to review calculations. The calculator used by the estimator should have at least the following features.

- Printed tape function
- Full four function capability (+ , − , ÷ , ×)
- Numerical capacity of 8 digits

Additional calculator features that are not essential but are valuable aids when estimating a project are:

- Full memory
- Percent key
- Square and square root key

In addition to standard lead pencils, the estimator should have a variety of colored pencils. The purpose of colored pencils is for color coding of all fixtures, equipment, and piping on the drawings. Color coding is a very important part of the takeoff procedure. Color coded items are readily identified should the plumbing estimator or an assistant have to check back on the drawings for progress or to take over the takeoff. Color coding also provides the estimator with a simple method of checking for completeness. It is recommended that the color codes be consistent for all the jobs estimated in the same office. The reader, of course, can create his or her own color code, but once a certain color code is established, it should remain the standard for all estimates within a firm–both in the shop and in the field. A sample color code follows:

Sample In-House Plumbing System Color Code

• Plumbing fixtures and trim		Red
• Equipment		Green
• Cold water		Blue
• Hot water		Red
• Sanitary waste and vent		Yellow
• Storm system		Brown
• Fire standpipe system		Orange
• Sprinkler system		Light green
• Medical gas systems:	Oxygen	Purple
	Nitrogen	Dark blue
	Nitrous Oxide	Light blue
	Vacuum	Violet
	Compressed Air	Dark green
• Natural gas system		Lavender
• Acid waste and vent system		Gold

Takeoff Forms (Quantity Sheets)

Takeoff forms or quantity sheets can save the estimator valuable time. All takeoff or quantity sheets should have certain basic information at the top of the sheet:

- Title of quantity sheets (plumbing fixtures, piping, equipment, valves, fittings, etc.)
- Project title and job number
- Estimator's name
- Checked by
- Date
- Page number

Many firms prefer to design their own takeoff and estimating forms or use or adapt published forms such as those available in *Means Forms for Contractors*. The sample takeoff and estimate in this book are recorded on forms that the authors have designed.

They are:

- Plumbing fixture quantity sheet
- Equipment quantity sheet
- Piping quantity sheet
- Fitting quantity sheet
- Valve and device quantity sheet

Plumbing Fixture Quantity Sheet

This form (shown in Figure 3.2) is usually the first in the series and allows for recording the number of fixtures by floor. The "Total" column to the right indicates the total number of a particular fixture in the entire building. The total column at the bottom shows the total fixtures of all types per floor.

Equipment Quantity Sheet

On this sheet (shown in Figure 3.3), the plumbing equipment from each system is listed with enough information included for proper identification. This sheet becomes very useful when ordering the equipment.

Piping Quantity Sheet

The piping in a particular system is broken down by diameter and linear feet of pipe. The figures for linear feet of pipe are scaled off from the drawings. The total linear feet of each pipe size appears at the bottom of each piping quantity sheet (Figure 3.4). The column to the right is divided into six boxes. In each box the total is entered under the appropriate heading for various operations or materials that might be required for that particular system; the divisions are:

- C.Y. excavation: Total cubic yards of required excavation.
- Lbs. of flashing: Total lbs. of roof or drain flashing material.
- Solder/flux: Total lbs. of solder and flux required to join pipe.
- Lbs. of lead: Total lbs. of caulking lead required to join pipe.
- Lbs. of oakum: Total lbs. of packing oakum required to make up the lead joints.
- Gas cylinders: Total number of gas cylinders required to melt lead or solder.

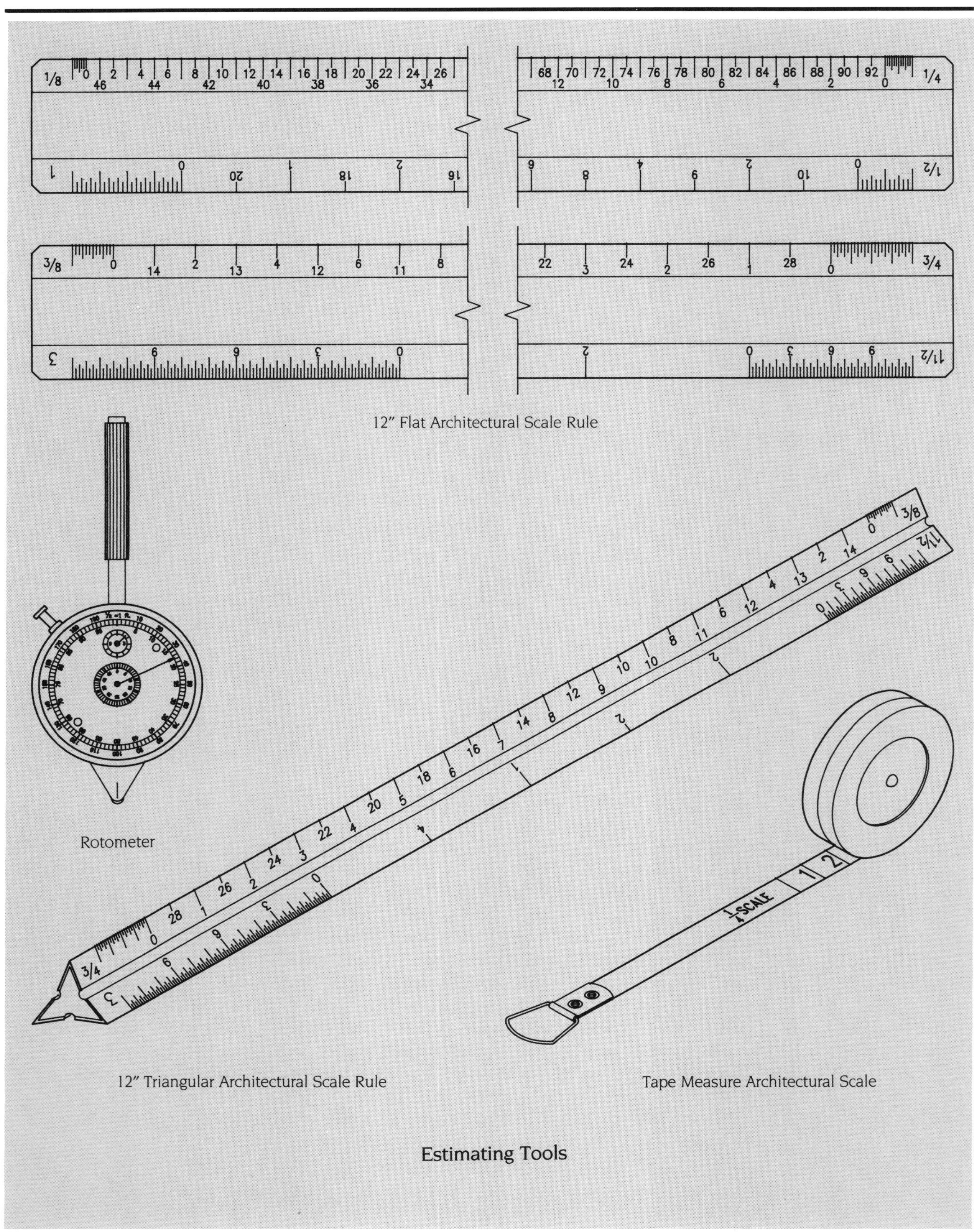

12" Flat Architectural Scale Rule
Rotometer
12" Triangular Architectural Scale Rule
Tape Measure Architectural Scale
Estimating Tools

Figure 3.1

PLUMBING FIXTURE QUANTITY SHEET	PROJECT	JOB NO.	ESTIMATOR	CHECKER	DATE	SHEET OF

FIXTURE TYPE	FLOOR										
	BASEMENT	FIRST	SECOND	THIRD	FOURTH	FIFTH	SIXTH	SEVENTH	EIGHTH	ROOF	TOTAL
TOTAL											

Figure 3.2

EQUIPMENT QUANTITY SHEET	PROJECT	JOB NO.	ESTIMATOR	CHECKER	DATE	SHEET OF

ITEM	QTY.	SYSTEM	CAPACITIES, DESCRIPTION AND OTHER INFORMATION

Figure 3.3

PIPING QUANTITY SHEET			SYSTEM				PROJECT			JOB NO.			ESTIMATOR			CHECKER	DATE	SHEET OF
PIPE SIZE																		
1/8″	1/4″	3/8″	1/2″	3/4″	1″	1-1/4″	1-1/2″	2″	2-1/2″	3″	4″	5″	6″	8″	10″	12″	C.Y. EXC.	
																	Lbs. of flashing	
																	Solder/flux	
																	Lbs. of lead	
																	Lbs. of oakum	
																	Gas cylinders	
																	TOTAL	

Figure 3.4

Of course, each box may not apply to every system. Where this is so, the estimator should simply enter "not applicable" in that particular box to remind himself that it has not been omitted.

Fitting Quantity Sheet

Like pipe, fittings are taken off by system and by pipe size. These are counted individually (See Figure 3.5), with their totals shown in the narrow columns to the right of each wide column.

Valve and Device Quantity Sheet

Valves and devices such as shock absorbers, vacuum breakers, strainers, etc., are listed by pipe size for a particular system and, like the fittings, are totaled in the narrow columns to the right. (See Figure 3.6).

Estimate Forms

Estimate forms aid an estimator in compiling and pricing out the estimate neatly and concisely by properly organizing the information. These sheets are the formal presentation sheets of an estimate. They contain work classifications, itemized quantities, material costs, and labor costs. Like quantity takeoff sheets, estimate forms should contain certain basic information on the top of the sheet:

- Firm name and address
- Classification
- Project title and location
- Date
- Architect/Engineer
- Type of estimate
- Estimate number
- Sheet number
- Estimator
- Checker

Each major system is subdivided into individual components. In the actual estimate to follow, each system is given a number (2, 3, 4, etc.), which is entered in the *Item* column, and each segment of that system is given a consecutive decimal number to identify it (e.g., .01, .02, .03, etc.). The total quantity of each component is transferred from the quantity sheets to be priced by material and labor costs. The *Labor* column is used to enter man-hours (M.H.), production units and totals, while the *Labor Cost* column is used to enter the labor dollar rate, along with the total labor cost.

A company's own historical cost data is, of course, the most accurate source for cost data, but published cost indexes, such as *Means Plumbing Cost Data*, are good sources of information that may be lacking from a firm's own data.

Estimate forms can also be obtained from published collections, such as *Means Forms for Contractors*. These forms can be used as is, or adapted to the specific needs and approaches of an individual firm. The sample estimates in this book are shown on forms designed by the authors for use in their firm. Figure 3.7 is a blank Estimate Sheet, which will be shown filled-in, in Chapter 6.

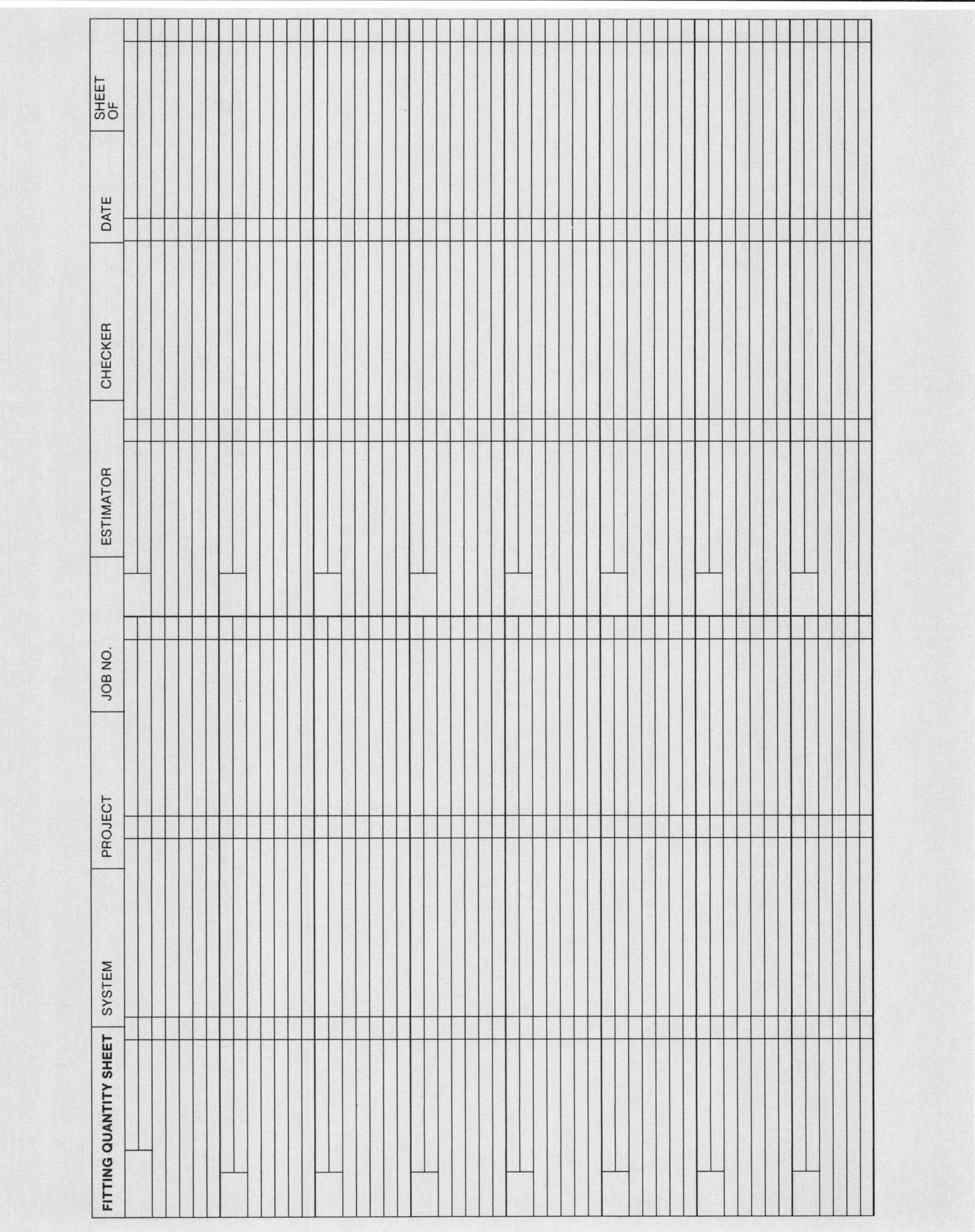
FITTING QUANTITY SHEET
SYSTEM
PROJECT
JOB NO.
ESTIMATOR
CHECKER
DATE
SHEET
OF

Figure 3.5

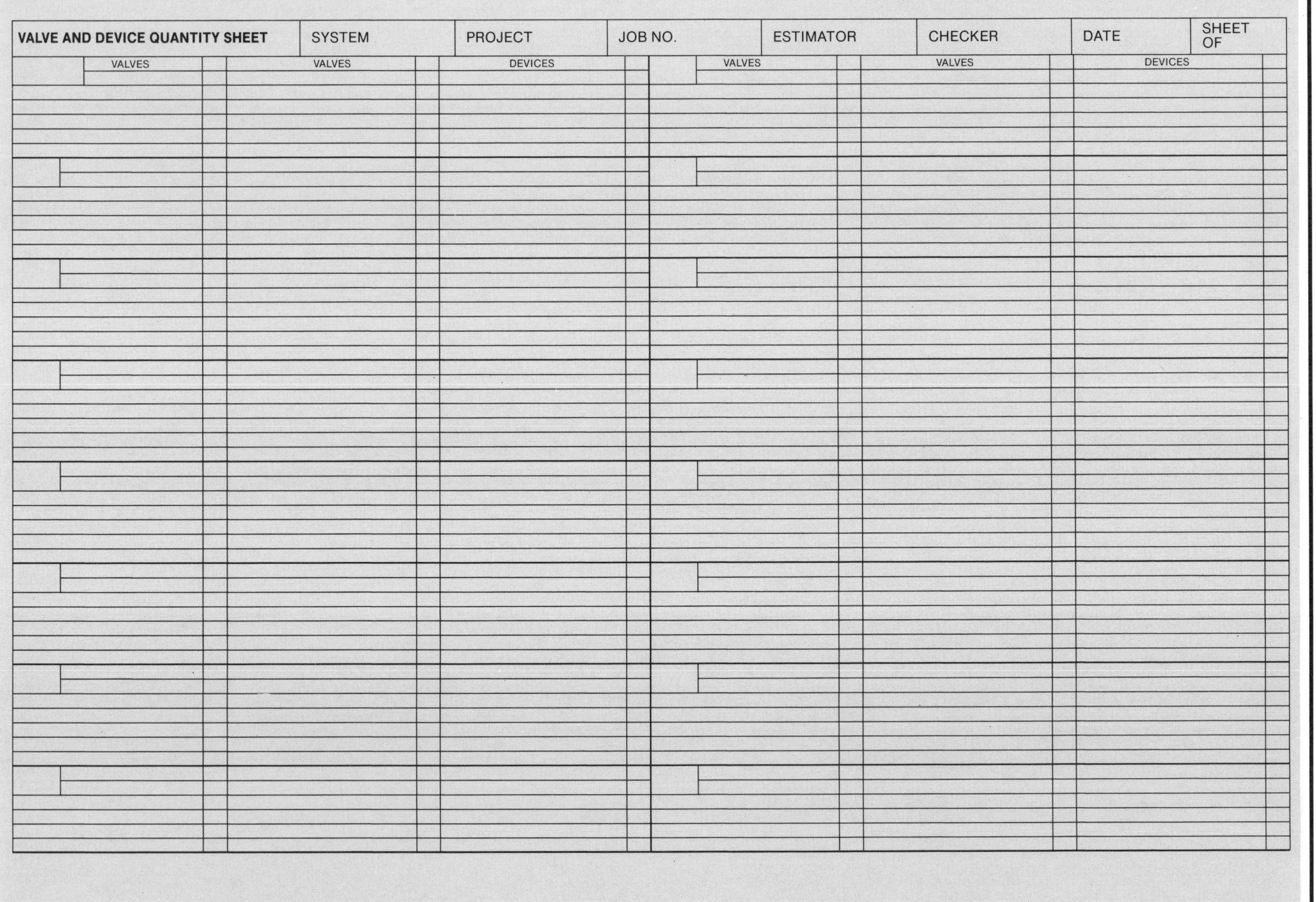

VALVE AND DEVICE QUANTITY SHEET

SYSTEM | PROJECT | JOB NO. | ESTIMATOR | CHECKER | DATE | SHEET OF

VALVES | VALVES | DEVICES | VALVES | VALVES | DEVICES

Figure 3.6

SHEET NO. ______

PROJECT ______ ESTIMATE NO. ______

LOCATION ______ CLASSIFICATION ______ DATE ______

ARCHITECT ______ ESTIMATOR ______ PRICED BY ______ CHECKED BY ______

DESCRIPTION	QUAN-TITY	UNIT	MATERIAL		LABOR				TOTAL COST MAT./LABOR
			UNIT COST	TOTAL COST	UNIT MH	TOTAL MH	UNIT RATE	TOTAL COST	

Figure 3.7

Summary Sheet

Every estimate contains a form called a *Summary Sheet*. On this form, the estimator summarizes all totals arrived at on the estimate forms, so the final estimated cost can be calculated. The Summary Sheet contains the totals of the applicable systems broken out by material and labor, a listing of job overhead costs, the contractor's profit, and finally, the total job cost. A sample of a Summary Sheet can be seen in Figure 3.8. The process of filling out estimate forms and summary sheets is discussed further in Chapters 5 and 6.

Plumbing Codes

Every project is designed according to a particular plumbing code. The plumbing codes are written to protect the public health by setting minimum standards and procedures to be followed in plumbing system design. Large cities such as New York and Baltimore write their own official plumbing codes, but in rural areas and small towns, where there might not be a local plumbing code, an existing one created elsewhere is generally adopted. There are a number of plumbing codes published that a town or municipality may want to use, such as:

- **Uniform Plumbing Code:** International Association of Plumbing and Mechanical Officials (IAPMO).
- **Basic Plumbing Code:** Building Officials and Code Administrators International Inc. (BOCA).
- **National Plumbing Code:** National Association of Plumbing, Heating, & Cooling Contractors (NAPHCC); American Society of Plumbing Engineers (ASPE).
- **Southern Standard Plumbing Code:** Southern Building Code Congress International (SBCCI).
- **Fire Codes:** National Fire Protection Association, Inc. (NFPA).

Addresses for obtaining the above codes appear in Appendix D.

The plumbing code is of vital concern to a plumbing estimator for a number of reasons. Every estimator should have a copy of the plumbing code that has jurisdiction over the project. In this way, the plumbing estimator can verify that the plans and specifications are designed and written according to that code. If they are not, and the estimator figures the project as designed and is awarded the contract for work, he or she may still be required to install the material according to the respective code, at a possible additional cost. In addition, the plumbing estimator can use the code as a guide to properly estimate projects with incomplete drawings or specifications.

Vendor Catalogs

Manufacturers of plumbing products all publish catalogs describing the items they manufacture. These vendor catalogs usually contain sketches, item descriptions, and model numbers of the manufacturers' full line of products. In addition, catalogs usually contain valuable engineering information and, in some cases, prices. The plumbing estimator should have a complete up-to-date library of vendor catalogs for reference purposes. Vendor catalogs are always free of charge and can be obtained by simply mailing or phoning in a request to the respective manufacturer. These catalogs are updated and estimators can request the latest product information on an ongoing basis.

Trade Price Sheets

To price a project correctly, an estimator needs up-to-date material costs. The prices of some materials change every day, and a price sheet even one month old may be completely outdated and useless. Items such as plumbing fixtures, valves, piping, and fittings, usually appear on printed trade price sheets for use by the plumbing estimator. These price sheets are usually distributed by plumbing wholesalers and manufacturers and may contain the discount allowed the plumbing trade. When pricing items subject to frequent fluctuation, one should include an appropriate margin. Large items, such as hot water generators and pumps, rarely appear on published price sheets. For these items, the estimator would call the manufacturer's sales representative for the price of the particular piece of equipment or materials specified. The plumbing estimator without current material prices leaves the firm open to the unnecessary risk of a mispriced estimate, resulting in lost contracts and money. A good backup reference for estimators who are unable to obtain a current price is the current edition of *Means Plumbing Cost Data*. This publication is also useful as a labor guide for unfamiliar methods or material installations.

Working Areas

Activity in contracting offices usually resembles the press room of a newspaper at a deadline. Unfortunately, the estimator cannot always have peace and quiet while trying to estimate a project. However, there are certain things an estimator can do to make the situation more bearable. The estimator should have a well lit office with a large drafting table and a reference table. Distractions such as typewriters and radios should be avoided if at all possible. An estimator constantly exposed to distractions will make mistakes, again, at the possible cost of lost contracts.

Summary Sheet

ABC PLUMBING COMPANY, INC.
CONTRACTORS
ANYWHERE, USA

SHEET NO. ______

PROJECT ______ ESTIMATE NO. ______

LOCATION ______ CLASSIFICATION ______ DATE ______

ARCHITECT ______ ESTIMATOR ______ PRICED BY ______ CHECKED BY ______

DESCRIPTION	QUAN-TITY	UNIT	MATERIAL		LABOR				TOTAL COST MAT./LABOR
			UNIT COST	TOTAL COST	UNIT MH	TOTAL MH	UNIT RATE	TOTAL COST	

Figure 3.8

Chapter 4

THE TAKEOFF

This chapter first discusses the prerequisites for performing the takeoff, such as reading the specifications, making notes, and scanning the drawings. The reader will learn the proper procedures for taking off a job and compiling a complete list of quantities. Finally, a sample job is used for a step-by-step analysis of an actual sample takeoff, complete with specifications, drawings, and quantity sheets.

Reading and Digesting Specifications

Specifications are the written instructions prepared by the design engineer that the contractor must follow in estimating and installing its portion of the work. It should be noted here that specifications generally take precedence over drawings. If any conflict of information occurs between the drawings and specifications, the specifications are the final word, unless otherwise stated by the engineer or architect through a written addendum to the contract.

Making Notes About Specifications

Before attempting any actual work, the estimator should spend time reading and digesting the specifications to fully understand the scope of work, the types of materials required, and any other requirements of a bidding contractor.

When reading the job specifications, it is advisable to make notes regarding anything unusual. Examples of noteworthy items include:

- Vaguely stated scope of work
- Noncompliance with plumbing code having jurisdiction
- Missing model numbers or equipment capacities

Becoming Familiar with the Drawings

Every estimator should have an overall "feel" for the job, in addition to knowledge of items listed in the specifications. Before beginning the takeoff, the estimator should scan all of the drawings in order to determine the complexity of the job, the approximate hours required to perform the work, and the method of design and construction used.

Making Notes About the Drawings

As with specifications, the estimator should also make notes about the drawings while scanning them. He or she should be sure that all required plans are accounted for in the drawing set; that the drawings are complete with respect to areas requiring plumbing, pipe sizing, details, and schedules; and that the designs are drawn according to code. If any of the three conditions is not met, the estimator should make the applicable notes and notify the design engineer for clarification.

Coordination of Drawings and Specifications

After reviewing the job specifications and drawings individually, the estimator should then verify that the two are compatible. Very often, design firms will have one person writing specifications for a job, and another person designing it. For various reasons, such as rushing to meet deadlines or drafting oversights, specifications and drawings can conflict at times. For example, the drawings may show a sump pump, while there is no mention of it in the specifications. These situations are infrequent with bid documents, but they can happen, and the estimator should be aware of them.

Taking Off Quantities From Drawings

The estimator should establish his or her own effective sequence for taking quantities off from drawings, and stick with it throughout his or her estimating career. The takeoff sequence the author has found best is shown below. This method is used on the sample takeoff that follows.

1. Plumbing fixtures
2. Equipment
3. Sanitary waste and vent system (pipe, fittings, devices) below grade
4. Sanitary waste and vent system (pipe, fittings, devices) above grade
5. Storm system (pipe, fittings, devices) below grade
6. Storm system (pipe, fittings, devices) above grade
7. Hot and cold water system (pipe, fittings, valves, devices)
8. Natural gas system (pipe, fittings, valves, devices)
9. Fire standpipe system (pipe, fittings, valves, devices)
10. Site work

Note: The sample project in this book does not have a sprinkler system or any other special system other than natural gas. The estimator will, of course, encounter projects that do include other systems. Special systems are taken off individually in the same manner shown for other systems.

Plumbing Fixtures

Plumbing fixtures are taken off by marking the fixture with a colored pencil on the drawings and then entering the fixture type onto the fixture quantity sheet (see Chapter 3, Figure 3.2). Fixture types are usually coded by the engineer to correspond with the codes in his specification, for example, P-1 water closet, P-2 lavatory, etc. Plumbing fixtures should be taken off separately for each floor. The quantity sheet includes columns to identify the floors each fixture type may appear on. This method aids the estimator in checking the fixture count, by totaling the columns down and the row across, and entering the single grand total in the lower right-hand corner, as shown on the sample takeoff. If a mistake was made, the estimator will arrive at two different totals, and should recheck the takeoff.

When taking off fixtures from the drawings, the estimator is automatically taking off fixture trim, since all trim required is called out in the specification under each fixture type. The counting of fixtures, as well as valves, fittings, and other devices throughout the job, is done by the following "slash" method. For example, if four P-1 water closets are shown on the basement plan, they are entered on the quantity sheet as ////. If five 1/2″ gate valves are shown on the basement plan for the water system, they are entered on the valve and device quantity sheet for that system as ~~////~~. This method eliminates the totaling of many one-

and two-digit numbers at the end of the takeoff. The estimator simply counts up each full block of slashes as 5 (////). This recording method is also known as the "picket fence" method.

Equipment

Due to the small amounts of equipment used for the plumbing portion of a project, equipment is taken off simply by marking the piece of equipment in colored pencil on the drawings and entering it on the equipment quantity sheet (Chapter 3, Figure 3.3). The equipment quantity sheet has *item of equipment, quantity, system*, and *capacity* columns, each to be filled out as the individual piece of equipment is taken off. It is important that the estimator fill in the system column because each piece of equipment will be transferred onto the estimate form to be priced with its appropriate system. Capacities for equipment can be found either on the drawings or in the specifications.

Sanitary Waste and Vent System (Below Grade)

Before taking off any piping, the estimator should take off all fittings and sleeves such as "Y"s, 1/8 bends, sweeps, cleanout deck plates, etc. Fittings are taken off by placing a line through them on the drawings with a colored pencil and entering them by size onto the fitting quantity sheet (Figure 3.5 in Chapter 3). Most below-grade sanitary piping in a building is comprised of cast iron soil pipe and fittings. The smallest size pipe manufactured in cast iron service is two inches. Therefore, there will not be any fittings less than two inches in diameter on the underground takeoff.

After the takeoff of fittings is complete, they are totaled in the columns provided on the right side of each size category, as shown on the sample takeoff forms.

The estimator is now ready to take off the underground sanitary piping by size and linear foot, passing through all of the fittings. By measuring through the overall length of the piping run, rather than taking off only the piping between fittings, the estimator allows for some waste, which is necessary for any contingency that may occur during installation of the piping system. As the pipe is being taken off, the estimator marks off the section of pipe on the drawing with a colored pencil and then enters the footage on the piping quantity sheet for below-grade sanitary under the appropriate size of pipe, as shown on the sample takeoff.

If excavation and backfill is specified to be performed by the plumber, the estimator is now ready to take off excavation. Underground pipe below a building is rarely deeper than 4'. Drawings that are considered final documents generally furnish the estimator with two measurements: a *finished floor elevation* and a *pipe invert*, which is the lowest elevation or bottom-most portion of the pipe. If these two measurements are given, the estimator can arrive at the depth of the pipe by subtracting the pipe invert from the finished floor elevation. With the pipe depth known, the estimator can calculate the cubic yards to be excavated by using the chart and method shown in Figures 1.23 and 1.24. If finished floor elevations and pipe inverts are not given, the estimator should assume a 4' burial. The number of calculated cubic yards of excavation is then placed in the extreme right-hand column of the piping quantity sheet, as shown on the sample takeoff at the end of this chapter. These quantities are later transferred to the estimate forms.

If the cast iron soil pipe is of lead-joint design, the estimator must determine the total pounds of lead, oakum (jute packing), and gas necessary to complete the installation. To do this, he or she must first have completed the piping and fitting takeoff in order to know the total number of joints required. Cast iron soil pipe is manufactured in 5' and 10' lengths. For estimating purposes and for figuring lead quantities, the 5' length is used. The amount of lead consumed per joint is determined by the diameter of pipe. (See Figure 4.1.)

Excavation and backfill are often performed by the prime or general contractor. The plumbing estimator should check the specifications and General Conditions to define responsibility for this part of the work and avoid costly duplication.

LEAD REQUIRED TO CAULK CAST IRON SOIL PIPE JOINTS					
Pipe & Fitting Diams. Inches	Lead Ring Depth Inches	Service Weight		Extra Heavy Weight	
		Cu. Ins.	Wt. Lbs.	Cu. Ins.	Wt. Lbs.
2	1	2.81	1.15	2.91	1.19
3	1	3.90	1.60	4.17	1.71
4	1	4.98	2.04	5.25	2.15
5	1	6.06	2.49	6.24	2.56
6	1	7.15	2.93	7.42	3.04
8	1.25	15.06	6.17	15.49	6.35
10	1.25	18.90	7.75	19.34	7.93
12	1.25	25.53	10.47	26.02	10.67
15	1.5	43.09	17.67	43.38	17.8

Figure 4.1

The following example will demonstrate how to estimate quantities of lead, oakum, and gas for cast iron soil pipe.

Let us assume we have taken off the following quantities of soil pipe and fittings for a project:

6″ XH cast iron soil pipe	–15 L.F.
4″ XH cast iron soil pipe	–10 L.F.
6″ x 4″ "Y"	–1 ea.
4″ 1/8 bend	–1 ea.
4″ sweep	–1 ea.

The estimator proceeds to calculate the lead, oakum, and gas as follows: (Note that each hub, rather than each opening, is the basis for the number of joints.)

15 L.F. of 6″ pipe (5′ lengths) = three 6″ joints x 3.04 lbs. per joint
= 9.12 lbs. of lead

10 L.F. of 4″ pipe (5′ lengths) = two 4″ joints x 2.15 lbs. per joint
= 4.30 lbs. of lead

6″ x 4″ "Y" = (one 6″ joint & one 4″ joint)
3.04 + 2.15 = 5.19 lbs. of lead

4″ 1/8 Bend = (one 4″ Joint) = 2.15 lbs. of lead

4″ Sweep = (one 4″ Joint) = 2.15 lbs. of lead

Total = 22.91 lbs. of lead

Oakum is usually estimated at one-tenth the weight of lead. Therefore, 22.91 lbs. of lead÷10 = 2.29 lbs. of oakum.

Gas consumption is approximately one (instopropane) cylinder per 200 lbs. of lead.

After calculating the lead, oakum, and gas, the estimator should enter all quantities in the columns provided on the piping quantity sheet to be transferred later to the estimate forms.

Note: The quantities of lead, oakum, and gas entered on the piping quantity sheet include all fittings taken off. The estimator must work with both the fittings and pipe quantity sheets to perform the exercise.

If the cast iron soil pipe is of the neoprene joint or clamp (hubless) design, it is suggested that the estimator:

1. Count the number of joints to arrive at a quantity of neoprene gaskets or clamps.
2. Price them based on an average size.

Sanitary Waste and Vent System (Above Grade)

Using the same takeoff procedure as the below-grade sanitary system, the estimator should begin taking off all fittings on a separate fitting quantity sheet for above-grade sanitary. (See sample fitting quantity sheet, Figure 3.5.) If hubless cast iron fittings are used, they are taken off in the same manner as bell and spigot pipe fittings.

After all fittings are taken off, the estimator can proceed with the above-grade sanitary piping. The above-grade piping takeoff procedure is similar to that previously explained for the underground. However, the estimator will have to take off the piping in two separate steps: (1) Horizontal runs and branches, and (2) risers and drops to fixtures and equipment.

Riser diagrams or floor plans often provide the estimator with dimensions showing heights floor-to-floor. With this information, the estimator can estimate the height of risers and approximate the lengths of drop pieces down to fixtures.

Horizontal piping and risers are taken off in separate operations because the estimator will most likely refer to two or more drawings, and the takeoff will be easier if done separately. However, the estimator can combine both the horizontal and riser quantities on one piping quantity sheet. If the drawings are not equipped with riser diagrams, the task becomes more difficult. All drawings are two-dimensional, and to take off risers and drop pieces, the estimator must try to visualize the drawings in a three-dimensional state.

Another item taken off for above-grade installations is *pipe hangers and supports*. After all the piping is taken off, the estimator can determine the quantities of hangers and supports by dividing the total linear footage of pipe in each size category by the recommended intervals stated in the pipe support section (shown in Figure 1.22), or as stated in the project specifications. This will give the estimator the approximate number of hanger assemblies required for the installation. The hanger quantities can be entered on the fitting quantity sheet until it is time to list them on the estimate forms.

Floor drains through a suspended slab and vents through the roof generally have to be flashed with either sheet metal or a membrane. If lead is used, four square feet of sheet lead per unit has to be carried in the estimate. Sheet lead can weigh either four or six pounds per square foot, depending on the engineer's specifications. To estimate the total pounds of sheet flashing required for a project, the estimator performs one of the following calculations:

Number of units x 4 lbs. x 4 SF = Total Pounds,

or Number of units x 6 lbs. x 4 SF = Total Pounds.

Once the sheet flashing quantity is calculated, the estimator enters the figure on the piping quantity sheet (Figure 3.4) under that heading. Other metallic flashing material is estimated similarly, but membrane flashing is calculated and priced by the square foot.

Hot and Cold Water System

On the hot and cold water system, fittings and sleeves are again the first items to be taken off. The fitting takeoff procedure is the same as outlined for the below-grade sanitary system. Copper water fittings in the reducing sizes are taken off as "x reducing." For example, if the estimator has a 3" x 2" x 2" tee, it is taken off as a 3" x reducing tee. See the fitting quantity sheet, Figure 3.5.

Valves and devices are the next item to be taken off. Valves are taken off according to type and size and are entered on the valve and device quantity sheet for hot and cold water, as shown on the sample takeoff. If items such as *access panels* are part of the contract, they should be taken off at this time and placed on the valve and device quantity sheet.

Water piping is taken off in a similar fashion as the sanitary piping above grade. The estimator first takes off mains and branches, and then proceeds with risers and drop pieces. The quantities are then entered onto the pipe quantity sheet for hot and cold water. (See the sample water piping quantity sheet at the end of the chapter.) Pipe hangers and supports are taken off by dividing the total linear footage of water piping in each size category (by the intervals recommended in Chapter 1, Figure 1.22) and are then entered on the water fitting quantity sheet, as shown on the sample takeoff.

Solder, flux, and gas, the materials used for joining water pipe and fittings, should now be estimated. Solder joint pipe and fittings are usually joined by soft (non-lead) solder. Solder, flux, and gas are difficult items to estimate, but using the chart in Figure 4.2, the estimator can arrive at a relatively accurate amount of solder and flux required for an installation. The estimator should count the number of joints required for each fitting and valve in its own respective size category. For example, a 2″ tee requires three 2″ joints and a 2″ ell requires two 2″ joints. The estimator should again refer to the chart in Figure 4.2 for the pounds of required solder per 100 joints. The total amounts of solder, flux, and gas can now be entered on the piping quantity sheet.

ESTIMATED POUNDS OF SOFT SOLDER REQUIRED TO MAKE 100 JOINTS*							
Size	3/8″	1/2″	3/4″	1″	1 1/4″	1 1/2″	2″
Pounds	.5	.75	1.0	1.4	1.7	1.9	2.4
Size	2 1/2″	3″	3 1/2″	4″	5″	6″	8″
Pounds	3.2	3.9	4.5	5.5	8.0	15.0	32.0

*Two oz. of flux will be required for each pound of solder. One tank of PRESTO gas will be required for every 500 joints.

Figure 4.2

Once the estimator has determined the total linear footage of water piping, he knows the total linear footage of pipe that requires insulation. All hot and cold water piping is usually insulated, and all the estimator needs to do to estimate insulation is multiply the cost of insulation by the actual footage of water piping taken off, plus fittings and valves. Insulation is usually estimated and installed by an appropriate insulation subcontractor.

Storm System Below and Above Grade

The storm system below and above grade is taken off in the same manner as the appropriate sanitary waste and vent system; the only difference is that the estimator should keep horizontal pipe offsets in hung ceilings separate since these sections of pipe are normally insulated to prevent condensation.

Fire Standpipe System and Natural Gas System

These two systems are taken off using the same procedure as the hot and cold water system. See the sample takeoff sheets for these systems.

Site Work

Site piping and fittings are taken off by size and system, and the quantities are entered on the respective quantity sheets. (See the sample site piping quantity takeoff sheets.) For drainage systems, the estimator takes off manholes and catch basins, and notes their depths. A top or rim elevation and a bottom or invert elevation are normally given at each manhole and catch basin. By subtracting the invert from the top elevation, the estimator will arrive at the depth of the manhole or catch basin. The estimator should also note connections of new sewers to existing sewers. Manholes, catch basins, and connections to existing sewers should be entered on the fitting quantity sheet. (See the sample site drainage fitting quantity sheets.)

Water service piping and fittings are taken off by size and entered on their respective quantity sheets. (See sample water piping quantity sheets.) Valves, or any wet connections or taps are then taken off and entered onto the valve quantity sheet as shown on the sample site estimate. Valves are taken off by size; for wet connections, the size of both the existing main and the new connection should be noted. For example, a new 4″ main connected to an existing 8″ main is taken off as an 8″ x 4″ wet connection. Taps are taken off based on the size of the new service.

Excavation is calculated as shown in the excavation section of Chapter 1. The estimator can determine the appropriate depth of drainage piping by the manhole and catch basin rim and invert elevations given on the drawings. Water piping excavation is based on an assumed depth of 4′, unless otherwise noted on the drawing. The cubic yards of excavation are then entered on the respective piping quantity sheet for each system.

Note: Excavation, backfill, and even site work piping may be subcontracted to other appropriate specialists. However, the estimator must still provide a responsible estimate for this work. Careful reading of the General Conditions or specifications will determine whether the site work is to be carried by the plumber or general contractor.

Items Related to the Plumbing Estimate

The following items, not included in every project, must be evaluated by the plumbing estimator. Valve tags, rigging, and pipe markers, when required, are always the work of the plumber. The number of valve tags should be the same as the number of valves.

The number of pipe markers is specified, based on designated intervals per lineal foot of pipe.

Rigging, the handling of large equipment, will be performed either by the plumber's own workers, or may be subcontracted (see Chapter 1 for more detail).

Piping painting and concrete pads are normally not part of the plumbing contract. However, the specifications may, in some instances, require the plumber to include concrete pads in his bid. In this case, prices would have to be solicited from the appropriate trade subcontractors. Pipe painting, other than stenciling, is not the work of the plumber. If, however, a cost is required for the bid, the appropriate subcontractor must be consulted. Concrete pads should be estimated as outlined in Chapter 1.

Once these figures are estimated they can be entered directly on the estimate forms. After all quantities are taken off and totaled on the quantity takeoff sheets, the figures should be rechecked by another individual. Upon completion, the person performing the check should initial the takeoff sheet in the space provided.

Sample Job

Imagine that you have been asked to bid on the "Three-Story Service Center," our sample project located in a medium to large U.S. city. Assume that you have received the following drawings and specifications for the purpose of performing a takeoff and estimate.

The building is a three-story, slab-on-grade structure of approximately 45,000 square feet. The superstructure is of steel frame construction with upper floor framing of bar joist, metal deck/concrete fill design. The interior partitions are to be constructed of 5/8" drywall with metal studs. The roofing system is of standard built-up design. Site soil conditions are good, consisting of soft clay and loose medium sand. Access to the site is excellent with required utilities along nearby roads.

You should now become familiar with the sample drawings in Figures 4.3 through 4.11. As mentioned in the Preface, it is assumed that you are familiar with architectural prints; therefore, elementary explanations are not necessary. However, you may want to refer to Appendix A for clarification of the plumbing fixtures and piping, fitting, valve, and device symbols found on the drawings.

Drawing Symbols

CO	Cleanout	RWC	Rainwater Conductor
MH	Manhole	VTR	Vent Thru Roof
Lav	Lavatory	Dn.	Down
W.C.	Water Closet	C.B.	Catch Basin
HWC	Handicapped Water Closet	RD	Roof Drain
UR	Urinal	Ⓔ	Existing
F.D.	Floor Drain	Ⓝ	New
RCP	Reinforced Concrete Pipe		

———————	Sanitary Sewer
— — — — — — —	Storm Sewer
——V———V——	Vent Pipe
———— – ————	Cold Water Pipe (CW)
———— – – ————	Hot Water Pipe (HW)
———— – – – ————	Hot Water Recirculation (HWR)
	Gate Valve
	Check Valve
	Balancing Valve
	Frost Proof Hydrant (FPH)

Rev.	Rev.
Project Name: 3 STORY SERVICE CENTER	
Drawing Name: FIRST FLOOR PLAN	
Scale: 1/8" = 1'-0"	
Drawn By: CWL	Date: 11-1-91
Approved By: JJM	Date: 11-8-91
Project Number: 67283	Drawing No.: A-1

Figure 4.3

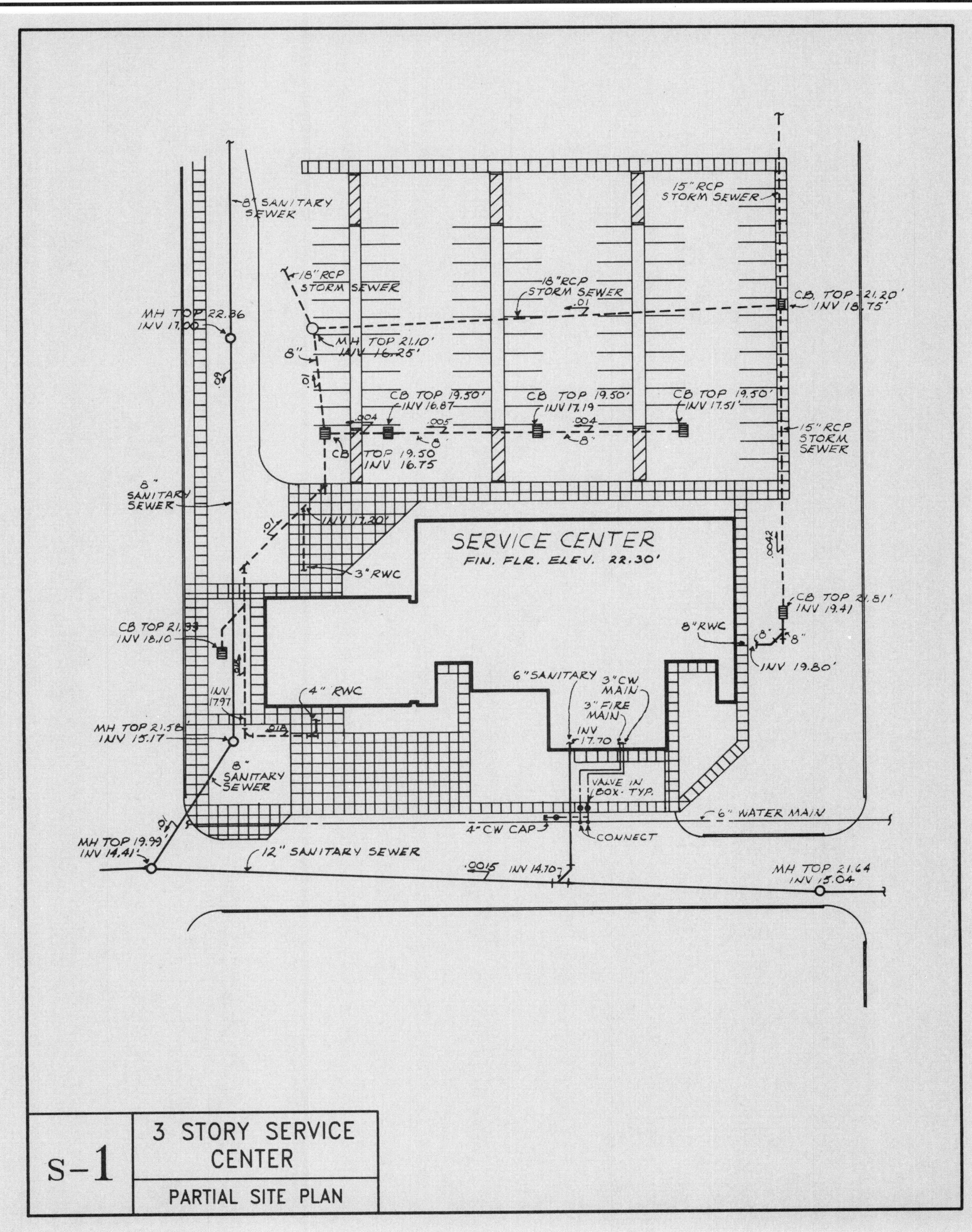
8" SANITARY SEWER
15" RCP STORM SEWER
18" RCP STORM SEWER
18" RCP STORM SEWER
.01
CB. TOP 21.20'
INV 18.75'
MH TOP 22.86
INV 17.00
MH TOP 21.10'
INV 16.25'
8"
CB TOP 19.50'
INV 16.87
CB TOP 19.50'
INV 17.19
CB TOP 19.50'
INV 17.51'
.004
.005
8"
CB TOP 19.50
INV 16.75
15" RCP STORM SEWER
8" SANITARY SEWER
INV 17.20'
SERVICE CENTER
FIN. FLR. ELEV. 22.30'
3" RWC
.0042
CB TOP 21.81'
INV 19.41
CB TOP 21.33
INV 18.10
8" RWC
INV 19.80'
6" SANITARY
3" CW MAIN
3" FIRE MAIN
INV 17.70
INV 17.97
4" RWC
MH TOP 21.58'
INV 15.17
.018
8" SANITARY SEWER
VALVE IN BOX - TYP.
6" WATER MAIN
4" CW CAP
CONNECT
MH TOP 19.99'
INV 14.41'
12" SANITARY SEWER
.0015
INV 14.70
MH TOP 21.64
INV 15.04
S-1
3 STORY SERVICE CENTER
PARTIAL SITE PLAN

Figure 4.4

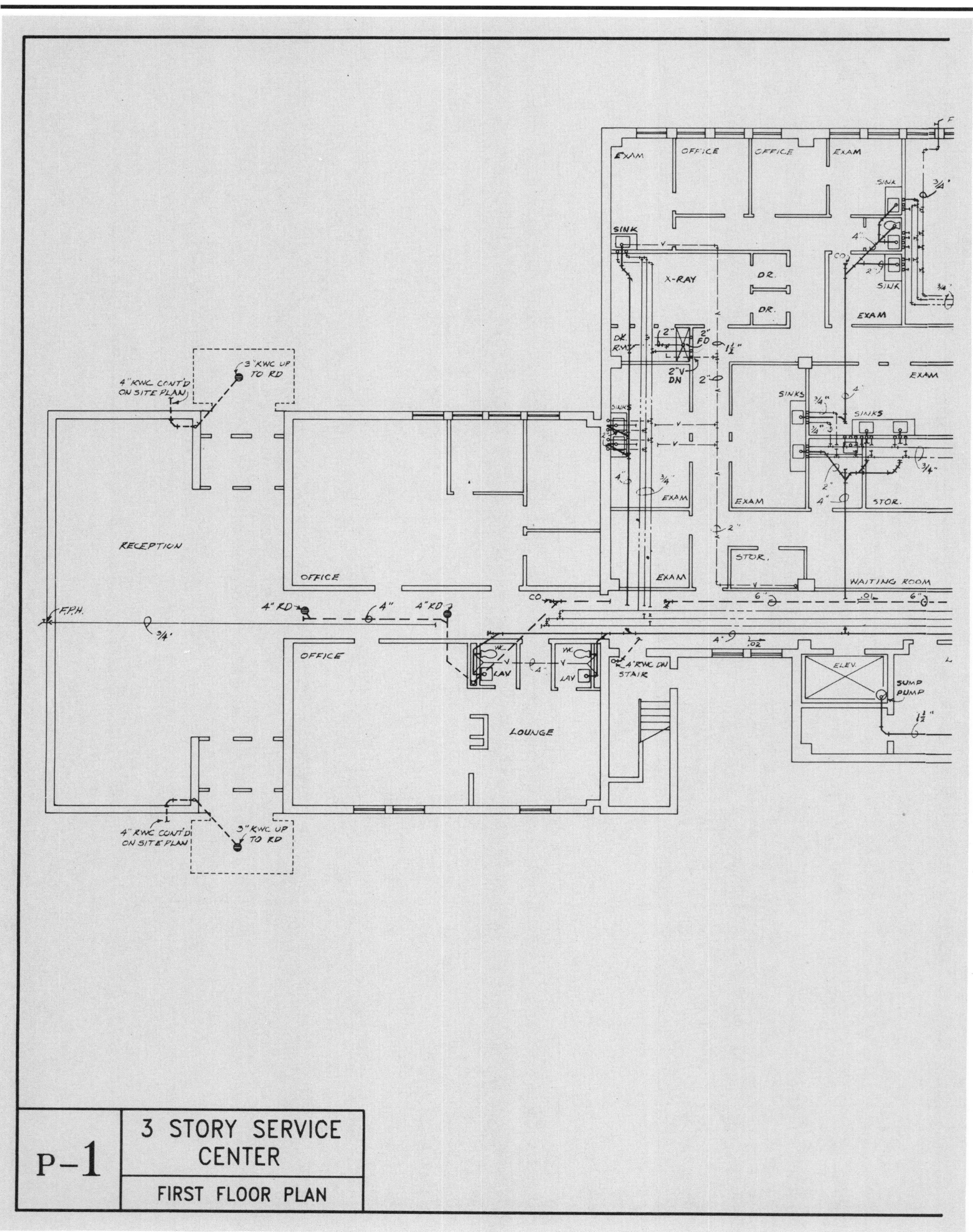
EXAM
OFFICE
OFFICE
EXAM
SINK
SINK
X-RAY
DR.
DR.
SINK
EXAM
EXAM
DK. RM.
SINKS
SINKS
SINKS
EXAM
EXAM
EXAM
STOR.
STOR.
EXAM
WAITING ROOM
3"KWC UP TO RD
4"KWC CONT'D ON SITE PLAN
RECEPTION
OFFICE
F.P.H.
4" RD
4"
4" RD
OFFICE
LAV
LAV
4"RWC DN
STAIR
ELEV.
SUMP PUMP
LOUNGE
4" RWC CONT'D ON SITE PLAN
3" KWC UP TO RD
P–1
3 STORY SERVICE CENTER
FIRST FLOOR PLAN
Figure 4.5

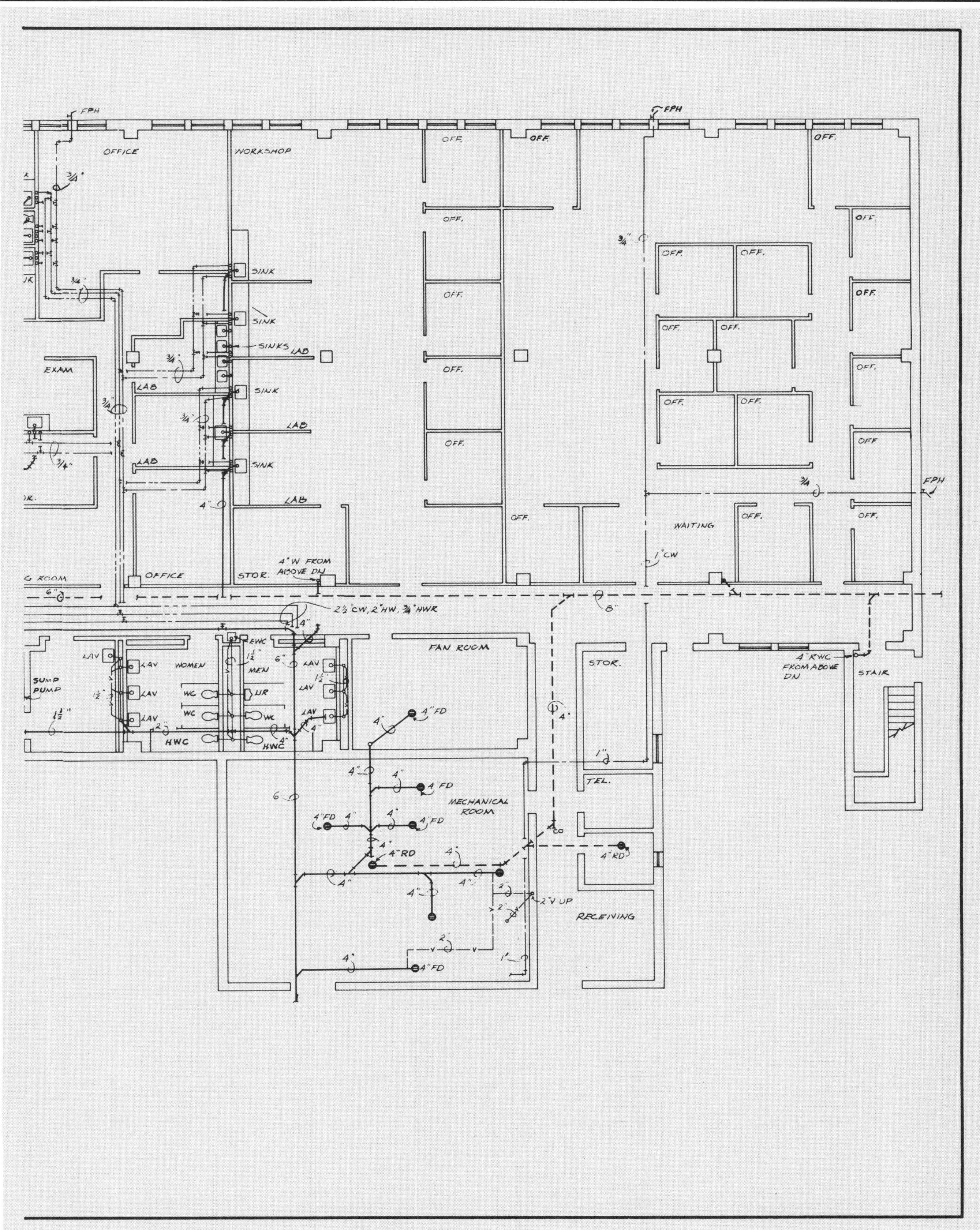

Figure 4.5 (cont'd.)

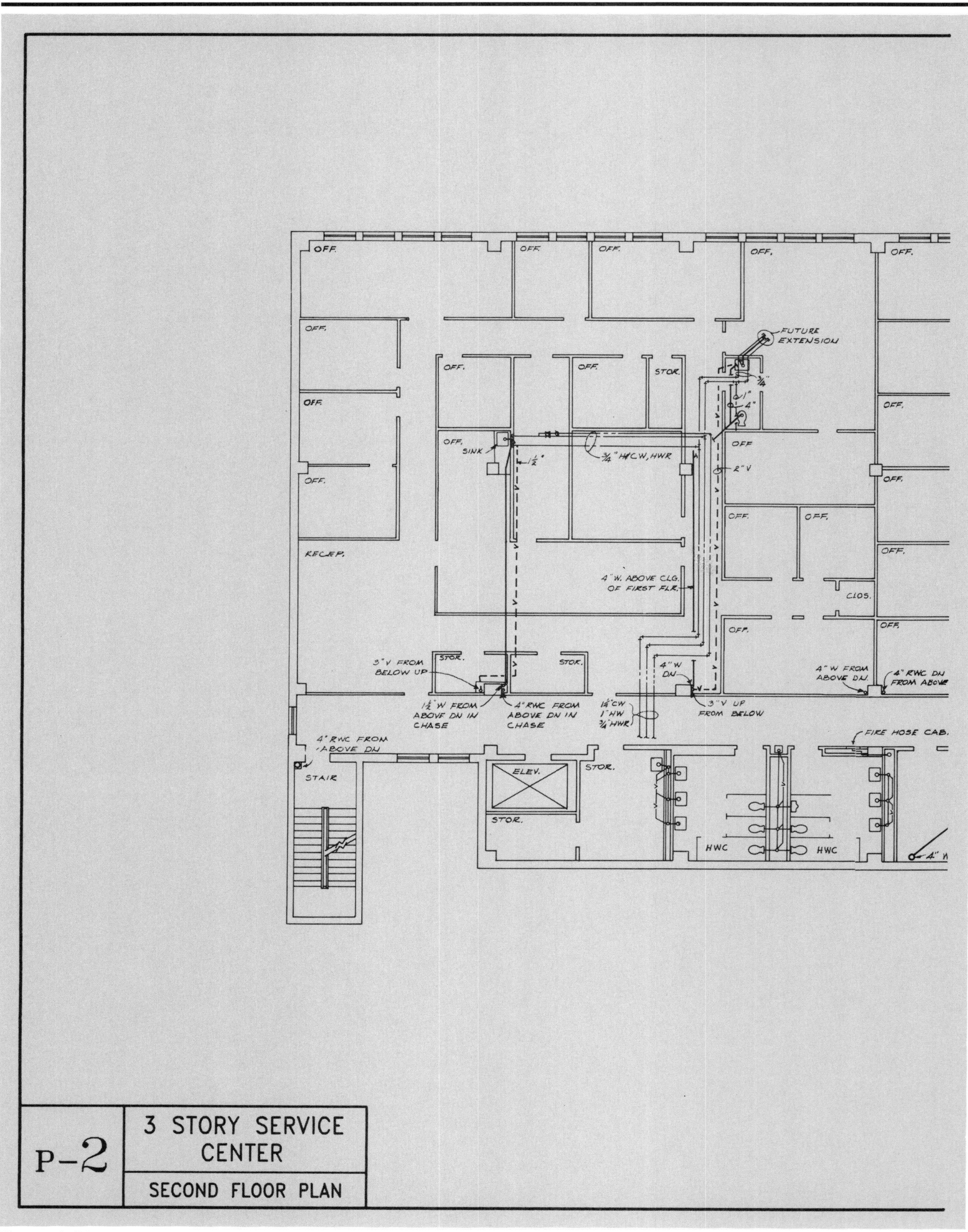

OFF.
FUTURE EXTENSION
STOR.
SINK
3/4" H&CW, HWR
2" V
RECEP.
4" W. ABOVE CLG. OF FIRST FLR.
CLOS.
3" V FROM BELOW UP
1½" W FROM ABOVE DN IN CHASE
4" RWC FROM ABOVE DN IN CHASE
1¼" CW
1" HW
¾" HWR
4" W DN
3" V UP FROM BELOW
4" W FROM ABOVE DN.
4" RWC DN FROM ABOVE
FIRE HOSE CAB.
4" RWC FROM ABOVE DN
STAIR
ELEV.
HWC
P-2
3 STORY SERVICE CENTER
SECOND FLOOR PLAN

Figure 4.6

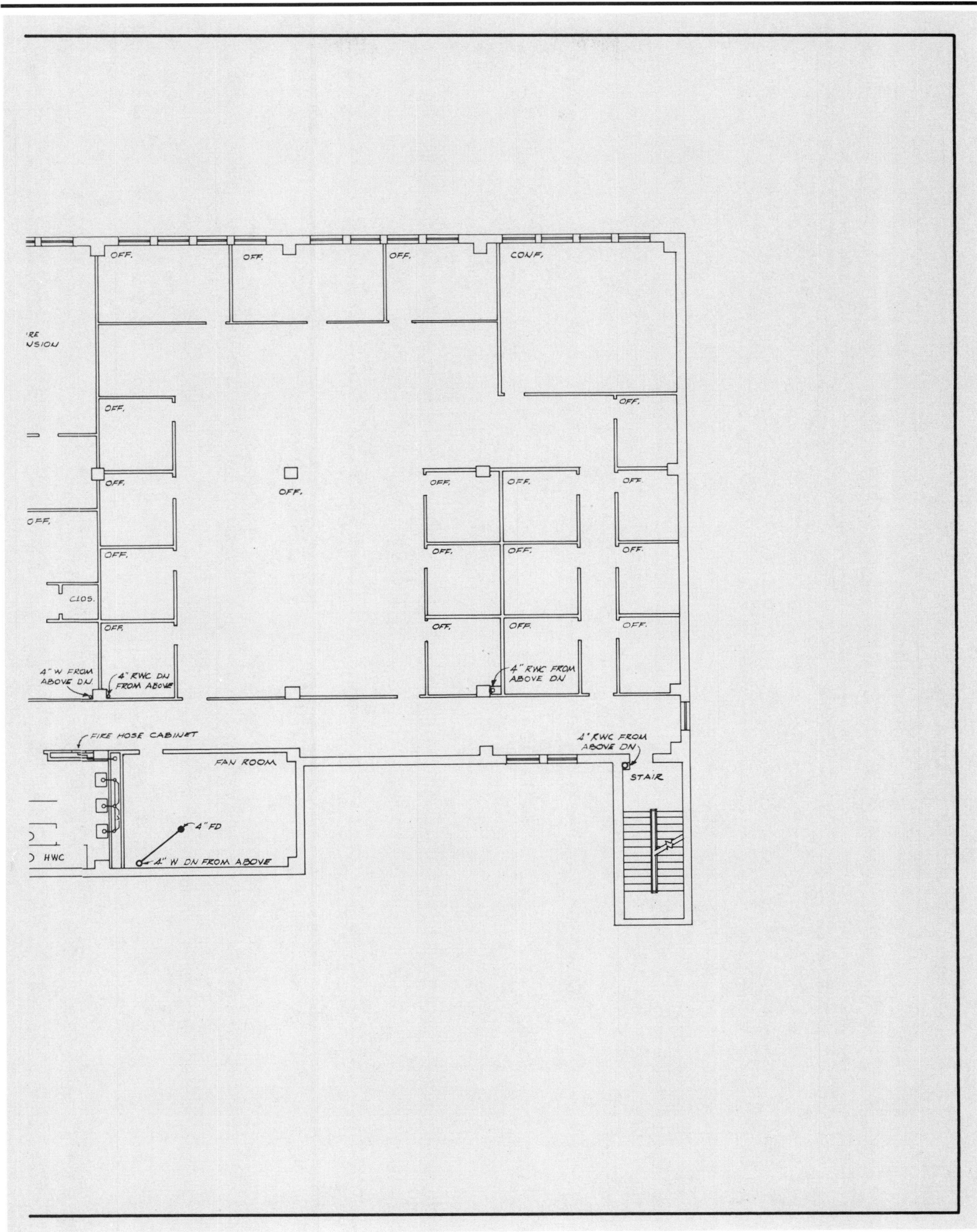

Figure 4.6 (cont'd.)

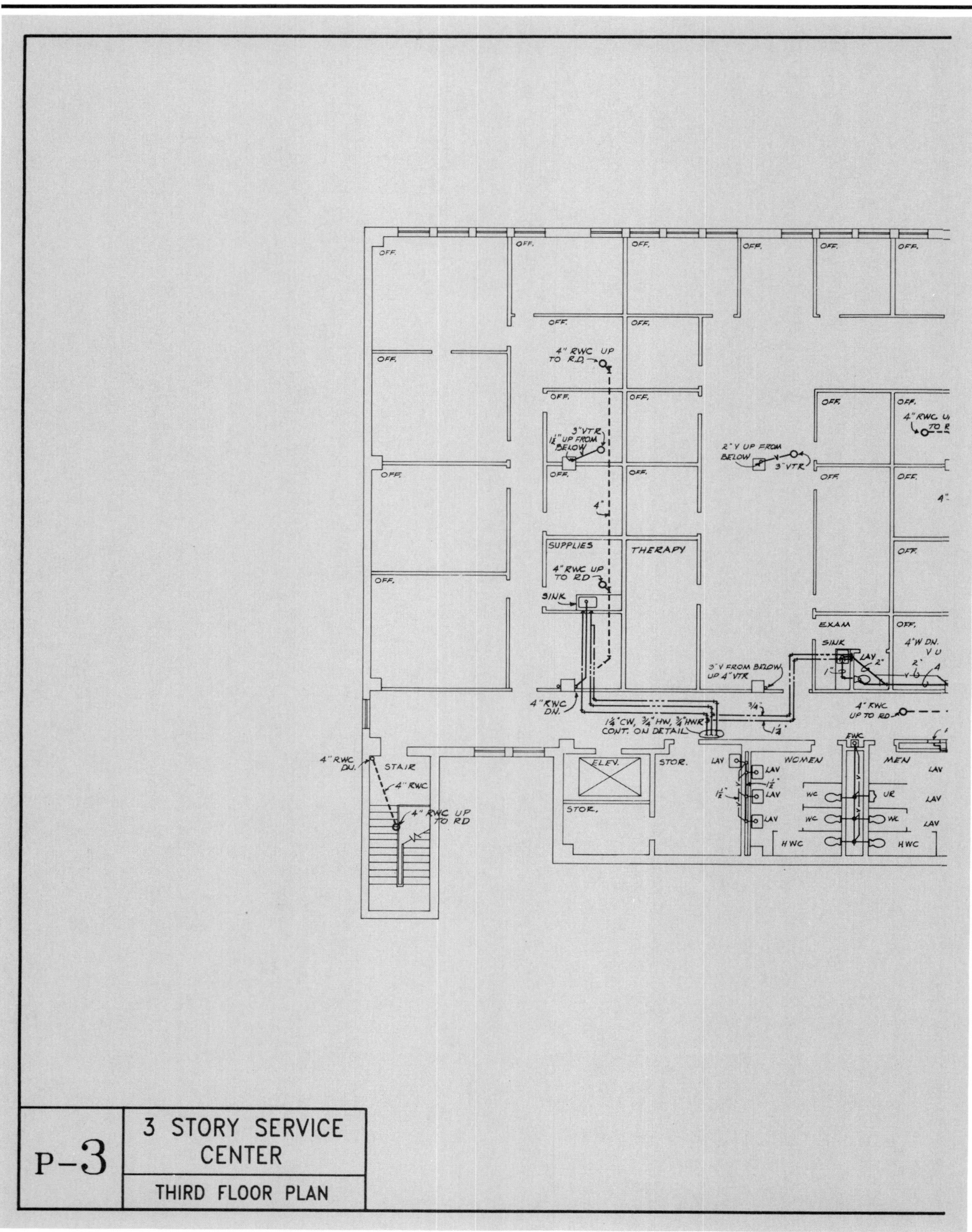
OFF.
4" RWC UP TO R.D.
3" VTR
1½" UP FROM BELOW
4"
2" V UP FROM BELOW
3" VTR
SUPPLIES
THERAPY
4" RWC UP TO RD
SINK
EXAM
4" W DN.
3" V FROM BELOW UP 4" VTR
4" RWC DN.
1¼" CW, ¾" HW, ¾" HWR CONT. ON DETAIL
4" RWC UP TO RD
4" RWC DN.
STAIR
4" RWC
4" RWC UP TO RD
ELEV.
STOR.
STOR.
WOMEN
MEN
LAV
WC
UR
HWC
EWC
P-3
3 STORY SERVICE CENTER
THIRD FLOOR PLAN

Figure 4.7

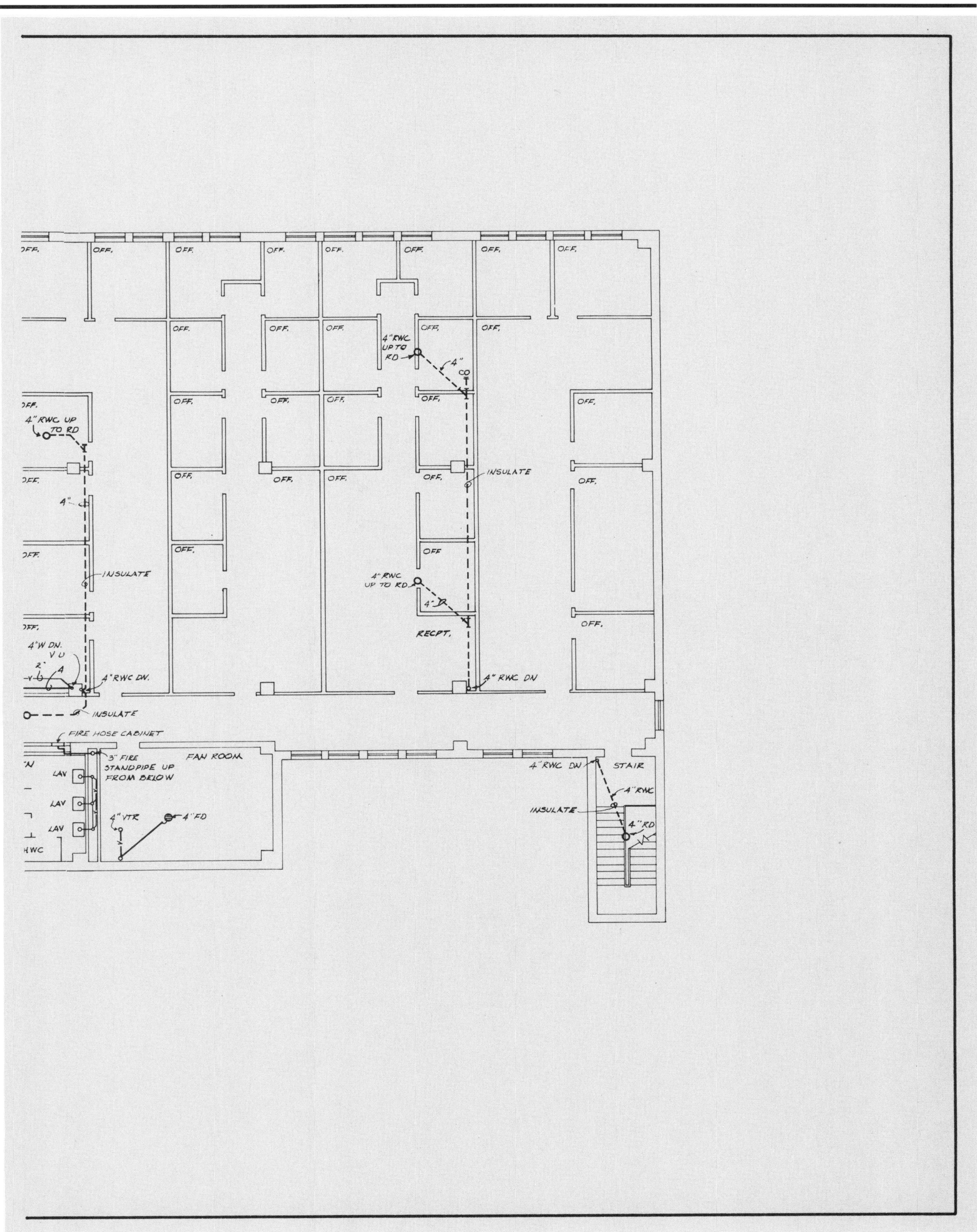

Figure 4.7 (cont'd.)

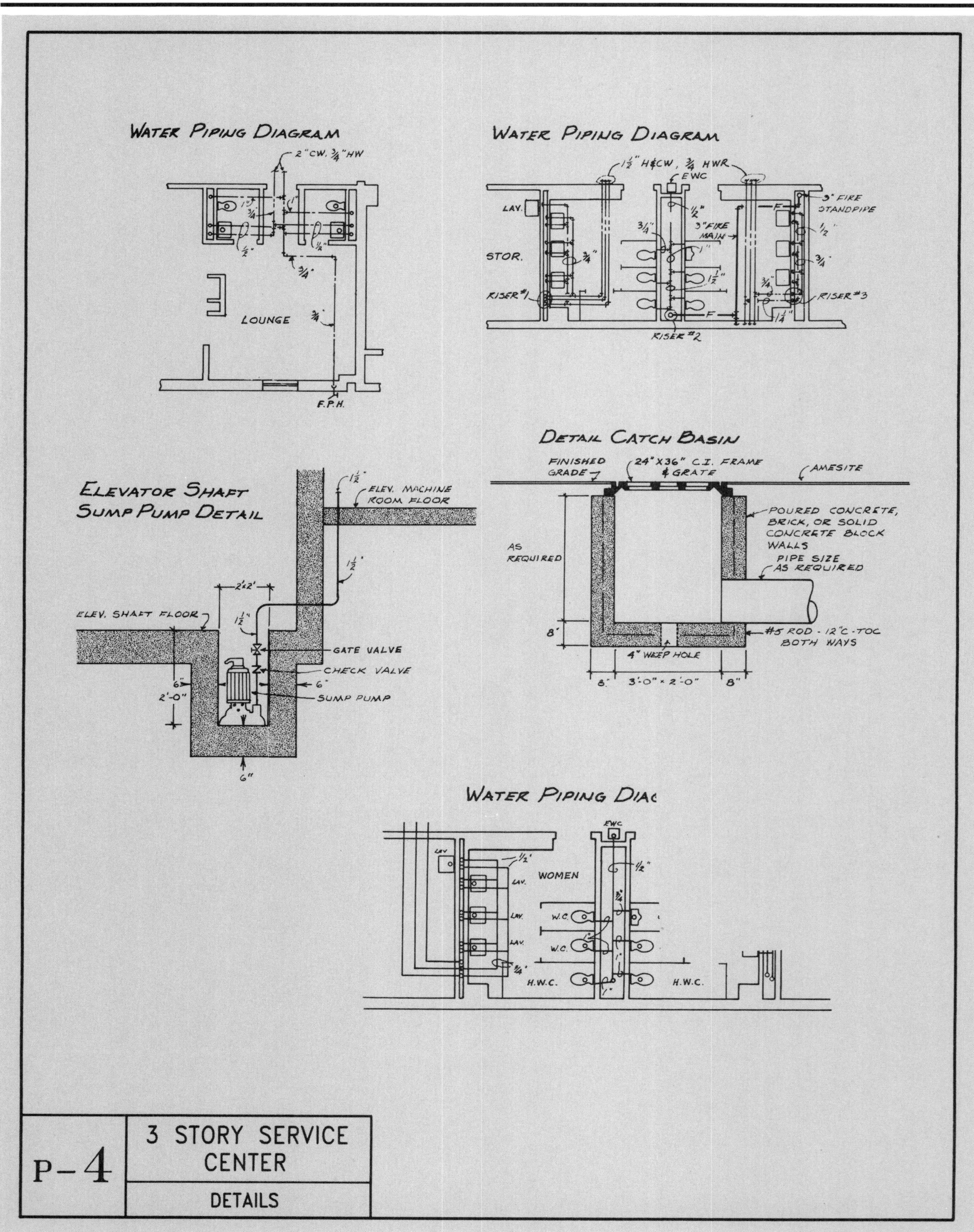

WATER PIPING DIAGRAM
2"CW. 3/4"HW
LOUNGE
F.P.H.
WATER PIPING DIAGRAM
1 1/2" H&CW, 3/4 HWR
EWC
LAV.
STOR.
3" FIRE STANDPIPE
3" FIRE MAIN
RISER #1
RISER #2
RISER #3
ELEVATOR SHAFT SUMP PUMP DETAIL
ELEV. MACHINE ROOM FLOOR
ELEV. SHAFT FLOOR
GATE VALVE
CHECK VALVE
SUMP PUMP
DETAIL CATCH BASIN
FINISHED GRADE
24"X36" C.I. FRAME & GRATE
AMESITE
POURED CONCRETE, BRICK, OR SOLID CONCRETE BLOCK WALLS
PIPE SIZE AS REQUIRED
AS REQUIRED
#5 ROD - 12"C-TOC BOTH WAYS
4" WEEP HOLE
3'-0" x 2'-0"
WATER PIPING DIAC
EWC
WOMEN
W.C.
H.W.C.
P-4
3 STORY SERVICE CENTER
DETAILS

Figure 4.8

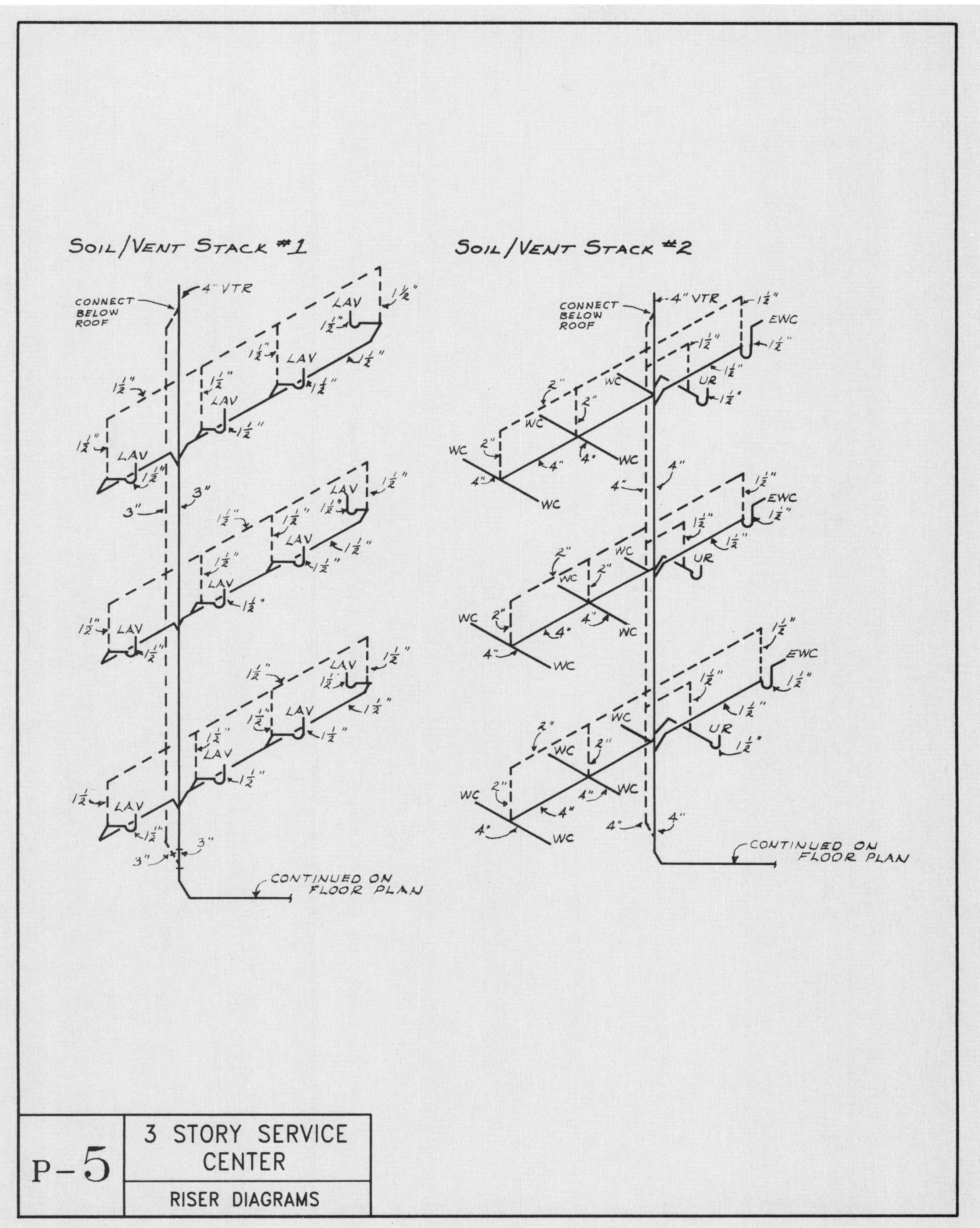
SOIL/VENT STACK #1
SOIL/VENT STACK #2
CONNECT BELOW ROOF
4" VTR
LAV
EWC
UR
WC
CONTINUED ON FLOOR PLAN
P-5
3 STORY SERVICE CENTER
RISER DIAGRAMS
Figure 4.9a

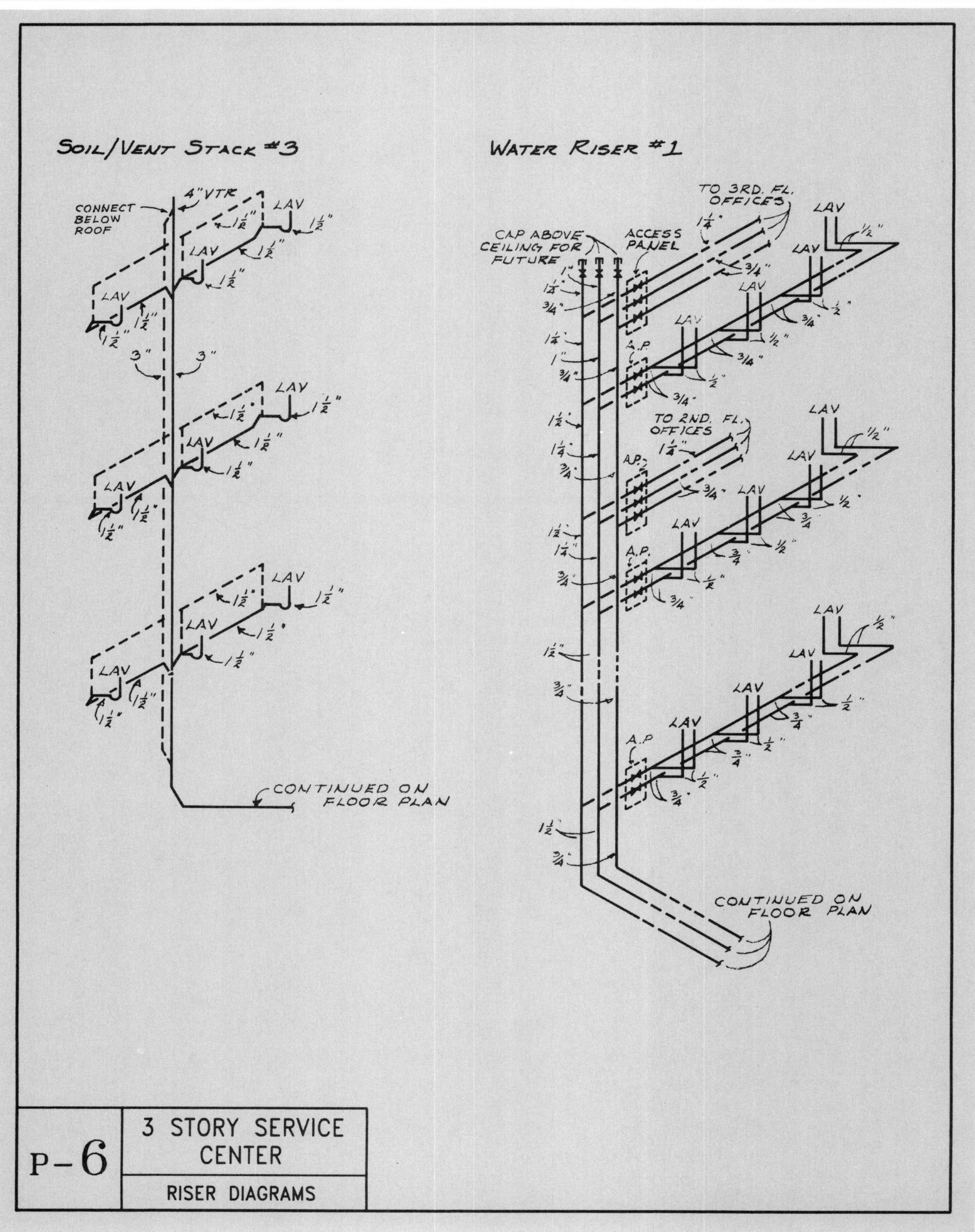

SOIL/VENT STACK #3
CONNECT BELOW ROOF
4" VTR
LAV
3"
CONTINUED ON FLOOR PLAN
WATER RISER #1
CAP ABOVE CEILING FOR FUTURE
ACCESS PANEL
TO 3RD. FL. OFFICES
TO 2ND. FL. OFFICES
A.P.
LAV
CONTINUED ON FLOOR PLAN
P-6
3 STORY SERVICE CENTER
RISER DIAGRAMS

Figure 4.9b

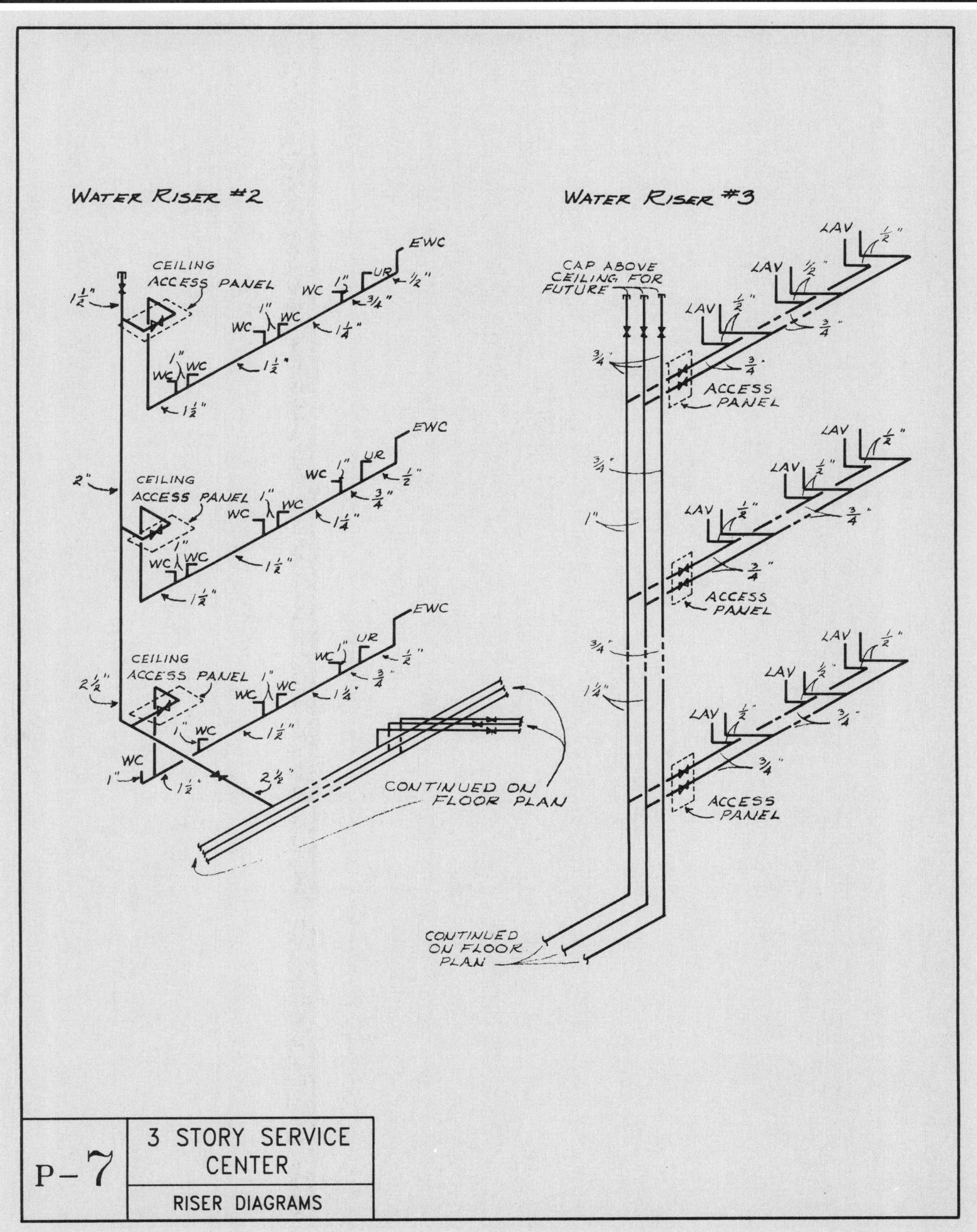
WATER RISER #2
WATER RISER #3
CEILING ACCESS PANEL
EWC
UR
WC
LAV
CAP ABOVE CEILING FOR FUTURE
ACCESS PANEL
CONTINUED ON FLOOR PLAN
P-7
3 STORY SERVICE CENTER
RISER DIAGRAMS

Figure 4.9c

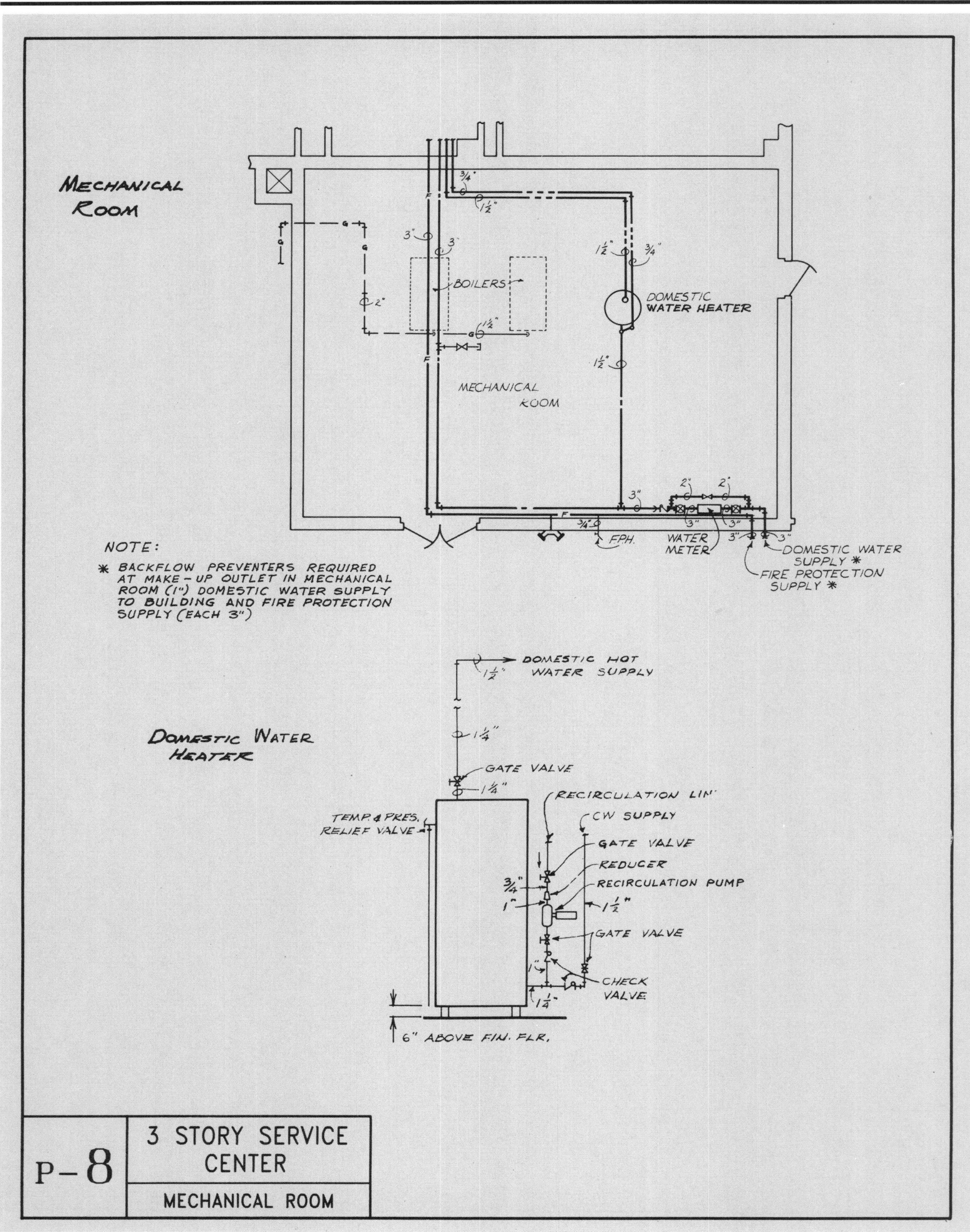
MECHANICAL ROOM
BOILERS
DOMESTIC WATER HEATER
MECHANICAL ROOM
F.P.H.
WATER METER
DOMESTIC WATER SUPPLY *
FIRE PROTECTION SUPPLY *
NOTE:
* BACKFLOW PREVENTERS REQUIRED AT MAKE-UP OUTLET IN MECHANICAL ROOM (1") DOMESTIC WATER SUPPLY TO BUILDING AND FIRE PROTECTION SUPPLY (EACH 3")
DOMESTIC WATER HEATER
DOMESTIC HOT WATER SUPPLY
GATE VALVE
TEMP. & PRES. RELIEF VALVE
RECIRCULATION LIN
CW SUPPLY
GATE VALVE
REDUCER
RECIRCULATION PUMP
GATE VALVE
CHECK VALVE
6" ABOVE FIN. FLR.
P-8
3 STORY SERVICE CENTER
MECHANICAL ROOM

Figure 4.10

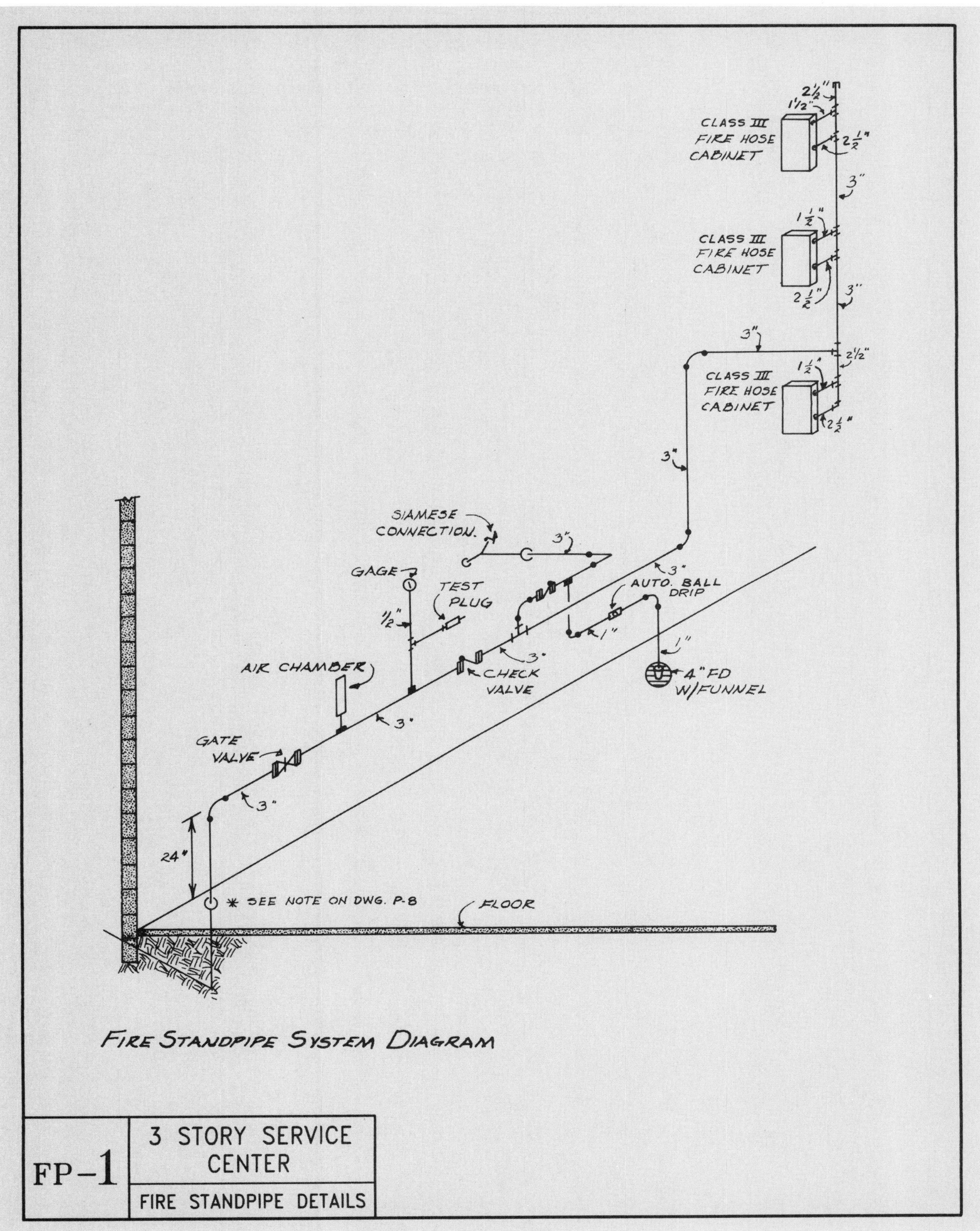
CLASS III
FIRE HOSE
CABINET
2½"
1½"
2½"
3"
CLASS III
FIRE HOSE
CABINET
1½"
2½"
3"
3"
2½"
CLASS III
FIRE HOSE
CABINET
1½"
2½"
3"
SIAMESE
CONNECTION.
3"
3"
GAGE
TEST
PLUG
½"
AUTO. BALL
DRIP
1"
1"
3"
AIR CHAMBER
CHECK
VALVE
4" FD
W/FUNNEL
3"
GATE
VALVE
3"
24"
* SEE NOTE ON DWG. P-8
FLOOR
FIRE STANDPIPE SYSTEM DIAGRAM
FP-1
3 STORY SERVICE
CENTER
FIRE STANDPIPE DETAILS

Figure 4.11

Following the drawings, you will find the sample specifications for the Three-Story Service Center (Figures 4.12 through 4.57). In the sample specifications there are numbered "specification notes" at the bottom of certain pages which correspond to the flagged and numbered sections within the body of the specification. The purpose of these notes is to extract and explain the most relevant portions of a specification.

SAMPLE JOB SPECIFICATIONS

Three-Story Service Center Index

DIVISION 15 - PLUMBING
SECTION 1
BASIC MATERIALS AND METHODS

PART 1: GENERAL

PART 2: MATERIALS

PART 3: EXECUTION

Figure 4.12

DIVISION 15 - PLUMBING

SECTION 1

BASIC MATERIALS AND METHODS

PART 1: GENERAL

1.01 NOTICE

A. General Conditions and Schedule of Drawings apply to and are hereby made part of this Section.

B. Contractor consult these Sections in detail as he will be responsible for and governed by conditions set forth therein and work indicated.

(1)

1.02 SCOPE

A. Work complete in all details including fixtures and equipment as hereinafter specified, with all appurtenances common to various systems generally consisting of piping, valves, hangers and supports, insulation, covering, structures, excavation and backfilling, cleaning, testing and such other material and work as is necessary, specified or required to form complete and properly operating systems as herein specified or indicated.

B. Following items are included in work required and are described hereinafter in detail:

1. Domestic water service, hot, cold and recirculating water piping.
2. Fire protection system water service and standpipe system.
3. Plumbing fixtures.
4. Building sanitary and storm water drainage.
5. Catch basins, storm water sewer and sanitary sewer.
6. Insulation.
7. Temporary Water.

(2)

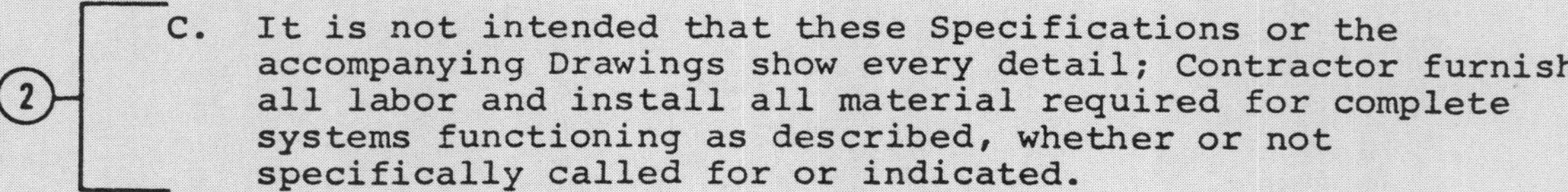

C. It is not intended that these Specifications or the accompanying Drawings show every detail; Contractor furnish all labor and install all material required for complete systems functioning as described, whether or not specifically called for or indicated.

SPECIFICATION NOTES

1. Estimator must take note of scope of work to see exactly what is required of him as a bidding contractor.
2. A note such as this should cause the estimator to work closely with the plumbing code having jurisdiction.

Figure 4.13

1.03 PLUMBING REFERENCES

A. Abbreviations

1. BTU - British Thermal Unit
2. cfm - cubic feet per minute
3. fpm - feet per minute
4. gal - gallon
5. gpm - gallons per minute
6. hp - horse power
7. lb - pound
8. psi - pounds per square inch
9. C - degree Centigrade
10. F - degree Fahrenheit
11. ft or ' - foot
12. gph - gallons per hour
13. in. or " - inch
14. wwp - water working pressure
15. sp - static pressure

B. Technical societies, trade organizations, governmental agencies.

1. AGA - American Gas Association
2. ASME - American Society of Mechanical Engineers
3. ASTM - American Society for Testing Materials
4. AWWA - American Water Works Association
5. NFPA - National Fire Protection Association
6. UL - Underwriters' Laboratories, Inc.
7. USA - USA Standards Institute

C. Definitions

1. "Provide" shall mean "furnish and install".
2. "Herein" shall mean "contents of a particular Division" where this term appears.
3. "Indicated" shall mean "indicated on Contract Drawings".
4. "Equal" shall mean "approved equal".
5. "Contractor" shall mean "Contractor or subcontractor for the work described".

Figure 4.14

Three-Story Service Center PLUMBING 1-3

1.04 SHOP DRAWINGS AND SAMPLES

A. Shop drawings

(3)

1. Furnish six (6) sets of shop drawings and pictorial or descriptive data.
2. Shop drawings marked with project designation.
3. Obtain approval within forty-five (45) days after signing respective Contract.
4. Data for respective trade submitted in separate folios.
5. Obtain approval of Architect before ordering.
6. Furnish performance curves showing efficiency, capacity, head and brake horsepower for all pumps, compressors and heat exchangers.
7. Furnish additional shop drawings and descriptive data, other than those listed herein, as requested by Architect.

B. Materials

1. Architect reserves right to require submission of samples of any or all articles or materials proposed to be used under these Specifications.

(4)

1.05 GOVERNING REQUIREMENTS

A. Mechanical installations comply with all applicable codes, ordinances, rules, regulations and laws in effect.

B. Following considered minimum requirements:

1. State Plumbing Code.
2. National Plumbing Code.
3. Occupational Safety and Health Administration.

C. Construction comply with Department of Labor, Bureau of Labor Standards, Safety and Health Regulations for Construction.

(5)

D. Contractor obtain and pay for all necessary permits for work, including sanitary and storm sewers, as part of Contract.

E. Contractor arrange and pay for all required inspections and furnish required certificates of inspection to Owner.

(6)

1.06 TESTS

A. Arrange and pay for all tests required by Authorities specified.

B. Contractor notify Architect three (3) working days before tests are made.

3. Indicates extent of shop drawing work, and helps estimate engineering cost when marking up estimate.
4. Indicates codes estimator must follow in his development of the estimate.
5. Indicates the bidding contractor is responsible for the paying of permits; aids in applying a dollar value for permits and fees in cost estimate.
6. Indicates to estimator that dollars must be included in estimate for testing systems.

Figure 4.15

C. Repeat tests after defects are corrected.

D. Drainage system.

1. Test applied before pipe is covered.
2. System filled with water and subjected to not less than 10' of hydrostatic head.
3. Water remain in system not less than 15 minutes with no leaks or lowering of water level.
4. Air test of 5 psi for 15 minutes acceptable in lieu of water test.

E. Interior water supply system

1. Hydrostatic pressure test of not less than 125 psi.
2. Test pressure applied for not less than one hour with no leaks.

F. Gas piping

1. Gas piping tested as required by local Gas Light Co. and State Plumbing Code.
2. Tests meet requirements of NFPA.

G. For other tests, see particular equipment specified.

1.07 PAINTING

A. Equipment

1. Equipment furnished factory-finished with colors as selected by Architect.

2. Contractor refinish equipment with matching finish when damaged during shipment or construction.

B. Piping and insulation covering

1. Piping and covering in masonry walls, trenches and underground painted with two coats of cut-back-asphaltum paint, except cast-iron pipe may have factory-applied coating.

2. Exposed piping painted as specified in Painting Section of this Specification.

C. Hangers, supports and insulation covering painted as specified in Painting Section of this Specification.

D. All surfaces to be painted must be thoroughly cleaned of rust, scale, grease and foreign matter.

Figure 4.16

Three-Story Service Center PLUMBING 1-5

1.08 TEMPORARY FACILITIES

A. Water

1. Provide temporary water supply in locations directed by General Contractor for drinking water and construction purposes.
2. Water for above purposes will be separately metered and paid for by General Contractor.

1.09 AS-BUILT DRAWINGS

A. As work progresses, record on one set of plumbing Drawings all changes from the installation originally indicated.

B. Record final location of underground lines by depth from finished grade.

C. Record offset distances from buildings, curbs, or edges of walks.

D. Locate piping from interior walls and floors.

E. Submit to Architect for approval and record the above required information in colored pencil on blueprints of Contract Drawings.

1.10 INSTRUCTING ATTENDANT

A. Verbal Instruction

1. After all tests and adjustments, Contractor instruct attendant or Owner's representative in all details of operation of respective system.
2. Supply attendants to operate the systems until Architect is satisfied that the systems have been installed in accordance with these Drawings and Specifications and are functioning properly.
3. Provide services of equipment manufacturer's engineer to instruct representative of Owner in operation and maintenance of Mechanical equipment and controls.

B. Written Instructions

1. Provide two (2) copies of printed instructions and diagrams covering operation and maintenance of each item of equipment and controls.
2. Instructions furnished in bound covers and posted at locations designated by Architect.
3. Diagrams include performance curves for all pumps, minimum size 8-1/2" x 11".

7. Indicates to estimator that temporary facilities are to be installed under his contract.

Figure 4.17

1.11 GUARANTEE

A. Contractor leave entire system installed under respective contracts in proper working order.

B. Contractor responsible for specified performance of all equipment.

C. Contractor replace any work or material which develop defects, except ordinary wear and tear, or fail to perform satisfactorily, within one (1) year from the date of final acceptance.

D. Date of final acceptance or partial acceptance of system determined by Architect.

PART 2: MATERIALS

2.01 MATERIAL & EQUIPMENT REQUIREMENTS

A. Design

1. Materials and equipment conform to capacity, efficiency design and material specified.
2. Equipment must meet dimension and space requirements.
3. Sizes and capacities indicated or specified are minimum requirements; Contractor may use larger sizes provided space requirements are met and do not result in additional installation, maintenance or operating costs to Owner.
4. Materials and appliances of types for which there are UL Standard requirements, listings or labels have such listing of UL, be so labeled, and conform to their requirements.

B. Materials

1. Equipment or material of the same type or classification shall be product of same manufacturer.
2. Provide all new materials new, of best of their respective kind, and conforming with accepted standards of trade.
3. Equipment and accessories not specifically described or identified by manufacturer's catalog number designed in conformity with applicable technical standards and specifications of societies, organizations and/or agencies listed herein, suitable for maximum working pressure and have neat and finished appearance.
4. In all cases where device or part of equipment is herein referred to in singular number, it is intended that such reference apply to as many such items as are

Figure 4.18

required to complete installation.
5. Manufacturer's names and catalog numbers are given to describe and illustrate type, quality and design of material and equipment required.
6. Data on comparable material and equipment of other than listed manufacturers may be submitted with written request for approval of Architect; if approved, Architect will issue Addenda to Specifications.
7. No request for above approval will be considered later than ten (10) days before bids are due.

2.02 PIPE AND FITTINGS

(8)

A. Schedule 40, black steel pipe and fittings.

1. Provide pipe of uniform thickness with smooth cylindrical interior.
2. Pipe conform with USA Standard B36.10.
3. Provide standard weight black banded malleable iron fittings.
4. Fittings conform with ASTM Standard A-47.

B. Copper pipe and fittings.

1. Provide Type L hard copper pipe for pipe 1-1/2" and smaller above ground.
2. Provide Type K hard copper pipe for pipe larger than 1-1/2" above ground.
3. Provide Type L or K, as specified herein, soft copper pipe underground. (9)
4. Pipe conform to ASTM Standard B-88.
5. Copper pipe fittings wrought, sweat type; no joints underground. (10)
6. Fittings conform to ASTM Standard B-62.

(13)

C. Cast-iron soil pipe and fittings.

1. Provide cast-iron soil pipe of extra heavy weight, bell and spigot pattern, factory-coated inside and out with coal-tar pitch varnish, cylindrical and smooth, free from sand holes, cracks, and other defects.
2. Pipe and fitting conform with USA Standard 40.1 and ASTM Standard A-74.
3. Hubless pipe and fittings as manufactured by Tyler Pipe Industries, or equal, acceptable above ground. (11)

D. Terra cotta pipe and fittings.

1. Provide extra strength, hub and spigot pattern, vitrified, impervious clay sewer pipe.

8. Indicates to estimator the type of piping and fittings specified.
9. Notice that engineer has given bidding contractor a choice of materials. Estimator can use least expensive alternate and yet comply with specifications.
10. Estimator cannot figure joints for underground copper.
11. Engineer again has given bidding contractor a choice.

Figure 4.19

2. Pipe sound and well burned, with clear ring, smooth and free from blisters, cracks, or large chips.
3. Pipe and fittings conform to ASTM Standard C-200.

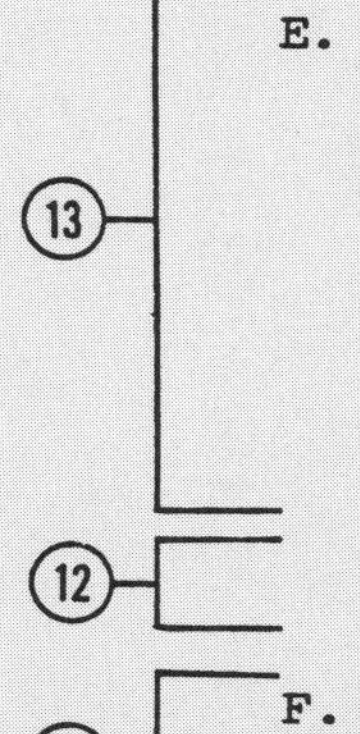

E. Class 250 ductile iron pressure pipe and fittings.

1. Provide pipe conforming to USA Standard A21 and A21.7.
2. Pipe of type with bolted mechanical joints.
3. Fittings conform to AWWA Specifications for Class D special castings or USA Standard A21.10 for Class 250 short-body fittings.
4. Pipe and fittings coated inside and out with coal-tar pitch varnish.
5. Provide cement lining as indicated conforming with AWWA Standard C104.

F. Galvanized Steel Schedule 40 pipe and fittings.

1. Provide pipe, of threaded, heavily and uniformly galvanized inside and outside.
2. Pipe conform to ASTM Standard A-53.
3. Provide galvanized cast iron recessed drainage fittings, screw pattern on waste and drain piping.
4. Provide galvanized, cast iron or malleable iron, flat banded pattern fittings on vent piping.

12. Cement lining is required for cast-iron water pipe. Estimator should figure accordingly.
13. Indicates to estimator type of piping and fittings specified.
14. Indicates to estimator type of piping and fittings specified.

Figure 4.20

14

G. Concrete pipe

1. Provide machine tongue and grooved reinforced concrete pipe with closed joints.
2. Pipe true circle, or uniform thickness and straight in direction of axis, sound, without cracks or large chips.
3. Pipe conform to ASTM Standard C76.

15

H. Valves

1. Provide valves of one manufacturer; Crane, Jenkins, Lunkenheimer or Walworth.

16

2. Valves designed for 125 psi wwp.
3. Provide gate valves for shut-off valves, 1" and larger.
4. Provide globe valves for all throttling valves.
5. Valves have manufacturer's name and working pressure cast integral.
6. Provide sleeve end type valves for solder joints on copper pipe.
7. Provide globe pattern valves for sizes 3/4" and smaller.
8. Gate valves conform to following:

   a. 2-1/2" and smaller: Bronze, inside screw non-rising spindle, solid or split wedge, screwed bonnet.
   b. 3" and larger: Bronze, outside screw and yoke, rising stem, bronze-mounted, solid or split bronze wedge, renewable seat rings and bolted bonnet, flanged.

9. Check valves conform to following:

   a. 2-1/2" and smaller: Bronze body, renewable composition disc, screwed top.
   b. 3" and larger: Bronze body, renewable seat ring, composition disc bolted at top, flanged.

10. Globe and angle valves conform to following:

   a. 2-1/2" and smaller: Bronze body, renewable composition disc, screwed bonnet.
   b. 3" and larger: Bronze body, bronze mounted with renewable seat ring and composition disc, outside screw and yoke, flanged.

11. Provide bronze body, bronze or brass mounted, double gate valve conforming to AWWA Standard Specifications, for valves in pipe underground; terminate valve stems in wrench nuts and furnish two (2) suitable keys.

12. Valves placed in accessible position and installed with stems vertical or as directed by Architect.

15. Indicates quality of valves specified.
16. Indicates types of valves, and types of valves for various size ranges specified.

Figure 4.21

13. Provide valve boxes for valves underground.

    a. Standard cast iron, adjustable shaft having minimum diameter of 5-1/4".
    b. Casting coated with two coats of coal-tar pitch varnish.
    c. Lids of all boxes bear the word "Water" or letter "W".

I. Unions.

1. Provide screwed pattern, galvanized malleable iron unions for sizes 2-1/2" and smaller.
2. Provide standard weight, flanged pattern, galvanized cast-iron unions sizes 3" and larger.
3. Unions suitable for 300 psi wwp and be of ground joint type with brass seat ring pressed into head piece.

J. Gaskets.

1. Provide full-faced rubber ring type, 1/16" thick gaskets for above ground; cast iron or malleable flanges.
2. Provide soft asbestos gaskets with graphited finish for fixture outlets to floor flanges.
3. Gaskets suitable for 125 psi wwp.

K. Nipples.

1. Provide nipples of same material as pipe or tubing on which they are installed.
2. Nipples extra strong when unthreaded portion is less than 1" long.
3. Running thread nipples are prohibited.

L. Cleanouts

1. Provide bodies conforming in thickness to that required for pipe on which installed.
2. Cleanouts extend not less than 1/4" above hub if installed on soil pipe.
3. Cleanouts have heavy brass plugs not less than 1/4" thick, provide with raised nut of rot less than 3/16" height for removal of plug.
4. Cleanouts terminate 2" below finished floor in cast brass cleanout frame installed flush with floor.

(17)

5. Provide Josam, or equal Wade or Zurn, frame and cover in floor.
6. Cleanouts in wall terminate 2" inside finished surface in chromium-plated brass or stainless steel flush deck plate, Josam, or equal Wade or Zurn.

17. Indicates quality of cleanouts to be provided.

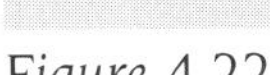

Figure 4.22

M. Traps.

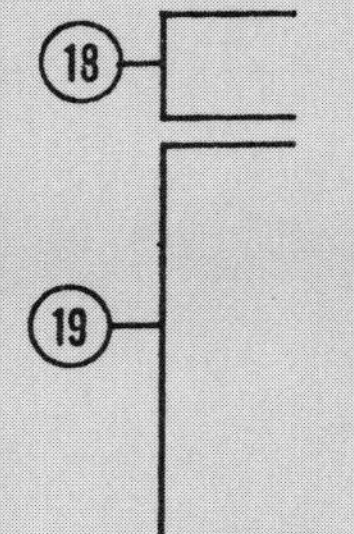

1. Provide traps, except on fixtures, cast iron and conforming to piping systems on which installed.
2. Provide 2-1/2" minimum and 4" maximum seal for traps.
3. Fixture traps, except water closets and urinals, have full size cleanout plugs below water line.
4. Traps self-cleaning type.
5. Running traps have vent hub on each side.
6. P-traps have vent hub on one side.
7. Traps below ground floor have cleanout extendeu to floor level.

N. Sleeves and Escutcheons.

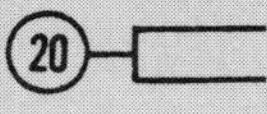

1. Provide steel or cast-iron pipe sleeves.
2. Provide one piece, chromium plated steel or brass, escutcheons.

(21)

O. Gauges.

1. Provide Ashcroft Series 10-10, or equal, crosby-Ashton Lonergron or Marsh gauges.
2. Gauges of bourdon tube type with bronze movement, white dial and black figures.
3. Provide aluminum case with close fitting friction ring, chromium plated, less back flange.
4. Scale approximately twice normal working pressure.
5. Gauges connected by means of brass pipe and fittings with brass shut-off cock.

P. Thermometers.

1. Provide Wexler Type AA5a, or equal, Moeller or Taylor thermometers.
2. Thermometer 9" scale red reading mercury type with brass, separable socket pattern, and 3/4" thread.
3. Provide 3-1/2" stem length inclined for visibility were located overhead.

(22)

Q. Joint Material.

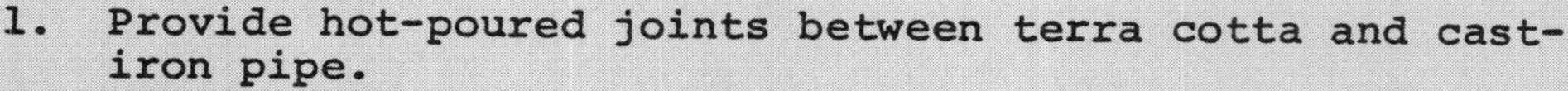
1. Provide hot-poured joints between terra cotta and cast-iron pipe.

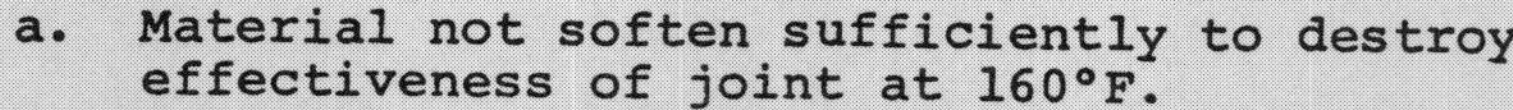
a. Material not soften sufficiently to destroy effectiveness of joint at 160°F.
b. Material not become brittle at low temperatures.
c. Material not soluble in any wastes normally carried by drainage system.
d. Material adhere tightly to pipe with no injury to

18. Indicates all traps may not be shown on drawings, estimator must include them.
19. Indicates size and types of traps required.
20. Indicates estimator must figure sleeves and describes type required.
21. Indicates type and quality of gages and thermometers.
22. Indicates a certain joining method required.

Figure 4.23

joint.

e. No deterioration when immersed 5 days in 1% solution of hydrochloric acid or 5% solution of caustic potash.

2. Provide dry twisted jute packing or substitute approved by architect, for joints between terra cotta and cast iron.
3. Provide mortar of 1:2 Portland Cement-sand mixture for concrete sewer pipe joints.
4. Provide neoprene rubber type joints for cast-iron "No-Hub" pipe.
5. Provide pure, soft, best quality lead for cast-iron pipe joints.
6. Provide tarred or white oakum packing for cast-iron soil pipe below floor; white oakum only used above finished floor level.
7. Provide soft solder, composition 95/5 for joints on copper tubing; flux for solder joints non-corrosive type.

(23)

R. Flashings.
1. Provide sheetlead for flashing of all pipe extending through roof.
2. Cylindrical part of flashing fit snugly over pipe and extend over top and turn inside pipe.
3. 6" flange extended on sides of cylinder.
4. Roof drain provided with 36" square of 4-lb lead flashing.

(24)

2.03 MACHINERY VIBRATION ISOLATORS

A. Isolate all moving machinery from the building structure.

B. Isolating material guaranteed to effectively prevent noise or vibration being transmitted into building structure.

C. Design isolators to suit vibration frequency to be absorbed; isolator units of area and distribution to obtain proper resiliency under machinery load and impact.

D. Where equipment is bolted through isolators, isolate bolt head from equipment base with resilient washer; also use resilient bushing for bolt hole in base.

E. Cork type isolation.

1. Provide continuous cork layer under entire base or individual pads, as recommended by manufacturer.
2. Use pure natural corkboard with grains running horizontally, uniform thickness, reputable manufacturer; board made of pure cork granules, compressed and baked without foreign binder, free from defects, uniform thickness as manufactured by Armstrong Cork Co., or equal, alsoacceptable.

23. See Note 22.
24. Indicates flashing is part of bidding contractor's work.

Figure 4.24

Three-Story Service Center PLUMBING 1-13

F. Fabricated vibration isolator units.

1. Provide manufacturers standard catalog products with printed load ratings.
2. Each unit consist of steel top and bottom members with intermediate isolating material of cork, rubber, or spring steel as specified or approved for particular installation.
3. Provide Korfund Co. "LK" Vibro-Isolator, or equal, for steel spring type isolator.
4. Provide Vibration Eliminator Co., Korfund Co., or equal, for cork and rubber type vibration isolator.

G. Should objectionable noise or vibration in excess of design be produced and transmitted to occupied portions of the building by apparatus, piping, or other parts of mechanical installation due to improper installation, installing Contractor make necessary changes and additions as approved, without cost to Owner.

(25)

2.04 EQUIPMENT FOUNDATIONS

A. Equipment foundations inside and outside of building will be furnished by General Contractor.

1. Respective contractor shall furnish information and material required forming and imbedding, including anchor bolts, sleeves and washers to be built into foundation.
2. Respective contractor shall furnish for approval shop drawings showing the recommended foundation requirements of the equipment manufacturer.

2.05 ANCHOR BOLTS

A. Provide foundation bolts, sleeves, washers, nuts and templates to locate position of bolts for machinery on foundations.

B. Provide hook type anchor bolts of proper size and length to suit equipment.

C. Set bolts in steel pipe sleeves of approximately twice the bolt diameter and one-half imbedded length of bolts, set flush with top of rough concrete.

D. Contractor furnishing equipment is responsible for location of anchor bolts.

25. Indicates to estimator that equipment foundations are by general contractor. However, Items 1 and 2 must be furnished.

Figure 4.25

2.06 EQUIPMENT SUPPORTS AND STANDS

A. Provide supporting structures of strength to safely withstand stresses to which subjected and distribute properly load and impact over building areas.

B. Conform to applicable technical society's standards, and to codes, regulations of agencies having jurisdiction.

C. Provide structural steel or pipe frames and structural members rigidly braced, and secured with flanges bolted to the floor for floor mounted tanks set over four feet above the floor.

D. Provide suspended platform, bracket or shelf as indicated for ceiling or wall mounting.

1. Construction of structural steel members steel plates and rods as required.
2. Brace and fasten to building structure or to inserts as approved.

E. Locate supports for tanks so as to avoid undue strain on shell and interference with pipe connections to tank outlets.

1. Check support locations for clearance to pull tubes of tanks containing tubes.
2. Where saddles are indicated or specified for tank supports, use cast-iron or welded steel saddles of curvature to fit tank and not less than 150° support.

F. Respective Contractor provide required supports for equipment provided by them.

G. Submit detailed shop drawings of all supports; obtain approval before fabricating or constructing.

2.07 FLEXIBLE PIPE CONNECTORS

A. Provide flexible connections as indicated or required in water heating systems.

1. Connectors constructed of flexible, braided seamless copper tubing with brass ips male ends.
2. Connectors as manufactured by American Brass Corp., American Metal Hose Branch "Flexpipe" or Flexonics Corp.

B. Install connectors per manufacturer's written installation directions.

Figure 4.26

2.08 HANGERS AND INSERTS

A. Provide inserts constructed of cast iron or fabricated galvanized iron or steel.

1. Inserts of type to receive machine bolt head or nut after installation and permit adjustment of this bolt in one horizontal direction.
2. Inserts suspended from concrete floor, accurately locate before concrete is poured to be flush with concrete surface when forms are removed.
3. Where inserts are not provided fasten hangers by means of approved expansion bolts.
4. Wood plug not acceptable.

(26)

B. Provide hangers of malleable iron clevis or split ring type with machine thread and provisions for vertical adjustment.

(27)

1. Provide steel, copper or copper plated hangers for supporting copper pipe; where unplated steel hangers are used, copper piping cleaned and wrapped with insulating tape at point of contact of hanger.
2. Wire, band iron, chain and perforated strap iron not permitted for pipe or conduit supports.

(28)

3. Support horizontal steel piping and conduit on hangers in accordance with following schedule:

Pipe Size	Rod Diameter	Maximum Spacing
Up to 1-1/4"	3/8"	8'-0"
1-1/2" and 2"	3/8"	10'-0"
2-1/2" and 3"	1/2"	10'-0"
4" and 5"	5/8"	12'-0"
6"	3/4"	12'-0"
8"	7/8"	14'-0"

(29)

4. Support horizontal copper pipe and tubing on not more than 10' centers, using rod diameters in schedule above. above.
5. Support vertical risers with finished ring clamps approximately 8' from floor, runouts from ceiling 3' from risers and at intervals not greater than 8' apart, adjusted to maintain true and uniform grade of pipe.
6. No piping supported from other piping or conduit.
7. Piping in trenches supported on rods imbedded in concrete or having foot supports; spacing as specified for hangers.
8. Do not install hangers in cells of cellular floor intended for wiring.
9. Trapeze hanger may be used where several pipes can be installed in parallel at same level, provide piping is not heating piping exceeding 215°F.

26. Indicates types of pipe supports to be provided.
27. See Note 26.
28. Indicates spacing requirements of piping supports.
29. General pipe support instructions.

Figure 4.27

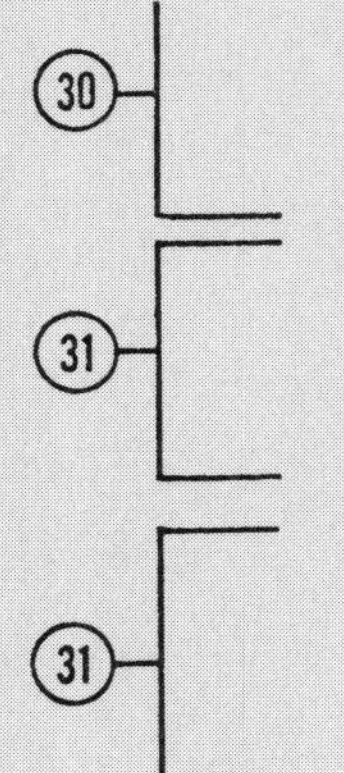

a. Hangers consist of two (2) horizontal steel channels bolted back to back with space between for hanger rods at each end, secured with washers and nuts.

b. Support from beam clamps on inserts.

c. Where provision for expansion and contraction in piping is required, use Fee & Mason Fig. 169 roller chairs, Fig. 160 pipe roller stands, or equal Grabler Mfg. Co. or Grinnell; fasten to trapeze channels.

d. Brace trapeze hangers as directed.

10. Support piping size 6" and larger by Grinnell Fig. 171 single roll type hangers with two rods and adjustable sockets, Grinnell Fig. 174 adjustable swivel pipe roll type hangers with one rod, or equal Fee & Mason Mfg. Co. or Grabler Mfg. Co., provide protection saddles.

11. All methods of supporting pipe work and equipment subject to approval of Architect.

2.09 MOTORS

A. Furnish, set and align all motors specified for driven equipment in Division 15 - Mechanical.

B. Motors conform with latest standards of IEEE and NEMA.

C. Motors designed for 60 Hz alternating current, voltage available, rated 40°C rise for continuous duty and equipped with alignment adjustment.

D. Connect motors 1/2 hp and larger for 3-phase operation unless otherwise indicated; connect smaller motors for 1-phase operation.

E. Motor load not less than 75% nor more than 100% of capacity when apparatus to which motors are connected is operating at specified capacity.

F. Nameplate voltage of motor same as voltage indicated and define upper limit; 5% less of nameplate voltage define lower limit.

2.10 MOTOR CONTROL EQUIPMENT

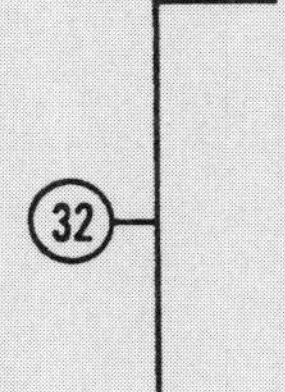

A. Motor control and starting equipment, including push-button and selector switches will be provided and connected by Electrical Contractor except as otherwise indicated or specified herein.

B. Mechanical Contractor check Division 16 - Electrical for motor control equipment requirements and meet all requirements specified therein for motor control equipment supplied by

30. Gives contractor option of using trapeze hangers for multiple lines; cost savings possible.
31. Indicates quality of hangers specified.
32. Indicates that estimator should coordinate with electrical drawings.

Figure 4.28

Mechanical Contractor.

2.11 ACCESS PANELS

33 A. Provide access panels of required size for walls and ceilings where required for access to concealed valves, and controls.

1. Access panels suitable for flush mounting with smooth covers primed for painting, except baked enamel finish in tile walls, color as selected by Architect.
2. Panels constructed of 16-gauge steel with 14-gauge doors with concealed hinges and tamperproof cylinder lock of dual latch type; four (4) keys for locks furnished and delivered to Owner.
3. Access panels 12" x 12" minimum except where space requirements dictate smaller.

B. Provide 1/4" iron plate with tumbler lock, suitable lift device and flush hinge in angle iron frame for access panels in floor; panels mounted flush with floor.

C. Access panels in walls mounted with bottom 18" above floor or as directed by Architect.

D. Contractor responsible for installation of panels as work progresses, including furnishing of all anchors.

E. Access panels as manufactured by Inland Steel Products, Co., or equal.

2.12 TAGS, CHARTS AND IDENTIFICATION

A. Provide black, numbered and stamped 1-1/2" brass or aluminum tags fastened to valve by brass chain and S-hook.

B. Provide stencils on pipe at each valve in location easily read from floor; stencils indicate contents, size and flow direction in accordance with the following:

1. Domestic cold water - CW
2. Domestic hot water - HW
3. Domestic Recir. water - HWR
4. Size of letters in accordance with USA Standard A-13 or HPACCNA.

34

C. Provide brass or aluminum name plates, 2-1/2" x 3/4" as manufactured by Seton Name Plate Co., or equal, for all equipment.

1. Tags secured to equipment by rivets or screws.
2. Suitable adhesive may be used except in Boiler Room, subject to approval of Architect.
3. Provide duplicate name plates on motor controls.

33. Indicates access panels are provided by bidding contractor.
34. Indicates valve tag, chart, and pipe identification requirements for job.

Figure 4.29

D. Identify further materials and flow in Boiler and Equipment Rooms by W. H. Brady Co., Style 1235, or equal, direction arrows.

1. Secure arrows to piping or covering at changes in direction and at approximately 20' maximum intervals.
2. Identify mains at one readily visible central location for each service by W. H. Brady, Co., Style 2, or equal, pipe marker.
3. Color identification of arrows as follows:

(34)

1) CW - Green
2) HW - Blue
3) HWR - Purple

E. Provide 1/8" scale diagrams showing location, number and service or function of each tagged item.

1. Frame diagrams in approved metal frames with clear acrylic front, hinges and locks.
2. Secure to wall where directed.
3. Provide two (2) additional separate copies permanently covered and bound.

2.13 INSULATION

A. Pipe insulation

1. Provide first quality insulation and covering on all piping as specified herein.

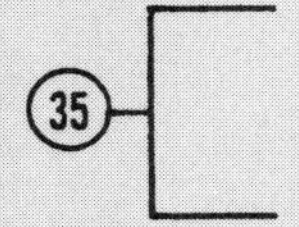

2. Insulate domestic cold, hot and recirculating water lines with 1/2" thickness fiberglass preformed sectional insulation with vapor barrier jacket consisting of .001" aluminum foil between layers of kraft paper.
3. Preformed fiberglass insulation have thermal conductivity not to exceed .22 BTU per square in. per °F per hour at mean temperature of 75°F.
4. Flanges, bends, fittings and valve bodies on insulated piping to be insulated with hydraulic setting cement insulation to same thickness as pipe insulation.

a. Coat cement with white vapor barrier lap cement wrapped with same jacket as piping insulation.
b. Jacket coated with white vapor barrier lap cement.
c. Jacket overlap adjacent jacket and be cemented thereto to maintain tight vapor barrier.

35. Indicates to estimator that all cold, hot and recirculating water piping must be insulated.

Figure 4.30

Three-Story Service Center PLUMBING 1-19

5. Leave uncovered all screwed or flanged unions, except on domestic cold water, or where exposed to freezing.

   a. Adjacent insulation beveled and covering applied in manner to provide access for wrenches without disturbing covering.
   b. Bring covering ends of insulation down over ends of insulation, terminate at least 1/2" from pipe union.

6. Insulate piping, fittings and valves in outside walls or wall chases, above ceiling or where otherwise exposed to freezing with 1-1/2" thickness insulation as specified herein.

7. Thoroughly clean all dirt, rust, dust, oil, paint or scale from all surfaces to be insulated.

8. Wrap piping in Boiler Room and where exposed with 40 lb. resin sized paper stapled in place.

   a. Paste 6 oz. canvas jacket over resin sized paper with Foster's No. 8142W adhesive, or equal.
   b. Where so finished, factory finish may be omitted and insulation secured with 16-gauge annealed wire on 12" centers or metal bands before applying paper.
   c. Cement canvas over fittings on smooth coat of cement.
   d. All exposed canvas covering finished glue sized for painting.

9. Apply all insulation in accordance with manufacturer's instructions and in workmanlike manner.

   a. Butt all sections of insulation tightly together to prevent open joints.
   b. Seal all jackets longitudinal and end overlap joints with white vapor barrier lap cement and, except where exposed, fasten with aluminum bands spaced not more than 18" apart, 3 bands per section.
   c. Seal joints between sections on vapor barrier jacket with factory supplied 4" wide sealing strips cemented as specified above.
   d. Trim ends of coverings true.
   e. Neatly finish ends with hydraulic setting cement insulation and canvas covering as specified for joints.
   f. No staples permitted in covering.
   g. Where insulation must be cut to clear joints, hangers or metal work, provide fiberglass between piping and hanger or metal work; fill opening with hydraulic setting cement to full diameter of covering.

Figure 4.31

h. All sections molded true to form and must be of proper size to fit snugly all pipes to which applied.

(36)

10. Insulate horizontal runs of storm water piping over finished ceilings with 1/2" thickness fiberglass, medium density flexible blanket insulation wrapped on piping.

11. Insulate all branch wastes from water coolers as specified for cold water piping.

2.14 PUMPS

(37)

A. Provide direct connected recirculating water pumps as indicated.

B. Provide pumps as manufactured by Bell & Gossett, Taco or Thrush.

C. Provide pumps 1 hp and larger to conform to the following:

1. Iron-body, bronze impeller, bronze-fitted with corrosion resistant steel shaft.

(38)

D. Provide pumps less than 1 hp to conform to the following:

1. All bronze construction.
2. Mount pump and motor in common housing designed for mounting in piping with flanged joints.
3. Single stage type.

E. All pumps conform to the following:

1. Pump and motor have sleeve bearings and mechanical seals.
2. Pump designed for 220°F water.
3. Finish pump, motor and base in manufacturer's standard factory finish.
4. Pump controlled as described under Automatic Temperature Control Section.

F. Obtain services of pump manufacturer for startup.

1. Obtain manufacturer's service representative to witness initial startup of pumps, check alignment, rotation and lubrication.
2. Representative check and report on pump suction and discharge pressures, current draw and rating of motor and ph of system water.
3. Submit report to Architect for approval.

36. Indicates estimator must figure on insulating horizontal storm piping offsets, and branch wastes from water coolers.
37. Indicates construction and manufacturer of recirculating pumps.
38. See Note 37.

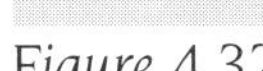
Figure 4.32

PART 3: EXECUTION

3.01 INSTALLATION REQUIREMENTS

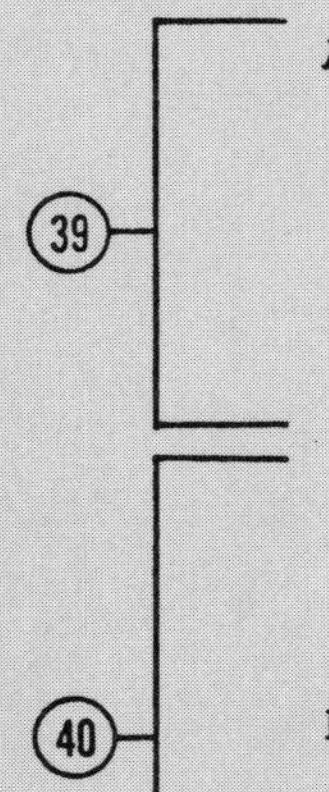

A. Contractors check all dimensions indicated immediately after award of contract, advise Architect promptly of discrepancies or interferences and obtain such measurements and information as may be required to satisfactorily install the work.

1. Before ordering any material or doing any work, Contractor verify all measurements and elevations at building site and be responsible for correctness of same.
2. Promptly submit any differences which may be found between field measurements and elevations and those indicated to the Architect for adjustment and approval before proceeding with work.

B. Contractors lay out their work and establish heights and grades in strict accordance with Drawings of building and finished site grades, and be responsible for accuracy of such layout.

C. Each Contractor consult with other concerned Contractors and Architect before any piping, ductwork, or conduit is installed.

1. Arrange work so that piping is kept as high as possible without interference.
2. Should Contractor fail to do so, or fail to agree, the decision of the Architect will be final.

D. Consider arrangement of piping, equipment and accessories approximate except where dimensioned.

1. Work installed generally as indicated and as directed by Architect.
2. Install piping as straight and direct as possible, parallel to or at right angles to building walls and other lines where exposed and properly spaced.
3. Install piping at uniform grade, supported on multiple hangers where practical, and adjusted to drop required.
4. Execute work in workmanlike manner so that it will present neat mechanical appearance when complete.
5. Right to make any reasonable changes in location, prior to rough-in or setting, to accommodate conditions arising during progress of work without additional cost to Owner, is reserved by Architect.

E. Align, level and adjust equipment for satisfactory operation; install so that connecting and disconnection of piping and accessories can be done readily, and so that all parts are easily accessible for inspection, operation and maintenance.

39. Indicates to estimator that close coordination with other trades necessary.
40. See Note 39.

Figure 4.33

F. Install material and equipment in accordance with manufacturer's written instructions and recommendations; submit such data to Architect prior to installation and consider this data part of these Specifications.

3.02 PIPING INSTALLATION

A. Cut piping accurately to measurements established at building and work into place without springing or forcing, properly clearing all windows, doors and supports.

1. Piping to have complete freedom of movement, except at anchor points, without causing stress or strain in pipe or any part of building during expansion and contraction.
2. Excessive cutting of building structure will not be permitted.
3. Use full-length pipe whenever possible.
4. Ream out pipe to full bore after cutting.
5. Where screwed joints are required, provide right hand, pipe standard, clean-cut, full-depth and tapering threads.
6. Make joints tight without caulking or use of lead or paint.

   a. Use of lubricant not permitted.
   b. Make up joints with "Teflon" tape.

7. Clean piping thoroughly before erection; clean after erection to remove foreign material from pipe.
8. Cap or plug open ends of piping during installation.
9. Copper piping and fittings mechanically clean, bright and fluxed.

B. Box unions, reducing bushings or caulking of joints will not be acceptable; use reducing fittings at all changes in pipe size.

C. Run piping as indicated.

1. Provide anchors and expansion bends as indicated or required.
2. Provide approved swing joints at mains and branch runouts to allow for expansion and contraction.
3. Do not project pipes beyond walls or limit lines more than necessary for installation.
4. Do not erect joints or fittings over any motor, switchboard, or other electrical equipment.
5. Adequately brace or clamp joints to prevent creeping or blowout.
6. Install piping in Boiler Room, Equipment Rooms and where exposed, close to ceiling; provide rise or drop in pipe for that purpose.
7. Run all piping, concealed, except in Boiler Room and Equipment Rooms.

Figure 4.34

8. Run mains carefully to insure unrestricted circulation and elimination of air pockets.

   a. Grade mains not less than 1" in 40'.
   b. Pitch pipe in direction indicated or required.

9. Architect reserves right to direct changes in run and details of piping as required by conditions encountered on site.

D. Use flange fittings in assembly of piping at equipment and in mains 3" and larger; provide union connections for pipe smaller than 3" and all connections to equipment.

E. Properly support pipe as specified herein; support piping underground by concrete or brick piers to prevent undue strain at joints, where disturbed earth is encountered.

(41) F. Provide sleeve on each pipe passing through walls, floors, partitions or ceilings.

1. Cut sleeve flush with surface, except as otherwise specified or required.
2. Provide sleeve one pipe size larger than pipe encased, except insulated pipes have sleeves of size to encase insulation.
3. Set sleeves in concrete or masonry during construction where possible.
4. Extend floor sleeves 1" above floor in toilets and other areas where water might be present.
5. Caulk sleeves embedded in concrete with graphite packing and an approved plastic and waterproofing compound.
6. Place escutcheon plate around pipe at exposed ends of sleeves in finished areas; secure with set screws.

G. After completion of installation, check piping for circulation and any excessive noise.

1. Promptly correct any defects.
2. Remove all concealed piping requiring repairs and have repairs to construction and finish made as required at respective Contractor's expense.

3.03 PROGRESS OF WORK

A. Mechanical and Electrical Contractors order progress of their work so as to conform to work of other trades.

B. Perform work underground as quickly as possible.

C. Complete all work within time specified for General Contract.

41. Indicates to estimator where sleeves are required.

Figure 4.35

3.04 CUTTING AND PATCHING

A. Install hangers, supports and pipe sleeves in floors, walls, partitions, ceilings, and roof slabs as construction progresses.

B. All cutting of concrete, brick or other material for passage of piping through floors, walls, partitions and ceilings will be done by General Contractor.

1. Respective Contractor deliver information to General Contractor for above purpose.
2. If respective Contractor delivers required information to General Contractor too late, or furnished information that is incorrect, or fails to order his work with General Construction, respective Contractor employ General Contractor to do cutting and patching required to install his work.

C. General Contractor will close openings around piping, duct-work and conduit with material equivalent to that removed.

D. Leave exposed surfaces in suitable condition for refinishing without further work.

E. Do not alter or cut any structural member without special permission of Architect.

3.05 CHASES, HOLES AND RECESSES

A. Mechanical and Electrical Contractors furnish to General Contractor, in advance of construction, exact details for provisions of chases, holes and recesses required for installation of all material and equipment furnished or installed by them.

B. Openings, recesses and chases required for such material and equipment will be provided by General Contractor.

3.06 DAMAGE TO OTHER WORK

A. Mechanical and Electrical Contractors responsible for damage to other work caused by their work or through neglect of their workmen.

B. Contractor who installed work do all patching and repairing, as directed by Architect; responsible Contractor pay cost of same.

42. Indicates to estimator that cutting is part of general contractor's work.

Figure 4.36

Three-Story Service Center PLUMBING 1-25

3.07 EXISTING SERVICES

A. Protect, brace and support existing active sewer, water, gas electric and other services where required for proper execution of work.

1. If existing active services are encountered that require relocation, make request in writing for determination; do not proceed with work until written directions are received.
2. Do not prevent or disturb operation of active services that are to remain.

B. Remove, cap or plug inactive services.

1. Notify utility companies or municipal agencies having jurisdiction.
2. Protect or remove the services as directed.

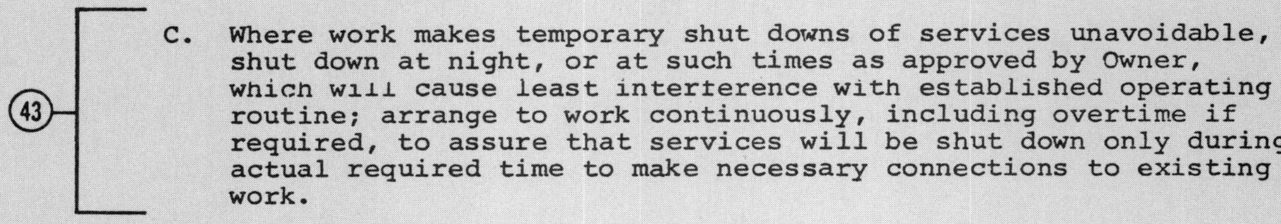

C. Where work makes temporary shut downs of services unavoidable, shut down at night, or at such times as approved by Owner, which will cause least interference with established operating routine; arrange to work continuously, including overtime if required, to assure that services will be shut down only during actual required time to make necessary connections to existing work.

3.08 EXCAVATION AND BACKFILL

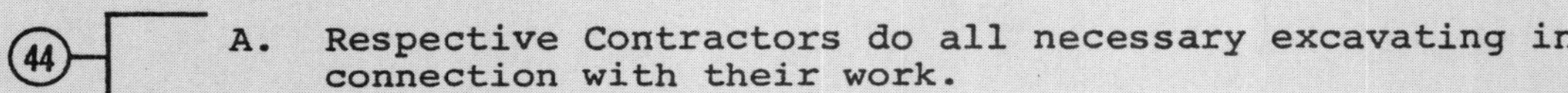

A. Respective Contractors do all necessary excavating in connection with their work.

1. Excavate bottom of trenches to exact depth and uniform grade in direction of flow so that pipes will be supported on solid bed of undisturbed earth, hubs, up grades, earth undercut at hubs so that each piece of pipe is supported throughout its entire length.
2. Refill excavation below required grade of piping with sand and firmly compact.
3. Excavate rock where encountered to grade of 4" below lowermost part of pipe grades specified.
4. Excavate principally with open-trench method.

   a. Excavate 12" wider than largest diameter of pipe, or tank, and to depths specified or required.
   b. Deposit materials excavated on sides of trenches and beyond reach of slides.
   c. Do not pile excavated material where it will interfere with traffic.
   d. Deposit all earth and other materials taken from trenches and not required for backfilling where directed.

43. Indicates to estimator that overtime costs may have to be included in his estimate.

44. Indicates to estimator that excavation and backfill is part of his contract.

Figure 4.37

e. Do not leave material where it will interfere with Owner's or other Contractor's operations.

5. Contractor provide shoring, bracing or sheet piling necessary to maintain banks of excavations.

a. Take out same as work progresses and filling in is accomplished, unless otherwise directed by Architect.
b. Arrangement of shoring must be such as to prevent any movement of trench banks and consequent strains on piping.
c. Provide shoring to prevent damage to work installed by other trades.

B. Exercise care to protect roots of trees to remain.

1. Do not cut any root greater than 1" in diameter.
2. Within branch spread of trees perform all trenching by hand.
3. Open trench only when utility can be installed immediately.
4. Prune injured roots cleanly.
5. Back fill as soon as possible after inspection and approval.
6. Perform all work under direction of Architect.

C. Contractors do all pumping required to keep their excavation free of water.

D. Suitably protect trenches and openings for underground work by signs, barricades or enclosures, and flashing.

1. Display lights at night until completion of work.
2. Contractor responsible during construction for all damage to underground piping or structures.

E. Install underground tanks and piping below frost line, but not less than 3' below finished grade to top of tank or piping, except as indicated.

F. After work in trenches has been completed, fill with good fine earth, free from cinders, stones or brickbats.

1. Apply fill in 6" layers and carefully tamp compactly in place before next layer.
2. Fill containing stone not acceptable.
3. Backfill with concrete, as specified herein, trenches which pass under or within 18" of column footings or wall foundations.

a. Concrete backfill under footings or foundations run full width of such structure and at least 6" below bottom of piping.
b. Before backfilling pipes spirally wrap with two layers

45. If shoring and pumping are required estimator must include these items in his estimate.
46. See Note 45.

Figure 4.38

Three-Story Service Center PLUMBING 1-27

of 1" hair felt wound in opposite directions or sleeved to prevent direct bearing on pipe.

(47) G. General Contractor will restore streets, pavements, and other finished surfaces damaged by work to their original condition after suitable backfill.

(48) H. General Contractor will remove rock as directed by Architect where it is encountered.

3.09 OWNER'S EQUIPMENT

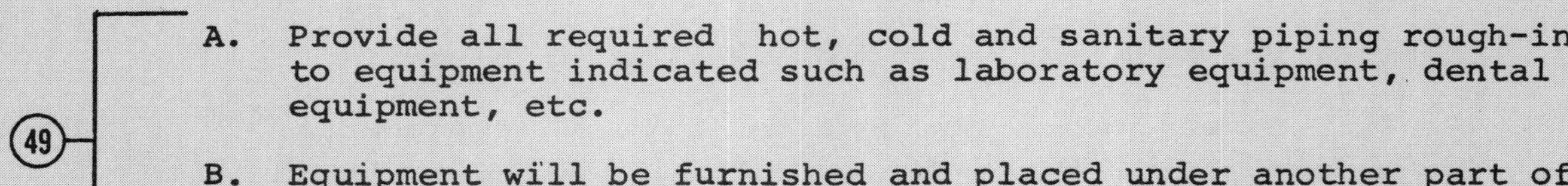

A. Provide all required hot, cold and sanitary piping rough-in to equipment indicated such as laboratory equipment, dental equipment, etc.

B. Equipment will be furnished and placed under another part of this Contract; make all final connections to equipment as part of this Contract.

C. Detail drawings will be furnished to Mechanical Contractor showing rough-in dimensions for waste and water connections.

1. This contractor responsible for correct installation of these services, in accordance with Drawings furnished and his field check.
2. Check information with equipment manufacturer where necessary.
3. Should installation of rough-in be incorrect, due to failure to check in above manner or incorrect installation, make necessary changes in rough-in without cost to Owner.

3.10 GAUGE & THERMOMETER INSTALLATION

A. Provide in readily visible location gauges and thermometers where indicated and as follows:

1. Circulating water pumps suction and discharge, one (1) gauge each, 0-70 ft.
2. Chilled water supply and return, one (1) thermometer each, 30-120°F.
3. Condenser water supply and return, one (1) thermometer each, 30-120°F.

B. Provide gauges and thermometers of types specified herein.

47. Indicates that restoration of site is by general contractor.
48. Indicates rock excavation is by general contractor.
49. Indicates that estimator will most likely encounter equipment furnished by other, but must be installed by bidding contractor. Necessary materials and labor must be included in estimate.

Figure 4.39

Three-Story Service Center Index

DIVISION 15 - PLUMBING

SECTION 2

WATER SUPPLY SYSTEM

PART 1: GENERAL

PART 2: MATERIALS

PART 3: EXECUTION

Figure 4.40

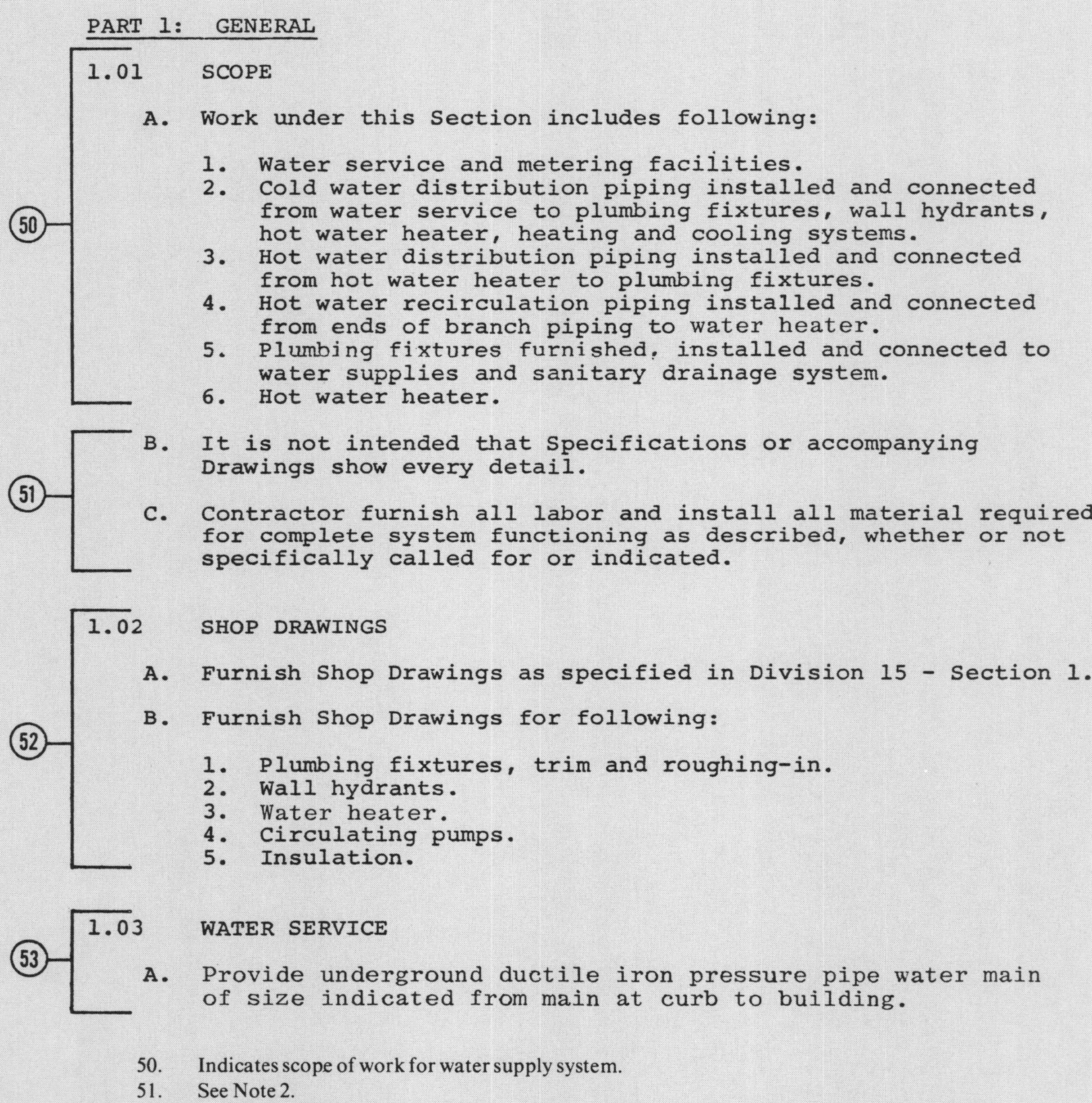

Three-Story Service Center PLUMBING 2-1

DIVISION 15 - MECHANICAL

SECTION 2

WATER SUPPLY SYSTEM

PART 1: GENERAL

(50)

1.01 SCOPE

A. Work under this Section includes following:

1. Water service and metering facilities.
2. Cold water distribution piping installed and connected from water service to plumbing fixtures, wall hydrants, hot water heater, heating and cooling systems.
3. Hot water distribution piping installed and connected from hot water heater to plumbing fixtures.
4. Hot water recirculation piping installed and connected from ends of branch piping to water heater.
5. Plumbing fixtures furnished, installed and connected to water supplies and sanitary drainage system.
6. Hot water heater.

(51)

B. It is not intended that Specifications or accompanying Drawings show every detail.

C. Contractor furnish all labor and install all material required for complete system functioning as described, whether or not specifically called for or indicated.

(52)

1.02 SHOP DRAWINGS

A. Furnish Shop Drawings as specified in Division 15 - Section 1.

B. Furnish Shop Drawings for following:

1. Plumbing fixtures, trim and roughing-in.
2. Wall hydrants.
3. Water heater.
4. Circulating pumps.
5. Insulation.

(53)

1.03 WATER SERVICE

A. Provide underground ductile iron pressure pipe water main of size indicated from main at curb to building.

50. Indicates scope of work for water supply system.
51. See Note 2.
52. Indicates which items require shop drawings.
53. Indicates type of piping specified for water main.

Figure 4.41

Three-Story Service Center PLUMBING 2-2

B. Provide all necessary accessories required by Water Company for their meter installation inside building.

1. Install gate valve at building entrance, valved bypass
(54) and spool piece for meter, as required by Water Company.
2. Arrange and pay for service, including service connection costs, meter and installation as part of Contract.

C. Provide tee in main as indicated for future connection of existing building.

PART 2: MATERIALS

2.01 WALL SUPPLY FITTINGS

A. Wall hydrants

1. Provide Josam Series 71000 , non-freeze type, wall hydrants for outside use.
2. Wall hydrant provided with 3/4", 45° angle nozzle, polished brass face, cast brass body, brass wall sleeve and pipe
(55) and loose key handle.

B. Inside hose bibbs

1. Provide Standard R7233 handle operated hose bibbs 3/4", all bronze, angle type.
2. Mount 18" above floor.

C. Approved manufacturers of wall supply fittings are American-Standard, Josam, Wade or Zurn.

2.02 WATER HEATER

A. Provide Jackson Model #GRE-120-T-H commercial, electric water heater.

1. Heater tank have minimum storage capacity of 120 gallons.
(56) 2. Heater designed for 150 psi wwp USA Standard.
3. Heater designed for 480-volt, 3-phase operation with 3 elements producing 18KW.
4. Provide glass- or stone-lined surfaces where exposed to water.
5. Provide all required fittings constructed of brass.
6. Casing constructed of "Bonderized" steel finished with baked-on enamel.
7. Provide fiberglass blanket type insulation between tank and casing.

54. Indicates water meter is part of bidding contractors work.
55. Indicates types and quality of wall hydrants and hose bibbs.
56. Indicates capacity, type and quality of hot water heater.

Figure 4.42

Three-Story Service Center PLUMBING 2-3

8. Heater have minimum recovery rate of 73.8 gph at 100° rise.
9. Water heater provided with the following:

   a. Adjustable thermostat with bulb immersed directly into water.
   b. High limit temperature control.
   (57) c. ASME spring loaded temperature-pressure relief valve, reset type set at 100 psi and 200°F.
   d. 3/4" drain valve.
   e. Magnesium anode rod.

10. Unit guaranteed for ten (10) years.
11. Entire unit approved by UL.

B. Approved manufacturers of water heater are Jackson, Ruud, A. O. Smith or Westinghouse.

2.03 PLUMBING FIXTURES

A. Provide fixtures of types hereinafter specified and of quantities indicated, making all required supply, waste, soil and vent connections with all fittings, supports, fastening devices, cocks, valves and traps leaving all in complete working order.

1. Provide carrier and fixture supports as required; install in walls as work progresses.
2. Contractor responsible for stability of all supports.
(58) 3. Wall-hung fixtures generally supported on fixture carriers.
4. Carriers as manufactured by Josam, Wade, or Zurn.

B. Trap all fixtures close to fixture so that discharge passes through not more than one trap before reaching house drain.

C. Provide fixtures clearly marked with manufacturer's name, trademark and quality or class of fixture; do not remove labels until work has been accepted.

D. Construction of fixtures conform to following except as specified otherwise:

1. White, twice-fired, vitreous china, non-absorbent, close grained, thoroughly vitrified, free from pores, unmarked, true and level.
2. Free from chips or flaws.
3. Fixture warranted not to craze, color or scale.
4. Exposed metal work chromium-plated, guaranteed against defects for one (1) year.
5. Strainers and screens of monel metal.
6. Fittings of best quality known to trade as No. 1 line.

57. See Note 56.
58. Indicates requirements and construction for plumbing fixtures.

Figure 4.43

7. Iron for enameled ware of best quality cast iron and of proper thickness to produce high grade quality.

E. Acceptable manufacturers for fixtures and trim are American Standard, Speakman, Crane Co., Eljer or Kohler.

(59) 1. American Standard and Speakman numbers are used herein to describe quality, type and finish desired.
2. Provide fixtures of one manufacturer for purposes of standardization.

F. Lavatories

1. Fixture - "Lucerne" No. 0350.132 for concealed arms, 20" x 18", 8" centers, front overflow, splash back; No. 0350.025 wall hanger with wall hanger where carrier installation is not possible.
2. Supply - Speakman S-4331 with "Autoflo" control, pop-up waste with 1-1/4" tailpiece and vandal-proof aerator; 2302.81 supplies 3/8" ips with key operated angle stops to wall, reducing couplings and escutcheons.
3. Trap - No. 4429.015 cast brass "P" trap with 1-1/4" inlet, 1-1/2" outlet and 4446.019 6" nipple.

(60) G. Urinal

1. Fixture - "Washbrook" No. 6500.011 wall-hung, washout type with integral extend shields, flush spreader, trap with cleanout and top spud inlet.
2. Flush valve - Speakman No. K9082 BSP "Si-Flo" flush valve with key-operated angle stop and vacuum breaker, 1" x 4" nipple, escutcheon, chromium-plated nuts, bolts and washer.

H. Water Closet (Wall-Hung)

1. Fixture - "Afwall" No. 2477.016, wall-hung, syphon jet, elongated bowl, 1-1/2" top spud.
2. Flush valve - Speakman No. K-9000 BSP flush valve with key-operated angle stop, vacuum breaker, 1" x 4" nipple, escutcheon, chromium-plated nuts, bolts and washers.
3. Seat - Church American-Standard No. 5320.114 "Moltex" heavy duty solid plastic open front seat with stainless steel check hinge.

I. Water Closet (Floor-Mounted)

1. Fixture - "New Madera" No. 2222.016, floor-mounted, siphon jet, elongated bowl, 1-1/2" top spud, cast-iron floor flange, china caps and bolts.

59. Indicates quality of fixtures specified.
60. Indicates types of fixtures along with manufacturer's model numbers for both fixtures and trim.

Figure 4.44

2. Flush valve - Speakman No. K-9000 BSP "Si-Flo" flush valve with key-operated angle stop and vacuum breaker.
3. Seat - Church American-Standard No. 5320.114 as specified for wall-hung water closet.

J. Service Sink

1. Fixture - "Lakewell" No. 7692.023, 22" x 18", wall hanger, plain black, enameled cast iron with 8379,018 rim guard.
2. Supply - Wall-mounted S-7115-ISVB double faucet with top brace, spout with bucket hook and hose end, integral stops, 5' of rubber hose.
3. Trap - Trap standard No. 7798.176 with cleanout.

K. Cabinet Sink

61 1. Fixture - Elkay No. LR-1918, single compartment, 18-gauge stainless steel, 19" x 18" self-rimmed with ledge.
2. Supply - Examination Rooms and Laboratories: Speakman S-7001, 3/8" gooseneck discharge nozzle, wrist action handles, 8" centers, cast drain plug, set screw plate and 1-1/4" tailpiece; other areas: Speakman S-4961 single control, brass swing nozzle, non-splash aerator indexed forged brass lever handle, 8" centers and Elkay LK99 drain and 1-1/4" tailpiece.
3. Trap - No. 4429.015 "P" trap with 1-1/4" inlet, 1-1/2" outlet, 4446.019 6" nipple and escutcheon.

L. Water Cooler

1. Fixture - Halsey-Taylor No. SW-8-A, or equal, surface wall-mounted, capacity of 8.0 gph at 90°F room temperature, 80°F inlet water and 50°F drinking water with 60% waste through precooler; include 1/5, 115-volt motor, hermetically sealed compressor, Freon-12 refrigerant, 10°F water temperature control adjustment, vinyl covering of color selected by Architect, steel housing, and electric cord with ground.
2. Mounting height as directed by Architect.
3. Unit include five (5) year warranty.

PART 3: EXECUTION

3.01 COLD WATER DISTRIBUTION

A. Install and connect cold water distribution from meter to water heater, plumbing fixtures, wall hydrants, hose bibbs, heating and cooling equipment, and as indicated.

61. See Note 60.

Figure 4.45

Three-Story Service Center PLUMBING 2-6

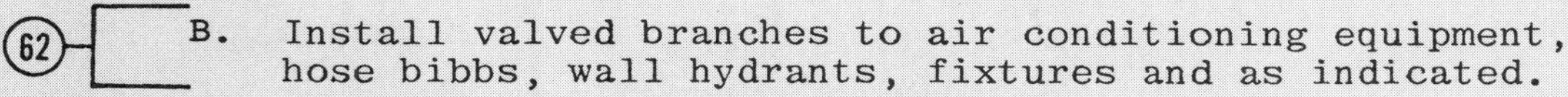

(62) B. Install valved branches to air conditioning equipment, hose bibbs, wall hydrants, fixtures and as indicated.

(63) C. All cold water lines installed with copper piping and fittings as specified herein, having nominal size indicated.

3.02 HOT WATER DISTRIBUTION

A. Hot water distribution piping installed and connected from water heater to plumbing fixtures and as indicated.

B. Install and connect hot water recirculation piping through circulation pump from water heater to valved connections at ends of distribution piping and as indicated.

(64) C. All hot water distribution lines installed with copper piping and fittings as specified herein, having nominal size indicated.

3.03 BRANCH SUPPLIES

A. Take branches and runouts to wall at all fixtures requiring water.

B. Provide branches from wall of size specified for fixture supplies.

(65) C. In no case provide branch runouts to fixtures less than following sizes:

Fixture	C.W.	H.W.
Water Closet	1"	-
Urinals	1"	-
Lavatories	1/2"	1/2"
Sinks	1/2"	1/2"
Water Coolers	1/2"	-

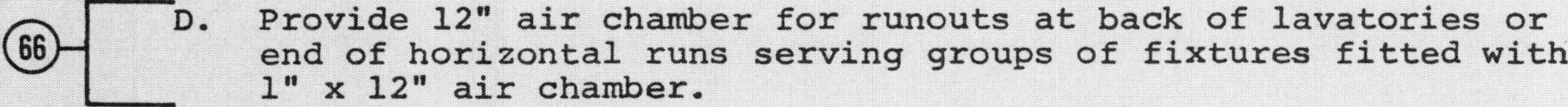

(66) D. Provide 12" air chamber for runouts at back of lavatories or end of horizontal runs serving groups of fixtures fitted with 1" x 12" air chamber.

(67) E. Place gate valves in all branches leading from mains to groups of fixtures and as indicated.

62. Indicates mentioned items require shut-off valves. These may not show up on drawings; however, estimator must include them.
63. Indicates pipe material to be used for cold water lines.
64. Indicates pipe material to be used for hot water lines.
65. Indicates minimum hot and cold water fixture connections.
66. Indicates air chambers to be used in lieu of mechanical shock absorbers; these are considerably less expensive.
67. Indicates all water branches are to be controlled with gate valves; these may not be shown on drawings; estimator must include them in estimate.

Figure 4.46

Three-Story Service Center Index

DIVISION 15 - PLUMBING

SECTION 3

SANITARY AND STORM WATER DRAINAGE SYSTEM

Figure 4.47

Three-Story Service Center PLUMBING 3-1

DIVISION 15 - PLUMBING

SECTION 3

SANITARY AND STORM WATER DRAINAGE SYSTEM

PART 1: GENERAL

(68)

1.01 SCOPE

A. Work under this Section includes the following:

1. Sanitary drainage and vent piping installed and connected from plumbing fixtures, floor drains and Owner's equipment.
2. Construction of sanitary sewer and connection to city sewer.
3. Storm water drainage piping installed and connected from roof drains to storm water sewer.
4. Construction of storm water sewer including yard basins, lampholes and connection to existing sewer.

(69)

B. It is not intended that Specifications or accompanying Drawings show every detail.

C. Contractor furnish all labor and install all material required for complete system functioning as described, whether or not specifically called for or indicated.

(70)

1.02 SHOP DRAWINGS

A. Furnish Shop Drawings as specified in Division 15 - Section 1.

B. Furnish Shop Drawings for following:

1. Cleanouts
2. Lampholes
3. Drains
4. Castings

1.03 CONNECTION OF SEWERS

A. Contractor arrange for connection of sanitary sewer with City agency.

(71)

B. Contractor pay all required fees and connection charges as part of his work.

68. Indicates scope of work for sanitary and storm system.
69. See Note 2.
70. Indicates which items require shop drawings.
71. See Note 5.

Figure 4.48

Three-Story Service Center PLUMBING 3-2

PART 2: MATERIALS

2.01 DRAINS

A. Provide drains connecting to the sanitary and storm water piping as indicated or specified herein.

B. Provide drains as manufactured by Josam, Wade or Zurn; Josam numbers are used herein to describe quality and type of drain required.

(72)

C. Floor Drains

1. Provide Series 32/00 cast-iron body floor drain for Boiler and Equipment Rooms; drain complete with loose set cast-iron anti-tilting grate with double drainage pattern and arranged for bottom outlet.
2. Provide Series 1465-U cast brass automatic trap seal valve with vacuum breaker for all floor drains.
3. Install trap seal valves with access panel and connected from nearest lavatory or sink to floor drains.
4. Provide all floor drains of inside caulk type.

D. Roof Drains

1. Provide Series 21540 cast-iron body roof drain with integral expansion joint with brass sleeve, removable low dome and sediment cup, non-puncturing flash clamp with integral gravel stop and arranged for bottom outlet.
2. Provide all roof drains with threaded bottom outlet.

2.02 LAMPHOLE COVER

A. Provide lamphole cover as manufactured by Josam, Wade or Zurn.

B. Provide Josam Series cast-iron lacquered lamphole cover complete with the following:

1. Serrated cut-off ferrule, rough brass raised head and screwed plug.
2. Rough cast brass round adjustable head have flanged rim and scoriated type tractor cover with vandal-proof screws.

(73)

2.03 SEWER MATERIALS

A. Provide brick for sewer structures conforming to applicable requirements of ASTM STandard C62, Grade SW.

1. Clean, used paving or building brick which conforms to above, or radial brick or concrete meeting requirements given herein, may be used for sewer structures.
2. Precast storm sewer structures meeting standards and quality described herein will be acceptable.

72. Indicates type and quality of lampholes, floor and roof drains.
73. Indicates materials manholes and catch basins are to be constructed of.

Figure 4.49

Three-Story Service Center PLUMBING 3-3

74 B. Provide concrete for sewer structures of 1:2:4 mix.

C. Provide mortar for masonry in sewer structures of 1:3 cement-sand mix, provided that hydrated lime may be substituted for, not to exceed 10%, by weight, of cement.

75 D. Provide sewer structure castings as indicated.

1. Castings for sewer structures in roadways comply with State Highway Department Standards.
2. Provide tough, even grained, soft gray iron sewer structures for other areas.

   a. Structures free from burnt-on sand and other injurious defects.
   b. Thoroughly clean and subject to hammer tests for soundness all castings before leaving foundry.
   c. Castings given two (2) coats of coal-tar pitch varnish.
   d. Provide locking devices for tops and gratings weighting less than 100 lbs.
   e. Provide same design for like structures.

PART 3: EXECUTION

76 3.01 BUILDING DRAINAGE AND VENT LINES

A. Provide soil, waste, vent and drain piping and fittings of types indicated or listed below.

1. Cast iron pipe and fittings below ground.

   a. Pipe and fittings below first floor, except as indicated.
   b. Pipe 2" and larger within the building and to 10' outside the building.

2. Hubless cast iron pipe and fittings.

   a. All soil waste and vent piping 1-1/2" and larger above finished floor.
   b. All vent piping 2-1/2" and smaller above finished first floor.

B. Building drains receive discharge of all stack, branch mains and runouts.

1. Arrange all horizontal mains, branches and runouts to present neat symmetrical appearance.
2. Provide support under vertical stacks.

C. Install mains at elevations and grades as indicated or directed.

74. See Note 73.
75. Indicates types of castings (manhole frames and covers) required.
76. Indicates type of piping required for sanitary and storm piping below grade in building, and for sanitary above grade in building.

Figure 4.50

Three-Story Service Center PLUMBING 3-4

1. Minimum grade of horizontal lines in building 1/4" per ft.
2. Make changes in direction and connection of drain, soil and waste lines with proper fittings.

3. Provide offsets and cleanouts as indicated or required for testing or cleaning.

D. Install branches as indicated to outlets for connection to plumbing fixtures, equipment and floor drains.

E. Continue risers as directly as possible to roof and have vent lines run parallel and cross-connected therewith.

F. Make offsets in main vent lines, if possible, not less than 45° to horizontal.

1. Connect vent lines at bottom with soil or waste pipes in such manner that accumulation of rust or scale will be washed by flow of water from fixtures.
2. Keep branch vents above tops of connecting fixtures to prevent use of these vent pipes as soil or waste pipes.
3. (78) Properly vent all traps to prevent syphoning.
4. Arrange vertical stacks as direct and straight as possible and locate with respect to wall so fittings will be well back of wall finish within rooms.
5. Fit vent lines which are less than 3" in diameter with increasers to 3" size before passing through roof.

(79)

G. Provide Y branches on soil and waste lines to all fixtures and connections.

1. Short TY branches permitted in vertical lines only.
2. Long quarter-bends and TY's may be used.
3. Short quarter-bends, double hubs, short increasers and flat offsets not permitted.
4. Fittings may be integral part of fixture supports.

H. Carry soil and wastes to floor for floor-mounted water closets and floor drains, all other branches carried to wall; provide minimum sizes as listed below:

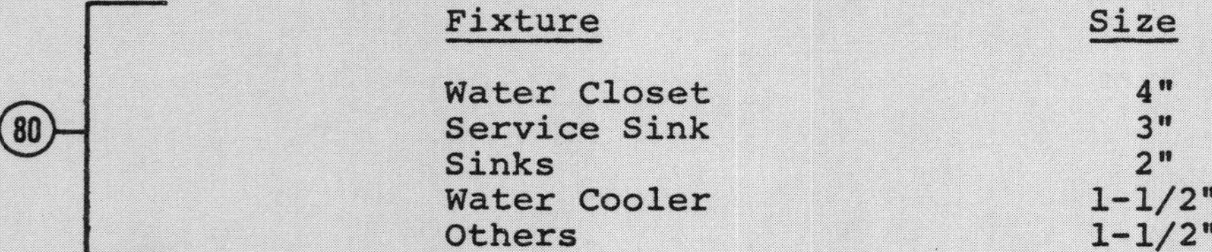

(80)

Fixture	Size
Water Closet	4"
Service Sink	3"
Sinks	2"
Water Cooler	1-1/2"
Others	1-1/2"

77. Indicates cleanout test tees required; these do not show on drawings.
78. Estimator must check drawings to see that all traps show venting.
79. Indicates any prohibited fittings on sanitary and storm systems in building. Also indicates acceptable fittings for certain applications.
80. Indicates minimum acceptable waste connections to fixtures.

Figure 4.51

(81) I. Install test cleanouts at base of all soil and waste lines.

J. Connect runouts to sanitary sewer 10' outside building.

1. Runouts extended with cast-iron pipe.
2. Make connection by inserting cast-iron soil pipe inside hub of terra cotta pipe not less than 6" or as far as possible in bend to form suitable bearing.

3.02 STORM WATER DRAINAGE

A. Install interior rainwater conductors with hubless cast iron pipe and fitting.

1. Install storm drainage piping below finished first floor with hubless cast iron pipe and fittings.
2. Piping installed generally as specified for sanitary building drainage piping.

B. Install test tee and cleanout at base of each riser.

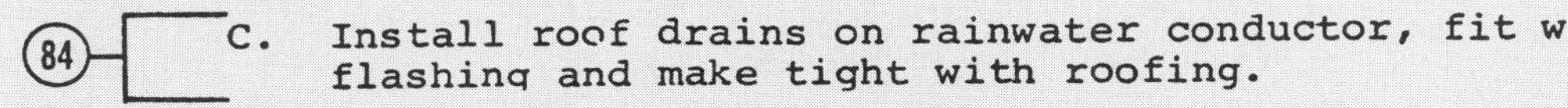

C. Install roof drains on rainwater conductor, fit with lead flashing and make tight with roofing.

D. Extend runouts with cast-iron pipe to approximately 10' outside of building and connect to storm sewer as specified for sanitary runouts.

3.03 SEWER CONSTRUCTION

A. Construct storm sewer to receive runouts from rainwater conductors, roof drains and catch basin and connect existing sewer as indicated.

B. Construct sanitary sewer to receiving building runouts from soil and waste piping and connect to City of Albany sanitary sewer.

C. Provide sanitary and storm sewer piping of types indicated or listed below.

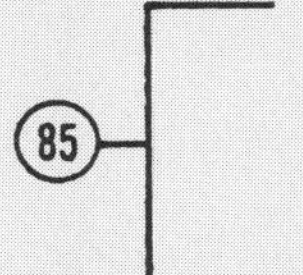

1. Sewers more than 10' outside of building of terra cotta pipe for sizes 12" and smaller.
2. Provide concrete pipe for sizes 15" and larger.
3. Provide cast-iron pipe for sizes 12" and smaller under roadways.

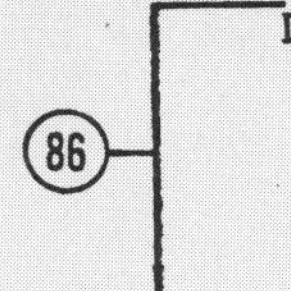

D. Construct catch basins of materials as specified herein.

1. Set basins in cement and locate at proper elevation to drain to finish grade.
2. Extend one length of cast-iron pipe from each catch to provide runout.

81. See Note 77.
82. Indicates piping material required for storm system (above grade) in building.
83. See Note 81.

Figure 4.52

Three-Story Service Center PLUMBING 3-6

3. Fit pipe with cast-iron T set bullheaded in vertical position within basin as indicated.

E. Install sanitary and storm sewer piping with minimum of 36" cover, except as indicated.

1. Commencing at lowest point in system lay sewer piping with bell upgrade.
2. Test pipe for soundness and clean interior and joint surfaces before lowering the pipe into trench.
3. Carefully check invert elevations of sewers to which connections are made.
4. Lay pipe in straight lines and on uniform grades between points where changes in alignment or grade are indicated.
5. Check line and invert grade of each pipe from top line carried on batter boards, not over 25' apart.
6. Fit pipes to form smooth uniform invert.
7. Keep stopper in pipe mouth when pipe laying is not in progress.

F. In jointing sewer pipe, comply fully with directions of manufacturer or pre-formed joint pipe.

1. Two lengths of pipe may be jointed vertically on bank provided they are lowered and laid without injury to joint.
2. In making cement joints in tongue and groove pipe, wet joint surfaces thoroughly.

   a. Spread mortar in lower half of groove end, over upper half of tongue.
   b. After pipe has been shoved home, fill remainder of joint space, inside and outside, with mortar and finish outside with bead or ring around pipe.

3. As soon as joint has set, start backfill operation as specified herein.

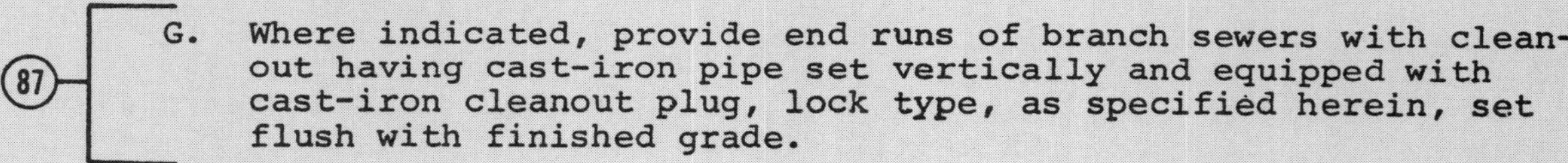

(87) G. Where indicated, provide end runs of branch sewers with clean-out having cast-iron pipe set vertically and equipped with cast-iron cleanout plug, lock type, as specified herein, set flush with finished grade.

84. Indicates type of flashing required for roof drains.
85. Indicates type of piping required for site drainage.
86. Indicates construction method for catch basins.
87. Indicates where cleanouts are required on site drainage system.

Figure 4.53

DIVISION 15 - PLUMBING

SECTION 4

FIRE PROTECTION SYSTEM

PART 1: GENERAL

PART 2: MATERIALS

PART 3: EXECUTION

Figure 4.54

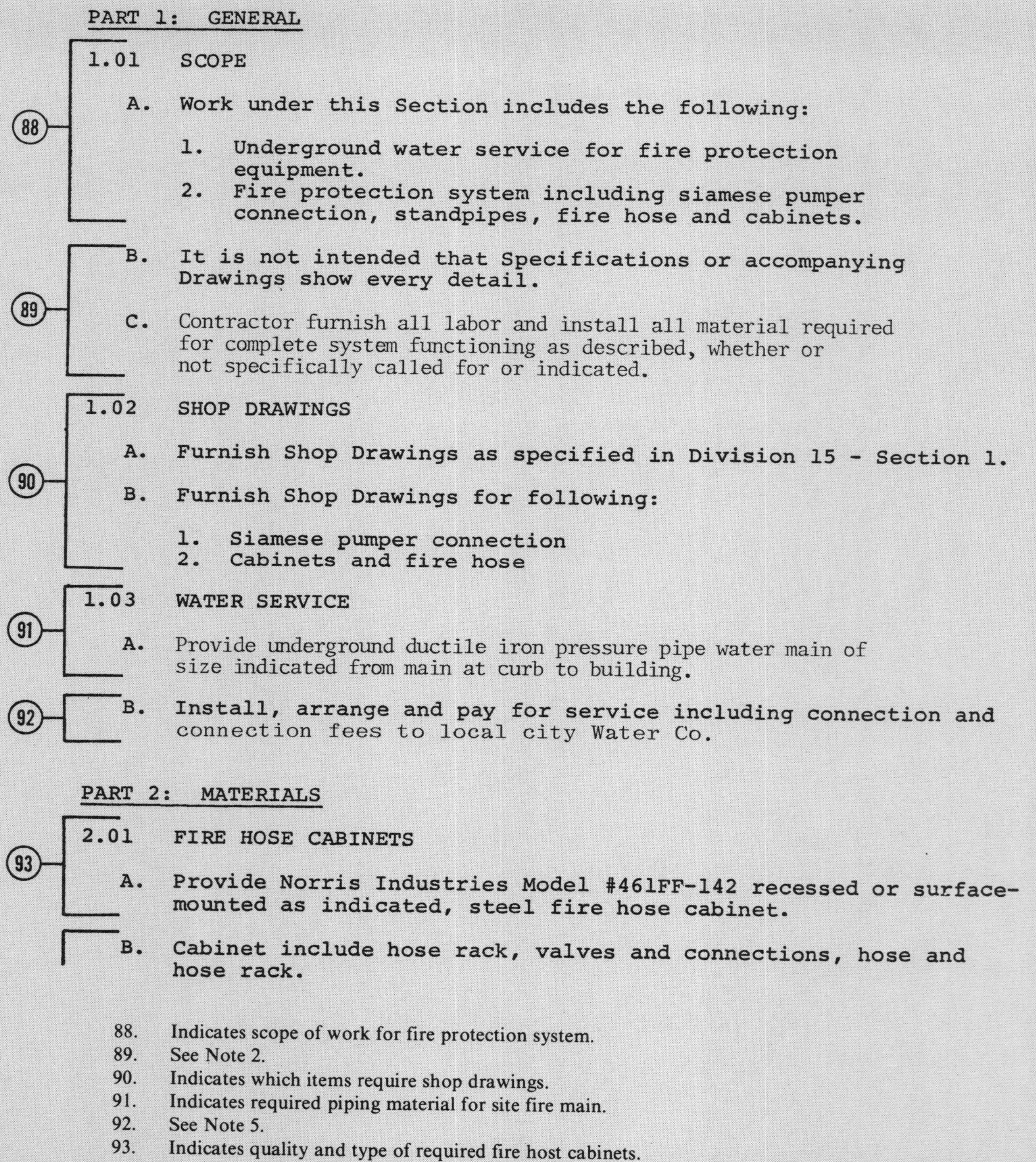

Three-Story Service Center PLUMBING 4-1

DIVISION 15 - PLUMBING

SECTION 4

FIRE PROTECTION SYSTEM

PART 1: GENERAL

1.01 SCOPE

88 A. Work under this Section includes the following:

1. Underground water service for fire protection equipment.
2. Fire protection system including siamese pumper connection, standpipes, fire hose and cabinets.

89 B. It is not intended that Specifications or accompanying Drawings show every detail.

C. Contractor furnish all labor and install all material required for complete system functioning as described, whether or not specifically called for or indicated.

90 1.02 SHOP DRAWINGS

A. Furnish Shop Drawings as specified in Division 15 - Section 1.

B. Furnish Shop Drawings for following:

1. Siamese pumper connection
2. Cabinets and fire hose

91 1.03 WATER SERVICE

A. Provide underground ductile iron pressure pipe water main of size indicated from main at curb to building.

92 B. Install, arrange and pay for service including connection and connection fees to local city Water Co.

PART 2: MATERIALS

93 2.01 FIRE HOSE CABINETS

A. Provide Norris Industries Model #461FF-142 recessed or surface-mounted as indicated, steel fire hose cabinet.

B. Cabinet include hose rack, valves and connections, hose and hose rack.

88. Indicates scope of work for fire protection system.
89. See Note 2.
90. Indicates which items require shop drawings.
91. Indicates required piping material for site fire main.
92. See Note 5.
93. Indicates quality and type of required fire host cabinets.

Figure 4.55

Three-Story Service Center PLUMBING 4-2

1. Provide two (2) valved hose connections in cabinet.

   a. Provide 2-1/2" bottom connection and 1-1/2" top connection.
   b. Fire hose connection conform to local fire company.

2. Provide one piece, swing type hose rack with steel pins and 100' of 1-1/2" single jacket, polyester rubber lined hose.

(94) a. Provide hose with adjustable hose rack and fog nozzle, all FM approved.

C. Construct cabinet of not less than 18-gauge steel.

1. Cabinet have continuous hinged steel door with glass front and chrome lever.
2. Finish cabinet inside with white enamel; provide rust resistant primer on door and trim.

D. Provide fire hose cabinets as manufactured by Norris Industries, Seco Manufacturing Inc., Elkhart Brass Co., or Fyr-Fyter Co.

2.02 SIAMESE PUMPER CONNECTION

A. Provide Seco Manufacturing Inc. No. 251, wall type Siamese pumper connection.

1. Unit constructed of highly polished brass.
2. Siamese pumper connection equipped with double clapper valves.
3. Provide "Standpipe" engraved on escutcheon plate.
(95) 4. Unit complete with brass plugs and chains of polished brass.

B. Provide 2-1/2" fire department inlets with threads to match local fire department.

C. Provide outlet size as indicated.

D. Provide Siamese pumper connection as manufactured by Seco Manufacturing, Inc., Elkhart Brass Co., or Fyr-Fyter Co.

<u>PART 3: EXECUTION</u>

3.01 STANDPIPE SYSTEM

A. Provide standpipe system as indicated connected from service entrance to fire hose cabinets.

94. See Note 93.
95. Indicates quality and type of required Siamese connection.

Figure 4.56

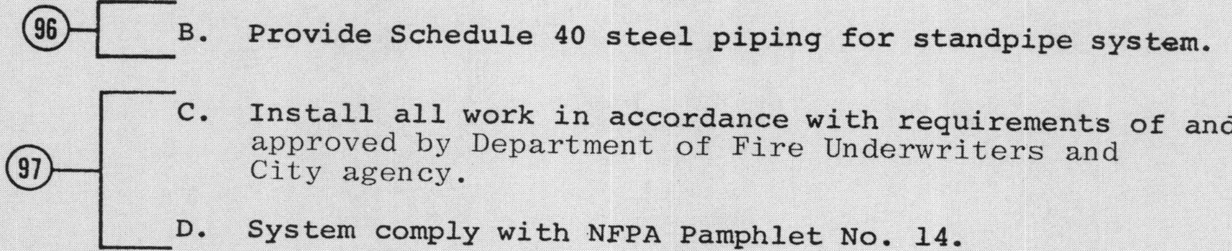

96. Indicates required piping material for fire standpipe system in building.
97. Indicates codes system may comply to.

Figure 4.57

After the specifications you will find the actual quantity takeoff for the plumbing work on the Three-Story Service Center (Figures 4.58 through 4.84). As with the specifications, there will be accompanying "takeoff notes" corresponding to numbered items flagged on the takeoff sheet.

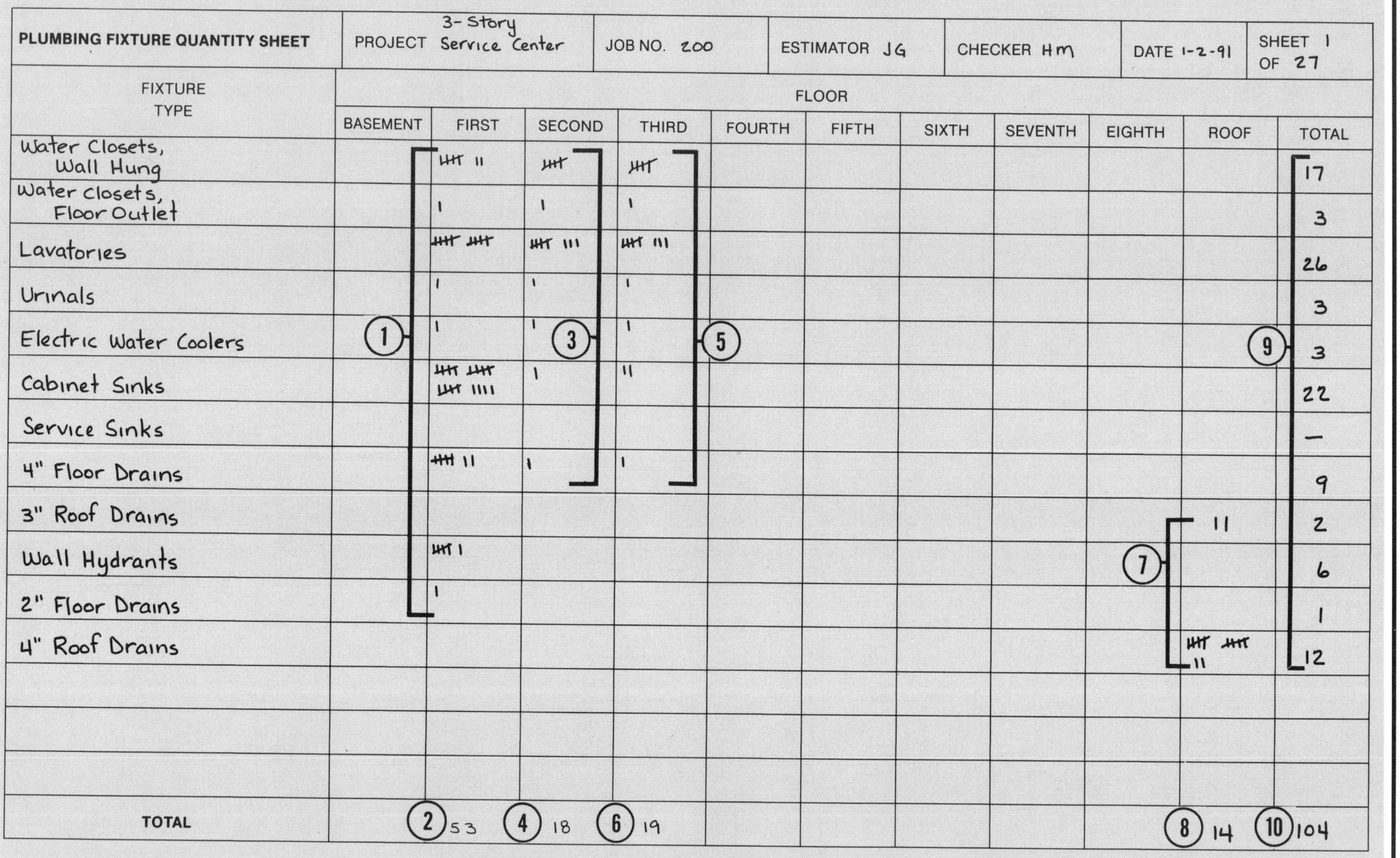

PLUMBING FIXTURE QUANTITY SHEET	PROJECT 3-Story Service Center		JOB NO. 200		ESTIMATOR JG		CHECKER HM		DATE 1-2-91	SHEET 1 OF 27
FIXTURE TYPE	FLOOR										
	BASEMENT	FIRST	SECOND	THIRD	FOURTH	FIFTH	SIXTH	SEVENTH	EIGHTH	ROOF	TOTAL
Water Closets, Wall Hung	(1)	HHT II	HHT	HHT							17
Water Closets, Floor Outlet		I	I	I							3
Lavatories		HHT HHT	HHT III	HHT III							26
Urinals		I	I	I							3
Electric Water Coolers		I	I (3)	I (5)							(9) 3
Cabinet Sinks		HHT HHT HHT IIII	I	II							22
Service Sinks											—
4" Floor Drains		HHT II	I	I							9
3" Roof Drains									(7)	II	2
Wall Hydrants		HHT I									6
2" Floor Drains		I									1
4" Roof Drains										HHT HHT II	12
TOTAL		(2) 53	(4) 18	(6) 19						(8) 14	(10) 104

TAKEOFF NOTES

1. Quantity of takeoff of all plumbing fixtures, by type, appearing on first floor plan P-1.
2. Total of Item 1.
3. Quantity takeoff of all plumbing fixtures, by type, appearing on second floor plan P-2.
4. Total of Item 3.
5. Quantity takeoff of all plumbing fixtures, by type, appearing on third floor plan P-3.
6. Total of Item 5.
7. Quantity takeoff of all roof drains appearing on plans P-1 and P-2.
8. Total of Item 7.
9. Totals of plumbing fixtures by type, on all floors.
10. Total of all plumbing fixtures on job.

Figure 4.58

EQUIPMENT QUANTITY SHEET | PROJECT 3-Story Service Center | JOB NO. 200 | ESTIMATOR JG | CHECKER HM | DATE 1-2-91 | SHEET 2 OF 27

ITEM	QTY.	SYSTEM	CAPACITIES, DESCRIPTION AND OTHER INFORMATION
3" Domestic Water Meter	1 (1)	Hot and Cold Water (5)	
Electric Domestic Hot Water Heater - H-3	1 (2)	Hot and Cold Water (5)	73 8 G.P.H. @ 100° Rise Recovery, 120 G.P.H. (3) Element, 18 KW, 480 V, 3-Phase Jackson 'H' Series # GRE 120-T-H (6)
Hot Water Circulation Pump - P-2	1 (3)	Hot and Cold Water (5)	In-line, Direct Connection, 1750 RPM, 1/6 H.P. 115 V, 1-Phase, Bell + Gossett # 7-PR (7)
Elevator Sump Pump	1 (4)	Sanitary (5)	9 G.P.M., 1/3 H.P., Simplex, 24 Ft. Head, 1750 RPM, 120 V, 1-Phase, Weil # SS-805-ND. (8)

TAKEOFF NOTES

1. 3" domestic water meter taken off mechanical equipment room plan P-3.
2. Electric hot water heater taken off mechanical equipment room plan P-3.
3. Hot water circulation pump taken off domestic hot water heater piping schematic plan P-3.
4. Elevator sump pump taken off first floor plan P-1.
5. Denotes applicable system for each item of equipment.
6. Capacity of hot water heater found in specification page 2-2.
7. Capacity of hot water circulation pump taken off domestic hot water heater piping schematic plan P-3.
8. Capacity for elevator sump pump was not given in drawings or specification. Estimator had to verify capacity with design engineer.

Figure 4.59

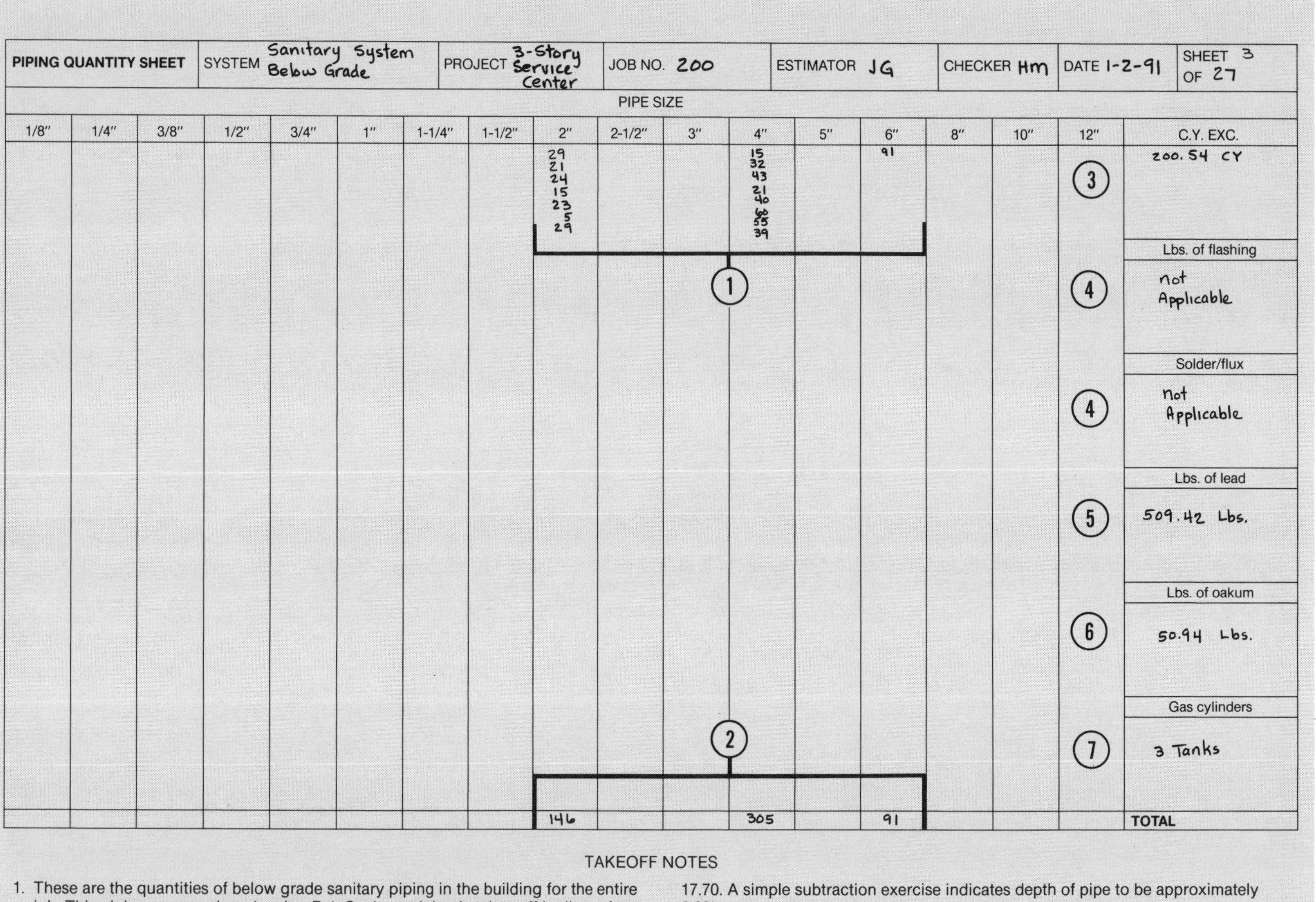

PIPING QUANTITY SHEET	SYSTEM Sanitary System Below Grade	PROJECT 3-Story Service Center	JOB NO. 200	ESTIMATOR JG	CHECKER HM	DATE 1-2-91	SHEET 3 OF 27

PIPE SIZE

1/8"	1/4"	3/8"	1/2"	3/4"	1"	1-1/4"	1-1/2"	2"	2-1/2"	3"	4"	5"	6"	8"	10"	12"	
								29 21 24 15 23 5 29			15 32 43 21 40 60 55 39		91			(3)	C.Y. EXC. 200.54 CY
								(1)								(4)	Lbs. of flashing not Applicable
																(4)	Solder/flux not Applicable
																(5)	Lbs. of lead 509.42 Lbs.
																(6)	Lbs. of oakum 50.94 Lbs.
								(2)								(7)	Gas cylinders 3 Tanks
								146			305		91				TOTAL

TAKEOFF NOTES

1. These are the quantities of below grade sanitary piping in the building for the entire job. This piping appeared on drawing P-1. Sanitary piping is taken off by linear foot and pipe size. Pipe is not taken off fitting to fitting; estimator passes through fittings which allows for waste. Material is cast-iron as per specification page 3-3.
2. Quantities of pipe are then totaled according to size and purchasing quantities.
3. Excavation was taken off according to method outlined in Figure 1.23 of text. Drawing P-1 indicates finish floor elevation is 22.30 and invert of outgoing sewer is 17.70. A simple subtraction exercise indicates depth of pipe to be approximately 2.60′.
4. This item not applicable to sanitary system.
5. Pounds of lead required; developed according to Figure 4.1 in text.
6. Pounds of oakum required; was developed according to method shown in Chapter 4.
7. Gas consumption was developed according to method shown in Chapter 4.

Figure 4.60

FITTING QUANTITY SHEET	SYSTEM Sanitary Below Grade	PROJECT 3 Story Service Center	JOB NO. 200	ESTIMATOR JG	CHECKER HM	DATE 1-2-91	SHEET 4 OF 27

Size	Fitting	Qty	Fitting	Qty
1/8" + 1/4"				
3/8"				
1/2"				
3/4"				
1"				
1 1/4"				
1 1/2"				
2"	2" 1/4 Bend - III	3	2" Cleanout Deck Plate - II	2
	2" Sanitary Tee - I	1	2" 'P' Trap - I	1
	2" 1/8 Bend - 𝍸 III	8	2" Pipe Sleeves - 𝍸 𝍸 𝍸 𝍸 II	22 — (2)
	2" Sweep - 𝍸 𝍸 𝍸 𝍸 IIII	24		
	2" 'Y' IIII	4		
2 1/2"				
3"				
4" (1)	4" 'P' Trap/w2" Vent - II	2	4"x2" Reducer - III	3
	4" 1/8 Bend - 𝍸 𝍸 I	11	4" Cleanout Deck Plate - IIII	4
	4" 'Y' - 𝍸 𝍸	10	4"x2" 'Y' - 𝍸 𝍸 𝍸 III	18
	4" 'P' Trap - 𝍸	5	4" Pipe Sleeves - 𝍸 𝍸 IIII	14 — (2)
	4" Sweep 𝍸 III	8		
	4" Long Turn 'TY' - II	2		
5"				
6"	6"x4" 'Y' 𝍸	5		
	6"x2" 'Y' I	1		
	6" 'Y' - I	1		
	6"x4" Reducer - I	1		
	6" 1/8 Bend - I	1		
8"				
10"				
12"				

TAKEOFF NOTES

1. These are the total quantities of cast-iron soil pipe fittings required for the below grade sanitary system. Fittings chosen according to specification page 1-7. Fittings are taken off according to method described in Chapter 4.
2. Pipe sleeves were taken off on all areas where pipe passed through walls, floors or ceiling as per specification page 1-23.

Figure 4.61

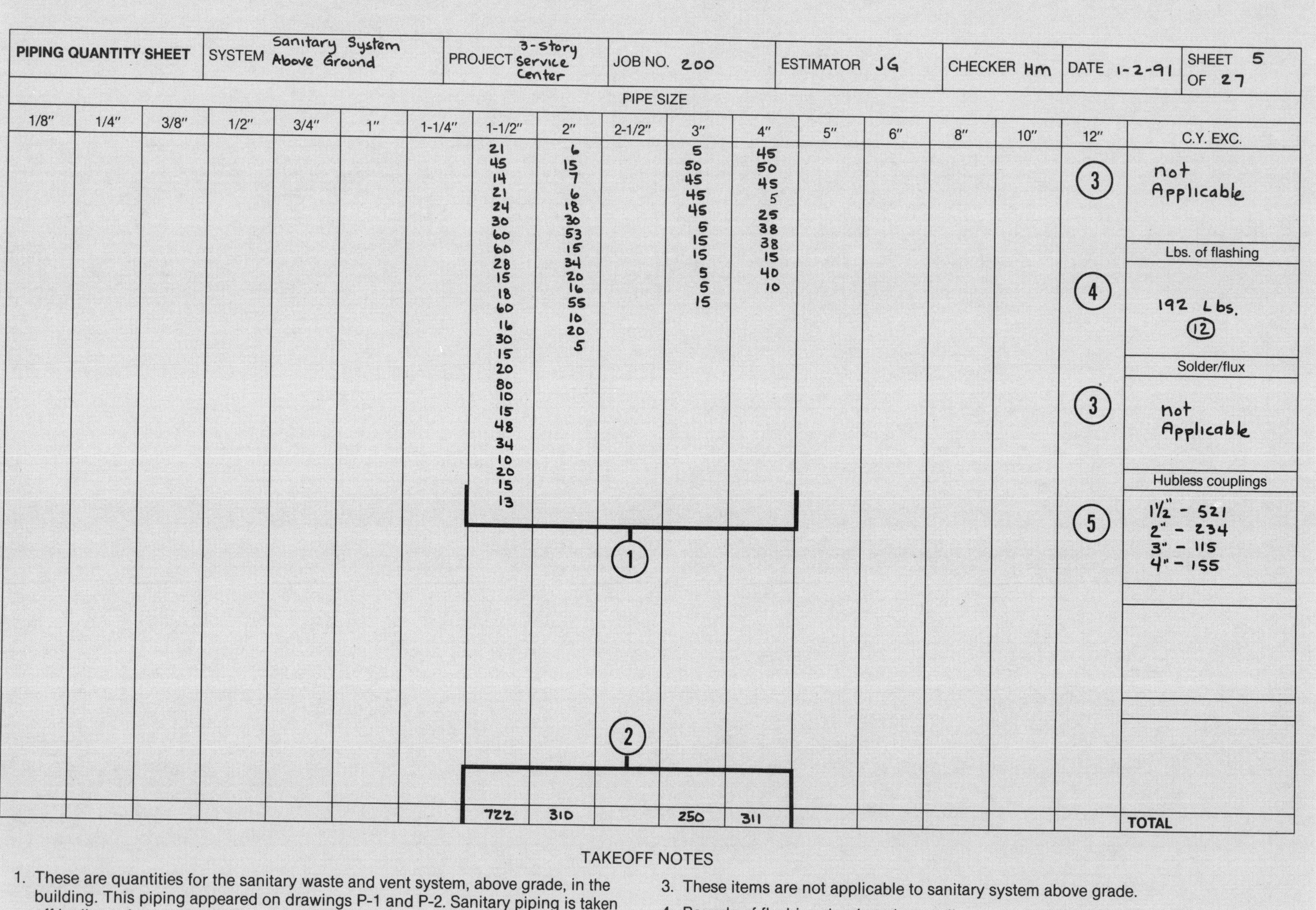

PIPING QUANTITY SHEET	SYSTEM Sanitary System Above Ground	PROJECT 3-Story Service Center	JOB NO. 200	ESTIMATOR JG	CHECKER Hm	DATE 1-2-91	SHEET 5 OF 27

PIPE SIZE

1/8"	1/4"	3/8"	1/2"	3/4"	1"	1-1/4"	1-1/2"	2"	2-1/2"	3"	4"	5"	6"	8"	10"	12"
							21 45 14 21 24 30 60 60 28 15 18 60 16 30 15 20 80 10 15 48 34 10 20 15 13	6 15 7 6 18 30 53 15 34 20 16 55 10 20 5	(1)	5 50 45 45 45 5 15 15 5 5 15	45 50 45 5 25 38 38 15 40 10					(3) (4) (3) (5)
									(2)							
							722	310		250	311					

C.Y. EXC.
not Applicable
Lbs. of flashing
192 Lbs. (12)
Solder/flux
not Applicable
Hubless couplings
1½" - 521 2" - 234 3" - 115 4" - 155
TOTAL

TAKEOFF NOTES

1. These are quantities for the sanitary waste and vent system, above grade, in the building. This piping appeared on drawings P-1 and P-2. Sanitary piping is taken off by linear foot and pipe size. Pipe is not taken off fitting to fitting. Material is hubless cast-iron soil pipe for 1-1/2" and larger as per specification page 3-3.
2. Quantities of pipe are then totaled according to size and purchasing quantities.
3. These items are not applicable to sanitary system above grade.
4. Pounds of flashing developed according to method described in Chapter 4; as per specification page 1-12.
5. Quantity of hubless pipe clamps required to complete installation.

Figure 4.62

FITTING QUANTITY SHEET	SYSTEM Sanitary System Above Grade	PROJECT 3 Story Service Center	JOB NO. 200	ESTIMATOR JG	CHECKER HM	DATE 1-3-91	SHEET 6 OF 27

Size rows with no entries: 1/8" + 1/4", 3/8", 1/2", 3/4", 1", 1 1/4", 2 1/2", 5", 6", 8", 10"

(1) HUBLESS SWCI

Size	Fitting	Qty	Fitting	Qty
1 1/2"	1 1/2" TY	25	1 1/2" Gate Valve - 1 (4)	1
1 1/2"	1 1/2 LTTY	6	1 1/2" Check Valve - 1 (4)	1
	1 1/2" Tee	15		
	1 1/2" Sweep	12		
	1 1/2" 1/8 Bend	20		
	1 1/2" 1/4 Bend	55		
2"	2 x 1 1/2" - LTTY	25	2 x 1 1/2" Tee	10
2"	2" Tee	4	2 x 1 1/2" Red.	22
	2" Sweep	7	2" C.O/Plug - 1	1
	2" 1/8 Bend	13		
	2" 1/4 Bend	11		
	2" Cross TY - 1	1		

(3)

Item	Qty
4" Pipe Sleeves	8
3" " "	17
1 1/2" " " 1	1

(2)

Item	Qty
4" Hanger Assemblies	62
3" " "	50
2" " "	26
1 1/2" " "	60

(1)

Size	Fitting	Qty	Fitting	Qty
3"	3"x2" Y	6	3x2 Cross Y	6
3"	3"x 1 1/2" Y	6	3x2 Red.	2
	3x2 TY - 1	1	3" Test Tee/Plug	2
	3x1 1/2 TY - 1	1	3x4 Increaser	2
	3" 1/8 Bend	2	3" Roof Coup.	2
	3" 1/4 Bend	3		
4"	4" Y	5	4" CO/Plug - 1	1
4"	4x3 Y	2	4" Roof Coup.	8
	4x2 Y	2		
	4" TY	2		
	4" Tee - 1	1		
	4x3 Tee	2		
	4x2 Tee	6		
	4" P Trap	2		
	4" Sweep	6		
	4" 1/8 Bend	4		
	4" 1/4 Bend - 1	1		
	4x3 Red. - 1	1		
	4" Closet Bend	3		
	4" Test Tee/Plug - 1	1		

(5)

Item	Qty
4" Dbl. Closet Carriers	6
4" Single Closet Carriers	5
Lavatory Carriers	26
Urinal Carriers	3

TAKEOFF NOTES

1. These are the total quantities of hubless cast-iron fittings required for the sanitary waste and vent system 1-1/2" in size and larger. Fittings chosen according to specification page 1-7. Fittings are taken off as described in Chapter 4.
2. Pipe supports were taken off according to Figure 1.22 in text.
3. Pipe sleeves were taken off on all areas where pipe passed through walls, floors, or ceiling as per specification page 1-23.
4. Valves for elevator sump pump were taken off elevator shaft pump detail on plan P-1.
5. Water closet carrier fittings were figured on all wall hung water closets. Double carrier fittings were used when water closets were positioned back to back. In addition, urinal and lavatory carriers were quantified.

Figure 4.63

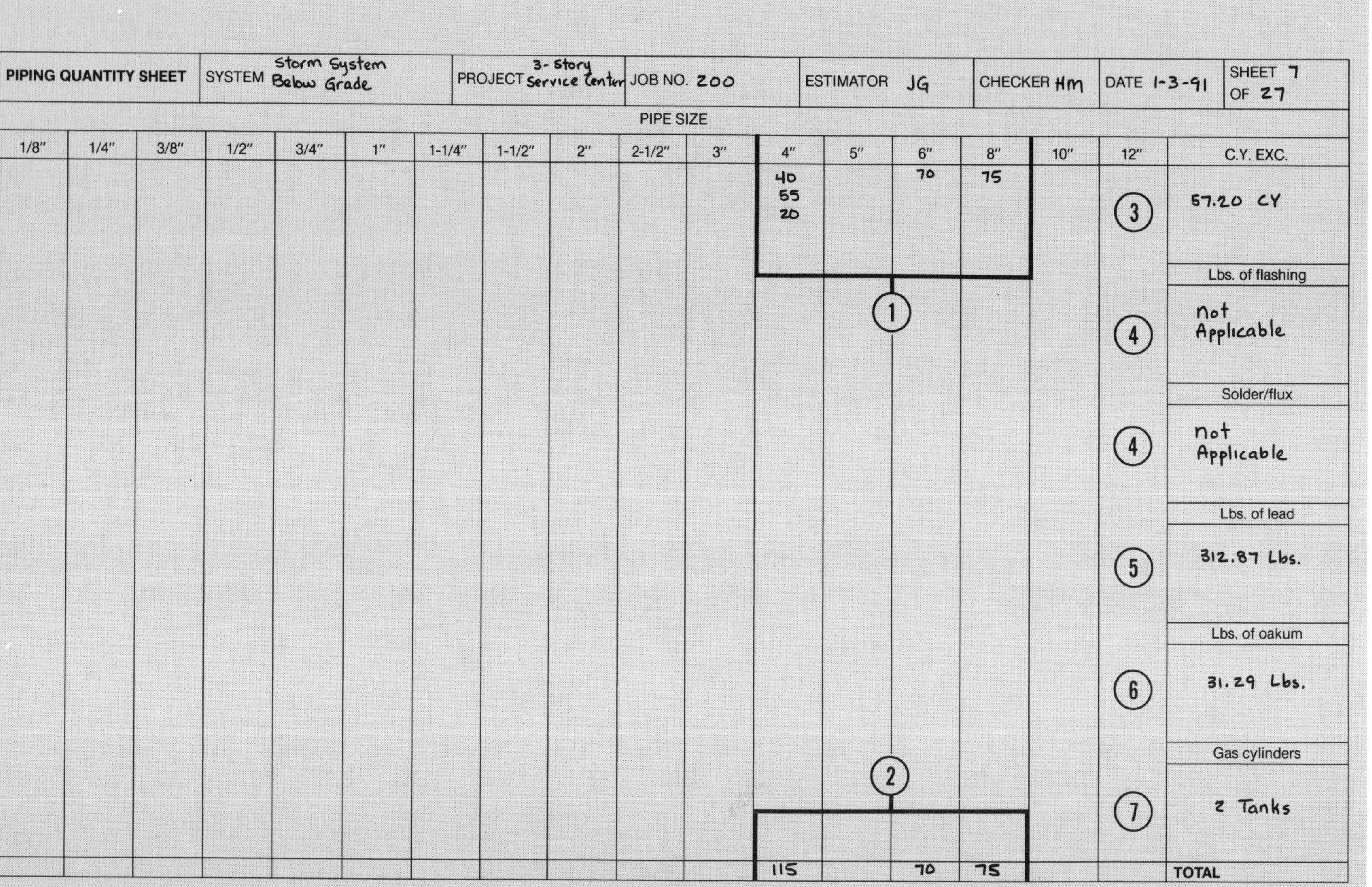

PIPING QUANTITY SHEET	SYSTEM Storm System Below Grade	PROJECT 3-Story Service Center	JOB NO. 200	ESTIMATOR JG	CHECKER HM	DATE 1-3-91	SHEET 7 OF 27

PIPE SIZE

1/8"	1/4"	3/8"	1/2"	3/4"	1"	1-1/4"	1-1/2"	2"	2-1/2"	3"	4"	5"	6"	8"	10"	12"	
																	C.Y. EXC.
											40 55 20		70	75		(3)	57.20 CY
												(1)					Lbs. of flashing
																(4)	Not Applicable
																	Solder/flux
																(4)	Not Applicable
																	Lbs. of lead
																(5)	312.87 Lbs.
																	Lbs. of oakum
																(6)	31.29 Lbs.
																	Gas cylinders
												(2)				(7)	2 Tanks
											115		70	75			TOTAL

TAKEOFF NOTES

1. These are the quantities of below grade storm piping in the building for the entire job. This piping appeared on drawing P-1. Storm piping is taken off by linear foot and pipe size. Pipe is not taken off fitting to fitting. Material is cast iron as per specification page 3-3.
2. Quantities of pipe are then totaled according to size and purchasing quantities.
3. Excavation was taken off according to method outlined in Figure 1.23 of text. Depth of pipe according to information given on drawing P-1 is 2.50'. (See Note 3 — sanitary below grade.)
4. These items not applicable to storm system below grade.
5. Pounds of lead required; developed according to Figure 4.1 in text.
6. Pounds of oakum required; developed according to method shown in Chapter 4.
7. Gas consumption developed according to method shown in Chapter 4.

Figure 4.64

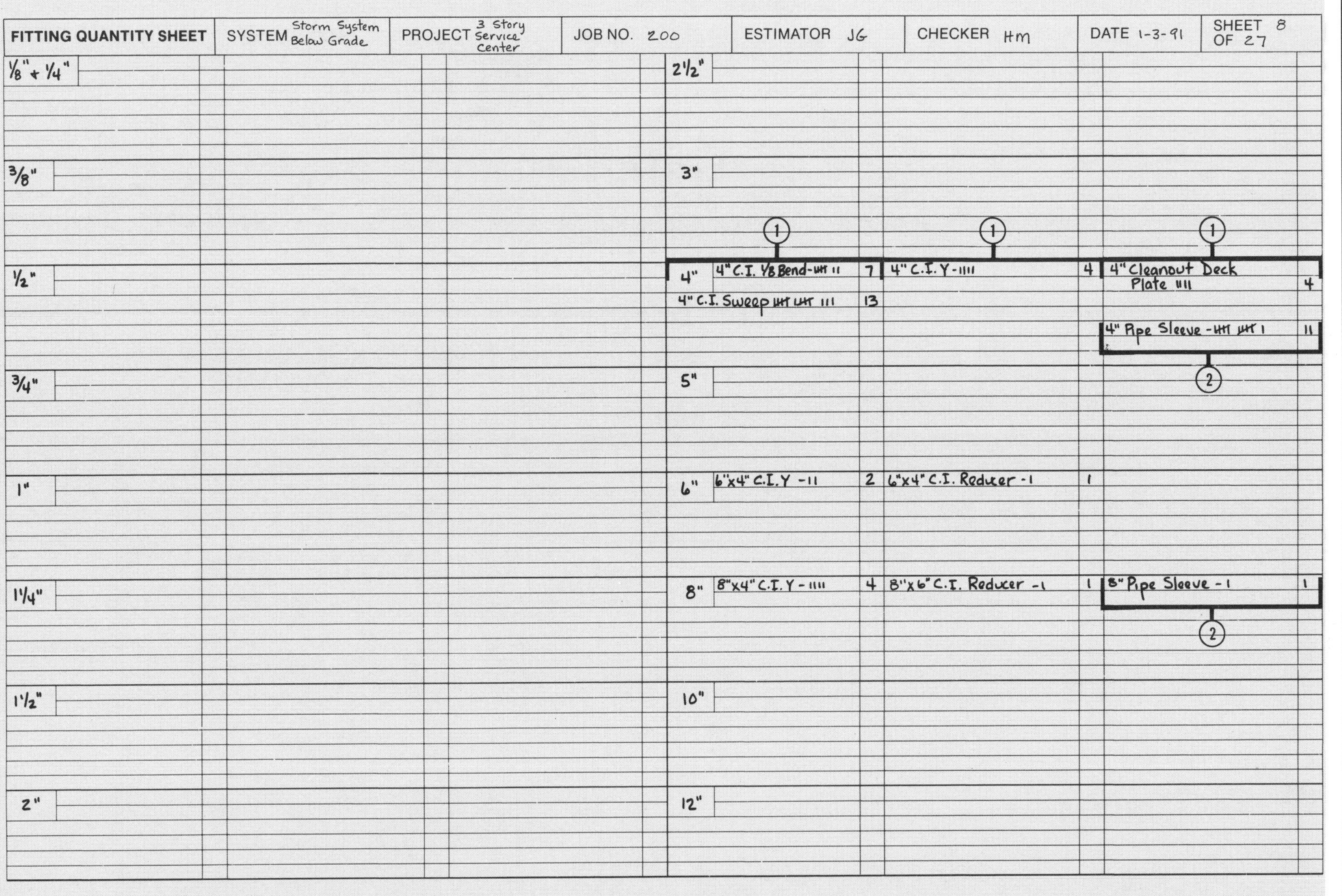

FITTING QUANTITY SHEET	SYSTEM Storm System Below Grade	PROJECT 3 Story Service Center	JOB NO. 200	ESTIMATOR JG	CHECKER HM	DATE 1-3-91	SHEET 8 OF 27

Size	Fitting	Qty	Fitting	Qty	Fitting	Qty
1/8" + 1/4"						
3/8"						
1/2"						
3/4"						
1"						
1 1/4"						
1 1/2"						
2"						
2 1/2"						
3"						
4"	4" C.I. 1/8 Bend - ||||/ || (1)	7	4" C.I. Y - |||| (1)	4	4" Cleanout Deck Plate |||| (1)	4
	4" C.I. Sweep ||||/ ||||/ |||	13			4" Pipe Sleeve - ||||/ ||||/ | (2)	11
5"						
6"	6"x4" C.I. Y - ||	2	6"x4" C.I. Reducer - |	1		
8"	8"x4" C.I. Y - ||||	4	8"x6" C.I. Reducer - |	1	8" Pipe Sleeve - | (2)	1
10"						
12"						

TAKEOFF NOTES

1. These are the total quantities of cast-iron soil pipe fittings required for the below grade storm system. Fittings chosen according to specification page 1-7. Fittings are taken off according to method described in Chapter 4.
2. Pipe sleeves were taken off on all areas where pipe passed through walls, floors, or ceiling as per specification page 1-23.

Figure 4.65

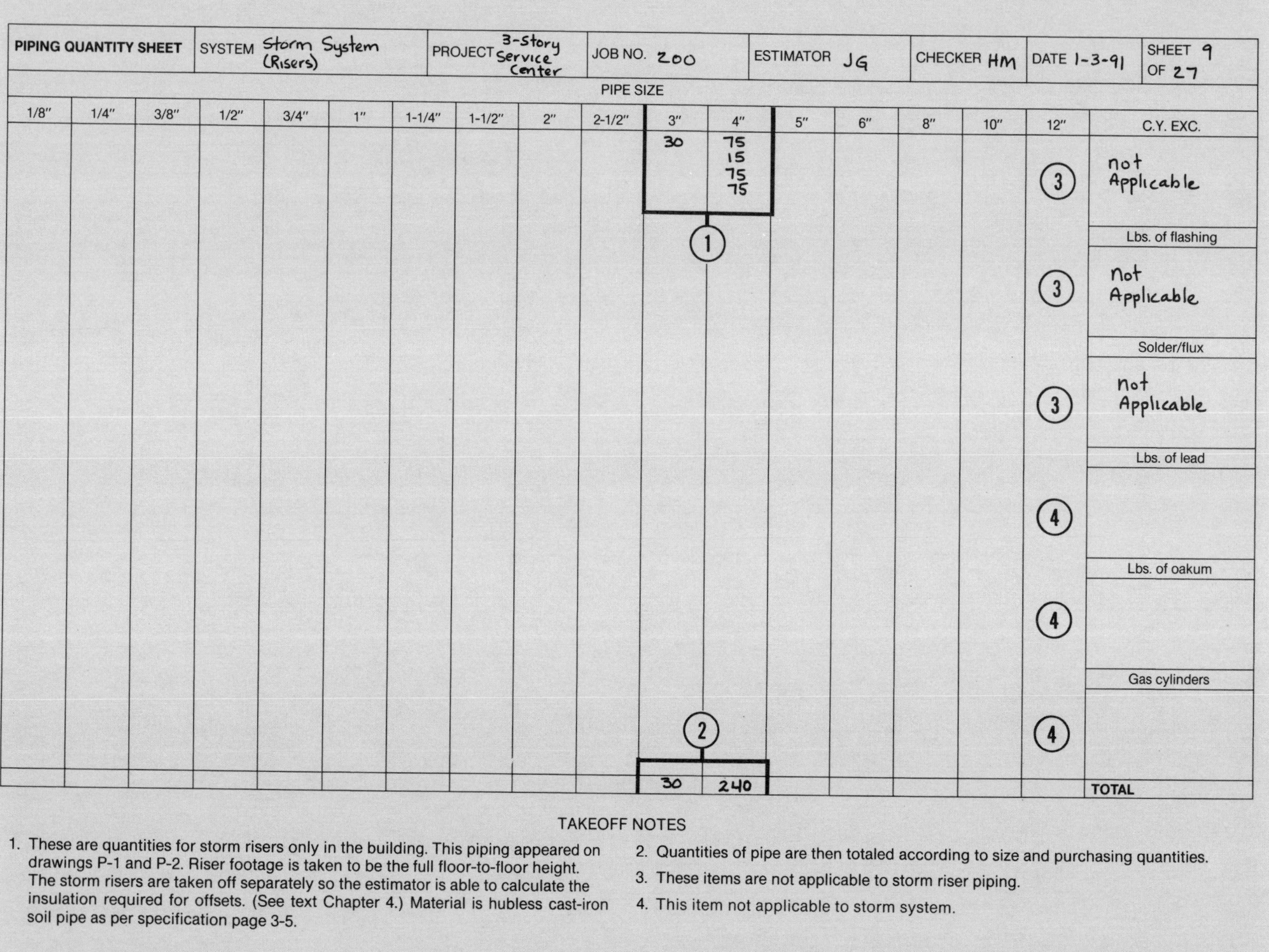

PIPING QUANTITY SHEET	SYSTEM Storm System (Risers)	PROJECT 3-Story Service Center	JOB NO. 200	ESTIMATOR JG	CHECKER HM	DATE 1-3-91	SHEET 9 OF 27

PIPE SIZE																	
1/8"	1/4"	3/8"	1/2"	3/4"	1"	1-1/4"	1-1/2"	2"	2-1/2"	3"	4"	5"	6"	8"	10"	12"	C.Y. EXC.
										30	75 15 75 75					(3)	not Applicable
										(1)							Lbs. of flashing
																(3)	not Applicable
																	Solder/flux
																(3)	not Applicable
																	Lbs. of lead
																(4)	
																	Lbs. of oakum
																(4)	
																	Gas cylinders
										(2)						(4)	
										30	240						TOTAL

TAKEOFF NOTES

1. These are quantities for storm risers only in the building. This piping appeared on drawings P-1 and P-2. Riser footage is taken to be the full floor-to-floor height. The storm risers are taken off separately so the estimator is able to calculate the insulation required for offsets. (See text Chapter 4.) Material is hubless cast-iron soil pipe as per specification page 3-5.
2. Quantities of pipe are then totaled according to size and purchasing quantities.
3. These items are not applicable to storm riser piping.
4. This item not applicable to storm system.

Figure 4.66

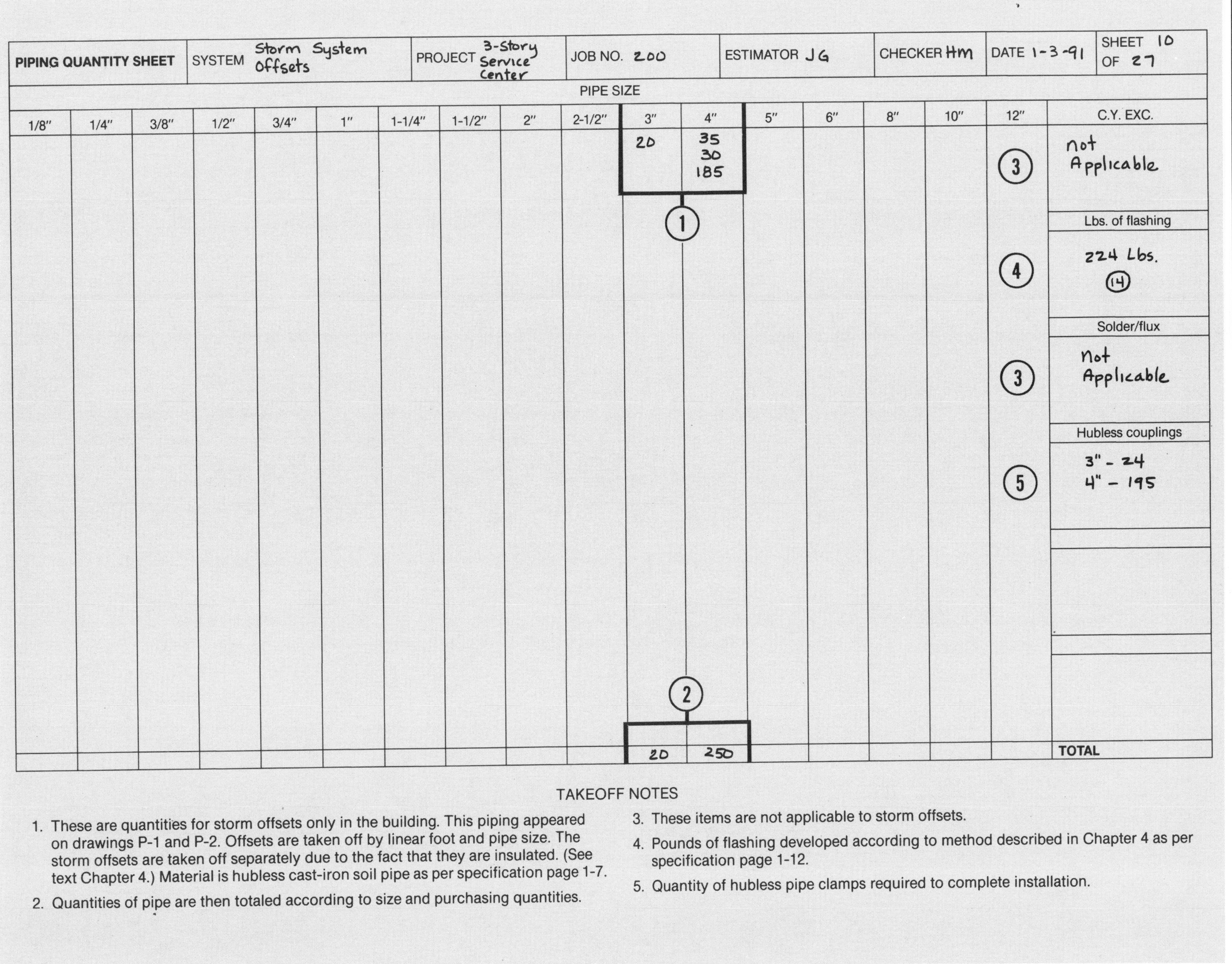

PIPING QUANTITY SHEET	SYSTEM Storm System Offsets	PROJECT 3-Story Service Center	JOB NO. 200	ESTIMATOR JG	CHECKER HM	DATE 1-3-91	SHEET 10 OF 27

PIPE SIZE																	
1/8"	1/4"	3/8"	1/2"	3/4"	1"	1-1/4"	1-1/2"	2"	2-1/2"	3"	4"	5"	6"	8"	10"	12"	C.Y. EXC.
										20	35 30 185					(3)	Not Applicable
										(1)							Lbs. of flashing
																(4)	224 Lbs. (14)
																	Solder/flux
																(3)	Not Applicable
																	Hubless couplings
																(5)	3" - 24 4" - 195
										(2)							
										20	250						TOTAL

TAKEOFF NOTES

1. These are quantities for storm offsets only in the building. This piping appeared on drawings P-1 and P-2. Offsets are taken off by linear foot and pipe size. The storm offsets are taken off separately due to the fact that they are insulated. (See text Chapter 4.) Material is hubless cast-iron soil pipe as per specification page 1-7.
2. Quantities of pipe are then totaled according to size and purchasing quantities.
3. These items are not applicable to storm offsets.
4. Pounds of flashing developed according to method described in Chapter 4 as per specification page 1-12.
5. Quantity of hubless pipe clamps required to complete installation.

Figure 4.67

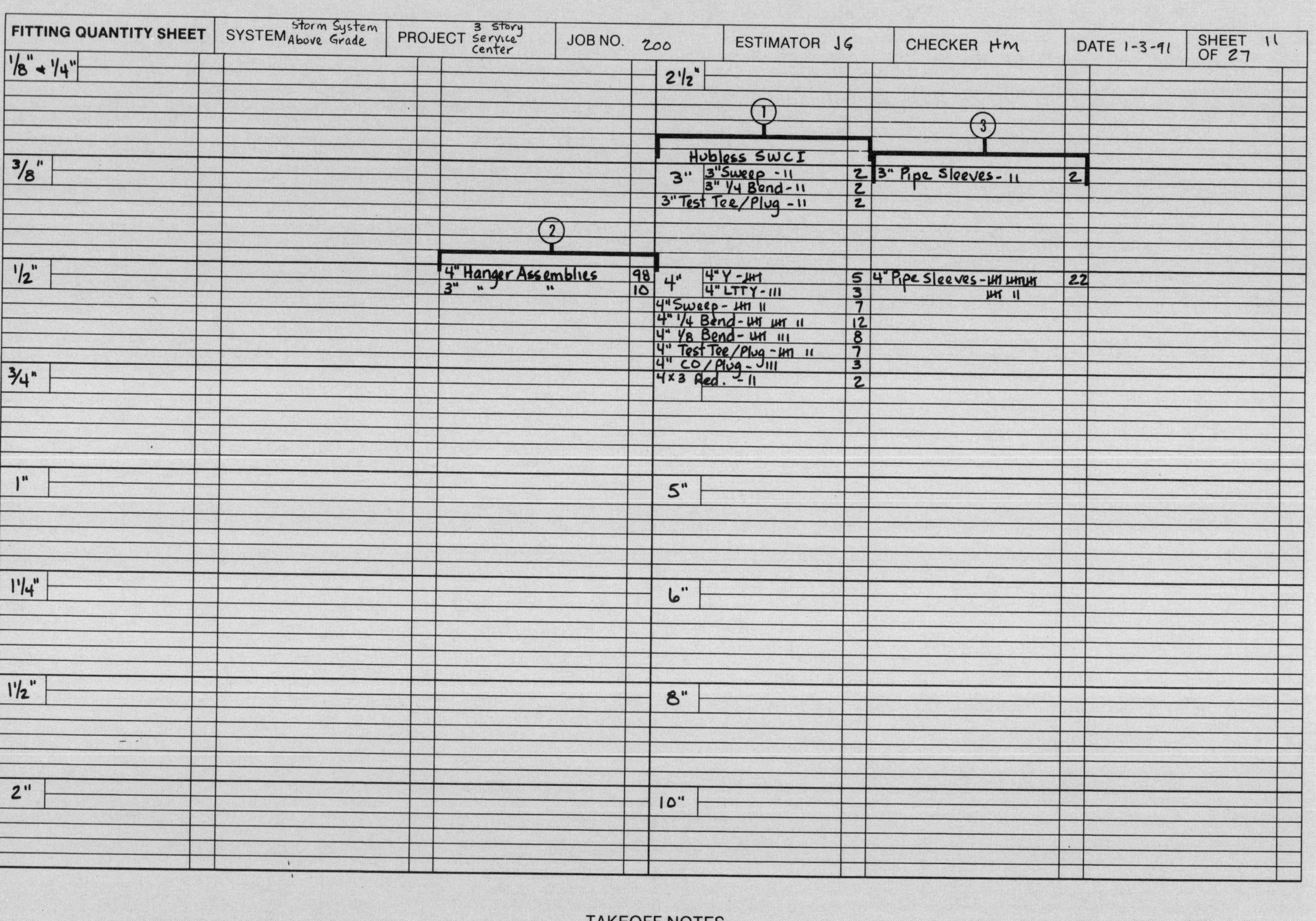

FITTING QUANTITY SHEET | SYSTEM Storm System Above Grade | PROJECT 3 Story Service Center | JOB NO. 200 | ESTIMATOR JG | CHECKER HM | DATE 1-3-91 | SHEET 11 OF 27

1/8" + 1/4"

3/8"

1/2"

3/4"

1"

1 1/4"

1 1/2"

2"

2 1/2"

(1) Hubless SWCI

		Qty
3"	3" Sweep - II	2
	3" 1/4 Bend - II	2
3" Test Tee/Plug - II		2
4"	4" Y - 卌	5
	4" LTTY - III	3
4" Sweep - 卌 II		7
4" 1/4 Bend - 卌 卌 II		12
4" 1/8 Bend - 卌 III		8
4" Test Tee/Plug - 卌 II		7
4" CO/Plug - III		3
4x3 Red. - II		2

(2)

	Qty
4" Hanger Assemblies	98
3" " "	10

(3)

	Qty
3" Pipe Sleeves - II	2
4" Pipe Sleeves - 卌 卌 卌 卌 II	22

5"

6"

8"

10"

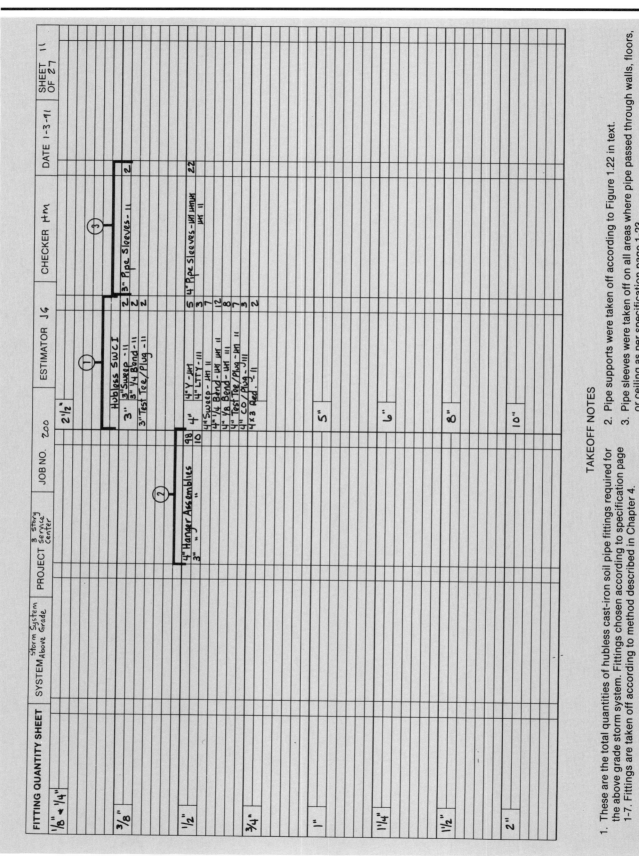

TAKEOFF NOTES

1. These are the total quantities of hubless cast-iron soil pipe fittings required for the above grade storm system. Fittings chosen according to specification page 1-7. Fittings are taken off according to method described in Chapter 4.
2. Pipe supports were taken off according to Figure 1.22 in text.
3. Pipe sleeves were taken off on all areas where pipe passed through walls, floors, or ceiling as per specification page 1-23.

Figure 4.68

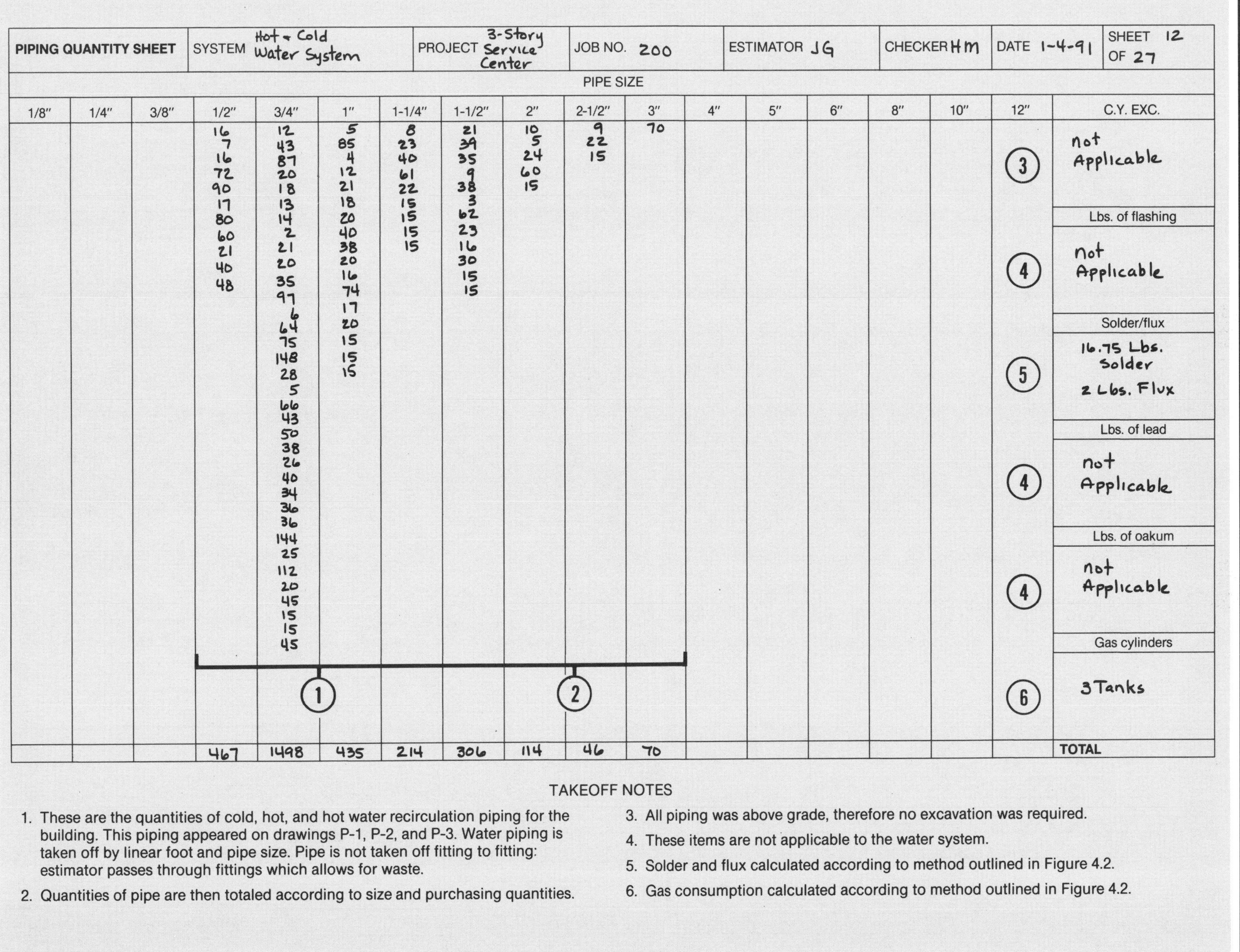

PIPING QUANTITY SHEET	SYSTEM Hot + Cold Water System	PROJECT 3-Story Service Center	JOB NO. 200	ESTIMATOR JG	CHECKER HM	DATE 1-4-91	SHEET 12 OF 27

PIPE SIZE																
1/8"	1/4"	3/8"	1/2"	3/4"	1"	1-1/4"	1-1/2"	2"	2-1/2"	3"	4"	5"	6"	8"	10"	12" / C.Y. EXC.
			16 7 16 72 90 17 80 60 21 40 48	12 43 87 20 18 13 14 2 21 20 35 97 6 64 75 148 28 5 66 43 50 38 26 40 34 36 36 144 25 112 20 45 15 15 45	5 85 4 12 21 18 20 40 38 20 16 74 17 20 15 15 15	8 23 40 61 22 15 15 15 15	21 39 35 9 38 3 62 23 16 30 15 15	10 5 24 60 15	9 22 15	70						(3) C.Y. EXC.: not Applicable (4) Lbs. of flashing: not Applicable (5) Solder/flux: 16.75 Lbs. solder, 2 Lbs. Flux (4) Lbs. of lead: not Applicable (4) Lbs. of oakum: not Applicable (6) Gas cylinders: 3 Tanks
			(1)						(2)							
			467	1498	435	214	306	114	46	70						TOTAL

TAKEOFF NOTES

1. These are the quantities of cold, hot, and hot water recirculation piping for the building. This piping appeared on drawings P-1, P-2, and P-3. Water piping is taken off by linear foot and pipe size. Pipe is not taken off fitting to fitting: estimator passes through fittings which allows for waste.
2. Quantities of pipe are then totaled according to size and purchasing quantities.
3. All piping was above grade, therefore no excavation was required.
4. These items are not applicable to the water system.
5. Solder and flux calculated according to method outlined in Figure 4.2.
6. Gas consumption calculated according to method outlined in Figure 4.2.

Figure 4.69

FITTING QUANTITY SHEET	SYSTEM Hot + Cold Water System	PROJECT 3 Story Service Center	JOB NO. 200	ESTIMATOR JG	CHECKER HM	DATE 1-4-91	SHEET 13 OF 27

Size	Fitting	Qty	Note
1/8" + 1/4"	Misc. Nipples	60	②
3/8"			
1/2"	1/2" Wrought Ell	143	①
	1/2" Wrought 45	29	①
	1/2" Wrought Tees	2	①
	1/2" Copper x Female Adapters	54	①
	1/2" Wrought Cap	2	①
	1/2" Wrought Couplings	10	
3/4"	3/4" Wrought Ells	58	①
	3/4" Wrought Tee	8	①
	3/4" Wrought Tee, Red.	53	①
	3/4" Wrought Cap	6	①
	3/4" Copper x Female Adapter	9	①
	3/4" Wrought 45	14	①
	3/4" x Red. Wrought Ells	2	①
	3/4" Wrought Couplings	29	③
1"	1" x Red Coupling	1	①
	1" Wrought Ell	35	①
	1" Red. Wrought Tee	11	①
	1" Wrought Tee	1	①
	1" Wrought Cap	1	①
	1" Copper x Female Adapter	18	①
	1" Wrought 45	2	①
	1" Wrought Coupling	12	①
1-1/4"	1-1/4 x Red. Wrought Tee	10	①
	1-1/4" Wrought Tee	1	①
	1-1/4" Wrought Ells	6	①
	1-1/4" Wrought Cap	1	①
	1-1/4" Wrought Coupling	7	①
	1-1/4" Wrought 45	1	①
1-1/2"	1-1/2" Wrought Ell	23	①
	1-1/2" x Red. Wrought Ell	1	①
	1-1/2" x Red. Wrought Tee	30	①
	1-1/2" Wrought 45	4	①
	1-1/2" Wrought Coupling	11	①
	1-1/2" Wrought Cap	1	①
	1-1/2" Pipe Sleeves	25	③
2	2" Wrought Ells	3	①
	2" Red. Wrought Tee	4	①
	2" Wrought Coupling	5	①
	2" Pipe Sleeve	1	③
2-1/2"	2-1/2" Red. Wrought Tee	3	①
	2-1/2" Wrought Ell	1	①
	2-1/2" Wrought Couplings	2	①
	2-1/2" Pipe Sleeve	1	③
3"	3" Wrought Ell	7	①
	3" Red. Wrought Tee	5	①
	3" Wrought Couplings	2	①
	3" Pipe Sleeve	2	③
4"			
5"			
6"			
8"			
10"			
12"			

Pipe Supports ④	Qty
3" Pipe Supports	7
2-1/2" " "	5
2" " "	12
1-1/2" " "	31
1-1/4" " "	36
1" " "	13
3/4" " "	250
1/2" " "	78

TAKEOFF NOTES

1. These are the total quantities of wrought copper solder joint fittings required for the hot and cold water system in the building. Fittings chosen according to specification page 1-7. Fittings are taken off according to method described in Chapter 4.
2. Pipe nipples were taken off all areas requiring threaded connections such as around roughing of fixtures and equipment. Size and length of nipples were not taken off since they will be priced on an average basis.
3. Pipe sleeves were taken off on all areas where pipe passed through walls, floors, or ceiling as per specification page 1-23.
4. Pipe supports were taken off according to Figure 1.22 in text.

Figure 4.70

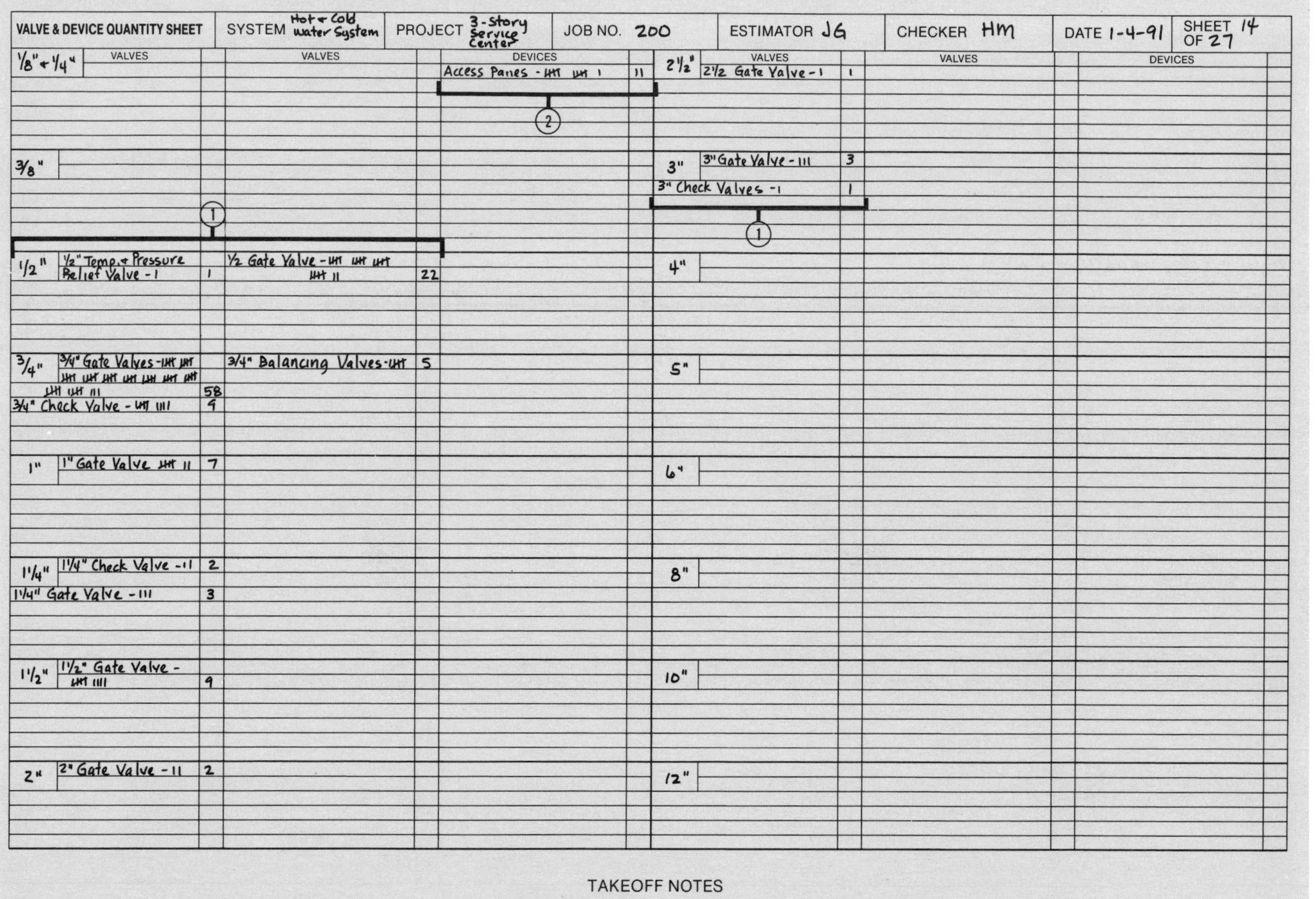

VALVE & DEVICE QUANTITY SHEET	SYSTEM Hot + Cold water System	PROJECT 3-Story Service Center	JOB NO. 200	ESTIMATOR JG	CHECKER HM	DATE 1-4-91	SHEET 14 OF 27

Size	VALVES	Qty	VALVES	Qty	DEVICES	Qty
1/8" + 1/4"					Access Panes - 卌 卌 I ②	11
3/8"						
1/2" ①	1/2" Temp. + Pressure Relief Valve - I	1	1/2 Gate Valve - 卌 卌 卌 卌 II	22		
3/4"	3/4" Gate Valves - 卌 卌 卌 卌 卌 卌 卌 卌 卌 卌 卌 III	58	3/4" Balancing Valves - 卌	5		
	3/4" Check Valve - 卌 IIII	9				
1"	1" Gate Valve 卌 II	7				
1 1/4"	1 1/4" Check Valve - II	2				
	1 1/4" Gate Valve - III	3				
1 1/2"	1 1/2" Gate Valve - 卌 IIII	9				
2"	2" Gate Valve - II	2				

Size	VALVES	Qty	VALVES	Qty	DEVICES	Qty
2 1/2"	2 1/2 Gate Valve - I	1				
3" ①	3" Gate Valve - III	3				
	3" Check Valves - I	1				
4"						
5"						
6"						
8"						
10"						
12"						

TAKEOFF NOTES

1. These are the total quantities of gate, check, balancing and relief valves required for the hot and cold water system. Valves appeared on all drawings P-1, P-2, and P-3. Valves are sized according to pipe line size. See Appendix C for valve symbols. Valve types are according to specification page 1-9.
2. Access panels were taken off riser diagrams on drawing P-2. See specification page 1-17 for information on access panels.

Figure 4.71

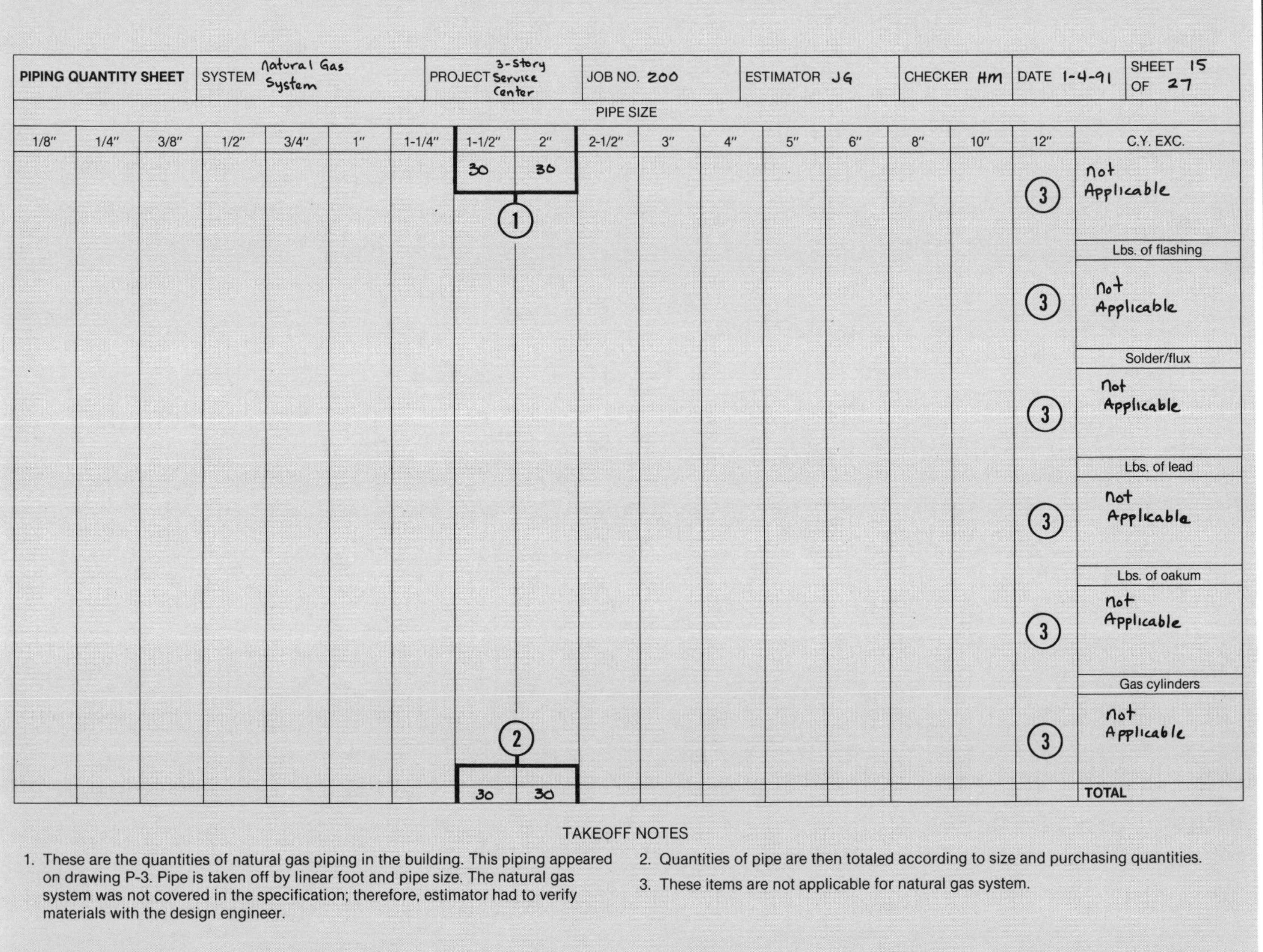

PIPING QUANTITY SHEET	SYSTEM Natural Gas System	PROJECT 3-Story Service Center	JOB NO. 200	ESTIMATOR JG	CHECKER HM	DATE 1-4-91	SHEET 15 OF 27

PIPE SIZE																	
1/8"	1/4"	3/8"	1/2"	3/4"	1"	1-1/4"	1-1/2"	2"	2-1/2"	3"	4"	5"	6"	8"	10"	12"	C.Y. EXC.
							30	30									
							(1)									(3)	Not Applicable
																	Lbs. of flashing
																(3)	Not Applicable
																	Solder/flux
																(3)	Not Applicable
																	Lbs. of lead
																(3)	Not Applicable
																	Lbs. of oakum
																(3)	Not Applicable
																	Gas cylinders
							(2)									(3)	Not Applicable
							30	30									TOTAL

TAKEOFF NOTES

1. These are the quantities of natural gas piping in the building. This piping appeared on drawing P-3. Pipe is taken off by linear foot and pipe size. The natural gas system was not covered in the specification; therefore, estimator had to verify materials with the design engineer.
2. Quantities of pipe are then totaled according to size and purchasing quantities.
3. These items are not applicable for natural gas system.

Figure 4.72

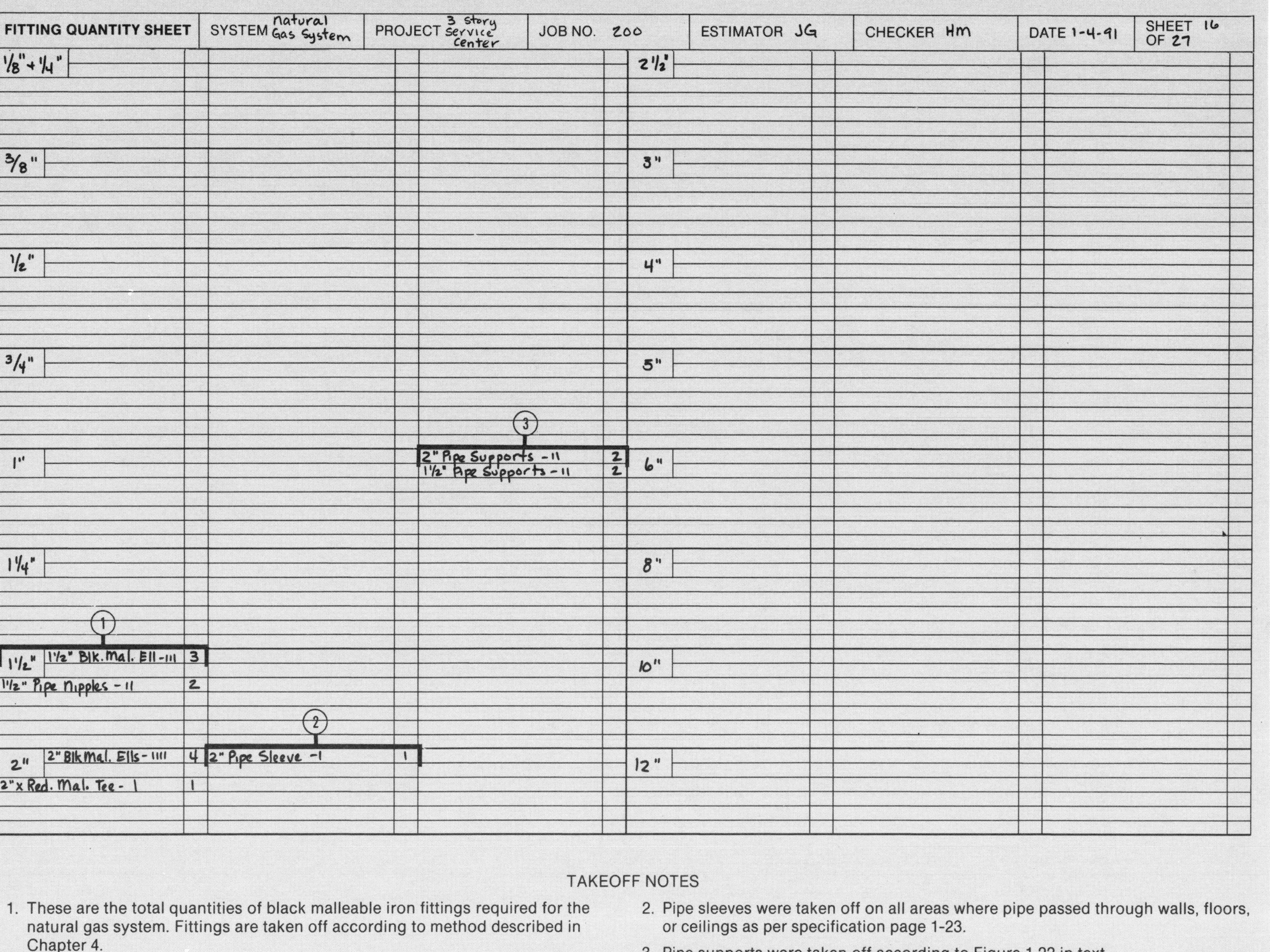

FITTING QUANTITY SHEET	SYSTEM Natural Gas System	PROJECT 3 Story Service Center	JOB NO. 200	ESTIMATOR JG	CHECKER HM	DATE 1-4-91	SHEET 16 OF 27

Size	Item	Qty	Item	Qty	Item	Qty
1/8" + 1/4"						
3/8"						
1/2"						
3/4"						
					(3)	
1"					2" Pipe Supports -11	2
					1½" Pipe Supports -11	2
1¼"						
	(1)					
1½"	1½" Blk. Mal. Ell -111	3				
	1½" Pipe nipples -11	2				
			(2)			
2"	2" Blk Mal. Ells -1111	4	2" Pipe Sleeve -1	1		
	2" x Red. Mal. Tee - 1	1				

Size						
2½"						
3"						
4"						
5"						
6"						
8"						
10"						
12"						

TAKEOFF NOTES

1. These are the total quantities of black malleable iron fittings required for the natural gas system. Fittings are taken off according to method described in Chapter 4.
2. Pipe sleeves were taken off on all areas where pipe passed through walls, floors, or ceilings as per specification page 1-23.
3. Pipe supports were taken off according to Figure 1.22 in text.

Figure 4.73

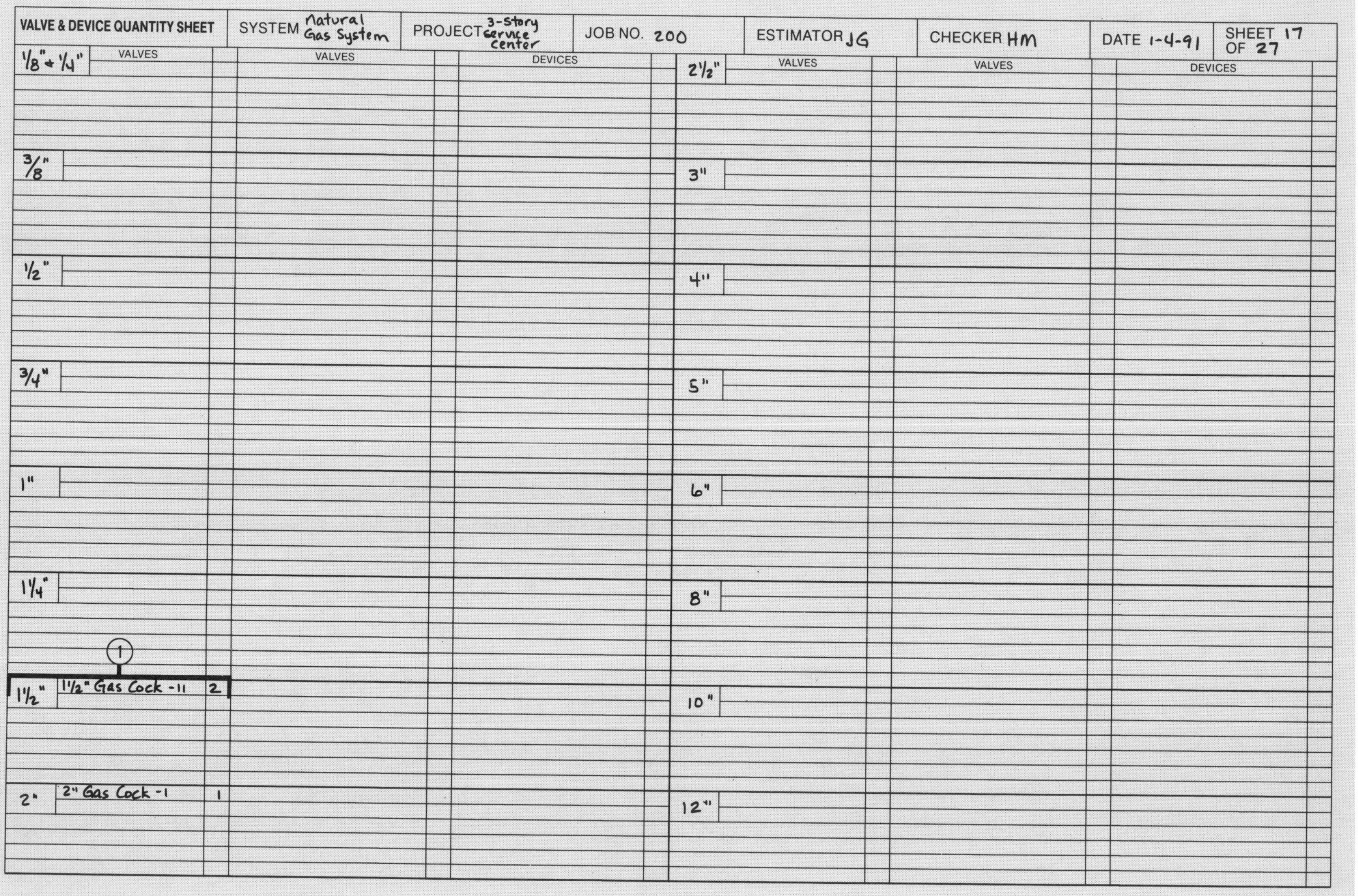

VALVE & DEVICE QUANTITY SHEET

SYSTEM Natural Gas System | PROJECT 3-Story Service Center | JOB NO. 200 | ESTIMATOR JG | CHECKER HM | DATE 1-4-91 | SHEET 17 OF 27

Size	VALVES	Qty	VALVES	DEVICES
1/8" + 1/4"				
3/8"				
1/2"				
3/4"				
1"				
1 1/4"				
1 1/2"	(1) 1 1/2" Gas Cock - 11	2		
2"	2" Gas Cock - 1	1		

Size	VALVES	VALVES	DEVICES
2 1/2"			
3"			
4"			
5"			
6"			
8"			
10"			
12"			

TAKEOFF NOTES

1. These are all the gas cocks required for the natural gas system. Gas cocks were taken off drawing P-3 mechanical equipment room.

Figure 4.74

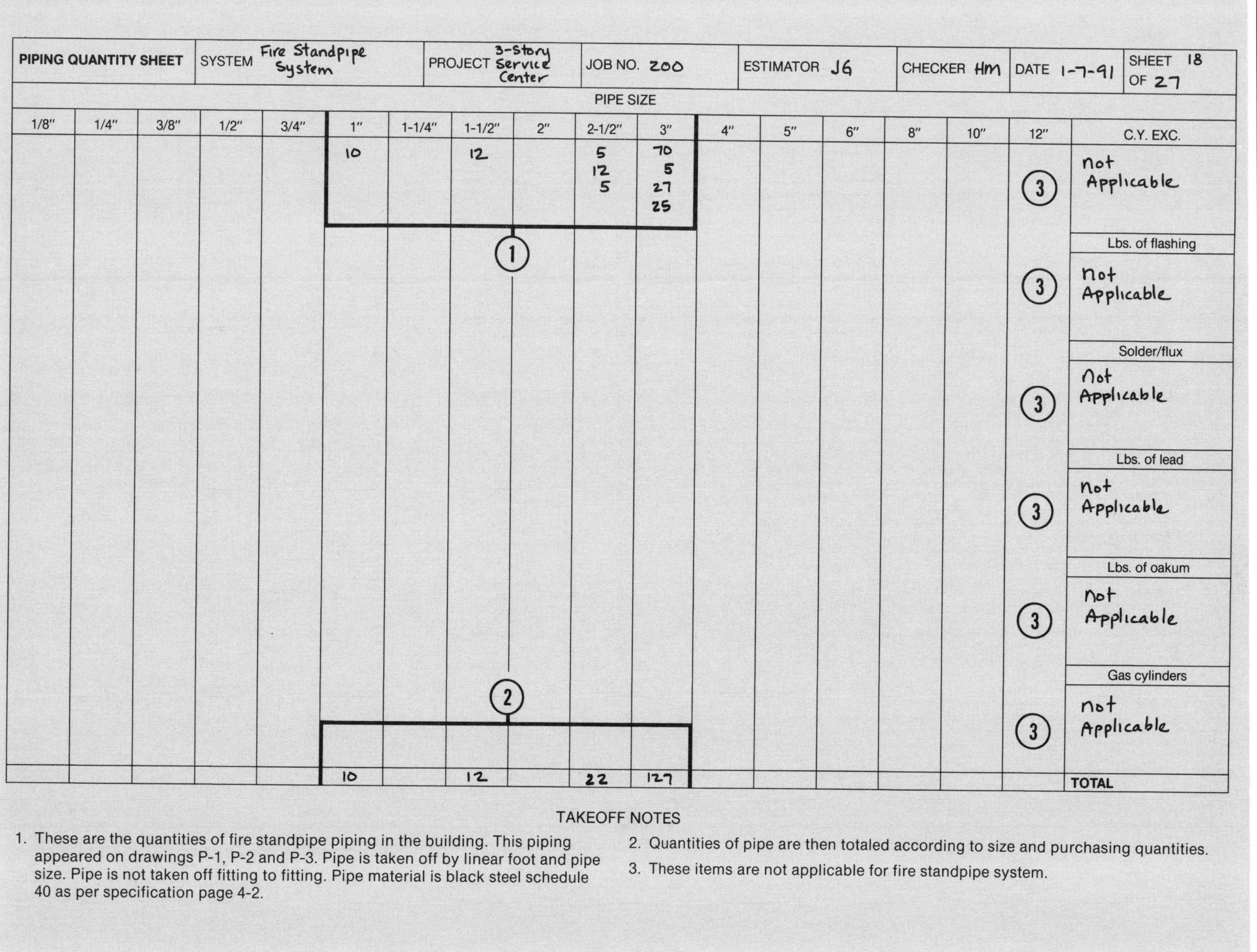

PIPING QUANTITY SHEET	SYSTEM Fire Standpipe System	PROJECT 3-Story Service Center	JOB NO. 200	ESTIMATOR JG	CHECKER HM	DATE 1-7-91	SHEET 18 OF 27

PIPE SIZE																
1/8"	1/4"	3/8"	1/2"	3/4"	1"	1-1/4"	1-1/2"	2"	2-1/2"	3"	4"	5"	6"	8"	10"	12"
					10		12		5 12 5	70 5 27 25						
					(1)											
					(2)											
					10		12		22	127						TOTAL

C.Y. EXC.	(3)	not Applicable
Lbs. of flashing	(3)	not Applicable
Solder/flux	(3)	not Applicable
Lbs. of lead	(3)	not Applicable
Lbs. of oakum	(3)	not Applicable
Gas cylinders	(3)	not Applicable

TAKEOFF NOTES

1. These are the quantities of fire standpipe piping in the building. This piping appeared on drawings P-1, P-2 and P-3. Pipe is taken off by linear foot and pipe size. Pipe is not taken off fitting to fitting. Pipe material is black steel schedule 40 as per specification page 4-2.
2. Quantities of pipe are then totaled according to size and purchasing quantities.
3. These items are not applicable for fire standpipe system.

Figure 4.75

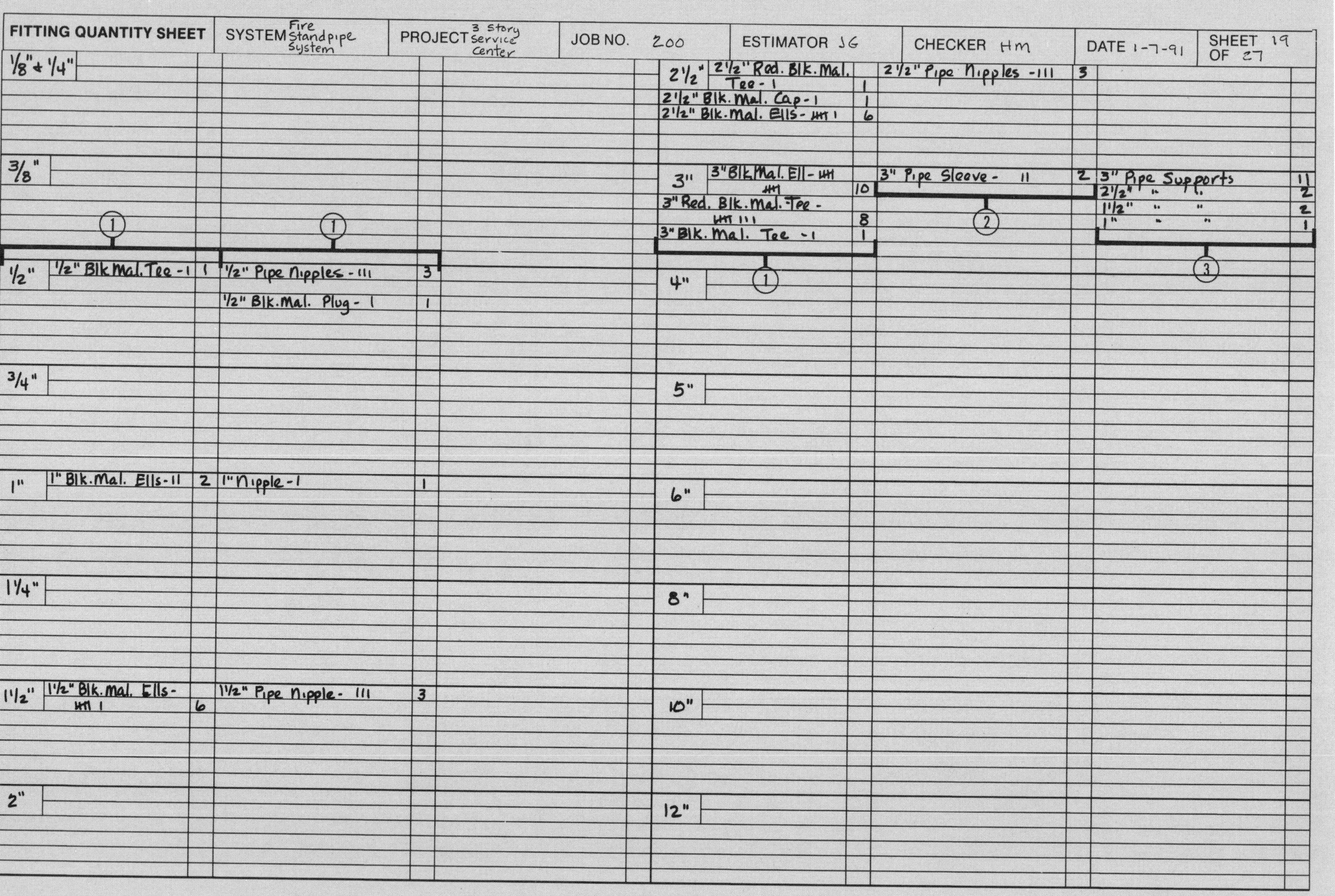

FITTING QUANTITY SHEET	SYSTEM Fire Standpipe System	PROJECT 3 Story Service Center	JOB NO. 200	ESTIMATOR JG	CHECKER HM	DATE 1-7-91	SHEET 19 OF 27

Size	Item	Qty	Item	Qty	Item	Qty
1/8" & 1/4"						
3/8"						
1/2"	1/2" Blk Mal. Tee - I	1	1/2" Pipe Nipples - III	3		
			1/2" Blk. Mal. Plug - I	1		
3/4"						
1"	1" Blk. Mal. Ells - II	2	1" Nipple - I	1		
1 1/4"						
1 1/2"	1 1/2" Blk. Mal. Ells - ~~HH~~ I	6	1 1/2" Pipe Nipple - III	3		
2"						
2 1/2"	2 1/2" Red. Blk. Mal. Tee - I	1	2 1/2" Pipe Nipples - III	3		
	2 1/2" Blk. Mal. Cap - I	1				
	2 1/2" Blk. Mal. Ells - ~~HH~~ I	6				
3"	3" Blk. Mal. Ell - ~~HH~~ ~~HH~~	10	3" Pipe Sleeve - II	2	3" Pipe Supports	11
	3" Red. Blk. Mal. Tee - ~~HH~~ III	8			2 1/2" " "	2
	3" Blk. Mal. Tee - I	1			1 1/2" " "	2
					1" " "	1
4"						
5"						
6"						
8"						
10"						
12"						

(Bracket notes: ① for the 1/2" group and the 3" fittings; ② for the pipe sleeves; ③ for the pipe supports.)

TAKEOFF NOTES

1. These are the total quantities of black malleable iron fittings required for the fire standpipe system. Fittings are taken off according to method described in Chapter 4.
2. Pipe sleeves were taken off on all areas where pipe passed through walls, floors, or ceilings as per specification page 1-23.
3. Pipe supports were taken off according to Figure 1.22 in text.

Figure 4.76

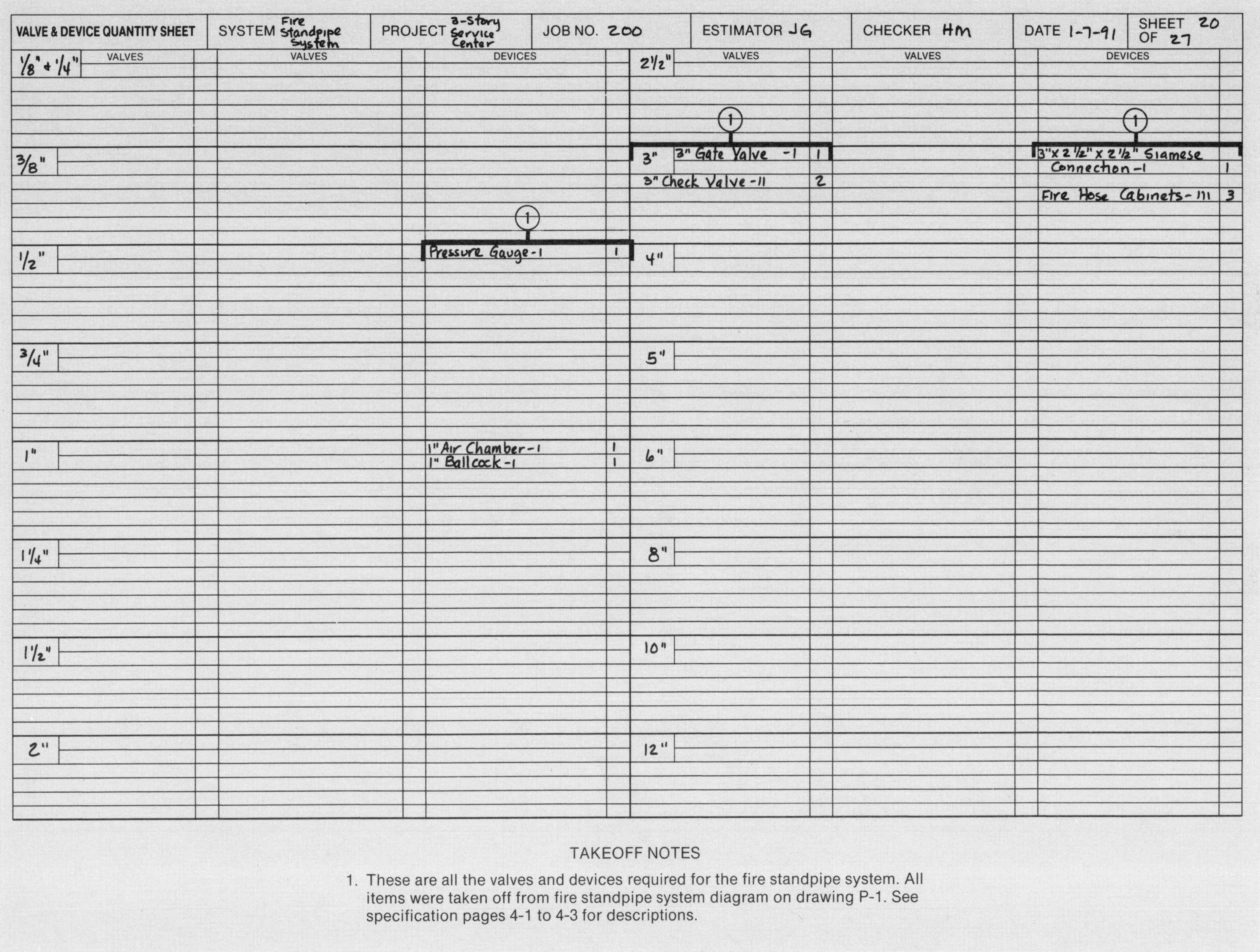

VALVE & DEVICE QUANTITY SHEET	SYSTEM Fire Standpipe System	PROJECT 3-Story Service Center	JOB NO. 200	ESTIMATOR JG	CHECKER HM	DATE 1-7-91	SHEET 20 OF 27

Size	VALVES	VALVES	DEVICES	Qty	Size	VALVES	Qty	VALVES	DEVICES	Qty
1/8" & 1/4"					2 1/2"					
3/8"					3"	(1) 3" Gate Valve -1	1		(1) 3"x 2 1/2" x 2 1/2" Siamese Connection-1	1
						3" Check Valve-11	2		Fire Hose Cabinets-111	3
1/2"			(1) Pressure Gauge-1	1	4"					
3/4"					5"					
1"			1" Air Chamber-1	1	6"					
			1" Ballcock-1	1						
1 1/4"					8"					
1 1/2"					10"					
2"					12"					

TAKEOFF NOTES

1. These are all the valves and devices required for the fire standpipe system. All items were taken off from fire standpipe system diagram on drawing P-1. See specification pages 4-1 to 4-3 for descriptions.

Figure 4.77

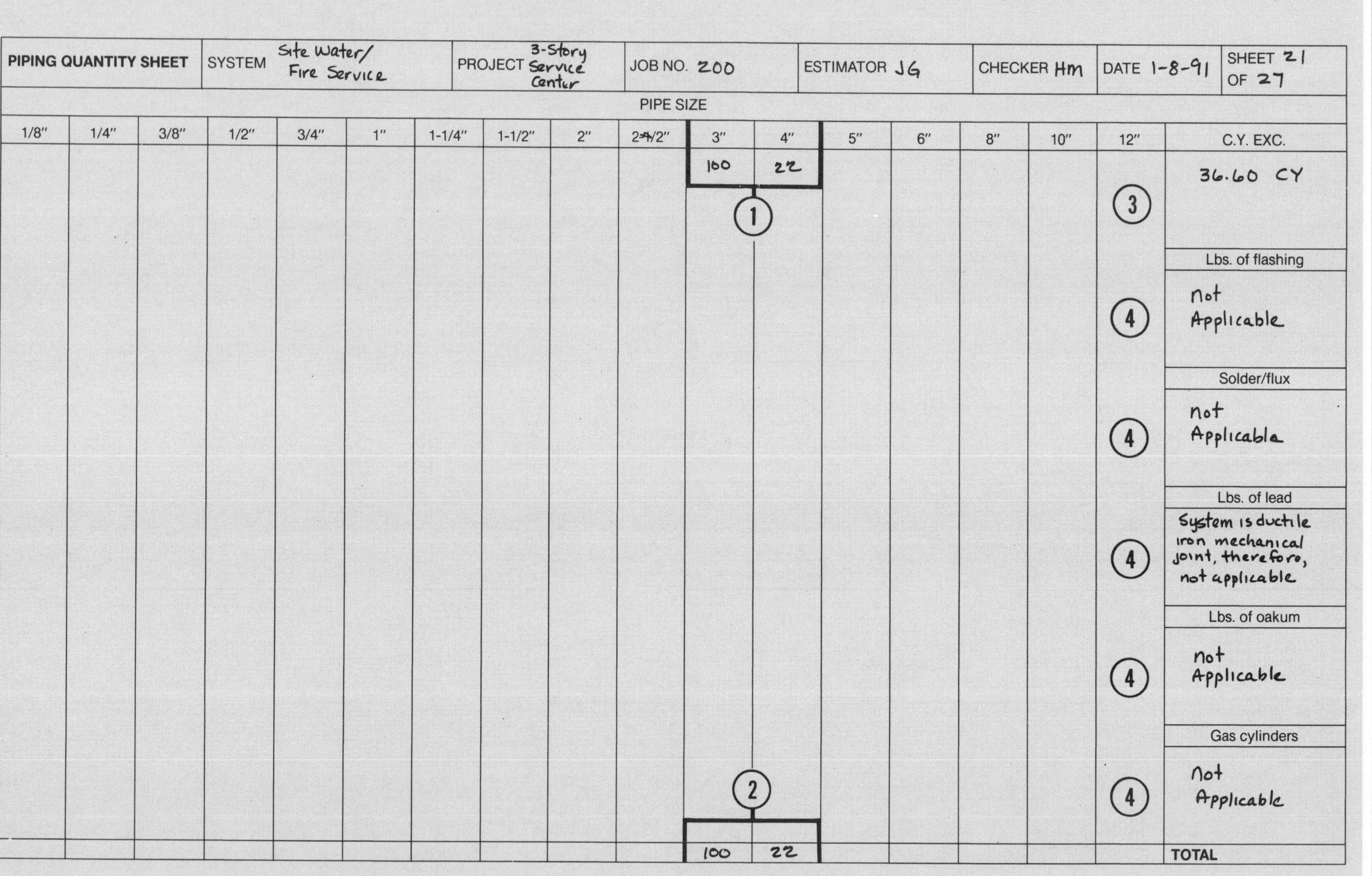

PIPING QUANTITY SHEET	SYSTEM Site Water/ Fire Service	PROJECT 3-Story Service Center	JOB NO. 200	ESTIMATOR JG	CHECKER HM	DATE 1-8-91	SHEET 21 OF 27

PIPE SIZE																	
1/8"	1/4"	3/8"	1/2"	3/4"	1"	1-1/4"	1-1/2"	2"	2-1/2"	3"	4"	5"	6"	8"	10"	12"	C.Y. EXC.
										100	22						
										(1)						(3)	36.60 CY
																	Lbs. of flashing
																(4)	Not Applicable
																	Solder/flux
																(4)	Not Applicable
																	Lbs. of lead
																(4)	System is ductile iron mechanical joint, therefore, not applicable
																	Lbs. of oakum
																(4)	Not Applicable
																	Gas cylinders
										(2)						(4)	Not Applicable
										100	22						TOTAL

TAKEOFF NOTES

1. These are the quantities of domestic water and fire protection mains on the site. This piping appears on the site plan on drawing P-1. Pipe is taken off by the linear foot. Material is ductile-iron water pipe as per specification pages 2-1 and 4-1.
2. Quantities of pipe are then totaled according to size and purchasing quantities.
3. Excavation was taken off according to method outlined in Figure 1.23 of text. Depth of pipe was assumed to be 4.00 feet.
4. These items are not applicable to water/fire mains.

Figure 4.78

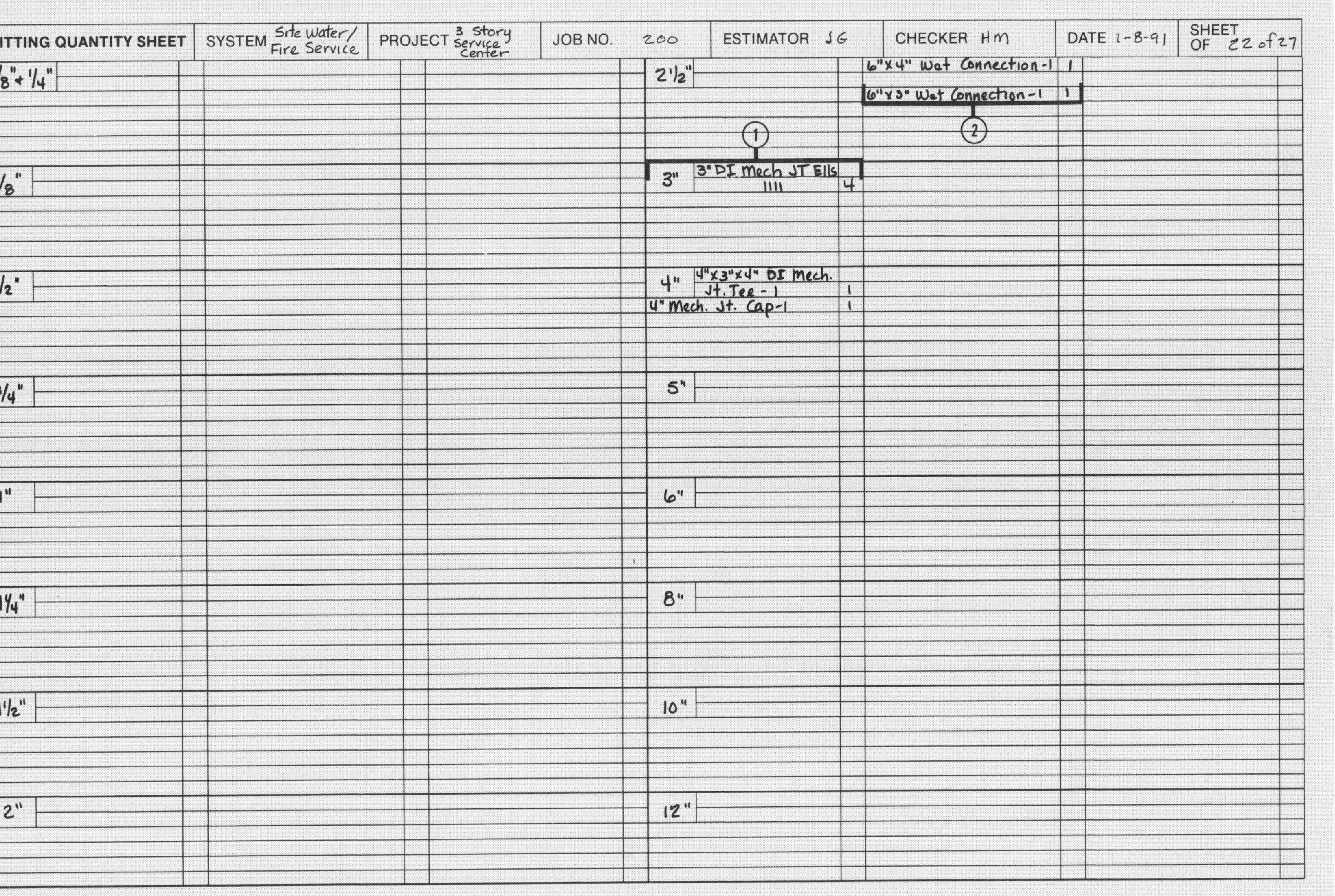

FITTING QUANTITY SHEET	SYSTEM Site Water/ Fire Service	PROJECT 3 Story Service Center	JOB NO. 200	ESTIMATOR JG	CHECKER HM	DATE 1-8-91	SHEET OF 22 of 27

Size	Item	Qty
1/8" + 1/4"		
3/8"		
1/2"		
3/4"		
1"		
1¼"		
1½"		
2"		
2½"	6"x4" Wet Connection-1 (2)	1
	6"x3" Wet Connection-1 (2)	1
3"	3" DI Mech JT Ells (1) 1111	4
4"	4"x3"x4" DI Mech. Jt. Tee-1	1
	4" Mech. Jt. Cap-1	1
5"		
6"		
8"		
10"		
12"		

TAKEOFF NOTES

1. These are the total quantities of ductile-iron mechanical joint fittings for site water and fire mains. Fittings are taken off according to method described in Chapter 4. Fittings chosen according to specification page 1-8.
2. Wet connections were taken off site plan on drawing P-1, according to specification pages 2-2 and 4-1.

Figure 4.79

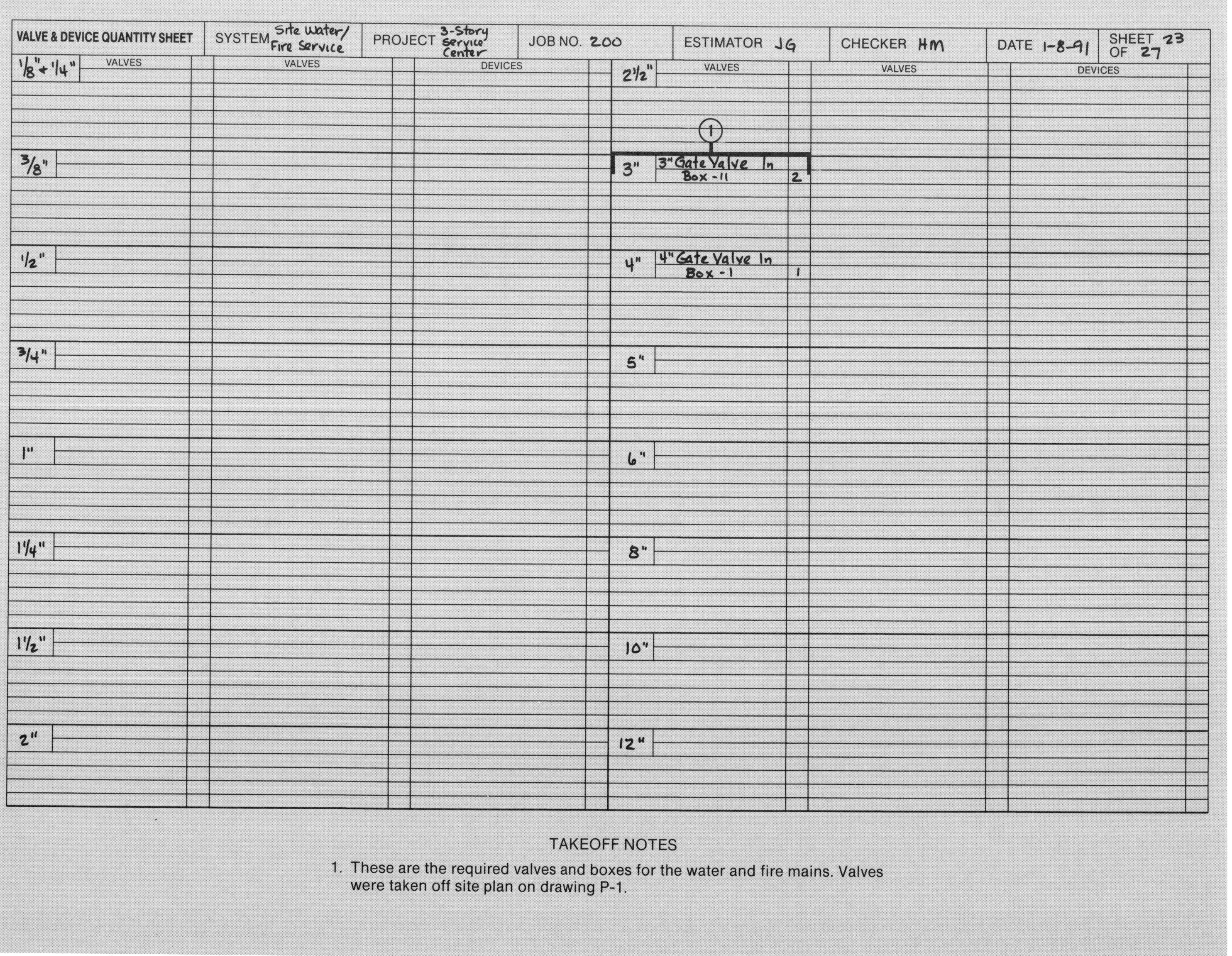

VALVE & DEVICE QUANTITY SHEET	SYSTEM Site Water/ Fire Service	PROJECT 3-Story Service Center	JOB NO. 200	ESTIMATOR JG	CHECKER HM	DATE 1-8-91	SHEET 23 OF 27

Size	VALVES		VALVES		DEVICES		Size	VALVES		VALVES		DEVICES	
1/8" + 1/4"							2½"						
3/8"							3"	3" Gate Valve In Box - 11 (1)	2				
1/2"							4"	4" Gate Valve In Box - 1	1				
3/4"							5"						
1"							6"						
1¼"							8"						
1½"							10"						
2"							12"						

TAKEOFF NOTES

1. These are the required valves and boxes for the water and fire mains. Valves were taken off site plan on drawing P-1.

Figure 4.80

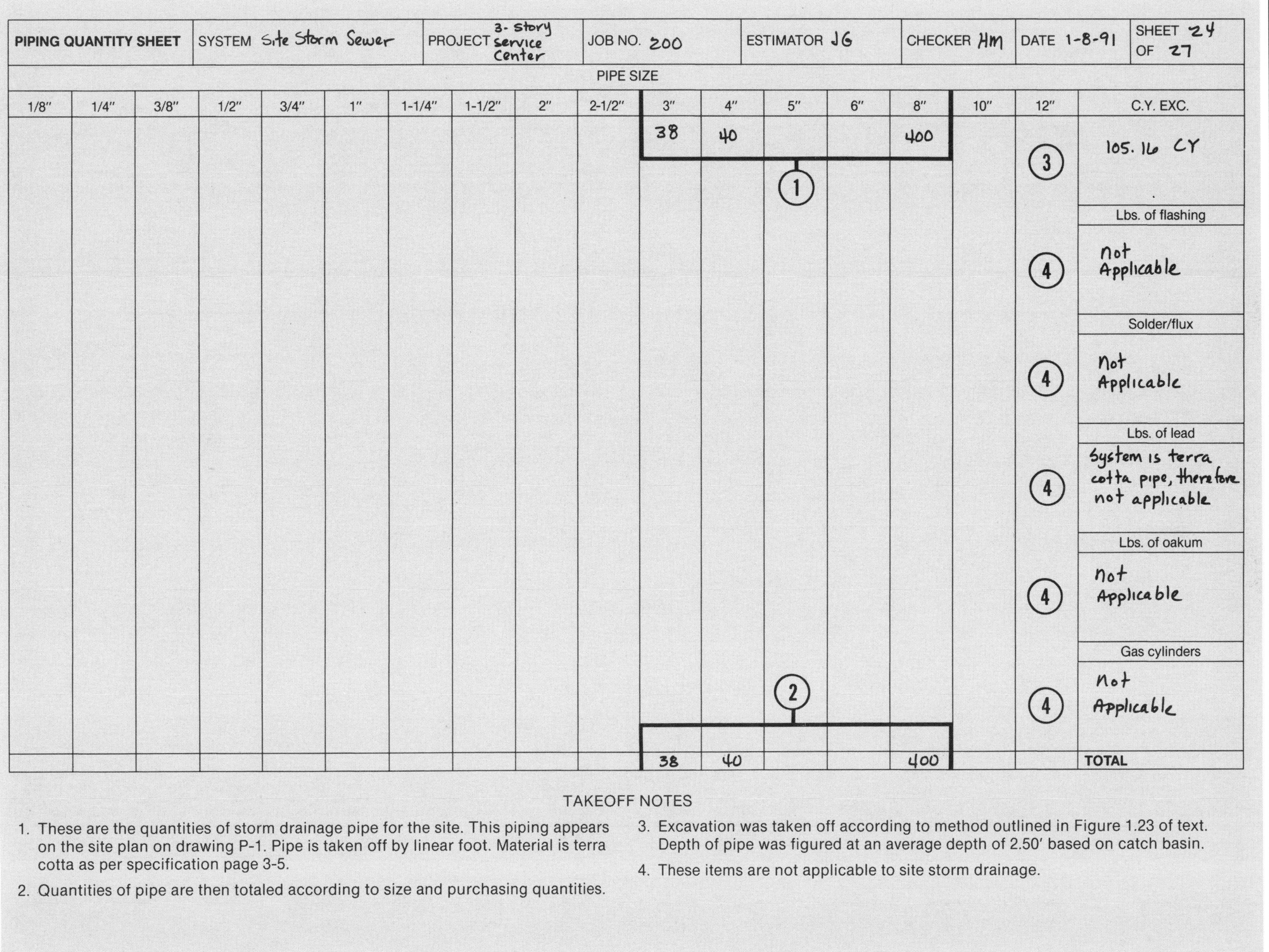

PIPING QUANTITY SHEET	SYSTEM Site Storm Sewer	PROJECT 3-story service Center	JOB NO. 200	ESTIMATOR JG	CHECKER HM	DATE 1-8-91	SHEET 24 OF 27

PIPE SIZE																	
1/8"	1/4"	3/8"	1/2"	3/4"	1"	1-1/4"	1-1/2"	2"	2-1/2"	3"	4"	5"	6"	8"	10"	12"	C.Y. EXC.
										38	40	(1)		400		(3)	105.16 CY
																	Lbs. of flashing
																(4)	Not Applicable
																	Solder/flux
																(4)	Not Applicable
																	Lbs. of lead
																(4)	System is terra cotta pipe, therefore not applicable
																	Lbs. of oakum
																(4)	Not Applicable
																	Gas cylinders
												(2)				(4)	Not Applicable
										38	40			400			TOTAL

TAKEOFF NOTES

1. These are the quantities of storm drainage pipe for the site. This piping appears on the site plan on drawing P-1. Pipe is taken off by linear foot. Material is terra cotta as per specification page 3-5.
2. Quantities of pipe are then totaled according to size and purchasing quantities.
3. Excavation was taken off according to method outlined in Figure 1.23 of text. Depth of pipe was figured at an average depth of 2.50′ based on catch basin.
4. These items are not applicable to site storm drainage.

Figure 4.81

FITTING QUANTITY SHEET	SYSTEM Site Storm Sewer	PROJECT 3 Story Service Center	JOB NO. 200	ESTIMATOR JG	CHECKER HM	DATE 1-8-91	SHEET 25 OF 27

Size	Fitting	Qty
1/8" & 1/4"		
3/8"		
1/2"		
3/4"		
1"		
1 1/4"		
1 1/2"		
2"		

Size	Fitting	Qty	Item	Qty
2 1/2"			Catch Basin 1.99 Ft. Deep	1
			" " 2.31 " "	1
			" " 2.63 " "	1
			" " 2.75 " "	1
			" " 3.23 " "	1
			Lampholes - |||| (2)	5
3"				
4"	(1) 4" 1/8 Bend - I	1	(3) Connect new 8" Storm Sewer to Existing catch basin	1
			Connect new catch basin to existing 8" storm sewer	1
5"				
6"				
8"	8" Y - ||||	5		
	8" Sweep - ||||	5		
	8" X 3" Y - I	1		
	8" 1/8 Bend - III	3		
	8" X 4" "Y" - I	1		
10"				
12"				

TAKEOFF NOTES

1. These are the total quantities of terra cotta fittings for the site storm drainage system. Fittings are taken off according to method described in Chapter 4. Fittings chosen according to specification page 1-7.
2. These are total quantity of catch basins and lampholes shown on site plan drawing P-1. Catch basin depths arrived at by subtracting bottom elevations from top or rim elevations which are shown on drawings.
3. These are required connections to existing sewers shown on site plan drawing P-1.

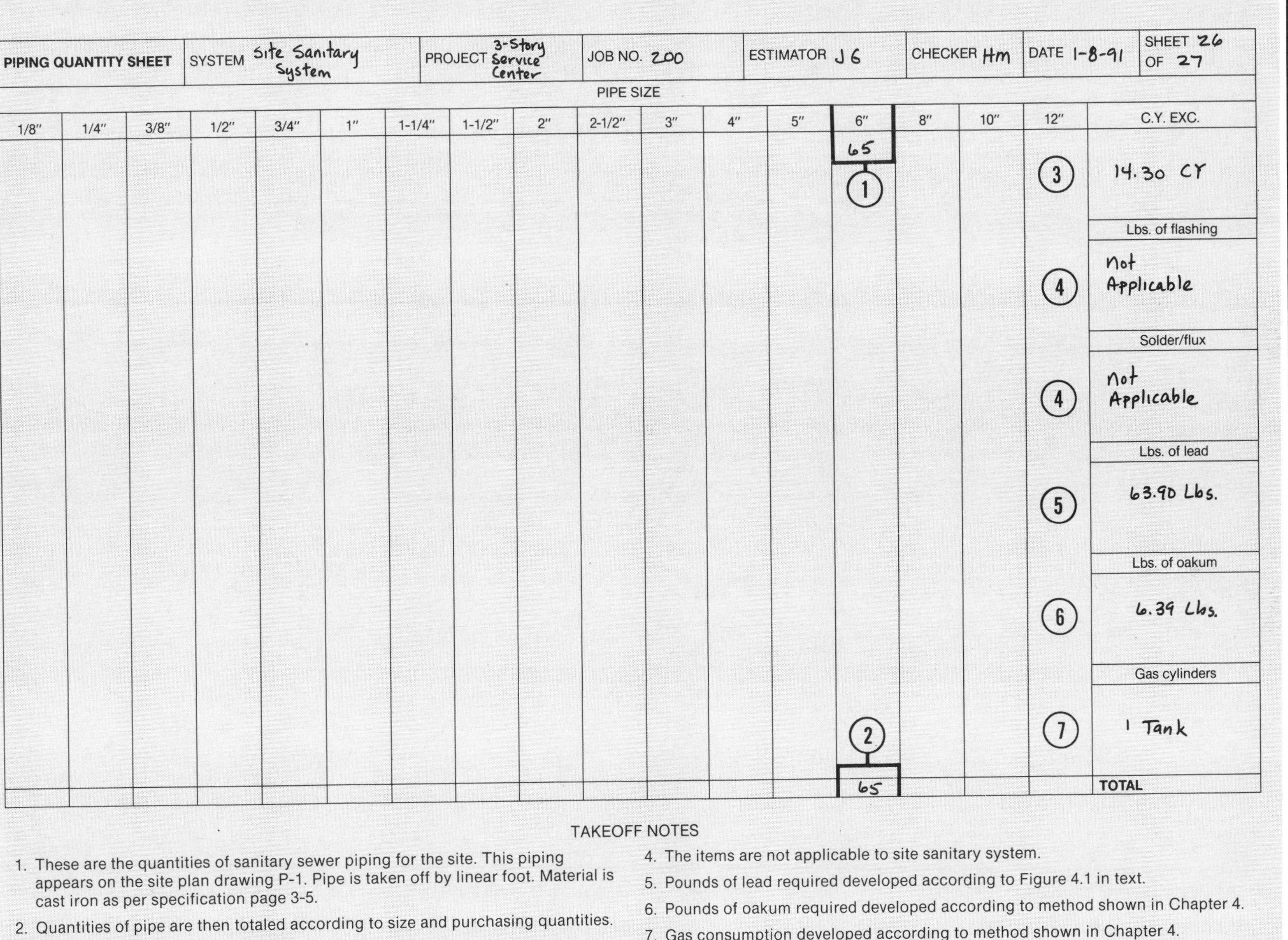

PIPING QUANTITY SHEET | SYSTEM Site Sanitary System | PROJECT 3-Story Service Center | JOB NO. 200 | ESTIMATOR J6 | CHECKER Hm | DATE 1-8-91 | SHEET 26 OF 27

PIPE SIZE

1/8"	1/4"	3/8"	1/2"	3/4"	1"	1-1/4"	1-1/2"	2"	2-1/2"	3"	4"	5"	6"	8"	10"	12"	C.Y. EXC.
													65 (1)			(3)	14.30 CY
																	Lbs. of flashing
																(4)	Not Applicable
																	Solder/flux
																(4)	Not Applicable
																	Lbs. of lead
																(5)	63.90 Lbs.
																	Lbs. of oakum
																(6)	6.39 Lbs.
																	Gas cylinders
													(2)			(7)	1 Tank
													65				**TOTAL**

TAKEOFF NOTES

1. These are the quantities of sanitary sewer piping for the site. This piping appears on the site plan drawing P-1. Pipe is taken off by linear foot. Material is cast iron as per specification page 3-5.
2. Quantities of pipe are then totaled according to size and purchasing quantities.
3. Excavation was taken off according to method outlined in Figure 1.23 of text.
4. The items are not applicable to site sanitary system.
5. Pounds of lead required developed according to Figure 4.1 in text.
6. Pounds of oakum required developed according to method shown in Chapter 4.
7. Gas consumption developed according to method shown in Chapter 4.

Figure 4.83

FITTING QUANTITY SHEET	SYSTEM Site Sanitary Sewer	PROJECT 3 Story Service Center	JOB NO. 200	ESTIMATOR JG	CHECKER HM	DATE 1-8-91	SHEET 27 OF 27

Size	Item	Qty	Note	Size	Item	Qty	Note
1/8" + 1/4"				2 1/2"			
3/8"				3"			
1/2"				4"			
3/4"				5"			
1"				6"	6" 1/8 Bend-1	1	(1)
					Connect new 6" Sewer to existing 12" Sewer -1	1	(2)
1 1/4"				8"			
1 1/2"				10"			
2"				12"	12" X 6" 'Y' -1	1	(1)

TAKEOFF NOTES

1. These are total quantities of cast-iron soil pipe fittings for site sanitary sewer. Fittings are taken off according to method shown in Chapter 4. Fittings chosen according to specification page 1-7.
2. This is required connection to existing sewer shown on site plan drawing P-1.

Figure 4.84

Chapter 5

WRITING UP AND PRICING THE ESTIMATE

With the takeoff complete and all quantities rechecked, the estimator is now ready to write up and price the estimate. This chapter will cover material pricing, including discounts, and labor. The second part of the chapter is a written estimate for the sample job.

Writing Up the Estimate

The estimate is written up on estimate forms similar to the one shown in Chapter 3, Figure 3.7. In addition to the basic information on the top of the form, the following columns are included:

1. **Item:** used for numbering entries.
2. **Classification of Work:** used to enter description of item to be priced.
3. **Quantity:** used to enter quantity and unit of measure. For example: *each, linear foot, pound allowance, percentage,* etc.
4. **Material:** used to enter material *unit* cost per item and then material *total* cost per item.
5. **Labor:** used to enter man-hour production unit per item, and total man-hours per item.
6. **Labor Cost:** used to enter the prevailing man-hour labor rate per item and the total labor cost per item.
7. **Total Cost:** used to enter total cost (material and labor).

The order in which the estimate is written up corresponds to the systems breakdown on the project summary sheet. (See summary sheet, Chapter 3, Figure 3.8.) To begin the write-up, the estimator transfers all quantities on the takeoff forms to the estimate forms, and draws a red line through the totals on the quantity takeoff as a check-off system to be sure that all items are accounted for.

The estimator must refer to the job specifications while writing up the estimate. This is necessary to account for items that are not specified on the takeoff forms, but must be priced. Items that fall into this category are:

- Plumbing fixture trim
- Painting (if required)
- Tags/charts/identification
- Pipe insulation

- Rigging
- Tests and adjustments

A good habit to acquire is numbering all estimate forms as shown on the sample estimate. This also holds true for all takeoff sheets. In this way, one can put the sheets in order quickly, and be sure that all pages are there.

The Art of Pricing

Although pricing the estimate usually takes less than half the time required for the takeoff, it is more demanding. A takeoff of the same job, performed by two different careful, competent estimators using the same plans, will probably differ only slightly. This is not the case with pricing. Many factors enter into the picture when an estimator prices a job. These are:

- Material costs and availability
- Size and location of job to be bid
- Volume of construction activity in area of job to be bid (if area is inactive, bidding may be very competitive)
- Other jobs currently under contract (workload)
- Labor availability in area of job to be bid
- Union or open shop area
- Labor contract expiration dates

The estimator pricing the job should have all of the above information before assigning any unit prices to the estimate. Pricing a job is more than just taking a material price and labor rate, entering them on the estimate form, and arriving at a bid price. For this reason, job pricing should be reserved for the senior estimator in a contracting office.

Material Pricing and Discounts

As previously mentioned, material costs are in a constant state of change. Therefore, it would be of little value to place any material cost data in this book other than that used for our sample estimate. However, we can discuss how materials are priced and how discounts are taken.

Materials should, of course, always be priced from the latest trade price sheets and quotes issued by a manufacturer. The estimator, however, must realize that the duration of the project might be two or three years. If awarded the job, purchase orders for materials should be issued immediately to ensure that the goods will be received at the current (bid) price. In addition to price sheets, published cost data, such as the current issue of *Means Plumbing Cost Data*, offers the estimator another material price source.

Plumbing contractors are often afforded what is called a *contractor's discount* on materials. Discounts are percentages deducted from list prices, and the amounts of discount vary according to the type and amount of material. For example, fixtures are discounted at a different rate than copper tubing. If a contractor purchases 25 fixtures, his or her rate of discount will be less than a contractor purchasing 250 fixtures.

To avoid confusion or misinterpretation, all prices in our sample estimate are net prices, showing no material discounts. However, it should be noted here that the estimator should apply all discounts afforded at the *bottom* of the material list on the estimate form. If the estimator has a list price of $25,000 for copper tubing and is granted a 25% discount, the bid or net price should be $18,750.

Composition of the Labor Man-Hour

The Man-Hour Production Table that is given in Appendix B is based on certain assumptions. On medium to large projects, work is performed by teams. The number of teams required depends on the size of the project and the stage of work being performed at a particular time. On a plumbing job of average size, a typical crew might be as follows:

1 foreman
4 journeymen plumbers
1 apprentice

On this crew, two men usually work at a specific task, such as installing a fixture or a length of copper tubing. Depending on the specific task, the two-man mix may differ. The number of man-hours shown on the table is a measure of an *average* team's productivity, including the time for supervision by the foreman. Conditions such as weather, hazards or job conditions, all of which affect production, have not been considered. The estimator should evaluate the particular project and adjust the production rates up or down accordingly.

Pricing the Sample Takeoff

Note the first item on page 1 of the estimate sheet (Figure 5.1):

"Water closet wall-hung, flush-valve, seat."

We see from the first page of Appendix B that 2.0 man-hours are required for its installation. This is placed in the labor column. Knowing that 17 units are required, a quick calculation will show that 17 x 2.0 = 34.0 man-hours total are required to install the wall-hung water closets.

To determine the labor cost, the total man-hours must be multiplied by the labor rate in dollars per hour. Appendix C contains a chart of prevailing wage rates for journeymen plumbers in principal U.S. cities. Since the sample project is located in Tampa, Florida, the hourly rate is shown to be $31.35. Thus,

34.0 man-hours x 31.35 per hour = $1,065.90,

which is the total labor cost shown for the water closet.

To this is added the material cost. In this case, the estimator found the current price per unit to be $239.00. The total material price is calculated to be:

17 x 239 = $4,063.00

We are now ready to go through a step-by-step calculation of material and labor costs for all the items transferred to the estimating forms from the takeoff forms in Figures 5.1 through 5.15.

ABC PLUMBING COMPANY, INC.
CONTRACTORS
ANYWHERE, USA

SHEET NO. 1 of 15

PROJECT Three Story Service Center — ESTIMATE NO.

LOCATION Anywhere, USA — CLASSIFICATION Plumbing — DATE 1-9-91

ARCHITECT Jarrett, Assoc. — ESTIMATOR JG — PRICED BY SG — CHECKED BY MG

DESCRIPTION	QUANTITY	UNIT	MATERIAL UNIT COST	MATERIAL TOTAL COST	LABOR UNIT MH	LABOR TOTAL MH	LABOR UNIT RATE	LABOR TOTAL COST	TOTAL COST MAT./LABOR
1. Plumbing Fixtures + Trim									
Water Closet - Wall Hung	17	Ea.	239	4063	2.0	34.0	31.35	1065.90	5128.90
Flush Valve w/Stop + V.B.							↓		
Toilet Seat									
Water Closet - Floor Outlet	3	Ea.	207	621	2.25	6.75		211.61	832.61
Flush Valve									
Toilet Seat									
Closet Flange w/Bolt, nuts, washers									
Wax Gasket									
Lavatories 20"x 18" Wall Hung	26	Ea.	210	5460	1.75	45.5		1426.43	6886.43
Faucet w/Pop-up Waste									
1½"x 1¼" 'P' Trap w/Tail Piece + Esc.									
Pr. 3/8" Supplies w/Angle Stops + Esc.									
Urinals - Wall Hung	3	Ea.	295	885	2.0	6.0		188.10	1073.10
Flush Valve w/Stop + V.B.									
Electric Water Coolers	3	Ea.	575	1725	3.0	9.0		282.15	2007.15
1½" x 1¼" 'P' Trap w/Tail Piece + Esc.									
3/8" Supply w/Angle Stop + Esc.									
Cabinet Sinks 19"x 18"	22	Ea.	300	6600	3.0	66.0	↓	2069.10	8669.10
Faucet w/Gooseneck Discharge									
nozzle + Wrist Action Handles									
8" Centerset + C.I. Drain Plug									
1¼" Tail Piece									
2" 'P' Trap w/Esc.									
Pr. 3/8" Supplies w/Angle Stop + Esc.									
Plumbing Fixtures + Trim									
Total Direct Cost				19354				5243.29	24597.29

Figure 5.1 *The costs shown in this sample estimate are used as examples only. The costs should not be used for estimating purposes.*

ABC PLUMBING COMPANY, INC.
CONTRACTORS
ANYWHERE, USA

SHEET NO. 2 of 15

PROJECT | ESTIMATE NO.

LOCATION | CLASSIFICATION | DATE

ARCHITECT | ESTIMATOR | PRICED BY | CHECKED BY

DESCRIPTION	QUANTITY	UNIT	MATERIAL		LABOR				TOTAL COST MAT./LABOR
			UNIT COST	TOTAL COST	UNIT MH	TOTAL MH	UNIT RATE	TOTAL COST	
2. Sanitary Waste/Vent System									
Below Ground									
6" XHCI Pipe B + S	95	LF	8.93	848.35	.21	19.95	31.35	625.43	1474.78
4" " " "	305		5.76	1756.80	.14	42.70		1334.38	3091.18
2" " " "	150		2.69	403.50	.08	12.0		376.20	779.70
6" XHCI Y	1	Ea.	36.62	36.62	2.11	2.11		66.15	102.77
6x4 Y	5		23.32	116.60	2.11	10.55		330.74	447.34
6x2 Y	1		16.95	16.95	2.11	2.11		66.15	83.10
4" Y	10		20.88	208.80	1.38	13.80		432.63	641.43
4x2 Y	18		13.52	248.36	1.38	24.84		778.73	1022.09
2" Y	4		5.77	23.08	.70	2.80		87.78	110.86
4" Long Turn TY	2		20.88	41.76	1.38	2.76		86.53	128.29
2" Tee	1		7.00	7.00	.70	.70		21.95	28.95
6" 1/8 Bend	1		12.98	12.98	1.06	1.06		33.23	46.21
4" 1/8 Bend	11		8.56	94.16	.70	7.70		241.40	335.56
2" 1/8 Bend	8		2.87	22.96	.36	2.88		90.29	113.25
4" Sweep	8		15.85	126.80	.70	5.60		175.59	302.36
2" Sweep	24		5.77	138.48	.36	8.64		270.86	409.34
2" 1/4 Bend	3		3.59	10.77	.36	1.08		33.86	44.63
4" 'P' Trap w/2" Vent	2		31.27	62.54	.70	1.40		43.89	106.43
4" 'P' Trap	5		17.98	89.90	.70	3.50		109.73	199.63
2" 'P' Trap	1		6.70	6.70	.36	.36		11.29	17.99
6x4 Reducer	1		8.72	8.72	1.06	1.06		33.23	41.95
4x2 Reducer	3		5.07	15.21	.70	2.10		65.84	81.05
Caulking Lead	510	Lbs.	1.04	530.40	–	–		–	530.40
Oakum	51	"	.95	48.45	–	–		–	48.45
Gas	3	CYL	12.00	36.00	–	–		–	36.00
4" Pipe Sleeves	14	Ea.	25.00	350.00	.50	7.0		219.45	569.45
2" " "	22	Ea.	12.00	264.00	.32	7.04		220.70	484.70
4" Floor Drains w/Trap Seal, Valve + Vac. Brk.	7	Ea.	100.00	700.00	1.25	8.75		274.31	974.31
2" " " " " " " "	1		89.00	89.00	1.25	1.25		39.19	128.19
4" Cleanout Deck Plate	4		55.00	220.00	.75	3.0		94.05	314.05
2" " " "	2		49.00	98.00	.75	1.50		47.03	145.03
Sanitary Waste/Vent - Below Ground									
Total Direct Cost				6627.89				6210.58	12838.47

Figure 5.2 *The costs shown in this sample estimate are used as examples only. The costs should not be used for estimating purposes.*

ABC PLUMBING COMPANY, INC.
CONTRACTORS
ANYWHERE, USA

SHEET NO. 3 of 15

PROJECT | ESTIMATE NO.

LOCATION | CLASSIFICATION | DATE

ARCHITECT | ESTIMATOR | PRICED BY | CHECKED BY

DESCRIPTION	QUANTITY	UNIT	MATERIAL		LABOR				TOTAL COST MAT./LABOR
			UNIT COST	TOTAL COST	UNIT MH	TOTAL MH	UNIT RATE	TOTAL COST	
3. Sanitary Waste/Vent System Above Ground									
4" SWCI Hubless Pipe	315	LF	2.97	935.55	.14	44.10	31.35	1382.54	2318.09
3" " " "	250	"	2.29	572.50	.10	25.0		783.75	1356.25
2" " " "	310	"	1.66	514.60	.07	21.70		680.30	1194.90
1½" " " "	725	"	1.58	1145.50	.04	29.0		909.15	2054.65
4" SWCI Hubless Y	5	Ea.	6.98	34.90	1.0	5.0		156.75	191.65
4x3 Y	2		5.83	11.66	1.0	2.0		62.70	74.36
4x2 Y	2		4.35	8.10	1.0	2.0		62.70	70.80
3x2 Y	6		3.39	20.34	.88	5.28		165.53	185.87
3x 1½ Y	6		3.39	20.34	.88	5.28		165.53	185.87
4" TY	2		6.19	12.38	1.0	2.0		62.70	75.08
3"x2" TY	1		3.67	3.67	.88	.88		27.59	31.26
3 x 1½ TY	1		3.67	3.67	.88	.88		27.59	31.26
1½" TY	25		2.95	73.75	.62	15.50		485.93	559.68
2x 1½ Long Turn TY	25		3.43	85.75	.75	18.75		587.81	673.56
1½" " " TY	6		3.15	18.90	.62	3.72		116.62	135.52
4" Tee	1		6.19	6.19	1.0	1.0		31.35	37.54
4x3 Tee	2		5.62	11.24	1.0	2.0		62.70	73.94
4x2 Tee	6		4.71	28.50	1.0	6.0		188.10	216.60
2" Tee	4		3.31	13.24	.75	3.0		94.05	107.29
2x Red. Tee	10		3.31	33.10	.75	7.50		235.13	268.25
1½" Tee	15		2.95	44.25	.62	9.30		291.56	335.81
4" P Trap	2		13.45	26.90	.66	1.32		41.38	68.28
4" Sweep	6		9.18	55.08	.66	3.96		124.15	179.23
2" Sweep	7		4.90	34.30	.49	3.43		107.53	141.83
1½" Sweep	12		4.83	57.96	.41	4.92		154.24	212.20
4" ⅛ Bend	4		3.35	13.40	.66	2.64		82.76	96.16
3" ⅛ Bend	2		2.55	5.10	.58	1.16		36.37	41.47
2" ⅛ Bend	13		1.79	23.27	.49	6.37		199.64	222.91
1½" ⅛ Bend	20		1.75	35.00	.41	8.20		257.07	292.07
4" ¼ Bend	1		4.67	4.67	.66	.66		20.69	25.36
3" ¼ Bend	3		3.11	9.33	.58	1.74		54.55	63.88
2" ¼ Bend	11		2.35	25.85	.49	5.39		168.98	194.83
1½" ¼ Bend	55		2.23	122.65	.41	22.55		706.94	829.59
3x2 Cross TY	6		7.06	42.36	1.17	7.02		220.08	262.44
2" Cross TY	1		4.99	4.99	1.0	1.0		31.35	36.34
4x3 Reducer	1		2.55	2.55	.66	.66		20.69	23.24
3x2 Reducer	2		1.67	3.34	.58	1.16		36.37	39.71
2x 1½ Reducer	22		1.63	35.86	.49	3.92		122.89	158.75
4" Closet Bends	3		13.85	41.55	1.0	3.0		94.05	135.60
continued				4142.29				9059.81	13202.10

Figure 5.3 *The costs shown in this sample estimate are used as examples only. The costs should not be used for estimating purposes.*

ABC PLUMBING COMPANY, INC.
CONTRACTORS
ANYWHERE, USA

SHEET NO. 4 of 15

PROJECT | ESTIMATE NO.

LOCATION | CLASSIFICATION | DATE

ARCHITECT | ESTIMATOR | PRICED BY | CHECKED BY

DESCRIPTION	QUAN-TITY	UNIT	MATERIAL UNIT COST	MATERIAL TOTAL COST	LABOR UNIT MH	LABOR TOTAL MH	LABOR UNIT RATE	LABOR TOTAL COST	TOTAL COST MAT./LABOR
3. Sanitary Waste/Vent - Aboveground - Continued	Brought Fwd.			4142.29				9059.81	13202.10
4" SWCI Hubless Test Tee Plug	1	Ea.	7.91	7.91	.66	.66	31.35	20.69	28.55
3"	2		4.75	9.50	.58	1.16		36.37	45.87
4" Co w/ Plug	1		3.75	3.75	.33	.33		10.35	14.10
2" C.O. w/ Plug	1		2.56	2.56	.25	.25		7.84	10.40
3x4 Increaser	2		4.27	8.54	.58	1.16		36.37	44.91
4" Roof Coupling	8		20.00	160.00	.66	5.28		165.53	325.53
3" Roof Coupling	2		17.00	34.00	.58	1.16		36.37	70.37
4" Hubless Coupling	155	Ea.	2.58	399.90	–	–		–	399.90
3"	115		2.23	256.45	–	–		–	256.45
2"	234		1.84	430.56	–	–		–	430.56
1½"	521		1.84	958.64	–	–		–	958.64
4" Double Water Closet Carriers	6	Ea.	290.	1740.00	2.0	12.0		376.20	2116.20
4" Single " "	5		156.	780.00	2.0	10.0		313.50	1093.50
Lavatory Carriers	26		97.	2522.00	2.0	52.0		1630.20	4152.20
Urinal Carriers	3		103.	309.00	1.5	4.5		141.08	450.08
4" Pipe Sleeves	8	Ea.	25.	200.00	.50	4.0		125.40	325.40
3" " "	17		18.	306.00	.45	7.65		239.83	545.83
1½" " "	1		11.	11.00	.28	.28		8.78	19.78
4" Hanger Assemblies	62	Ea.	7.11	440.82	.36	22.32		699.73	1140.55
3" " "	50		6.43	321.50	.36	18.0		564.30	885.80
2" " "	26		5.70	148.20	.36	9.36		293.44	441.64
1½" " "	60		5.66	339.60	.36	21.60		677.16	1016.76
Sump Pump - Simplex	1	Ea.	175.	175.00	6.0	6.0		188.10	363.10
9 GPM, 1/3 HP, 24' Head, 1750 RPM, 120V, 1Ø									
1½" Gate Valve	1	Ea.	24.	24.00	.66	.66		165.53	189.53
1½" Check Valve	1	Ea.	28.	28.00	.66	.66		165.53	193.53
4" Floor Drains w/Trap Seal Valve + V.B.	2	Ea.	100.	200.00	1.25	2.50		78.38	278.38
Sheetlead Flashing (12)	192	Lbs.	1.10	211.20	1.0	12.0		376.20	587.40
Sanitary Waste/Vent Above Ground Total Direct Cost				14,170.42				15,416.64	29,587.06

Figure 5.4 *The costs shown in this sample estimate are used as examples only. The costs should not be used for estimating purposes.*

ABC PLUMBING COMPANY, INC.
CONTRACTORS
ANYWHERE, USA

SHEET NO. 5 of 15

PROJECT | ESTIMATE NO.

LOCATION | CLASSIFICATION | DATE

ARCHITECT | ESTIMATOR | PRICED BY | CHECKED BY

DESCRIPTION	QUANTITY	UNIT	MATERIAL UNIT COST	MATERIAL TOTAL COST	LABOR UNIT MH	LABOR TOTAL MH	LABOR UNIT RATE	LABOR TOTAL COST	TOTAL COST MAT./LABOR
4. Storm System- Below Ground									
8" XHCI Pipe B & S	75	LF	13.44	1008.	.32	24.0	31.35	752.40	1760.40
6" " " "	70		8.93	625.10	.21	14.70		460.85	1085.95
4" " " "	115		5.76	662.40	.14	16.10		504.74	1167.14
8"x4" XHCI Y	4	Ea.	43.48	173.92	3.13	12.52		392.50	566.42
6 x 4 Y	2		23.32	46.64	2.11	4.22		132.30	178.94
4" Y	4		20.88	83.52	1.38	5.52		173.05	256.57
4" Sweep	13		15.85	206.05	.70	9.10		285.29	491.34
4" 1/8 Bend	7		8.56	59.92	.70	4.90		153.62	213.54
8 x 6 Reducer	1		19.73	19.73	1.57	1.57		49.22	68.95
6 x 4 Reducer	1		8.72	8.72	1.06	1.06		33.23	41.95
4" Cleanout Deck Plate	4	Ea.	55.	220.	.75	3.0		94.05	314.05
8" Pipe Sleeves	1	Ea.	40.	40.	.63	.63		19.75	59.75
4" Pipe Sleeves	11	Ea.	25.	275.	.40	4.40		137.94	412.94
Caulking Lead	315	Lbs.	1.04	327.60	–	–		–	327.60
Oakum	32	Lbs.	.95	30.40	–	–		–	30.40
Gas	2	Cyl.	12.	24.	–	–		–	24.00
Storm System- Below Ground Total Direct Cost				3811.00				3188.94	6999.94

Figure 5.5 *The costs shown in this sample estimate are used as examples only. The costs should not be used for estimating purposes.*

ABC PLUMBING COMPANY, INC.
CONTRACTORS
ANYWHERE, USA

SHEET NO. 6 of 15

ESTIMATE NO.

PROJECT

LOCATION CLASSIFICATION DATE

ARCHITECT ESTIMATOR PRICED BY CHECKED BY

DESCRIPTION	QUANTITY	UNIT	MATERIAL UNIT COST	MATERIAL TOTAL COST	LABOR UNIT MH	LABOR TOTAL MH	LABOR UNIT RATE	LABOR TOTAL COST	TOTAL COST MAT./LABOR
5. Storm System-Above Ground									
4" SWCI Hubless Pipe	490	LF	2.97	1455.30	.14	6.86	31.35	215.06	1670.36
3" " "	50	LF	2.29	114.50	.10	5.0		156.75	271.25
4" SWCI Hubless Long Turn TY	3	Ea.	9.70	29.10	1.0	3.0		94.05	123.15
4" Y	5		6.98	34.90	1.0	5.0		156.75	191.65
4" Sweep	7		9.18	64.26	.66	4.62		144.84	209.10
3" Sweep	2		5.55	11.10	.58	1.16		36.37	47.47
4" 1/4 Bend	12		4.67	56.04	.66	7.92		248.29	304.33
3" 1/4 Bend	2		3.11	6.22	.58	1.16		36.37	42.59
4" 1/8 Bend	8		3.35	26.80	.66	5.28		165.53	192.33
4" Test Tee w/ Plug	7		7.91	55.37	.66	4.62		144.84	200.21
3" " " " "	2		4.75	9.50	.58	1.16		36.37	45.87
4" C.O. w/ Plug	3		3.75	11.25	.33	.99		31.04	42.29
4x3 Reducer	2		2.55	5.10	.66	1.32		41.38	46.48
4" Hubless Couplings	195	Ea.	2.58	503.10	–	–		–	503.10
3" " "	24	Ea.	2.23	53.52	–	–		–	53.52
4" Pipe Sleeves	22	Ea.	25.	550.	.40	8.80		275.88	825.88
3" " "	2	Ea.	18.	36.	.32	.64		20.06	56.06
4" Hanger Assemblies	98	Ea.	7.11	696.78	.36	35.28		1106.03	1802.81
3" " "	10	Ea.	6.43	64.30	.36	3.60		112.86	177.16
4" Roof Drains w/Integral Expansion Jt. Brass Sleeve, Sediment Cup, Flashing, Clamp + Gravel Stop	12	Ea.	165.	1980.	1.50	18.0		564.30	2544.30
3" Roof Drains - Same as 4"	2	Ea.	155.	310.	1.50	3.0		94.05	404.05
Sheet Lead Flashing (14)	224	Lbs.	1.10	246.40	1.0	14.0		438.90	685.30
Storm System- Above Ground Total Direct Cost				6319.54				4119.72	10,439.26

Figure 5.6 *The costs shown in this sample estimate are used as examples only. The costs should not be used for estimating purposes.*

ABC PLUMBING COMPANY, INC.
CONTRACTORS
ANYWHERE, USA

SHEET NO. 7 of 15

PROJECT ESTIMATE NO.

LOCATION CLASSIFICATION DATE

ARCHITECT ESTIMATOR PRICED BY CHECKED BY

DESCRIPTION	QUANTITY	UNIT	MATERIAL UNIT COST	MATERIAL TOTAL COST	LABOR UNIT MH	LABOR TOTAL MH	LABOR UNIT RATE	LABOR TOTAL COST	TOTAL COST MAT./LABOR
6. Hot + Cold Water System									
3" Type "K" Copper	70	LF	7.10	497.	.12	8.40	31.35	263.34	760.34
2½" " " "	50		5.14	257.	.09	4.50		141.08	398.08
2" " " "	115		3.55	408.25	.06	6.90		216.32	624.57
1½" Type "L" Copper	305		1.94	591.70	.06	18.30		573.71	1165.41
1¼" " " "	215		1.52	326.80	.05	10.75		337.01	663.81
1" " " "	435		1.12	487.20	.04	17.40		545.49	1032.69
¾" " " "	1500		.80	1200.	.03	45.0		1410.75	2610.75
½" " " "	470		.51	239.70	.03	14.10		442.04	681.74
3" Copper Wrot Ells	7	Ea.	18.15	127.05	.89	6.23		195.31	322.36
2½"	1		12.90	12.90	.70	.70		21.95	34.85
2"	3		6.83	20.49	.57	1.71		53.61	74.10
1½"	23		3.75	86.25	.50	11.50		360.53	446.78
1¼"	6		2.65	15.90	.43	2.58		80.88	96.78
1"	35		1.54	53.90	.39	13.65		427.93	481.83
¾"	58		.65	37.70	.32	18.56		581.86	619.56
½"	143		.29	41.47	.29	41.47		1300.08	1341.55
3 x Red. Tee	5		30.50	152.50	1.34	6.70		210.05	362.55
2½ x Red.	3		27.50	82.50	1.05	3.15		98.75	181.25
2 x Red.	4		9.05	36.20	.86	3.44		107.84	144.04
1½ x Red.	30		6.08	182.40	.75	22.50		705.38	887.78
1¼ x Red.	10		5.35	53.50	.65	6.50		203.78	257.28
1 x Red.	11		3.68	40.48	.59	6.49		203.46	243.94
¾ x Red.	53		1.11	58.83	.48	25.44		797.54	856.37
1¼"	1		5.55	5.55	.65	.65		20.38	25.93
1"	1		3.50	3.50	.59	.59		18.50	22.00
¾"	8		1.71	13.68	.48	3.84		120.38	134.06
½"	2		.49	.98	.43	.86		26.96	27.94
1½" 45	4		3.78	15.12	.50	2.0		62.70	77.82
1¼"	1		3.15	3.15	.43	.43		13.48	16.63
1"	2		2.29	4.58	.39	.78		24.45	29.03
¾"	14		.89	12.46	.32	4.48		140.45	152.91
½"	29		.53	15.37	.29	8.41		263.65	279.02
1½ x Red. Ell	1		10.60	10.60	.50	.50		15.68	26.28
¾ x Red. Ell	2		1.64	3.28	.32	.64		20.06	23.34
1½" Cap	1		1.81	1.81	.25	.25		7.84	9.65
1¼"	1		1.25	1.25	.22	.22		6.90	8.15
1"	1		.87	.87	.20	.20		6.27	7.14
¾"	6		.35	2.10	.16	.96		30.10	32.20
½"	2		.20	.40	.15	.30		9.41	9.81
Continued				5104.42				10,065.90	15,170.32

Figure 5.7 *The costs shown in this sample estimate are used as examples only. The costs should not be used for estimating purposes.*

ABC PLUMBING COMPANY, INC.
CONTRACTORS
ANYWHERE, USA

SHEET NO. 8 of 15

PROJECT | ESTIMATE NO.

LOCATION | CLASSIFICATION | DATE

ARCHITECT | ESTIMATOR | PRICED BY | CHECKED BY

DESCRIPTION	QUANTITY	UNIT	MATERIAL UNIT COST	MATERIAL TOTAL COST	LABOR UNIT MH	LABOR TOTAL MH	LABOR UNIT RATE	LABOR TOTAL COST	TOTAL COST MAT./LABOR
6. Hot & Cold Water - Continued	Brought Fwd.			5104.42				10065.90	15170.32
3" Copper Wrot Coupling	2	Ea.	11.15	22.30	.89	1.78	31.35	55.80	78.10
2½"	2		6.08	12.16	.70	1.40		43.89	56.05
2"	5		3.40	17.00	.57	2.85		89.35	106.35
1½"	11		2.74	30.14	.50	5.50		172.43	202.57
1¼"	7		1.71	11.97	.43	3.01		94.36	106.33
1"	12		.98	11.76	.39	4.68		146.72	158.48
3/4"	29		.48	13.92	.32	9.28		290.93	304.85
1/2"	10		.24	2.40	.29	2.90		90.92	93.32
1 x Red. XFE Adapters	1		1.45	1.45	.39	.39		12.23	13.68
1"	18		2.70	48.60	.20	3.60		112.86	161.46
3/4"	9		1.32	11.88	.16	1.44		45.14	57.02
1/2"	54		.94	50.76	.15	8.10		253.94	304.70
Miscellaneous Brass Nipples	60	Ea.	8.87	532.20	.04	2.40		75.24	607.44
3" Pipe Sleeves	2	Ea.	20.	40.	.45	.90		28.22	68.22
2½"	1		17.	17.	.40	.40		12.54	29.54
2"	1		14.	14.	.32	.32		10.03	24.03
1½"	25		12.	300.	.28	7.0		219.45	519.45
3" Hanger Assemblies	7	Ea.	9.32	65.24	.36	2.52		79.00	144.24
2½"	5		8.59	42.95	.36	1.80		56.43	99.38
2"	12		6.07	72.84	.36	4.32		135.43	208.27
1½"	31		5.63	174.53	.36	11.16		349.87	524.40
1¼"	36		5.53	199.08	.36	12.96		406.30	605.38
1"	13		5.40	70.20	.36	4.68		146.72	216.92
3/4"	250		5.21	1302.50	.36	90.0		2821.50	4124.00
1/2"	78		5.07	395.46	.36	28.08		880.31	1275.77
Solder 95/5	17	Lbs.	11.80	200.60	–	–		–	200.60
Flux	2	"	4.05	8.10	–	–		–	8.10
Gas	3	Cyl.	12.	36.	–	–		–	36.00
Access Panels	11	Ea.	30.	330.	1.0	11.0		344.85	674.85
Continued				9139.46				17040.36	26179.82

Figure 5.8 *The costs shown in this sample estimate are used as examples only. The costs should not be used for estimating purposes.*

ABC PLUMBING COMPANY, INC.
CONTRACTORS
ANYWHERE, USA

SHEET NO. 9 of 15

PROJECT — ESTIMATE NO.

LOCATION — CLASSIFICATION — DATE

ARCHITECT — ESTIMATOR — PRICED BY — CHECKED BY

			MATERIAL		LABOR				TOTAL
DESCRIPTION	QUANTITY	UNIT	UNIT COST	TOTAL COST	UNIT MH	TOTAL MH	UNIT RATE	TOTAL COST	TOTAL COST MAT./LABOR
6. Hot + Cold Water - Continued	Brought Fwd.			9139.46				17040.36	26,179.82
3" Gate Valves	3	Ea.	166.	498.	.98	2.94	31.35	92.17	590.17
2½"	1		119.	119.	.77	.77		24.14	143.14
2"	2		56.	112.	.63	1.26		39.50	151.50
1½"	9		35.	315.	.54	4.86		152.36	467.36
1¼"	3		29.	87.	.47	1.41		44.20	131.20
1"	7		21.	147.	.41	2.87		89.97	236.97
¾"	58		16.	928.	.34	19.72		618.22	1546.22
½"	22		13.	286.	.30	6.60		206.91	492.91
3" Check Valve	1		155.	155.	.98	.98		30.72	185.72
1¼"	2		30.	60.	.47	.94		29.47	89.47
¾"	9		14.	126.	.34	3.06		95.93	221.93
¾" Balancing Valve	5		17.	85.	.34	1.70		53.30	138.30
½" Temp. + Press. Relief Valve	1		9.	9.	.30	.30		9.41	18.41
¾" Non-Freeze Wall Hydrants	6		75.	450.	.50	3.0		94.05	544.05
3" Domestic Compound Water Meter	1	Ea.	750.	750.	2.50	2.50		78.38	828.38
Elec. Hot Water Heater - 73.8 GPH	1	Ea.	650.	650.	6.0	6.0		188.10	838.10
@ 100° Rise Recov. 120 GPH (3) Element									
18 KW, 480 V, 3Φ									
¾" HW Circulator Pump - Inline Direct	1	Ea.	230.	230.	1.25	1.25		39.19	269.19
Conn. 1750 RPM, 1/6 HP, 115V, 1Φ									
Hot + Cold Water System									
Total Direct Cost				14,146.40				18,926.38	33,072.84

Figure 5.9 *The costs shown in this sample estimate are used as examples only. The costs should not be used for estimating purposes.*

ABC PLUMBING COMPANY, INC.
CONTRACTORS
ANYWHERE, USA

SHEET NO. 10 of 15

PROJECT | ESTIMATE NO.

LOCATION | CLASSIFICATION | DATE

ARCHITECT | ESTIMATOR | PRICED BY | CHECKED BY

DESCRIPTION	QUANTITY	UNIT	MATERIAL UNIT COST	MATERIAL TOTAL COST	LABOR UNIT MH	LABOR TOTAL MH	LABOR UNIT RATE	LABOR TOTAL COST	TOTAL COST MAT./LABOR
7. Natural Gas System									
2" Black Steel Sch. 40 Pipe	30	LF	2.83	84.90	.07	2.10	31.35	65.84	150.74
1½" " " " " "	30	"	2.09	62.70	.06	1.80	↓	56.43	119.13
2" Black Mal. Ells	4	Ea.	3.61	14.44	.67	2.68		84.02	98.46
1½" " " "	3	"	2.46	7.38	.57	1.71		53.61	60.99
2 x Red. " " Tee	1	"	6.03	6.03	1.01	1.01		31.66	37.69
1½" Black Nipples	2	Ea.	3.98	7.96	.03	.06		1.88	9.84
2" Pipe Sleeves	1	Ea.	12.	12.	.32	.32		10.03	22.03
2" Hanger Assemblies	2	Ea.	5.70	11.40	.36	.72		22.57	33.97
1½" " "	2	"	5.66	11.32	.36	.72		22.57	33.89
2" Gas Cocks	1	Ea.	32.	32.	.80	.80		25.08	57.08
1½" " "	2	"	23.	46.	.75	1.50	↓	47.03	93.03
Natural Gas System									
Total Direct Cost				296.13				420.72	716.85

Figure 5.10 *The costs shown in this sample estimate are used as examples only. The costs should not be used for estimating purposes.*

ABC PLUMBING COMPANY, INC.
CONTRACTORS
ANYWHERE, USA

SHEET NO. 11 of 15

PROJECT | ESTIMATE NO.

LOCATION | CLASSIFICATION | DATE

ARCHITECT | ESTIMATOR | PRICED BY | CHECKED BY

DESCRIPTION	QUANTITY	UNIT	MATERIAL UNIT COST	MATERIAL TOTAL COST	LABOR UNIT MH	LABOR TOTAL MH	LABOR UNIT RATE	LABOR TOTAL COST	TOTAL COST MAT./LABOR
8. Fire Standpipe System									
3" Black Steel Sch. 40 Pipe	130	LF	5.93	770.90	.11	14.30	31.35	448.31	1219.21
2½"	25		4.52	113.00	.10	2.50		78.38	191.38
1½"	15		2.09	31.35	.06	.90		28.22	59.57
1"	10		1.36	13.60	.04	.40		12.54	26.14
3" Black Mal. Ells	10	Ea.	13.69	136.90	1.62	16.20		507.87	644.77
2½"	6		9.17	55.02	1.35	8.10		253.94	308.96
1½"	6		2.46	14.76	.57	3.42		107.22	121.98
1"	2		1.14	2.28	.47	.94		29.47	31.75
3 x Red. Tee	8		19.43	155.44	2.44	19.52		611.95	767.39
3"	1		21.24	21.24	2.44	2.44		76.49	97.73
2½ x Red.	1		14.55	14.55	2.03	2.03		63.64	78.19
½"	1		.75	.75	.58	.58		18.18	18.93
2½" Cap	1		4.71	4.71	.65	.65		20.38	25.09
½" Plug	1		.90	.90	.19	.19		5.96	6.86
2½" Blk. Nipples	3	Ea.	10.49	31.47	.05	.15		4.70	36.17
1½"	3		3.98	11.94	.04	.12		3.76	15.70
1"	1		2.72	2.72	.03	.03		.94	3.66
½"	3		1.51	4.53	.03	.09		2.82	7.35
3" Pipe Sleeves	2	Ea.	18.00	36.00	.45	.90		28.22	64.22
3" Hanger Assemblies	11	Ea.	18.00	198.00	.36	3.96		124.15	322.15
2½"	2		15.00	30.00	.36	.72		22.57	52.57
1½"	2		11.00	22.00	.36	.72		22.57	44.57
1"	1		7.00	7.00	.36	.36		11.29	18.29
3" I.B. OS+Y Valve	1	Ea.	152.	152.00	2.05	2.05		64.27	216.27
3" Check Valve	2		132.	264.00	2.05	4.10		128.54	392.54
3"x 2½" x 2½" Siamese Conn.	1		320.	320.00	3.0	3.0		94.05	414.05
Fire Hose Cabinet w/Rack + Valves	3		350.	1050.00	3.0	9.0		282.15	1332.15
Pressure Gauge	1		75.	75.00	.30	.30		9.41	84.41
1" Air Chamber	1		15.	15.00	.30	.30		9.41	24.41
1" Auto Ball Drip	1		35.	35.00	.30	.30		9.41	44.41
Fire Standpipe System Total Direct Cost				3590.06				3080.81	6670.87

Figure 5.11 *The costs shown in this sample estimate are used as examples only. The costs should not be used for estimating purposes.*

ABC PLUMBING COMPANY, INC.
CONTRACTORS
ANYWHERE, USA

SHEET NO. 12 of 15

PROJECT | ESTIMATE NO.

LOCATION | CLASSIFICATION | DATE

ARCHITECT | ESTIMATOR | PRICED BY | CHECKED BY

DESCRIPTION	QUANTITY	UNIT	MATERIAL UNIT COST	MATERIAL TOTAL COST	LABOR UNIT MH	LABOR TOTAL MH	LABOR UNIT RATE	LABOR TOTAL COST	TOTAL COST MAT./LABOR
9. Insulation									
4" Pipe Insulation 1/2" Thick (Storm)	250	LF	2.85	712.50	.073	18.25	31.90	582.18	1294.68
3" "	20		2.40	48.00	.070	1.40		44.66	92.66
3" (Water)	70		2.40	168.00	.070	4.90		156.31	324.31
2 1/2"	50		2.10	105.00	.067	3.35		106.87	211.87
2"	115		1.90	218.50	.065	7.48		238.61	457.11
1 1/2"	305		1.70	518.50	.055	16.78		535.28	1053.78
1 1/4"	215		1.60	344.00	.050	10.75		342.93	686.93
1"	435		1.52	661.20	.050	21.75		693.83	1355.03
3/4"	1500		1.46	2190.00	.045	67.50		2153.25	4343.25
1/2"	470		1.35	634.50	.045	21.15		674.69	1309.19
Insulation									
Total Direct Cost				5600.20				5528.61	11128.81

Figure 5.12 *The costs shown in this sample estimate are used as examples only. The costs should not be used for estimating purposes.*

ABC PLUMBING COMPANY, INC.
CONTRACTORS
ANYWHERE, USA

SHEET NO. 13 of 15

PROJECT ESTIMATE NO.

LOCATION CLASSIFICATION DATE

ARCHITECT ESTIMATOR PRICED BY CHECKED BY

DESCRIPTION	QUAN-TITY	UNIT	MATERIAL UNIT COST	MATERIAL TOTAL COST	LABOR UNIT MH	LABOR TOTAL MH	LABOR UNIT RATE	LABOR TOTAL COST	TOTAL COST MAT./LABOR
10. Sitework									
10A Water + Fire Service									
4" Ductile Iron Pipe Cem. Lined m.J.	22	LF	8.36	183.92	.13	2.86	31.35	89.66	273.58
3" " " " " " "	100	"	7.68	768.00	.11	11.0		344.85	1112.85
4" Ductile Iron M.J. Cem. Lined Cap	1	Ea.	9.95	9.95	Incl.	with Pipe		—	9.95
4x3 " " " " " Tee	1	"	89.80	89.80	"	"	"	—	89.80
3" " " " " " Ell	4	"	29.30	117.20	"	"	"	—	117.20
4" m.J. Gate Valve w/Box	1	Ea.	408.	408.00	3.0	3.0		94.05	502.05
3" " " " "	2	"	353.	706.00	3.0	6.0		188.10	894.10
6x4 Wet Connection	1	Ea.	795.	795.00	3.0	3.0		94.05	889.05
6x3 " "	1	"	795.	795.00	3.0	3.0		94.05	889.05
Water + Fire Service									
Total Direct Cost				3872.87				904.76	4777.63

Figure 5.13 *The costs shown in this sample estimate are used as examples only. The costs should not be used for estimating purposes.*

ABC PLUMBING COMPANY, INC.
CONTRACTORS
ANYWHERE, USA

SHEET NO. 14 of 15

PROJECT | ESTIMATE NO.
LOCATION | CLASSIFICATION | DATE
ARCHITECT | ESTIMATOR | PRICED BY | CHECKED BY

DESCRIPTION	QUANTITY	UNIT	MATERIAL UNIT COST	MATERIAL TOTAL COST	LABOR UNIT MH	LABOR TOTAL MH	LABOR UNIT RATE	LABOR TOTAL COST	TOTAL COST MAT./LABOR
10. Sitework - Continued									
10B Storm Sewer									
8" XH Terracotta Pipe	400	LF	2.67	1068.	.12	48.0	31.35	1504.80	2572.80
4" " " "	40	"	1.03	41.20	.10	4.0	↓	125.40	166.60
3" Bituminous Fibre Pipe	40	"	1.16	46.40	.10	4.0		125.40	171.80
8" Terracotta Y	5	Ea.	29.40	147.	Incl.	with pipe		–	147.00
8x4 Y	1	↓	29.40	29.40	↓	↓		–	29.40
8x3 Y	1		29.40	29.40				–	29.40
8" Sweep	5		29.40	147.				–	147.00
8" 1/8 Bend	3		29.40	88.20				–	88.20
4" 1/8 Bend	1		12.10	12.10				–	12.10
Catch Basins 1.99 Ft. Dp.	1	Ea.	575.	575.00	4.0	4.0		125.40	700.40
2.31	1	↓	↓	↓	↓	↓		↓	↓
2.63	1								
2.75	1								
3.23	1								
Lamp Holes	5	Ea.	50.	250.00	3.0	15.0		470.25	720.25
Connect new 8" storm sewer to existing catch basin	1	Ea.	50.	50.00	6.0	6.0		188.10	238.10
Connect new catch basin to existing 8" storm sewer	1	Ea.	50.	50.00	6.0	6.0	↓	188.10	238.10
Storm Sewer Total Direct Cost				4833.70				3229.05	8062.75

Figure 5.14 The costs shown in this sample estimate are used as examples only. The costs should not be used for estimating purposes.

ABC PLUMBING COMPANY, INC.
CONTRACTORS
ANYWHERE, USA

SHEET NO. 15 of 15

PROJECT | ESTIMATE NO.
LOCATION | CLASSIFICATION | DATE
ARCHITECT | ESTIMATOR | PRICED BY | CHECKED BY

DESCRIPTION	QUANTITY	UNIT	MATERIAL UNIT COST	MATERIAL TOTAL COST	LABOR UNIT MH	LABOR TOTAL MH	LABOR UNIT RATE	LABOR TOTAL COST	TOTAL COST MAT./LABOR
10. Sitework- Continued									
10C Sanitary Sewer									
6" XHCI Soil Pipe B & S	65	LF	8.93	580.45	.21	13.65	31.35	427.93	1008.38
12"x6" XHCI Y	1	Ea.	108.05	108.05	5.46	5.46		171.17	279.22
6" 1/8 Bend	1	"	12.98	12.98	1.06	1.06		33.23	46.21
Connect new 6" Sanitary Sewer to existing 12" Sewer	1	Ea.	75.	75.00	6.0	6.0		188.10	263.10
Caulking Lead	65	Lbs.	1.04	67.60	–	–		–	67.60
Oakum	6	"	.95	5.70	–	–		–	5.70
Gas	1	Cyl.	12.	12.00	–	–		–	12.00
Sanitary Sewer Total Direct Cost				861.78				820.43	1682.21

Figure 5.15 *The costs shown in this sample estimate are used as examples only. The costs should not be used for estimating purposes.*

Chapter 6

MARKING UP AND COMPLETING THE ESTIMATE

The estimator has now arrived at direct costs for all the systems within the estimate, direct cost being the cost *of a project prior to the addition of any supplementary expenses*, such as overhead and profit. At this point, the estimator transfers all the direct cost totals, both material and labor, onto the project summary sheet to apply the necessary markups. *Markups* are all the supplementary costs necessary to arrive at a bid price.

Breakdown of Markups

The following is a list of items that comprise the markup of most plumbing estimates:

1. *Sales tax (material only)*: At this writing, some states are contemplating changes that would base sales tax on the *total contract bid* or *selling price* rather than on material only.
2. *Field overhead*
   a. Temporary facilities
   b. Trailer field office
   c. Tools
   d. Engineering/shop drawings
   e. Job supervision
3. *Office overhead*
4. *Permits and fees*
5. *Insurance*
6. *Bid bond*
7. *Profit*

Sales Tax

This is the prescribed local tax imposed on all purchased materials. The amount of sales tax to be included in the estimate is determined by the cost of materials and the tax rate in the area of the project. (In some areas there are both city and state sales taxes.)

Field Overhead

These items are the overhead costs attributed to the particular job being bid.

1. **Temporary Facilities:** For the plumbing contractor, temporary facilities are the provision of water and/or sanitary facilities during construction. Depending on the particular project requirements, temporary water and sanitary facilities may mean providing only a

fresh water outlet and a rented portable toilet. On the other hand, temporary facilities may mean providing metered water to the construction site with cold water outlets on every floor, in addition to working toilets in a temporary structure on the site or in the building under construction. There is a wide range of possibilities regarding temporary facilities, from relatively inexpensive to very expensive set-ups. Temporary facilities should be estimated on an individual project basis. The estimator should take great care in interpreting the temporary facilities section in the job specifications. When estimated, temporary facilities costs should be entered as a lump sum cost on the summary sheet (Figures 6.1 and 6.2).

Summary Sheet

ABC PLUMBING COMPANY, INC.
CONTRACTORS
ANYWHERE, USA

SHEET NO.

PROJECT ESTIMATE NO.

LOCATION CLASSIFICATION DATE

ARCHITECT ESTIMATOR PRICED BY CHECKED BY

DESCRIPTION	QUAN-TITY	UNIT	MATERIAL		LABOR				TOTAL COST MAT./LABOR
			UNIT COST	TOTAL COST	UNIT MH	TOTAL MH	UNIT RATE	TOTAL COST	

Figure 6.1

2. **Trailer Field Office:** A prime contractor on a project usually includes in the bid provisions for a field office or trailer. The field office is furnished with office equipment such as plan tables, desks, file cabinets, and telephones, all of which become part of the field office expense. To estimate field office expenses, the estimator must envision the duration of the project to calculate trailer rentals, office equipment rentals, telephone charges, light, and power charges.
3. **Tools:** An allowance for small tools should be included in the field overhead expenses. Tools such as pipe wrenches, caulking irons, and pipe threading machines inevitably get worn out, damaged, stolen, or lost. The tool allowance can be estimated by consulting the purchasing records for small tools on previous projects, usually expressed as a percentage of the project labor.
4. **Engineering and Shop Drawings:** In anticipation of being awarded the contract, the estimator should include in the field overhead costs an allowance for engineering and shop drawings. This allowance should cover the expenses incurred by the contractor to develop dimensioned layout drawings necessary to coordinate the project. The allowance should also include the preparation of any reçord, or "as-built," drawing sets furnished to the owner.
5. **Job Supervision:** This is time charged by foremen and others for supervising productive labor. Depending on the project, the estimator may want to carry this cost at the full salary of the superintendent every week for the duration of the project, at full salary part-time, or at partial salary full-time.

Depending on the project, field overhead can range from 5% to 15% of the total direct cost of the job.

Office Overhead

A contractor incurs project-related expenses in running the main office, shop, and yard. Examples of these expenses are rent; utilities; wages for draftsmen, secretaries, clerks and estimators; taxes, stationery and office equipment. The office overhead, depending on the project, can range from two to four percent of the sum of the total direct cost and field overhead.

Permits and Fees

Most local municipalities require the plumbing contractor to obtain permits for installation of plumbing, based on the number of fixtures. Depending on local jurisdiction, permits may range in cost from one to ten dollars per fixture.

Insurance

The insurance the plumbing contractor will have to carry depends on local laws and project requirements. The different types of insurance the plumbing contractor may be required to obtain are:

- Public liability
- Property damage
- Fire Insurance

Worker's compensation and liablility insurance are usually carried in the hourly wage rate. (See Wage Rate Table, Appendix C) Insurance can be estimated at 1-1/2% of the subtotal cost on the summary sheet (Figures 6.1 and 6.2).

Bid Bond

When required, a bid bond is furnished by the contractor at the time of bid as proof that he or she will accept the contract for work if chosen to do the work. The cost of the bid bond is usually between two and four percent of the subtotal cost on the summary sheet (Figures 6.1 and 6.2).

Profit

This is the amount a contractor hopes to gain for performing the work. Profit is usually a percentage of the total material, labor, and overhead costs. The percentage of profit that the contractor allows usually depends on the size and type of job. Generally, the larger the project, the smaller the profit mark-up. Another factor that determines the contractor's profit percentage is, of course, need. If the shop is rather slow, it may need to bid the job very tight to ensure success. In a recession, the main goal is often to merely keep the workers busy and on the payroll. The percentage of profit mark-up for a plumbing job can range from 5% to 15%.

Contingencies

Very often a contractor may be required to bid on a project which has incomplete drawings and specifications or other unknown factors. It is very important that the estimator keep both mental and written notes regarding these unknowns, which should be evaluated during the pricing stage. If vague projects come into the office, it is to the contractor's advantage to give them to the most seasoned estimator to scrutinize. An estimator with many years of experience can readily pick up any missing items on the drawings or in the specifications, and assign properly weighted contingency costs to cover these unknown factors. Contingency factors are generally added immediately after the direct costs and prior to any mark-ups.

Marking Up and Completing Sample Estimate

The summary sheet of our sample estimate (Figure 6.2) is ready to be filled out with the appropriate markups to complete the estimate.

ABC PLUMBING COMPANY, INC.
CONTRACTORS
ANYWHERE, USA

SHEET NO. 1 of 1

PROJECT 3-Story Service Center — ESTIMATE NO.

LOCATION Anywhere, USA — CLASSIFICATION — DATE 1-9-91

ARCHITECT Jarrett Assoc. — ESTIMATOR JG — PRICED BY SG — CHECKED BY mS

DESCRIPTION	QUANTITY	UNIT	MATERIAL UNIT COST	MATERIAL TOTAL COST	LABOR UNIT MH	LABOR TOTAL MH	LABOR UNIT RATE	LABOR TOTAL COST	TOTAL COST MAT./LABOR
1. Plumbing Fixtures + Trim				19354.00				5243.29	24597.29
2. Sanitary Waste/Vent - Below Ground				6627.89				6210.58	12838.47
3. Sanitary Waste/Vent - Above Ground				14170.42				15416.64	29587.06
4. Storm System - Below Ground				3811.00				3188.94	6999.94
5. Storm System - Above Ground				6319.54				4119.72	10439.26
6. Hot + Cold Water System				14146.46				18926.38	33072.84
7. Natural Gas System				296.13				420.72	716.85
8. Fire Protection System				3590.06				3080.81	6670.87
9. Insulation				5600.20				5528.61	11128.81
10. Sitework									
10A Domestic Water + Fire Service				3872.87				904.76	4777.63
10B Storm Sewer				4833.70				3229.05	8062.75
10C Sanitary Sewer				861.78				820.43	1682.21
11. Test + Adjustment (Included with Labor)				—				—	—
Tags, Charts, Pipe Identification				500.00				750.00	1250.00
Excavation + Backfill									
Sanitary	201	CY		—			5.00	1005.00	1005.00
Storm	57	↓		—			↓	285.00	285.00
Site Water	37	↓		—			↓	185.00	185.00
Site Storm	105	↓		—			↓	525.00	525.00
Site Sanitary	14	↓		—			↓	70.00	70.00
Sales Tax (material Only) 7%				5878.88				—	5878.88
Direct Job Cost				89862.93				69909.93	159772.86
Field Overhead									
Temporary Facilities									2500.00
Trailer/Field Office									4000.00
Tools									1500.00
Engineering/Shop Drawings									1200.00
Job Supervision									7000.00
Office Overhead 2.5%									4400.00
Subtotal Cost									180372.86
Permits + Fees 74 Fixt. @ $5.00 Ea.									370.00
Insurance 1.5%									2705.00
Bid Bond 2.0%									3807.00
Profit 10%									18725.49
Total Job Cost									205980.35

Figure 6.2 *The costs shown in this sample estimate are used as examples only. The costs should not be used for estimating purposes.*

The estimator must now transfer the total material and labor direct costs for each system from the estimating sheets to the summary sheets. Once this is done, sales tax (when applicable) is entered in the Material column of the summary. The estimator then adds the material and labor costs for each system and enters the totals into the Total column. The next calculation is adding the Material, Labor, and Total columns down, with their respective totals entered on the line labeled *direct project cost*. As a check, the material and labor direct costs, when added together, should equal the total direct project cost as shown in the Total column.

The estimator is now ready to add the appropriate markups, shown on the summary sheet (Figure 6.2). This involves calculating and entering field and overhead costs in the Total column. These figures are then added to the direct job cost and the sum entered as a subtotal cost. Permits, insurance, bid bond, and profit are now calculated and entered in the Total column. The sum of these figures and the subtotal cost is the total project cost (bid price).

Submitting the Estimate

With the estimate complete, the plumbing contractor is now prepared to submit the bid to the respective owner, agency or general contractor. In submitting a bid, the plumbing contractor will function either as a prime or subcontractor. A prime contractor is generally directly responsible to the owner or agency. A subcontractor usually furnishes an estimate for work to a general contractor, to become part of one bid price. The subcontractor is responsible to the general contractor only for its portion of work as called for in the plans, specifications, and general conditions for the total project. Whether one is acting as a prime contractor or subcontractor, there are various ways to submit an estimate, some of which are described below.

Competitive and Negotiated Bids

Competitive bids are responses to formal announcements made by government agencies or owners requesting bids from any contractors who can meet their requirements. A contractor bidding competitively must estimate strictly according to plans and specifications. Bid closing dates and times are strictly adhered to in competitive bidding, and many bids have been refused because the contractor was seconds late to the bid-opening session. Almost all large projects will be bid in the competitive manner.

Negotiated bids are quite different from competitive bids, as demonstrated by the following example. A general contractor or owner has had good results on past jobs using two or three particular plumbing contractors in the area. Not wanting to tamper with success, the general contractor may invite only these contractors to bid on the next job.

Unlike competitive bidding, negotiated bid closing dates and times may not be firm. The plumbing contractor may suggest to the general contractor or owner alternate methods of design which will save the owner money and, at the same time, ensure the lowest possible bid. These contractor-owner communications are often held prior to the bid date.

Cover Letter (List of Exceptions)

Cover letters defining exactly what the contractor has or has not figured into the estimate are commonplace in negotiated bidding. As previously mentioned, competitive bids require the bidder to estimate strictly by plans and specifications, and cover letters with lists of exceptions are not required or permitted. In the informality of negotiated bidding, however, it is good practice for a cover letter to accompany the bid price to explain all inclusions and exclusions.

Value Engineering Analysis

Every estimator should use a value engineering approach while visualizing the project. Unaware of the true meaning of value engineering, many people often misinterpret it as a simple cost-cutting exercise. Alphonse Dell'Isola defined value engineering in his book, *Value Engineering in the Construction Industry*, as "a systematic approach to obtaining optimum value for every dollar spent. Through a system of investigation, unnecessary expenditures are avoided, resulting in improved value and economy."

The use of value engineering by plumbing contractors can result in considerable cost savings and reduced installation time. In the process of applying value engineering to a project, the estimator should place all alternate design schemes and material substitutions on an idea-listing sheet. It might also be advantageous for the estimator to conduct a brainstorming session with other estimators and/or engineers in the firm to obtain their ideas. The brainstorming session should be a free-thinking exercise, with all ideas entered into the listing; once all ideas are reported, they should be analyzed further for acceptance or rejection. Ideas that involve code violations should be rejected immediately. Life-cycle costs must also be analyzed in this stage; for example, vitrified clay pipe may initially cost less than cast iron soil pipe, but will it have the same life expectancy as the structure? If not, and a new installation is required after 10 or 15 years, the idea has cost money, not saved it. Once all acceptable ideas have been listed, the estimator should present them to the owner and architect for final approval.

Unfortunately, the contractor has little hope of applying value engineering to jobs bid competitively until after being awarded the contract. Having to bid by plan and specification, the contractor is locked into figuring the job as designed on the bid documents. In this case, he or she can only hope that any perceived value engineering ideas can be implemented after construction has begun.

Due to its informality, negotiated bidding is very conducive to a value engineering exercise, which can mean the difference in getting or losing the job.

Some expensive specifications that are often noticed in brainstorming a plumbing job are:

1. Fixtures are not designed in back-to-back groups wherever possible.
2. One large capacity hot water generator and hot water recirculation line are designed when small, isolated water heaters will suffice, eliminating the high-cost generator and recirculation pump, piping, and insulation.
3. Cast iron bell and spigot pipe is specified for above grade soil, waste, and storm lines. Consider the use of hubless soil pipe, D.W.V. copper, or D.W.V. PVC ABS drainage pipe and fittings.
4. Galvanized steel pipe is specified for above grade soil, waste, and storm lines. Consider the use of hubless cast iron soil pipe, D.W.V. copper, or PVC drainage pipe and fittings.

Typed or Handwritten Estimate

With the possible exception of the summary sheet, all estimates should remain in handwritten form. Typing is an extra operation, requiring the transfer of figures to other sheets, and allowing for unnecessary errors in transposition. A neatly printed estimate can be read as easily as a typewritten one. Numerical figures should not be typewritten in any circumstances, as a slip of the finger can cause 1,000 L.F. to read 10,000 L.F. Clients are interested in the *bottom line figure* on an estimate. It is the low bid, not whether the estimate is typewritten or handwritten, that will determine who will be awarded the contract.

Coordination with Other Trades

For the plumbing contractor who is the successful low bidder, close coordination before and during construction with other trades, such as structural, heating, ventilating, air-conditioning, and electrical, will be necessary. Upon winning the contract, the plumbing contractor should request two complete sets of architectural, structural, mechanical, and electrical drawings. When shop drawings are being developed showing exact locations for items such as sleeves, fixtures, piping runs, and equipment, it is imperative that the layout draftsman have these other drawings to ensure that the plumbing installation will not interfere with the other trades. A properly coordinated project will make for fewer delays and change orders, and costs will be kept to a minimum.

Chapter 7

OTHER PLUMBING ESTIMATES

Five types of plumbing estimates are discussed in this chapter.

1. Change order analysis
2. Estimating additions and alterations
3. Budget estimating
4. Assemblies approach to plumbing costs
5. Computer estimates

Any of the above should be attempted only by an estimator with considerable experience. For those who may be unfamiliar with these situations, this chapter explains the circumstances under which each estimate would be used, and the proper approach to be taken.

Change Order Analysis

A change order is any change in the original bid drawings or specifications. There are various reasons why change orders occur, such as errors or omissions from drawings, or simply the owner finding additional or less work necessary to meet the program requirements.

To estimate a change order, both the original and revised documents are needed. The estimator takes off the changed areas only in both the original and revised drawings and keeps each takeoff separate. In preparing a change order estimate, one must carefully take off *only* the items which are changed, to avoid listing materials or labor twice for the same work. Once the takeoffs are complete, the estimator prepares two estimates—one according to the original design and the other according to the revised design.

There are factors affecting change order pricing that did not affect the original bid. For example, a plumbing contractor can include delivery or returned-item charges paid on materials that are not usable due to the change. The contractor can also price any added materials at current prices while crediting the original material at the discounted price prevailing at bid time. This assumes that the cost of goods purchased at the time of the change order will be higher than for those at the time of the bid. The plumbing contractor can also charge for labor inefficiencies caused by the disruption of installation due to the change.

The estimator has now prepared two estimates showing direct costs. If the difference between the two estimates results in a *net addition*, the contractor adds the appropriate overhead and profit. If the difference results in a net *credit* (unless otherwise noted in the job specifications or by previous written agreement), the contractor does not deduct any original estimated overhead or profit.

Estimating Additions and Alterations

Because of unknown conditions within an existing structure, additions and alterations represent the most uncertain type of estimating in the construction industry. The first thing an estimator must do is visit the site. By doing so, one can determine many important facts that will influence the project estimate. Some of the items the estimator should look for on a site visit are:

- How the existing structure is built
- Locations of existing pipelines
- Difficulty in gaining access to hidden pipelines
- Condition of the building (poorly or well maintained)
- Any unusual conditions in the building or on the site that might make working more difficult, such as very high ceilings, flooded basements, crawl spaces, occupant use, etc.
- Difficulty in getting new equipment through existing entrance ways or corridors, or up stairwells or elevators

With a full understanding of site conditions, the estimator is ready to estimate the project. It should be noted that although most alteration drawings should show existing services, such representations cannot be accepted as accurate. The design engineer for the new work may have been working with old or very poor plans and may have had difficulty in interpreting them.

The estimator must be sure to allow enough labor and material costs to cover any unknowns that might exist.

The plumbing estimator must also determine costs for the removal and relocation of fixtures and piping, in addition to connections to existing services. If piping is very old, the estimator must take care not to underestimate the necessary removal time. On the surface, removals may seem easier than new installations, but if the contractor disrupts functioning lines during the installation, it must assume responsibility for any damages. Connections to existing lines are generally expensive in terms of time, and the estimator should take them off based on the size of the existing line being cut.

The labor required to install new items, such as fixtures and piping, on an alteration is generally greater than the cost of installing the same item on a new construction project. The estimator must realize that piping production will drop considerably due to expected interference from the existing structure (including the necessity of handling short measures of pipe rather than full lengths).

Reading the specifications is another very important part of estimating alterations work. The estimator should check to determine whether cutting and/or patching of existing walls and floors are part of the plumbing contract. The estimator should also check the specifications and general conditions for clauses stating responsibility for items such as dust control and noise abatement. On alteration work, certain parts of the job very often must be done at specified times during the day or night so as not to disrupt the daily functions of the building. If this is so, the estimator must figure any necessary overtime charges for workers performing during off hours. After the estimator has priced the alteration, overhead and profit are added. The percentages here might differ due to the nature of the job.

Budget Estimating

An estimator occasionally is required to calculate a plumbing cost for a project based on nothing more than architectural plans. The two methods of measurement used to budget-estimate plumbing are *cost per square foot of building* and *cost per fixture*. Taking off the plumbing fixtures or square footage from the architectural plan is not a difficult task, but allocating the right costs can be a tremendous challenge.

Accurate budget estimates must be based on historical cost information. Published cost data, such as *Means Plumbing Cost Data* can be helpful for this information. Another approach is to gather data from one's own past projects to compile an historical cost base. To do so, the contractor should fill out a cost data sheet similar to that in Figure 7.1 after completion of each project. After a period of time, the contractor will have developed a method from which to budget-estimate other similar types of projects.

COST DATA SHEET

JOB NAME ______________________ JOB NO. ____________

TYPE OF BUILDING ______________________ LOCATION ____________

SF ______________________ COST/SF ____________

FIXTURES ______________________ $/FIXTURE ____________

	$	% OF JOB	$/SF
PLUMBING FIXTURES AND TRIM			
EQUIPMENT			
HOT AND COLD WATER (DOMESTIC)			
SANITARY (ABOVE AND BELOW GRADE)			
GAS PIPING			
VALVES, FLASHING AND MISCELLANEOUS			
HANGERS, SLEEVES AND INSERTS			
INSULATION			
TEST-ADJUSTMENTS AND MISCELLANEOUS			
EXCAVATION AND BACKFILL			
SPRINKLER SYSTEM			
KITCHEN EQUIPMENT			
FIRE STANDPIPE SYSTEM			
LAB AND SPECIAL PIPING SYSTEM			
SITEWORK			
OVERHEAD			
PROFIT			
SALES TAX			
TOTAL COST			

NOTES

Figure 7.1

Filling out a cost data sheet is done as follows:

1. Enter job name, number, and location.
2. Enter type of building, i.e., library, hospital, etc.
3. Enter gross square foot area (s.f.)
4. Enter fixture count. (Total amount of plumbing fixtures on job. Floor and roof drains are valued at one half of a fixture.)
5. Enter from Estimate Summary Sheet dollar values for applicable items in the $ column.
6. Enter the percentage each item represents of the total value of the project in the **% of job** column. The sum of these items should equal 100%.
7. Enter cost per square foot for each item in the **$/s.f.** column.
8. Enter cost per square foot for whole project in **cost/s.f.** space. The sum of item 7 should equal cost/s.f.
9. Enter cost per fixture in **$/fixture** space. Cost per fixture is the total job cost, including mark-ups, divided by the number of fixtures.
10. Note that space is provided in Figure 7.1 for any unusual features a particular job may have, such as alterations, a packaged sewage treatment plant on the site, or kitchen equipment to be furnished or installed.

Plumbing costs vary from building type to building type. Therefore, for data to be valid, comparisons should be made with similar types of building usage and construction.

Assemblies Approach

Another method of plumbing estimating is the assemblies approach, which is helpful in developing plumbing costs for pre-bid estimates.

Costs shown in Figure 7.3 are based on the *gross square foot area* of a building. These costs are for budget and information purposes only and represent national average materials, productivity, and job conditions in mid-1999. The estimator should analyze the particular job conditions and adjust costs accordingly.

The following section is a guide for standard computations to accurately determine square footage of a building. See Figure 7.2 for the Gross Square Foot Area Value chart.

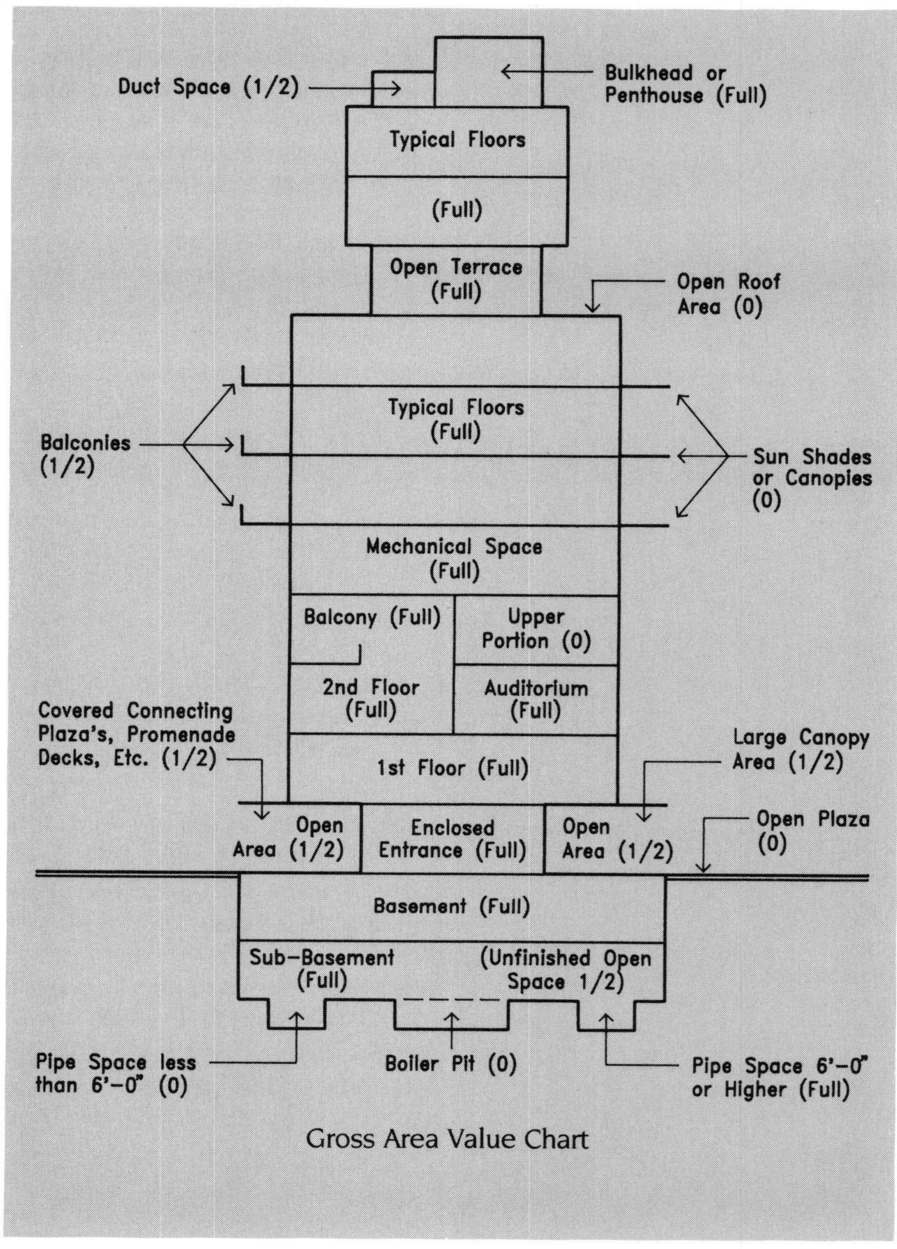

Gross Area Value Chart

Figure 7.2

1. FULL AREAS
   Square footage is determined by measuring the following spaces (from outside to outside of exterior walls):
   a. Basements or sub-basements having full height, including but not duplicating elevator pits, boiler rooms or sump pits, and other spaces which are below floor level.
   b. Pipe spaces 6'0" high or over.
   c. Enclosed spaces (four sides) of open entrance terraces beneath the upper floors, as in a structure of stilt design.
   d. All intermediate floors.
   e. Mezzanines and interior balconies.
   f. Mechanical spaces.
   g. Penthouses.
   h. Any full height space above roof, i.e., stair bulkheads, machine rooms, etc.
   i. Totally enclosed connecting plazas, passageways, promenade decks, etc.
2. HALF AREAS
   The following spaces will be considered at one-half their actual values:
   a. Exterior wall balconies with entrances to the interior of the building.
   b. Attached porches, open on three sides.
   c. Exterior entrance canopies of significant size and structure.
   d. Unenclosed spaces of entrance terrace beneath buildings of stilt design.
   e. Unfinished open basements with concrete floors.
   f. Covered (no walls) connecting plazas, passageways, promenade decks, etc.
3. AREAS TO BE INCLUDED
   a. Stairwell openings.
   b. Elevator shaft openings.
4. AREAS NOT TO BE INCLUDED
   a. Open spaces that go beyond one or more floors, such as the upper spaces of auditoriums, gymnasiums, swimming pools, large architectural stairwells, lecture halls or other rooms.
   b. Interior courts or yards.
   c. Catwalks.
   d. Unoccupied or unfinished attic spaces.
   e. Roofs.
   f. Open air spaces of roof entrance terraces or walkways.
   g. Other enclosed spaces (or structures) not attached to the building.
   h. Window canopies or sun shades.
   i. Crawl spaces (with or without concrete floors)
   j. Pipe spaces less than 6'0" high.

The plumbing work in a building is comprised of a group of subsystems, each generally complete in and of itself, and each serving a particular purpose. The plumbing composite services are presented in matrix charts, which in turn are organized by a subsystem and building-type categories. All costs presented are per gross square foot of building area (see Figure 7.3) where building gross area determinations are based upon the gross area value chart presented in Figure 7.2.

Building Type	Domest Water	Sanitary	Storm	Acid	Fire Stan	Gas	Med Gas	Fixtures	Misc	Total 1999 Avg Costs
Apartments: Low Rise (5 Stories)	0.86	1.01	0.24		0.09	0.17		2.30	0.09	4.76
High Rise (10 Stories)	0.85	0.97	0.19		0.05	0.16		2.19	0.09	4.50
Bank: Main	0.56	0.63	0.33		0.16			1.49	0.04	3.21
Branch	0.41	0.48	0.30					1.05	0.04	2.28
College: Classroom	0.89	1.07	0.50		0.16	0.05	0.09	1.32	0.09	4.17
Dining Hall	0.81	1.02	0.49		0.16	0.09		1.22	0.08	3.87
Laboratory	1.04	1.23	0.50	0.68	0.16	0.06	0.17	1.35	0.27	5.46
Library	0.41	0.43	0.28		0.09			0.81	0.02	2.04
Student Union	0.85	1.02	0.50		0.16			1.18	0.04	3.75
Auditorium										
Gymnasium										
Commercial: Dept Store	0.18	0.19	0.27					0.41	0.02	1.07
Shopping Center	0.38	0.42	0.27					0.56	0.02	1.81
Dormitories	0.89	1.07	0.50		0.16			1.44	0.09	4.15
Hospital: General/Small	1.17	1.48	0.19	0.39	0.08	0.06	0.24	2.06	0.09	5.84
General/Large	1.44	1.56	0.49	0.23	0.08		0.32	2.68	0.10	6.90
Infirmary	1.20	1.32	0.19	0.30	0.16	0.05	0.09	2.16	0.03	5.50
Medical Center	1.49	1.66	0.49	0.50	0.23	0.09	0.33	2.72	0.10	7.61
Nursing Home	1.17	1.39	0.25	0.39	0.16	0.16	0.12	2.33	0.03	6.00
Laboratory: Research	1.61	1.97	0.41	0.91	0.16	0.16	0.48	1.35	0.27	7.32
Manufacturing: Heavy	0.19	0.29	0.33	0.09	0.09	0.06	0.05	0.41	0.02	1.53
Light	0.18	0.19	0.33	0.05	0.08	0.03	0.03	0.40	0.02	1.31
Process	0.24	0.25	0.34	0.09	0.09	0.06	0.12	0.41	0.03	1.63
Motel/Hotel: Low Rise	0.86	1.01	0.24					1.92	0.02	4.05
High Rise	0.91	1.04	0.35		0.12	0.19		2.48	0.13	5.22
Museum	0.41	0.43	0.28		0.08			0.81	0.02	2.03
Office: Public - Low Rise	0.48	0.54	0.25		0.08			1.61	0.03	2.99
High Rise	0.46	0.49	0.19		0.05			1.57	0.04	2.80
Private -Low Rise	0.41	0.47	0.25		0.08			1.44	0.02	2.67
High Rise	0.46	0.49	0.19		0.05			1.57	0.04	2.80
Parking Garage	0.09	0.10	0.17		0.03			0.02	0.02	0.43
Power Plant	1.04	1.26	0.30		0.16		0.17	0.09	0.09	3.11
School: Primary	0.72	0.75	0.49		0.16	0.05		1.32	0.05	3.54
Secondary	0.75	0.79	0.49	0.09	0.16	0.08	0.14	1.36	0.03	3.89
Vocational	0.73	0.77	0.49	0.08	0.16	0.09	0.09	1.36	0.03	3.80
Theater	0.19	0.24	0.27					0.42	0.03	1.15
Warehouse	0.18	0.33	0.33		0.09			0.42	0.04	1.39

Plumbing Cost Relationships per S.F. of Building Area

Figure 7.3

The building types generally represent a single broad functional use and assume the space allocations typically found in such a building. The costs for each subsystem include all primary, secondary, and branch piping; connections; typical medium quality fixtures (anything that accepts and disposes of a fluid); insulation, etc. to 5' of the building wall—in short, all costs associated with the subsystem. Special "process" piping costs for production or manufacturing activities are not included.

To determine the composite plumbing cost for a project, the costs for the specified subsystems are selected and added. The process is illustrated by the two following examples:

1. The project is a dining hall with domestic water, sanitary water, minimal storm water, fire standpipe, and gas kitchen. The cost figures to use are those found opposite the building type "College Dining Hall." In the case of the storm water sub-system, a judgment must be made as to what "minimal" means. For this example, assume it means 40% less than what would typically be expected. The composite plumbing price would then be:

SUBSYSTEM	$
Domestic Water	.81
Sanitary	1.02
Storm Water ($.49 x .60)	.29
Fire Standpipe	.16
Gas	.09
Fixtures	1.22
Miscellaneous	.08
Plumbing Composite Cost	$ 3.67

2. The project is a twenty-story tower on a three-story base. The top ten floors of the tower are apartments, the bottom ten floors are an office building, and the base is a shopping center. An area analysis indicates that the three functional use categories represent these percentages of the total gross area: apartment, 35%, office, 35%, shopping center 30%. All subsystems are typical for the space served and of average quality. There are gas appliances in the apartments. The composite price is determined by the subsystem prices for each functional space category factored according to its relative percentage of the total buliding area. The composite schedule for the plumbing cost is as shown in figure 7.4.

Computerized Estimating Systems

More and more estimators are starting to harness power of the computer as an aid in preparing estimates. Therefore, this chapter will survey some of the systems currently available. No attempt is being made to teach the use of such systems; that would be beyond the scope of this book.

Two important points should be emphasized. First, although computers make estimating easier and faster, their use by a person inexperienced in estimating techniques can lead to in accurate results. Remember the guiding principle of all computer applications: Garbage in, Garbage out. If the information put into the computer is flawed, no amount of computer manipulation will correct it. A thorough understanding of estimating is needed to properly use computerized estimating systems.

Second, while the use of a computer can be faster in many cases, this is not always so. For example, small estimates may be accomplished as quickly by hand. It may also take a while to learn the intricacies of a new computer program, and this learning curve must be taken into account. Different programs will take varying amounts of time to learn.

Most offices using computerized estimating systems utilize small desktop microcomputers. While there are programs available for larger and more powerful types of computers, the principles involved are the same, and the desktop computers have adequate power to handle large and complex estimates. The basic microcomputer consists of a box housing the hard disk, or electronic "brains," a video display device, and a keyboard to enter information into the system. More sophisticated systems have other devices to input information into the computer, such as a mouse, which is a gadget that fits in the palm of a user's hand and is moved around on a desktop, and a digitizer, which is a "pad" of sensitive material laid out on a desk upon which drawings may be placed and "traced" into the computer with a special stylus. Some people have a preference for one device over another; both allow faster input of this type of data than with a keyboard.

	$	Factor	Subtotal	$	Factor	Subtotal	$	Factor	Subtotal	Weighted Total
Domestic Water	.81	.35	.284	.46	.35	.161	.38	.30	.114	0.56
Sanitary	1.02	.35	.357	.49	.35	.172	.42	.30	.126	0.66
Storm Water	.49	.35	.172	.19	.35	.067	.27	.30	.081	0.32
Fire Standpipe	.16	.35	.056	.05	.35	.018	.16	.30	.048	0.12
Gas	.16	.35	.056	—	—	—	—	—	—	0.06
Fixtures	1.22	.35	.427	1.57	.35	.550	.56	.30	.168	1.15
Miscellaneous	.08	.35	.028	.04	.35	.014	.02	.30	.006	0.05
Plumbing Composite Total										2.92

Composite Schedule for Plumbing Costs for 20-Story Tower

Figure 7.4

The four classes of estimating programs surveyed on the following pages range from the ultra-simple adaptation of a spreadsheet program to systems that automate almost all aspects of the process.

Spreadsheet Applications

A simple yet powerful tool for computerizing the estimating process is the computer spreadsheet program. (Some well-known programs are Lotus 1-2-3,™ Quattro,™ and Excel.™). A computer spreadsheet is a variation on an accountant's ledger sheet, consisting of a matrix of rows and columns of blank spaces called cells (shown as rows 1 thru 12 and columns A thru J, for example). Each cell can act as a label or be related to another cell mathematically. For example, in Figure 7.5, cell A4 (column A, row 4) contains a label with a description: 4" SWCI hubless pipe. The next cell horizontally, B4, contains a quantity: 10. Continuing horizontally, one encounters a label: LF, and a number: $4.16. The next cell, E4, contains the material total cost which is a formula: QUANTITY times UNIT PRICE or in spreadsheet language, B4 times D4 (the formula is not displayed, only the result). In this manner an estimate spreadsheet can be built up containing labels, numbers, and formulas. Cells J9, J10, and J12 contain formulas which respectively sum the prices for each line item, add markups and total the estimate.

	A	B	C	D	E	F	G	H	I	J
1				MATERIAL			LABOR			TOTAL COST
2	DESCRIPTION	QTY	UNIT	UNIT COST	TOTAL COST	UNIT MH	TOTAL MH	UNIT RATE	TOTAL	MAT/LAB
3										
4	4" SWCI HUBLESS PIPE	10	LF	$4.16	$41.60	0.14	1.40	$47.03	$65.84	$107.44
5	4" SWCI HUBLESS "Y"	1	EA	$9.77	$ 9.77	1.00	1.00	$47.03	$47.03	$56.80
6	4" SWCI HUBLESS COUPLINGS	4	EA	$3.61	$14.44					$14.44
7	4" HANGAR ASSEMBLY	3	EA	$9.24	$27.72	0.36	1.08	$47.03	$50.79	$78.51
8										
9									SUBTOTAL:	$257.19
10									OVERHEAD & PROFIT @ 21%:	$54.01
11										
12									TOTAL:	$311.20

Figure 7.5

The usefulness of the computer spreadsheet will only come into play after the quantity takeoff and pricing. These will still have to be done manually. Once entered, however, the power of the computer can be brought to bear not only in computing extensions and totals for large estimates, but in making adjustments to individual line items. Once entered, a formula such as that in cell E4 stays as the mathematical formula B4 times D4. If the value of B4 or D4 changes, the value displayed in E4 changes accordingly. "What-if" analyses can be played on a spreadsheet by varying some numbers and seeing what results. One may vary unit prices to estimate future costs or vary quantities to perform value engineering or least-cost studies.

To use a spreadsheet effectively, one must familiarize oneself with the ins and outs of the particular computer program being used. Since most offices have spreadsheets for other purposes such as accounting, the cost involved in set-up for estimating is solely the time required for personnel to learn the program.

Library-Based Applications

The previous example (Figure 7.5) involved a broad-use commercial package, tailored for estimating. There are other programs which are vastly tailored more specialized and exclusively oriented to estimating, such as Means CostWorks®. Such programs also require an estimator to manually take off quantities, but have libraries of cost information from which cost items needed for a particular estimate may be selected. In the case of Means CostWorks®, the format follows the layout of the annual cost data books they publish and can be updated yearly. An estimator enters various pieces of information about the cost item selected, such as quantity, whether or not the item is being subcontracted, in what city the work is taking place, markups, etc. The program will then compute the cost extensions and totals and print out numerous reports ranging from the brief summaries to detailed breakdowns (see Figure 7.6).

These library-based applications free an estimator from the burden of researching prices by allowing easy use of a database of national costs adjusted to local areas. Modifications can be made to allow for price or man-hour adjustment. In this way, in-house information maintained by a contractor can be incorporated into the database, as can costs for high-priced or unusually complicated specialty work. These kinds of programs are generally inexpensive, but since they are specialized, must be purchased specifically for estimating. They are easy to learn, but require some basic familiarity with computers.

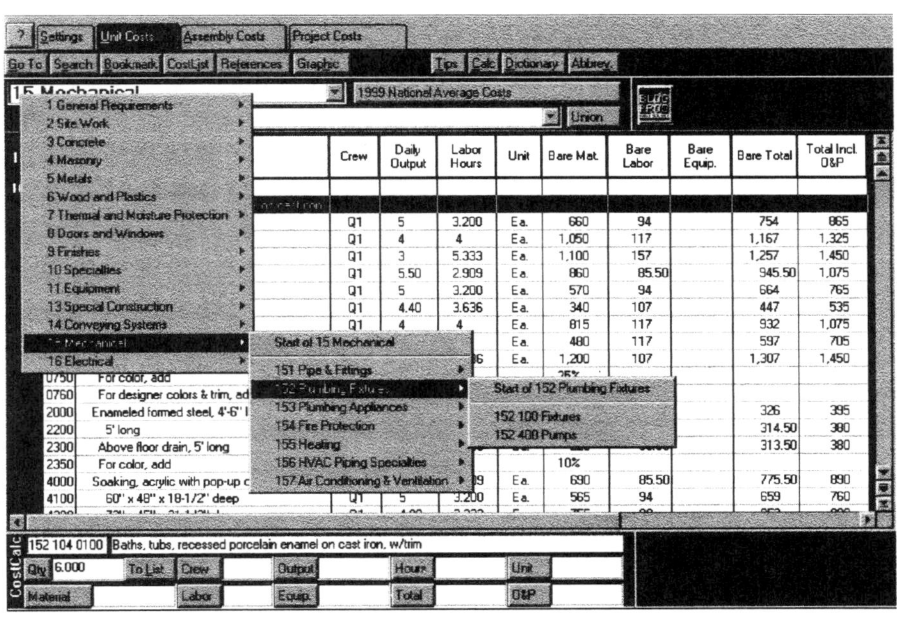

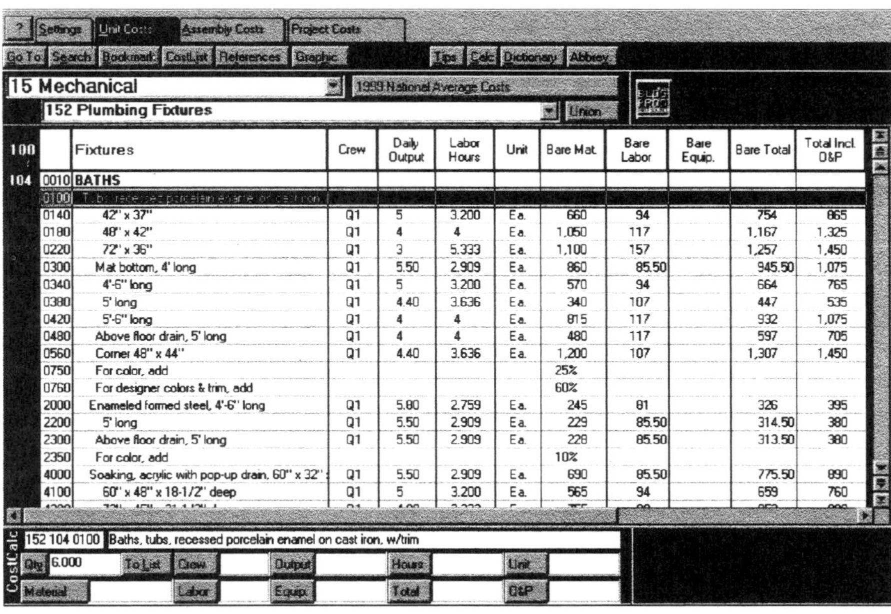

A user has the option of selecting line items from within the standard CSI code divisions, subdivisions and major classifications for use in estimates. The database has all the standard line items contained in the Means Cost Data books.

Figure 7.6

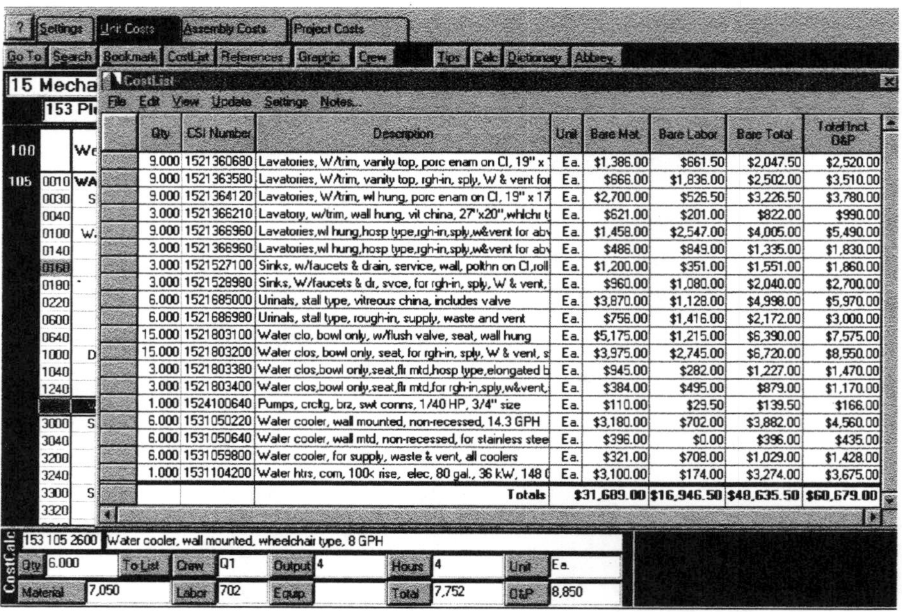

Qty	CSI Number	Description	Unit	Bare Mat.	Bare Labor	Bare Total	Total Incl. O&P
9.000	1521360680	Lavatories, W/trim, vanity top, porc enam on CI, 19" x	Ea.	$1,386.00	$661.50	$2,047.50	$2,520.00
9.000	1521363580	Lavatories, W/trim, vanity top, rgh-in, sply, W & vent fo	Ea.	$666.00	$1,836.00	$2,502.00	$3,510.00
9.000	1521364120	Lavatories, W/trim, wl hung, porc enam on CI, 19" x 17	Ea.	$2,700.00	$526.50	$3,226.50	$3,780.00
3.000	1521366210	Lavatory, w/trim, wall hung, vit china, 27"x20",whlchr t	Ea.	$621.00	$201.00	$822.00	$990.00
9.000	1521366960	Lavatories,wl hung,hosp type,rgh-in,sply,w&vent for ab	Ea.	$1,458.00	$2,547.00	$4,005.00	$5,490.00
3.000	1521366960	Lavatories,wl hung,hosp type,rgh-in,sply,w&vent for ab	Ea.	$486.00	$849.00	$1,335.00	$1,830.00
3.000	1521527100	Sinks, w/faucets & drain, service, wall, polthn on CI,roll	Ea.	$1,200.00	$351.00	$1,551.00	$1,860.00
3.000	1521528980	Sinks, W/faucets & dr, svce, for rgh-in, sply, W & vent,	Ea.	$960.00	$1,080.00	$2,040.00	$2,700.00
6.000	1521685000	Urinals, stall type, vitreous china, includes valve	Ea.	$3,870.00	$1,128.00	$4,998.00	$5,970.00
6.000	1521686980	Urinals, stall type, rough-in, supply, waste and vent	Ea.	$756.00	$1,416.00	$2,172.00	$3,000.00
15.000	1521803100	Water clo, bowl only, w/flush valve, seat, wall hung	Ea.	$5,175.00	$1,215.00	$6,390.00	$7,575.00
15.000	1521803200	Water clos, bowl only, seat, for rgh-in, sply, W & vent, s	Ea.	$3,975.00	$2,745.00	$6,720.00	$8,550.00
3.000	1521803380	Water clos,bowl only,seat,flr mtd,hosp type,elongated b	Ea.	$945.00	$282.00	$1,227.00	$1,470.00
3.000	1521803400	Water clos,bowl only,seat,flr mtd,for rgh-in,sply,w&vent,	Ea.	$384.00	$495.00	$879.00	$1,170.00
1.000	1524100640	Pumps, crcltg, brz, swt conns, 1/40 HP, 3/4" size	Ea.	$110.00	$29.50	$139.50	$166.00
6.000	1531050220	Water cooler, wall mounted, non-recessed, 14.3 GPH	Ea.	$3,180.00	$702.00	$3,882.00	$4,560.00
6.000	1531050640	Water cooler, wall mtd, non-recessed, for stainless stee	Ea.	$396.00	$0.00	$396.00	$435.00
6.000	1531059800	Water cooler, for supply, waste & vent, all coolers	Ea.	$321.00	$708.00	$1,029.00	$1,428.00
1.000	1531104200	Water htrs, com, 100< rise, elec, 80 gal., 36 kW, 148 (	Ea.	$3,100.00	$174.00	$3,274.00	$3,675.00
		Totals		$31,689.00	$16,946.50	$48,635.50	$60,679.00

Each line item, whether selected from among those in the program's database or input by the user, can have a number of attributes (quantity, material cost, labor cost, overhead and profit, etc.) associated with it as shown in the figure above.

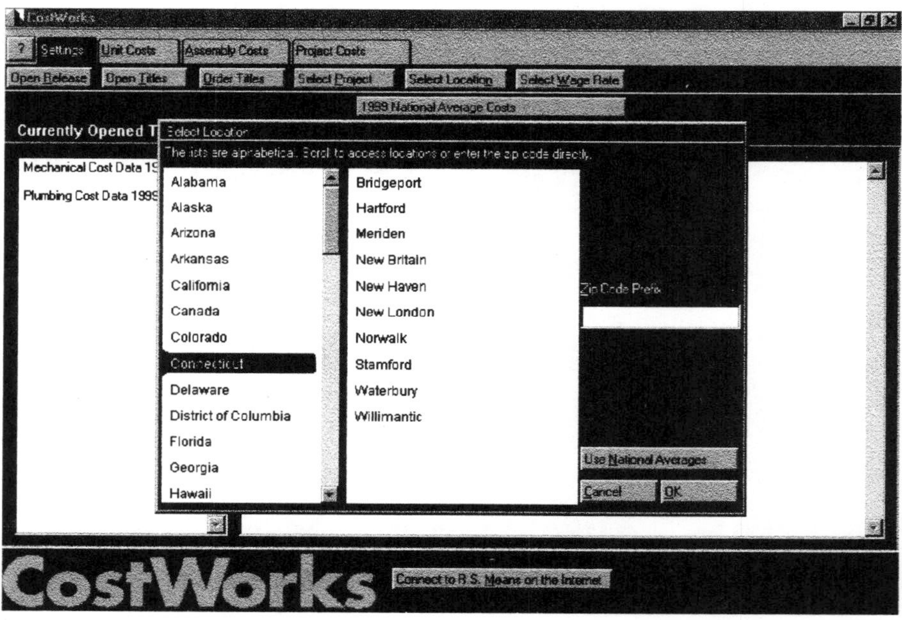

Special cost factors can be used to adjust the estimate to local economic conditions. The figure above shows several cities available in Connecticut. The user selects a city and the program automatically revises the estimate using the appropriate cost factor.

Figure 7.6 (cont'd.)

Input Device Applications

There are several programs currently on the market which take the library-based applications one step further by allowing direct input from a drawing to the computer. They usually use a digitizer to trace drawings directly into the computer. If a building perimeter is traced, wall length, building area and volume are computed automatically. The system will look up costs, man-hour and crew size information from a library database and produce numerous reports.

This type of system eliminates the double work of taking off quantities manually and then typing them into the computer. The takeoff is faster, but care should be exercised since a mistake can throw off the estimate just as easily as in the manual method and might be harder to find. These systems are highly specialized and the program itself might cost several times more than the computer hardware it runs on. They also require that time and effort be spent in learning all the features, and usually take much longer than the previous two types of applications.

Another feature commonly found in these more sophisticated programs is the ability to take the data generated by the takeoff and put it in a format that allows the same "what-if" analyses as spreadsheets. Some programs allow the cost and man-hour data to be used to prepare realistic cost-loaded construction schedules and for budget and payment tracking throughout a project.

Direct Input From CAD

No discussion of computer-aided estimating could be complete without mention of programs that allow direct input from computer-aided design packages (CAD). As long as drawings are still generated by manual draftsmen, the information will have to be manually taken off or entered into the computer with a digitizer. When the drawing is done on a computer screen, however, the takeoff can proceed automatically and simultaneously with the design. Once quantified, the program proceeds in a similar manner to the above-described applications (using database cost information, generating reports, producing schedules, etc.).

These applications are highly specialized, are the most expensive to purchase and set up, and require the user to be somewhat familiar with CAD systems as well as estimating. They are not yet a common sight in construction offices, but are definitely the wave of the future.

Chapter 8

USING MEANS PLUMBING COST DATA

There are occasions when a plumbing contractor or estimator is required to prepare an estimate without the benefit of finished plans and specifications. These estimates are usually for budget or preplanning purposes.

The data required for these early estimates may be readily available from the contractor's own records of past projects, especially if the plumbing contractor specializes in a particular type of building, such as hospitals or schools. Analysis of this data may reveal that for a hospital, the plumbing will cost so many dollars per hospital bed; or, in the case of a school, a cost per student or per classroom. The contractor might also maintain historical records based on dollars per square foot, particularly in the case of fire protection. These historical costs must be continually updated in order to be useful and accurate.

Many contractors or designers may not have records of similar, past projects to use as a basis for a budget estimate. They would have to find an outside source for this information, such as the cost data published by R.S. Means in both book and electronic format. R.S. Means Company, Inc. has been compiling and publishing construction cost data on an annual basis since 1942. This data is based on actual construction costs gathered from across the United States and Canada.

Four Levels of Estimates

Means Plumbing Cost Data furnishes information (both historical and current) for four stages of estimating: forecasting, budgeting, planning, and bidding. For the conceptual stage, order of magnitude estimates and data are covered. As the design progresses, the estimator uses the square foot or cubic foot data. When the design has progressed to the stage that occupancy is established and the number of plumbing fixtures or toilet rooms has been determined, an assemblies estimate comes into play. The final completed bid documents containing plans and specifications provide the estimator with the opportunity to perform an accurate unit-by-unit takeoff, estimate, and bid. Unit price information is presented for this level of estimate.

Building construction estimators use these four basic types of estimates, which may be referred to by different names and may not be recognized by all as definitive. Most estimators, however, will agree that each type has its place in the construction estimating process. The following paragraphs briefly describe these estimate types. Further details may be found later in the chapter.

Order of Magnitude Estimates

Order of magnitude costs are defined in relation to the usable units that have been designed for a facility. If, for example, a hospital administrator is planning to enlarge a hospital, he needs to know the projected cost per bed. If an estimator knows the quantity of beds in a proposed hospital (or number of apartments in an apartment building, or tons of air-conditioning in a facility), the cost of the project can be estimated. It is a very quick method, and accuracy may be plus or minus 20%.

Square Foot and Cubic Foot Estimates

This type is most useful when the proposed size and use of a planned building are known, but no further details. This method can be completed within an hour or two. Depending on the source of cost information, an accuracy of plus or minus 15% can be realized.

Assemblies Estimates

An assemblies estimate is best used as a budgetary tool in the planning stages of a project when some parameters have been decided (e.g., occupancy, fixture requirements, etc.). This type of estimate could require as much as one day to complete. Because more specific information is known about the project, a plus or minus of 10% accuracy can be attained from an assemblies level estimate.

Unit Price Estimates

Working drawings and full specifications are required to complete a unit price estimate. It is the most accurate of the four types, but is also the most time-consuming to prepare. Used primarily for bidding purposes, the accuracy of a unit price estimate can be plus or minus 5%. (This means, theoretically, that all bids based on a complete set of bid documents should be within 5% of the average proposal.)

Figure 8.1 demonstrates the relative relationship of required time versus resultant accuracy of a complete estimate for each of these four basic types. It should be recognized that, as an estimator and his company gain repetitive experience on similar or identical projects, the accuracy of all four types of estimates should improve dramatically. In fact, given enough experience, square foot and assemblies estimates may closely approach the accuracy of unit price estimates.

Data Format

The major portion of *Means Plumbing Cost Data* is the Unit Price section, Section A. This is the primary source of unit cost data and is orgainized according to the CSI division index. This index was developed by representatives of all parties concerned with the building construction industry and has been accepted by the American Institute of Architects (AIA), the Associated General Contractors of America, Inc. (AGC), and the Construction Specifications Institute, Inc. (CSI). In *Means Plumbing Cost Data*, relevant parts of other divisions are included along with Division 15-Mechanical. For example, items from Divisions 1, 2, 3, 4, 5, 6, 7, 8, 10, 11, 12, 13, 14, and 16 all appear in addition to the Division 15 entries.

CSI MasterFormat Divisions:

Division 1 - General Requirements
Division 2 - Site Work
Division 3 - Concrete
Division 4 - Masonry
Division 5 - Metals
Division 6 - Wood & Plastics
Division 7 - Moisture-Thermal Control
Division 8 - Doors, Windows & Glass
Division 9 - Finishes
Division 10 - Specialties
Division 11 - Equipment
Division 12 - Furnishings
Division 13 - Special Construction
Division 14 - Conveying Systems
Division 15 - Mechanical
Division 16 - Electrical

In addition to the 16 CSI divisions of the Unit Price section, Division 17, Square Foot and Cubic Foot Costs, presents consolidated data from over 10,200 actual reported construction projects and provides information based on total project costs as well as costs for major components.

Section B, Assemblies Cost Tables, contains over 3,000 costs for mechanical and appropriate related assemblies, or systems. Components of the systems are fully detailed and accompanied by illustrations.

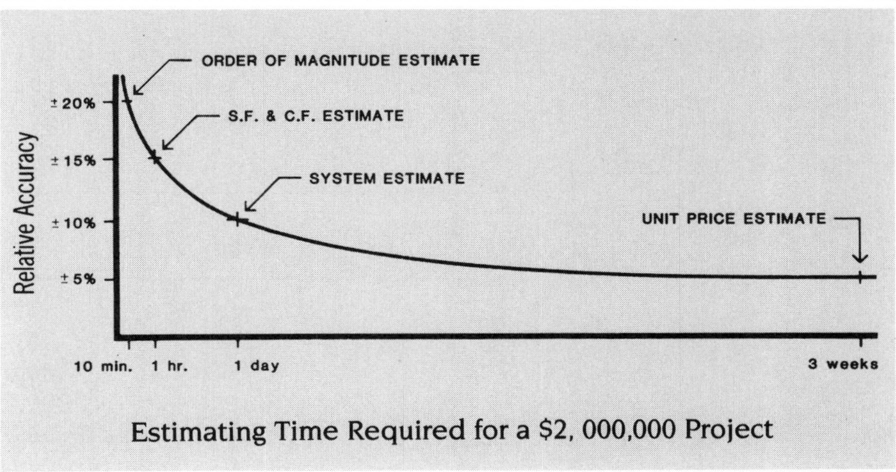

Figure 8.1

Section C contains tables and reference charts. It also provides estimating procedures and explanations of cost development which support and supplement the unit price and systems cost data. Also in Section C are the City Cost Factors and Zip Code Centers, representing the compilation of construction data for 930 major U.S. and Canadian cities and postal zones. Cost factors are given for each city, by trade, relative to the national average.

The prices presented in *Means Plumbing Cost Data* are national averages. Material and equipment costs are developed through annual contact with manufacturers, dealers, distributors, and contractors throughout the United States and Canada. Means' staff of engineers is constantly updating prices and keeping abreast of changes and fluctuations within the industry. Labor rates are the national average of each trade as determined from union agreements from 30 major U.S. cities. Throughout the calendar year, as new wage agreements are negotiated, labor costs should be factored accordingly.

Following is a list of factors and assumptions on which the costs presented in *Means Plumbing Cost Data* have been based:

- **Quality:** The costs are based on methods, materials, and workmanship in accordance with U.S. Government standards and represent good, sound construction practice.
- **Overtime:** The costs, as presented, include no allowance for overtime. If overtime or premium time is anticipated, labor costs must be factored accordingly.
- **Productivity:** The daily output and man-hour figures are based on an eight hour workday, during daylight hours.
- **Size of Project:** Costs in *Means Plumbing Cost Data* are based on commercial and industrial buildings for which total project costs are $1,000,000 and up. Large residential projects are also included.
- **Local Factors:** Weather conditions, season of the year, local union restrictions, and unusual building code requirements can all have a significant impact on construction costs. The availability of a skilled labor force, sufficient materials, and even adequate energy and utilities will also affect costs. These factors vary in impact and are not necessarily dependent upon location. They must be reviewed for each project in every area.

In presenting prices in *Means Plumbing Cost Data*, certain rounding rules are employed to make the numbers easy to use without significantly affecting accuracy. The rules are used consistently and are as follows:

Prices From	To	Rounded To Nearest
$ 0.01	$ 5.00	$ 0.01
5.01	20.00	0.05
20.01	100.00	1.00
100.01	1,000.00	5.00
1,000.01	10,000.00	25.00
10,000.01	50,000.00	100.00
50,000.01	up	500.00

Unit Price Costs

The Unit Price section of *Means Plumbing Cost Data* contains a great deal of information in addition to the unit cost for each construction component. Figure 8.2 is a typical page showing costs for fire valves. Note that prices are included for several types of valves, each in a wide range of size and capacity ratings. In addition, appropriate crews, workers, and productivity data are indicated. The information and cost data is broken down and itemized in this way to provide for the most detailed pricing possible. Both the unit price and the systems sections include detailed illustrations. The reference numbers enclosed in the squares refer the user to an appropriate assemblies section or reference table.

Within each individual line item, there is a description of the construction component, information regarding typical crews designated to perform the work and productivity shown as daily output and as labor-hours. Costs are presented in two ways: "bare," or unburdened costs, and costs with markups for overhead and profit. Figure 8.3 is a graphic representation of how to use the Unit Price section as presented in *Means Plumbing Cost Data*.

Line Numbers

Every construction item in the Means unit price cost data books has a unique line number. This line number acts as an address so that each item can be quickly located and/or referenced. The numbering system is based on the CSI MasterFormat classification by division. In Figure 8.3, note the bold number in reverse type, "151". This number represents the major subdivision, in this case "Pipe & Fittings", of the major CSI Division 15-Mechanical. Within each subdivision, the data is broken down into major classifications. These major classifications are listed alphabetically and are designated by bold type for both numbers and descriptions. Each item, or line, is further defined by an individual number. As shown in Figure 8.3, the full line number for each item consists of: a major CSI subdivision number a major classification number—an item line number. Each full line number describes a unique construction element. For example, in Figure 8.2, the line number for a 2", slow close, bronze butterfly valve is 154-160-1180.

Line Description

Each line has a text description of the item for which costs are listed. The description may be self-contained and all inclusive or, if indented, the complete description for a line is dependent upon the information provided above. All indented items are delineations (by size, color, material, etc.) or breakdowns of previously described items. An index is provided in the back of *Means Plumbing Cost Data* to aid in locating particular items.

Crew

For each construction element, (each line item), a minimum typical crew is designated as appropriate to perform the work. The crew may include one or more trades, foremen, craftsmen and helpers, and any equipment required for proper installation of the described item. If an individual trade installs the item using only hand tools, the smallest efficient

154 | Fire Protection

		154 100 | Fire Systems	CREW	DAILY OUTPUT	LABOR-HOURS	UNIT	1999 BARE COSTS MAT.	LABOR	EQUIP.	TOTAL	TOTAL INCL O&P	
145	0820	2500 GPM, 150 psi, 365 HP, 8" pump	Q-13	.26	123	Ea.	83,000	3,825		86,825	97,000	145
	0850	3000 GPM, 100 psi, 250 HP, 8" pump		.28	114		81,500	3,550		85,050	95,500	
	0900	3000 GPM, 150 psi, 384 HP, 10" pump		.20	160		95,000	4,950		99,950	112,000	
	0950	3500 GPM, 100 psi, 300 HP, 10" pump		.24	133		97,500	4,125		101,625	113,500	
	1000	3500 GPM, 150 psi, 518 HP, 10" pump		.20	160		137,500	4,950		142,450	159,000	
	3000	Electric										
	3100	250 GPM, 55 psi, 15 HP, 3,550 RPM, 2" pump	Q-13	.70	45.714	Ea.	10,700	1,425		12,125	14,000	
	3200	500 GPM, 50 psi, 27 HP, 1770 RPM, 4" pump		.68	47.059		13,300	1,450		14,750	16,800	
	3250	500 GPM, 100 psi, 47 HP, 3550 RPM, 3" pump		.66	48.485		16,100	1,500		17,600	20,000	
	3300	500 GPM, 125 psi, 64 HP, 3550 RPM, 3" pump		.62	51.613		17,700	1,600		19,300	21,800	
	3350	750 GPM, 50 psi, 44 HP, 1,770 RPM, 5" pump		.64	50		19,400	1,550		20,950	23,700	
	3400	750 GPM, 100 psi, 66 HP, 3550 RPM, 4" pump		.58	55.172		17,200	1,700		18,900	21,500	
	3450	750 GPM, 165 psi, 120 HP, 3550 RPM, 4" pump		.56	57.143		22,400	1,775		24,175	27,300	
	3500	1000 GPM, 50 psi, 48 HP 1770 RPM, 5" pump		.60	53.333		19,400	1,650		21,050	23,900	
	3550	1000 GPM, 100 psi, 86 HP, 3550 RPM, 5" pump		.54	59.259		21,800	1,825		23,625	26,700	
	3600	1000 GPM, 150 psi, 142 HP, 3550 RPM, 5" pump		.50	64		24,700	1,975		26,675	30,100	
	3650	1000 GPM, 200 psi, 245 HP, 1770 RPM, 6" pump		.36	88.889		53,500	2,750		56,250	62,500	
	3660	1250 GPM, 75 psi, 75 HP, 1770 RPM, 5" pump		.55	58.182		19,900	1,800		21,700	24,600	
	3700	1500 GPM, 50 psi, 66 HP, 1770 RPM, 6" pump		.50	64		20,900	1,975		22,875	26,000	
	3750	1500 GPM, 100 psi, 139 HP, 1770 RPM, 6" pump		.46	69.565		23,700	2,150		25,850	29,300	
	3800	1500 GPM, 150 psi, 200 HP, 1770 RPM, 6" pump		.36	88.889		50,000	2,750		52,750	59,000	
	3850	1500 GPM, 200 psi, 279 HP, 1770 RPM, 6" pump		.32	100		55,000	3,100		58,100	65,000	
	3900	2000 GPM, 100 psi, 167 HP, 1770 RPM, 6" pump		.34	94.118		30,200	2,925		33,125	37,700	
	3950	2000 GPM, 150 psi, 292 HP, 1770 RPM, 6" pump		.28	114		40,500	3,550		44,050	49,900	
	4000	2500 GPM, 100 psi, 213 HP, 1770 RPM, 8" pump		.30	106		33,100	3,300		36,400	41,400	
	4040	2500 GPM, 135 psi, 339 HP, 1770 RPM, 8" pump		.26	123		47,300	3,825		51,125	58,000	
	4100	3000 GPM, 100 psi, 250 HP, 1770 RPM, 8" pump		.28	114		39,600	3,550		43,150	49,000	
	4150	3000 GPM, 140 psi, 428 HP, 1770 RPM, 10" pump		.24	133		63,000	4,125		67,125	75,500	
	4200	3500 GPM, 100 psi, 300 HP, 1770 RPM, 10" pump		.26	123		49,100	3,825		52,925	60,000	
	4250	3500 GPM, 140 psi, 450 HP, 1770 RPM, 10" pump		.24	133		63,000	4,125		67,125	75,500	
	5000	For jockey pump 1", 3 HP, with control, add	Q-12	2	8		2,375	234		2,609	2,975	
160	0010	**FIRE VALVES** A8.2-310										160
	0020	Angle, combination pressure adjustable/restricting, rough brass										
	0030	1-1/2" A8.2-320	1 Spri	12	.667	Ea.	36.50	21.50		58	73	
	0040	2-1/2"	"	7	1.143	"	73.50	37		110.50	138	
	0050	For polished brass, add A8.2-390					30%					
	0060	For polished chrome, add					40%					
	0080	Wheel handle, 300 lb., 1-1/2" R154-310	1 Spri	12	.667	Ea.	22.50	21.50		44	57.50	
	0090	2-1/2"	"	7	1.143	"	55	37		92	117	
	0100	For polished brass, add R154-320					35%					
	0110	For polished chrome, add					50%					
	1000	Ball drip, automatic, rough brass, 1/2"	1 Spri	20	.400	Ea.	6.65	13		19.65	27	
	1010	3/4"	"	20	.400	"	7.70	13		20.70	28	
	1100	Butterfly, 175 lb., sprinkler system, FM/UL, threaded, bronze										
	1120	Slow close										
	1150	1" size	1 Spri	19	.421	Ea.	72	13.70		85.70	100	
	1160	1-1/4" size		15	.533		78.50	17.35		95.85	113	
	1170	1-1/2" size		13	.615		100	20		120	141	
	1180	2" size		11	.727		126	23.50		149.50	175	
	1190	2-1/2" size	Q-12	15	1.067		178	31		209	244	
	1230	For supervisory switch kit, all sizes										
	1240	One circuit, add	1 Spri	48	.167	Ea.	54.50	5.40		59.90	68	
	1250	Two circuits, add	"	40	.200	"	54.50	6.50		61	70	
	1280	Quarter turn for trim										
	1300	1/2" size	1 Spri	22	.364	Ea.	8.90	11.80		20.70	27.50	

From Means Plumbing Cost Data 1999

Figure 8.2

How to Use the Unit Price Pages

The following is a detailed explanation of a sample entry in the Unit Price Section. Next to each bold number below is the item being described with appropriate component of the sample entry following in parenthesis. Some prices are listed as bare costs, others as costs that include overhead and profit of the installing contractor. In most cases, if the work is to be subcontracted, the general contractor will need to add an additional markup (R.S. Means suggests using 10%) to the figures in the column "Total Incl. O&P."

1 Division Number/Title (151/Pipe and Fittings)

Use the Unit Price Section Table of Contents to locate specific items. The sections are classified according to the CSI MasterFormat.

Line Numbers (151 960 1090)

Each unit price line item has been assigned a unique 10-digit code based on the 5-digit CSI MasterFormat classification.

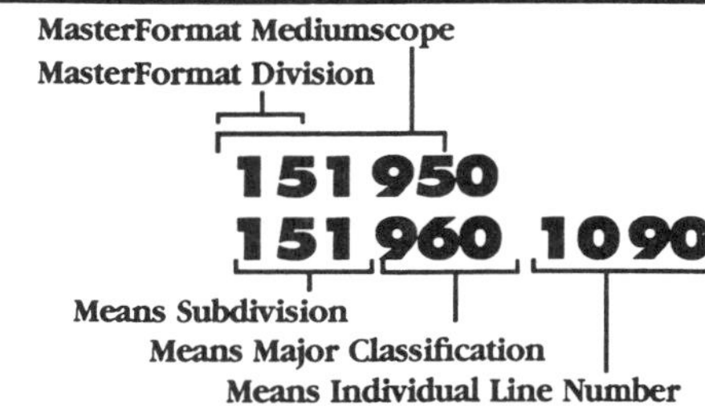

3 Description (Valves, Iron Body)

Each line item is described in detail. Sub-items and additional sizes are indented beneath the appropriate line items. The first line or two after the main item (in boldface) may contain descriptive information that pertains to all line items beneath this boldface listing.

4 Reference Number Information

R151 -090 You'll see reference numbers shown in bold squares at the beginning of some major classifications. These refer to related items in the Reference Section, visually identified by a vertical gray bar on the edge of pages.

The relation may be: (1) an estimating procedure that should be read before estimating, (2) an alternate pricing method, or (3) technical information.

The "R" designates the Reference Section. The numbers refer to the MasterFormat classification system. An "A" denotes the Assemblies section and the numbers refer to the UniFormat classification system.

Example: The square number above is directing you to refer to the reference number R151-090. This particular reference number provides technical data on valve selection.

151 | Pipe & Fittings

151 950 | Valves				CREW	DAILY OUTPUT	LABOR-HOURS	UNIT	1999 BARE COSTS MAT.	LABOR	EQUIP.	TOTAL	TOTAL INCL O&P	
960	0010	VALVES, IRON BODY	R151 -090				Ea.						960
	0020	For g[illegible] see D[illegible]sion 151-801											
	0560	Butterfly, [illegible]e, pneu[illegible]atic operator, 2" size		Stpi	14	.571		221	18.70		239.70	272	
	0570	[illegible]ze		Q-1	8	[illegible]		[illegible]	[illegible]		[illegible]	340	
	1050	3" size						116	58.50		174.50	217	
	1060	4" size						145	94		239	300	
	1070	5" size		[illegible]	5	[illegible]		175	146		321	415	
	1080	6" size			5	4.800		198	146		344	[illegible]	
	1090	8" size		Q-2	4.50	5.333		264	162		426	535	
	1100	10" size			4	6		[illegible]	[illegible]		[illegible]	[illegible]	
	[illegible]	[illegible]			3	8		460	243		703	[illegible]	
	1200	Wafer type, lever actuator, 200 lb.											
	1220	2" size		[illegible]	14	.571		73	18.65		91.65	[illegible]	
	1230	[illegible]		Q-1	9	1.778		76	52		128	163	
	1240	3" size			8	2		80.50	58.50		139	178	

From Means Plumbing Cost Data 1999

Figure 8.3

Crew (Q-2)

The "Crew" column designates the typical trade or crew used to install the item. If an installation can be accomplished by one trade and requires no power equipment, that trade and the number of workers are listed (for example, "2 Plum"). If an installation requires a composite crew, a crew code designation is listed (for example, "Q-2"). You'll find full details on all composite crews in the Crew Listings.

- For a complete list of all trades utilized in this book and their abbreviations, see the inside back cover.

Crews

Crew No.	Bare Costs		Incl. Subs O & P		Cost Per Labor-Hour	
Crew Q-2	Hr.	Daily	Hr.	Daily	Bare Costs	Incl. O&P
2 Plumbers	$32.60	$521.60	$49.40	$790.40	$30.43	$46.12
1 Plumber Apprentice	26.10	208.80	39.55	316.40		
24 L.H., Daily Totals		$730.40		$1106.80	$30.43	$46.12

Productivity: Daily Output (4.50)/ Labor-Hours (5.333)

The "Daily Output" represents the typical number of units the designated crew will install in a normal 8-hour day. To find out the number of days the given crew would require to complete the installation, divide your quantity by the daily output. For example:

Quantity	÷	Daily Output	=	Duration
10 Ea.	÷	4.50 Ea./ Crew Day	=	2.22 Crew Days

The "Labor-Hours" figure represents the number of labor-hours required to install one unit of work. To find out the number of labor-hours required for your particular task, multiply the quantity of the item times the number of labor-hours shown. For example:

Quantity	x	Productivity Rate	=	Duration
10 Ea.	x	5.333 Labor-Hours/Ea.	=	53.33 Labor-Hours

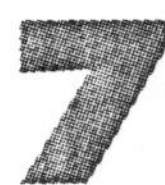

Unit (Ea.)

The abbreviated designation indicates the unit of measure upon which the price, production, and crew are based (Ea. = Each). For a complete listing of abbreviations refer to the Abbreviations Listing in the Reference Section of this book.

Bare Costs:

Mat. (Bare Material Cost) (264)

The unit material cost is the "bare" material cost with no overhead and profit included. *Costs shown reflect national average material prices for January of the current year and include delivery to the job site. No sales taxes are included.*

Labor (162)

The unit labor cost is derived by multiplying bare labor-hour costs for Crew Q-2 by labor-hour units. The bare labor-hour cost is found in the Crew Section under Q-2. (If a trade is listed, the hourly labor cost—the wage rate—is found on the inside back cover.)

Labor-Hour Cost Crew Q-2	x	Labor-Hour Units	=	Labor
$30.43	x	5.333	=	$162.28

Equip. (Equipment) (0)

Equipment costs for each crew are listed in the description of each crew. Tools or equipment whose value justifies purchase or ownership by a contractor are considered overhead as shown on the inside back cover. The unit equipment cost is derived by multiplying the bare equipment hourly cost by the labor-hour units.

Equipment Cost Crew Q-2	x	Labor-Hour Units	=	Equip.
$0	x	5.333	=	$0

Total (426)

The total of the bare costs is the arithmetic total of the three previous columns: mat., labor, and equip.

Material	+	Labor	+	Equip.	=	Total
$264	+	$162	+	$0	=	$426

Total Costs Including O&P

This figure is the sum of the bare material cost plus 10% for profit; the bare labor cost plus total overhead and profit (per the inside back cover or, if a crew is listed, from the crew listings); and the bare equipment cost plus 10% for profit.

Material is Bare Material Cost + 10% = $264 + $26.40	=	$290
Labor for Crew Q-2 = Labor-Hour Cost ($46.12) x Labor-Hour Units (5.333)	=	$246
Equip. is Bare Equip. Cost + 10% = $0 + $0	=	$ 0
Total (Rounded)	=	$530

Figure 8.3 (*cont'd.*)

number of tradesmen will be indicated (1 Plum, 2 Spri, etc.). Abbreviations for trades are shown in Figure 8.4. If more than one trade is required to install the item and/or if powered equipment is needed, a crew number will be designated (Q-19, Q-8, etc.). A complete listing of crews is presented in the Reference pages of *Means Plumbing Cost Data* (see Figure 8.5). On these pages, each crew is broken down into the following components:

1. Number and type of workers designated.
2. Number, size, and type of any equipment required.
3. Hourly labor costs listed two ways: "bare," the base rate including fringe benefits only; and "including overhead and profit," the installing contractor's billing rate. (See Figure 8.4 from the inside back cover of *Means Plumbing Cost Data* for labor rate information).
4. Daily equipment costs, based on the weekly equipment rental cost divided by 5, plus the hourly operating cost, times 8 hours. This cost is listed two ways: as a bare cost and with a 10% markup to cover handling and management costs.
5. Labor and equipment are broken down further into: cost per man-hour for labor, and cost per man-hour, for the equipment.
6. The total daily man-hours for the crew.
7. The total bare costs per day for the crew, including equipment.
8. The total daily cost of the crew including the installing contractor's overhead and profit.

The total daily cost of the required crew is used to calculate the unit installation cost for each item (for both bare costs and cost including overhead and profit).

The crew designation does not mean that this is the only crew that can perform the work. Crew size and content have been developed and chosen based on practical experience and feedback from contractors. These designations represent a labor and equipment makeup commonly found in the industry. The most appropriate crew for a given task is best determined based on particular project requirements. Unit costs may vary if crew sizes or content are significantly changed.

Figure 8.6 is a page from Division 16 of *Means Plumbing Cost Data*. This page lists the equipment costs used in the presentation and calculation of the crew costs and unit price data. Rental costs are shown as daily, weekly, and monthly rates. The Hourly Operating Cost represents the cost of fuel, lubrication, and routine maintenance. Equipment costs used in the crews are calculated as follows:

Line Number:	016-420-7800
Equipment:	Electric Welder, 300 Amp.
Rent per week:	\$205.00
Hourly Operating Cost:	\$1.09

$$\frac{\text{Weekly rental}}{\text{5 days}} + (\text{Hourly Oper. Cost} \times 8\ \text{hrs/day}) = \text{Daily Equipment Costs}$$

$$\frac{205}{5} + (\$1.09 \times 8) = \$49.72 \text{ per day}$$

Installing Contractor's Overhead & Profit

Below are the **average** installing contractor's percentage mark-ups applied to base labor rates to arrive at typical billing rates.

Column A: Labor rates are based on union wages averaged for 30 major U.S. cities. Base rates including fringe benefits are listed hourly and daily. These figures are the sum of the wage rate and employer-paid fringe benefits such as vacation pay, employer-paid health and welfare costs, pension costs, plus appropriate training and industry advancement funds costs.

Column B: Workers' Compensation rates are the national average of state rates established for each trade.

Column C: Column C lists average fixed overhead figures for all trades. Included are Federal and State Unemployment costs set at 7.0%; Social Security Taxes (FICA) set at 7.65%; Builder's Risk Insurance costs set at 0.34%; and Public Liability costs set at 1.55%. All the percentages except those for Social Security Taxes vary from state to state as well as from company to company.

Columns D and E: Percentages in Columns D and E are based on the presumption that the installing contractor has annual billing of $1,500,000 and up. Overhead percentages may increase with smaller annual billing. The overhead percentages for any given contractor may vary greatly and depend on a number of factors, such as the contractor's annual volume, engineering and logistical support costs, and staff requirements. The figures for overhead and profit will also vary depending on the type of job, the job location, and the prevailing economic conditions. All factors should be examined very carefully for each job.

Column F: Column F lists the total of Columns B, C, D, and E.

Column G: Column G is Column A (hourly base labor rate) multiplied by the percentage in Column F (O&P percentage).

Column H: Column H is the total of Column A (hourly base labor rate) plus Column G (Total O&P).

Column I: Column I is Column H multiplied by eight hours.

		A		B	C	D	E	F	G	H	I
		Base Rate Incl. Fringes		Workers' Comp. Ins.	Average Fixed Overhead	Overhead		Total Overhead & Profit		Rate with O & P	
Abbr.	Trade	Hourly	Daily				Profit	%	Amount	Hourly	Daily
Skwk	Skilled Workers Average (35 trades)	$28.05	$224.40	18.3%	16.5%	13.0%	10%	57.8%	$16.20	$44.25	$354.00
	Helpers Average (5 trades)	20.85	166.80	19.7		11.0		57.2	11.95	32.80	262.40
	Foreman Average, Inside ($.50 over trade)	28.55	228.40	18.3		13.0		57.8	16.50	45.05	360.40
	Foreman Average, Outside ($2.00 over trade)	30.05	240.40	18.3		13.0		57.8	17.35	47.40	379.20
Clab	Common Building Laborers	21.45	171.60	19.9		11.0		57.4	12.30	33.75	270.00
Asbe	Asbestos/Insulation Workers/Pipe Coverers	30.45	243.60	18.9		16.0		61.4	18.70	49.15	393.20
Boil	Boilermakers	32.85	262.80	16.6		16.0		59.1	19.40	52.25	418.00
Bric	Bricklayers	27.60	220.80	18.0		11.0		55.5	15.30	42.90	343.20
Brhe	Bricklayer Helpers	21.60	172.80	18.0		11.0		55.5	12.00	33.60	268.80
Carp	Carpenters	27.30	218.40	19.9		11.0		57.4	15.65	42.95	343.60
Cefi	Cement Finishers	26.15	209.20	11.7		11.0		49.2	12.85	39.00	312.00
Elec	Electricians	31.90	255.20	7.0		16.0		49.5	15.80	47.70	381.60
Elev	Elevator Constructors	33.15	265.20	8.9		16.0		51.4	17.05	50.20	401.60
Eqhv	Equipment Operators, Crane or Shovel	29.35	234.80	11.6		14.0		52.1	15.30	44.65	357.20
Eqmd	Equipment Operators, Medium Equipment	28.40	227.20	11.6		14.0		52.1	14.80	43.20	345.60
Eqlt	Equipment Operators, Light Equipment	27.20	217.60	11.6		14.0		52.1	14.15	41.35	330.80
Eqol	Equipment Operators, Oilers	24.05	192.40	11.6		14.0		52.1	12.55	36.60	292.80
Eqmm	Equipment Operators, Master Mechanics	30.05	240.40	11.6		14.0		52.1	15.65	45.70	365.60
Glaz	Glaziers	26.60	212.80	14.7		11.0		52.2	13.90	40.50	324.00
Lath	Lathers	26.80	214.40	12.4		11.0		49.9	13.35	40.15	321.20
Marb	Marble Setters	27.50	220.00	18.0		11.0		55.5	15.25	42.75	342.00
Mill	Millwrights	28.75	230.00	11.9		11.0		49.4	14.20	42.95	343.60
Mstz	Mosaic & Terrazzo Workers	26.55	212.40	10.3		11.0		47.8	12.70	39.25	314.00
Pord	Painters, Ordinary	24.90	199.20	15.6		11.0		53.1	13.20	38.10	304.80
Psst	Painters, Structural Steel	26.00	208.00	51.6		11.0		89.1	23.15	49.15	393.20
Pape	Paper Hangers	25.10	200.80	15.6		11.0		53.1	13.35	38.45	307.60
Pile	Pile Drivers	27.20	217.60	30.3		16.0		72.8	19.80	47.00	376.00
Plas	Plasterers	25.70	205.60	15.8		11.0		53.3	13.70	39.40	315.20
Plah	Plasterer Helpers	21.60	172.80	15.8		11.0		53.3	11.50	33.10	264.80
Plum	Plumbers	32.60	260.80	9.0		16.0		51.5	16.80	49.40	395.20
Rodm	Rodmen (Reinforcing)	30.40	243.20	32.6		14.0		73.1	22.20	52.60	420.80
Rofc	Roofers, Composition	24.10	192.80	34.6		11.0		72.1	17.40	41.50	332.00
Rots	Roofers, Tile & Slate	24.20	193.60	34.6		11.0		72.1	17.45	41.65	333.20
Rohe	Roofers, Helpers (Composition)	18.10	144.80	34.6		11.0		72.1	13.05	31.15	249.20
Shee	Sheet Metal Workers	31.75	254.00	12.8		16.0		55.3	17.55	49.30	394.40
Spri	Sprinkler Installers	32.50	260.00	9.1		16.0		51.6	16.75	49.25	394.00
Stpi	Steamfitters or Pipefitters	32.75	262.00	9.0		16.0		51.5	16.85	49.60	396.80
Ston	Stone Masons	27.70	221.60	18.0		11.0		55.5	15.35	43.05	344.40
Sswk	Structural Steel Workers	30.60	244.80	42.8		14.0		83.3	25.50	56.10	448.80
Tilf	Tile Layers	26.65	213.20	10.3		11.0		47.8	12.75	39.40	315.20
Tilh	Tile Layers Helpers	21.45	171.60	10.3		11.0		47.8	10.25	31.70	253.60
Trlt	Truck Drivers, Light	21.75	174.00	15.6		11.0		53.1	11.55	33.30	266.40
Trhv	Truck Drivers, Heavy	22.10	176.80	15.6		11.0		53.1	11.75	33.85	270.80
Sswl	Welders, Structural Steel	30.60	244.80	42.8		14.0		83.3	25.50	56.10	448.80
Wrck	*Wrecking	21.45	171.60	42.5		11.0		80.0	17.15	38.60	308.80

* Not included in averages

From Means Plumbing Cost Data 1999

Figure 8.4

Crews

Crew No.	Bare Costs Hr.	Bare Costs Daily	Incl. Subs O & P Hr.	Incl. Subs O & P Daily	Cost Per Labor-Hour Bare Costs	Cost Per Labor-Hour Incl. O&P
Crew J-4	**Hr.**	**Daily**	**Hr.**	**Daily**	**Bare Costs**	**Incl. O&P**
1 Tile Layer	$26.65	$213.20	$39.40	$315.20	$24.05	$35.55
1 Tile Layer Helper	21.45	171.60	31.70	253.60		
16 L.H., Daily Totals		$384.80		$568.80	$24.05	$35.55
Crew K-1	**Hr.**	**Daily**	**Hr.**	**Daily**	**Bare Costs**	**Incl. O&P**
1 Carpenter	$27.30	$218.40	$42.95	$343.60	$24.52	$38.13
1 Truck Driver (light)	21.75	174.00	33.30	266.40		
1 Truck w/Power Equip.		179.45		197.40	11.22	12.34
16 L.H., Daily Totals		$571.85		$807.40	$35.74	$50.47
Crew K-2	**Hr.**	**Daily**	**Hr.**	**Daily**	**Bare Costs**	**Incl. O&P**
1 Struc. Steel Foreman	$32.60	$260.80	$59.75	$478.00	$28.32	$49.72
1 Struc. Steel Worker	30.60	244.80	56.10	448.80		
1 Truck Driver (light)	21.75	174.00	33.30	266.40		
1 Truck w/Power Equip.		179.45		197.40	7.48	8.22
24 L.H., Daily Totals		$859.05		$1390.60	$35.80	$57.94
Crew L-1	**Hr.**	**Daily**	**Hr.**	**Daily**	**Bare Costs**	**Incl. O&P**
1 Electrician	$31.90	$255.20	$47.70	$381.60	$32.25	$48.55
1 Plumber	32.60	260.80	49.40	395.20		
16 L.H., Daily Totals		$516.00		$776.80	$32.25	$48.55
Crew L-2	**Hr.**	**Daily**	**Hr.**	**Daily**	**Bare Costs**	**Incl. O&P**
1 Carpenter	$27.30	$218.40	$42.95	$343.60	$24.08	$37.88
1 Carpenter Helper	20.85	166.80	32.80	262.40		
16 L.H., Daily Totals		$385.20		$606.00	$24.08	$37.88
Crew L-3	**Hr.**	**Daily**	**Hr.**	**Daily**	**Bare Costs**	**Incl. O&P**
1 Carpenter	$27.30	$218.40	$42.95	$343.60	$29.56	$45.73
.5 Electrician	31.90	127.60	47.70	190.80		
.5 Sheet Metal Worker	31.75	127.00	49.30	197.20		
16 L.H., Daily Totals		$473.00		$731.60	$29.56	$45.73
Crew L-3A	**Hr.**	**Daily**	**Hr.**	**Daily**	**Bare Costs**	**Incl. O&P**
1 Carpenter Foreman (outside)	$29.30	$234.40	$46.10	$368.80	$30.12	$47.17
.5 Sheet Metal Worker	31.75	127.00	49.30	197.20		
12 L.H., Daily Totals		$361.40		$566.00	$30.12	$47.17
Crew L-4	**Hr.**	**Daily**	**Hr.**	**Daily**	**Bare Costs**	**Incl. O&P**
2 Skilled Workers	$28.05	$448.80	$44.25	$708.00	$25.65	$40.43
1 Helper	20.85	166.80	32.80	262.40		
24 L.H., Daily Totals		$615.60		$970.40	$25.65	$40.43
Crew L-5	**Hr.**	**Daily**	**Hr.**	**Daily**	**Bare Costs**	**Incl. O&P**
1 Struc. Steel Foreman	$32.60	$260.80	$59.75	$478.00	$30.71	$54.99
5 Struc. Steel Workers	30.60	1224.00	56.10	2244.00		
1 Equip. Oper. (crane)	29.35	234.80	44.65	357.20		
1 Hyd. Crane, 25 Ton		549.35		604.30	9.81	10.79
56 L.H., Daily Totals		$2268.95		$3683.50	$40.52	$65.78
Crew L-5A	**Hr.**	**Daily**	**Hr.**	**Daily**	**Bare Costs**	**Incl. O&P**
1 Structural Steel Foreman	$32.60	$260.80	$59.75	$478.00	$30.79	$54.15
2 Structural Steel Worker	30.60	489.60	56.10	897.60		
1 Equip. Oper. (crane)	29.35	234.80	44.65	357.20		
1 Crane,SP, 25 Ton		547.90		602.70	17.12	18.83
32 L.H., Daily Totals		$1533.10		$2335.50	$47.91	$72.98

Crew No.	Bare Costs Hr.	Bare Costs Daily	Incl. Subs O & P Hr.	Incl. Subs O & P Daily	Cost Per Labor-Hour Bare Costs	Cost Per Labor-Hour Incl. O&P
Crew L-6	**Hr.**	**Daily**	**Hr.**	**Daily**	**Bare Costs**	**Incl. O&P**
1 Plumber	$32.60	$260.80	$49.40	$395.20	$32.37	$48.83
.5 Electrician	31.90	127.60	47.70	190.80		
12 L.H., Daily Totals		$388.40		$586.00	$32.37	$48.83
Crew L-7	**Hr.**	**Daily**	**Hr.**	**Daily**	**Bare Costs**	**Incl. O&P**
2 Carpenters	$27.30	$436.80	$42.95	$687.20	$26.29	$41.00
1 Building Laborer	21.45	171.60	33.75	270.00		
.5 Electrician	31.90	127.60	47.70	190.80		
28 L.H., Daily Totals		$736.00		$1148.00	$26.29	$41.00
Crew L-8	**Hr.**	**Daily**	**Hr.**	**Daily**	**Bare Costs**	**Incl. O&P**
2 Carpenters	$27.30	$436.80	$42.95	$687.20	$28.36	$44.24
.5 Plumber	32.60	130.40	49.40	197.60		
20 L.H., Daily Totals		$567.20		$884.80	$28.36	$44.24
Crew L-9	**Hr.**	**Daily**	**Hr.**	**Daily**	**Bare Costs**	**Incl. O&P**
1 Labor Foreman (inside)	$21.95	$175.60	$34.55	$276.40	$24.76	$40.44
2 Building Laborers	21.45	343.20	33.75	540.00		
1 Struc. Steel Worker	30.60	244.80	56.10	448.80		
.5 Electrician	31.90	127.60	47.70	190.80		
36 L.H., Daily Totals		$891.20		$1456.00	$24.76	$40.44
Crew L-10	**Hr.**	**Daily**	**Hr.**	**Daily**	**Bare Costs**	**Incl. O&P**
1 Structural Steel Foreman	$32.60	$260.80	$59.75	$478.00	$30.85	$53.50
1 Structural Steel Worker	30.60	244.80	56.10	448.80		
1 Equip. Oper. (crane)	29.35	234.80	44.65	357.20		
1 Hyd. Crane, 12 Ton		443.45		487.80	18.48	20.32
24 L.H., Daily Totals		$1183.85		$1771.80	$49.33	$73.82
Crew M-1	**Hr.**	**Daily**	**Hr.**	**Daily**	**Bare Costs**	**Incl. O&P**
3 Elevator Constructors	$33.15	$795.60	$50.20	$1204.80	$31.49	$47.68
1 Elevator Apprentice	26.50	212.00	40.10	320.80		
5 Hand Tools		85.00		93.50	2.66	2.92
32 L.H., Daily Totals		$1092.60		$1619.10	$34.15	$50.60
Crew Q-1	**Hr.**	**Daily**	**Hr.**	**Daily**	**Bare Costs**	**Incl. O&P**
1 Plumber	$32.60	$260.80	$49.40	$395.20	$29.35	$44.48
1 Plumber Apprentice	26.10	208.80	39.55	316.40		
16 L.H., Daily Totals		$469.60		$711.60	$29.35	$44.48
Crew Q-1C	**Hr.**	**Daily**	**Hr.**	**Daily**	**Bare Costs**	**Incl. O&P**
1 Plumber	$32.60	$260.80	$49.40	$395.20	$29.03	$44.05
1 Plumber Apprentice	26.10	208.80	39.55	316.40		
1 Equip. Oper. (medium)	28.40	227.20	43.20	345.60		
1 Trencher, Chain		535.90		589.50	22.33	24.56
24 L.H., Daily Totals		$1232.70		$1646.70	$51.36	$68.61
Crew Q-2	**Hr.**	**Daily**	**Hr.**	**Daily**	**Bare Costs**	**Incl. O&P**
2 Plumbers	$32.60	$521.60	$49.40	$790.40	$30.43	$46.12
1 Plumber Apprentice	26.10	208.80	39.55	316.40		
24 L.H., Daily Totals		$730.40		$1106.80	$30.43	$46.12
Crew Q-3	**Hr.**	**Daily**	**Hr.**	**Daily**	**Bare Costs**	**Incl. O&P**
1 Plumber Foreman (ins)	$33.10	$264.80	$50.15	$401.20	$31.10	$47.13
2 Plumbers	32.60	521.60	49.40	790.40		
1 Plumber Apprentice	26.10	208.80	39.55	316.40		
32 L.H., Daily Totals		$995.20		$1508.00	$31.10	$47.13

From Means Plumbing Cost Data 1999

Figure 8.5

016 | Material & Equipment

016 400 | Equipment Rental

			UNIT	HOURLY OPER. COST	RENT PER DAY	RENT PER WEEK	RENT PER MONTH	CREW EQUIPMENT COST/DAY	
420	7700	Welder, electric, 200 amp	Ea.	.81	31.50	95	285	25.50	420
	7800	300 amp		1.09	68.50	205	615	49.70	
	7900	Gas engine, 200 amp		4.33	51.50	155	465	65.65	
	8000	300 amp		5.17	68.50	205	615	82.35	
	8100	Wheelbarrow, any size	↓		8.35	25	75	5	
460	0010	LIFTING AND HOISTING EQUIPMENT RENTAL R016 -410							460
	0100	without operators							
	0200	Crane, climbing, 106' jib, 6000 lb. capacity, 410 FPM	Ea.	26.58	1,225	3,650	11,000	942.65	
	0300	101' jib, 10,250 lb. capacity, 270 FPM	"	35.34	1,550	4,650	14,000	1,213	
	0400	Tower, static, 130' high, 106' jib,							
	0500	6200 lb. capacity at 400 FPM	Ea.	53.48	1,425	4,250	12,800	1,278	
	0600	Crawler, cable, 1/2 C.Y., 15 tons at 12' radius		19	535	1,600	4,800	472	
	0700	3/4 C.Y., 20 tons at 12' radius		20.20	550	1,650	4,950	491.60	
	0800	1 C.Y., 25 tons at 12' radius		20.85	565	1,700	5,100	506.80	
	0900	Crawler, cable, 1-1/2 C.Y., 40 tons at 12' radius		30.54	765	2,300	6,900	704.30	
	1000	2 C.Y., 50 tons at 12' radius		35.59	935	2,800	8,400	844.70	
	1100	3 C.Y., 75 tons at 12' radius		43.66	965	2,900	8,700	929.30	
	1200	100 ton capacity, standard boom		41.43	1,325	4,000	12,000	1,131	
	1300	165 ton capacity, standard boom		64.77	2,175	6,500	19,500	1,818	
	1400	200 ton capacity, 150' boom		120.73	2,325	7,000	21,000	2,366	
	1500	450' boom		135.50	3,000	9,000	27,000	2,884	
	1600	Truck mounted, cable operated, 6 x 4, 20 tons at 10' radius		14.07	665	2,000	6,000	512.55	
	1700	25 tons at 10' radius		20.80	1,075	3,200	9,600	806.40	
	1800	8 x 4, 30 tons at 10' radius		28.61	600	1,800	5,400	588.90	
	1900	40 tons at 12' radius		29.34	765	2,300	6,900	694.70	
	2000	8 x 4, 60 tons at 15' radius		44.87	900	2,700	8,100	898.95	
	2050	82 tons at 15' radius		45.56	1,625	4,900	14,700	1,344	
	2100	90 tons at 15' radius		48.95	1,025	3,100	9,300	1,012	
	2200	115 tons at 15' radius		51.15	1,875	5,600	16,800	1,529	
	2300	150 tons at 18' radius		76.61	1,575	4,700	14,100	1,553	
	2350	165 tons at 18' radius		77.65	2,200	6,600	19,800	1,941	
	2400	Truck mounted, hydraulic, 12 ton capacity		22.93	435	1,300	3,900	443.45	
	2500	25 ton capacity		23.67	600	1,800	5,400	549.35	
	2550	33 ton capacity		24.37	835	2,500	7,500	694.95	
	2600	55 ton capacity		34.14	865	2,600	7,800	793.10	
	2700	80 ton capacity		37.29	1,325	4,000	12,000	1,098	
	2800	Self-propelled, 4 x 4, with telescoping boom, 5 ton		10.18	315	950	2,850	271.45	
	2900	12-1/2 ton capacity		16.42	435	1,300	3,900	391.35	
	3000	15 ton capacity		18.20	485	1,450	4,350	435.60	
	3100	25 ton capacity		20.99	635	1,900	5,700	547.90	
	3200	Derricks, guy, 20 ton capacity, 60' boom, 75' mast		8.70	292	875	2,625	244.60	
	3300	100' boom, 115' mast		16.39	515	1,550	4,650	441.10	
	3400	Stiffleg, 20 ton capacity, 70' boom, 37' mast		11.56	385	1,150	3,450	322.50	
	3500	100' boom, 47' mast		18.06	625	1,875	5,625	519.50	
	3550	Helicopter, small, lift to 1250 lbs. maximum		257.50	2,425	7,250	21,800	3,510	
	3600	Hoists, chain type, overhead, manual, 3/4 ton		.06	6	18	54	4.10	
	3900	10 ton		.25	25	75	225	17	
	4000	Hoist and tower, 5000 lb. cap., portable electric, 40' high		4.03	172	515	1,550	135.25	
	4100	For each added 10' section, add			11.65	35	105	7	
	4200	Hoist and single tubular tower, 5000 lb. electric, 100' high		5.41	237	710	2,125	185.30	
	4300	For each added 6'-6" section, add		.73	20	60	180	17.85	
	4400	Hoist and double tubular tower, 5000 lb., 100' high		5.77	250	750	2,250	196.15	
	4500	For each added 6'-6" section, add		.06	16.65	50	150	10.50	
	4550	Hoist and tower, mast type, 6000 lb., 100' high		5.34	275	825	2,475	207.70	
	4570	For each added 10' section, add		.15	15	45	135	10.20	
	4600	Hoist and tower, personnel, electric, 2000 lb., 100' @ 125 FPM		10.04	685	2,050	6,150	490.30	
	4700	3000 lb., 100' @ 200 FPM	↓	10.79	735	2,200	6,600	526.30	

From Means Plumbing Cost Data 1999

Figure 8.6

Units

The unit column (see Figures 8.4 and 8.5) defines the component for which the costs have been calculated. It is this "unit" on which Unit Price Estimating is based. The units as used represent standard estimating and quantity takeoff procedures. However, the estimator should always check to be sure that the units taken off are the same as those priced. A list of standard abbreviations is included at the back of *Means Plumbing Cost Data*.

Bare Costs

The four columns listed under "Bare Costs," — "Material," "Labor," "Equipment," and "Total" represent the actual cost of construction items to the contractor. In other words, bare costs are those which do not include the overhead and profit of the installing contractor, whether it is a subcontractor or a general contracting company using its own crews.

Material: Material costs are based on the national average contractor purchase price delivered to the job site. Delivered costs are assumed to be within a 20-mile radius of metropolitan areas. No sales tax is included in the material prices because of variations from state to state.

The prices are based on quantities that would normally be purchased for complete buildings or projects costing $1,000,000 and up. Prices for small quantities must be adjusted accordingly. If more current costs for materials are available for the appropriate location, it is recommended that adjustments be made to the unit costs to reflect any cost difference.

Labor: Labor costs are calculated by multiplying the "Bare Labor Cost" per labor hour times the number of labor-hours, from the "Labor-Hours" column. The "Bare" labor rate is determined by adding the base rate plus fringe benefits. The base rate is the actual hourly wage of a worker used in figuring payroll. It is from this figure that employee deductions are taken (Federal withholding, FICA, State withholding). Fringe benefits include all employer-paid benefits, above and beyond the payroll amount (employer-paid health, vacation pay, pension, profit sharing). The "Bare Labor Cost" is, therefore, the actual amount that the contractor must pay directly for construction workers. Figure 8.4 shows labor rates for the 35 construction trades plus skilled worker, helper, and foreman averages. These rates are the averages of union wage agreements effective January 1 of the current year from 30 major cities in the United States. The "Bare Labor Cost" for each trade, as used in *Means Plumbing Cost Data*, is shown in column "A" as the base rate including fringes. Refer to the "Crew" column to determine what rate is used to calculate the "Bare Labor Cost" for a particular line item.

Equipment: Equipment costs are calculated by multiplying the "Bare Equipment Cost" per man-hour, from the appropriate "Crew" listing, times the man-hours in the "Man-Hours" column. The calculation of the equipment portion of installation costs is outlined earlier in this chapter.

Total Bare Costs

This column simply represents the arithmetic sum of the bare material, labor, and equipment costs. This total is the average cost to the contractor for the particular item of construction, supplied and installed, or "in place." No overhead and/or profit is included.

Total Including Overhead and Profit

This column represents the total cost of an item including the installation contractor's overhead and profit. The installing contractor could be either the prime mechanical contractor or a subcontractor. If these costs are used for an item to be installed by a subcontractor, the prime mechanical contractor should include an additional percentage (usually 10% to 20%) to cover the expenses of supervision and management. Consideration must be given also to sub-subcontractors who often appear in mechanical contracting. An example might be an electrical sub to the Temperature Control Subcontractor who, of course, is a sub to the HVAC contractor. Each contractor has his own overhead and profit markup. The costs in the "Total Including Overhead and Profit" are the arithmetical sum of the following three calculations:

- Bare Material Cost plus 10%
- Labor Cost, including overhead and profit, per labor-hour times the number of labor-hours
- Equipment Costs, including overhead and profit, per labor-hour times the number of labor-hours

The Labor and Equipment Costs, including overhead and profit are found in the appropriate crew listings. The overhead and profit percentage factor for Labor is obtained from Column F in Figure 8.4. The overhead and profit for Equipment is 10% of "Bare" cost.

Labor costs are increased by percentages for overhead and profit, depending on trade as shown in Figure 8.4. The resulting rates are listed in the right-hand columns of the same figure. Note that the percentage increase for overhead and profit for plumbers is 51.5% of the base rate. The following items are included in the increase for overhead and profit, as shown in Figure 8.4

Workers' Compensation and Employer's Liability: Workers' Compensation and Employer's Liability Insurance rates vary from state to state and are tied into the construction trade safety records in that particular state. Rates also vary by trade according to the hazard involved (see Figure 8.7, average insurance rates as of January, 1999). The proper authorities will most likely keep the contractor well informed of the rates and obligations.

State and Federal Unemployment Insurance: The employer's tax rate is adjusted by a merit-rating system according to the number of former employees applying for benefits. Contractors who find it possible to offer a maximum of steady employment can enjoy a reduction in the unemployment tax rate.

Employer-Paid Social Security (FICA): The tax rate is adjusted annually by the federal government. It is a percentage of an employee's salary up to a maximum annual contribution.

Builder's Risk and Public Liability: These insurance-rates vary according to the trades involved and the state in which the work is done.

Overhead: The column listed as "Overhead" provides percentages to be added for office or operating overhead. This is the cost of doing business. The percentages are presented as national averages by trade as shown in Figure 8.4. Note that the operating overhead costs are applied to labor only in *Means Plumbing Cost Data*.

R010-060 Workers' Compensation Insurance Rates by Trade

The table below tabulates the national averages for Workers' Compensation insurance rates by trade and type of building. The average "Insurance Rate" is multiplied by the "% of Building Cost" for each trade. This produces the "Workers' Compensation Cost" by % of total labor cost, to be added for each trade by building type to determine the weighted average Workers' Compensation rate for the building types analyzed.

Trade	Insurance Rate (% Labor Cost) Range	Average	% of Building Cost Office Bldgs.	Schools & Apts.	Mfg.	Workers' Compensation Office Bldgs.	Schools & Apts.	Mfg.
Excavation, Grading, etc.	4.0 % to 26.6%	11.6%	4.8%	4.9%	4.5%	0.56%	0.57%	0.52%
Piles & Foundations	8.1 to 80.1	30.3	7.1	5.2	8.7	2.15	1.58	2.64
Concrete	7.2 to 39.4	19.1	5.0	14.8	3.7	0.96	2.83	0.71
Masonry	5.3 to 48.6	18.0	6.9	7.5	1.9	1.24	1.35	0.34
Structural Steel	8.1 to 132.9	42.8	10.7	3.9	17.6	4.58	1.67	7.53
Miscellaneous & Ornamental Metals	5.4 to 34.0	14.1	2.8	4.0	3.6	0.39	0.56	0.51
Carpentry & Millwork	7.0 to 49.9	19.9	3.7	4.0	0.5	0.74	0.80	0.10
Metal or Composition Siding	7.3 to 36.7	18.3	2.3	0.3	4.3	0.42	0.05	0.79
Roofing	8.1 to 88.8	34.6	2.3	2.6	3.1	0.80	0.90	1.07
Doors & Hardware	3.6 to 28.8	11.8	0.9	1.4	0.4	0.11	0.17	0.05
Sash & Glazing	5.3 to 30.0	14.7	3.5	4.0	1.0	0.51	0.59	0.15
Lath & Plaster	5.5 to 37.4	15.8	3.3	6.9	0.8	0.52	1.09	0.13
Tile, Marble & Floors	3.3 to 29.5	10.3	2.6	3.0	0.5	0.27	0.31	0.05
Acoustical Ceilings	4.2 to 26.7	12.4	2.4	0.2	0.3	0.30	0.02	0.04
Painting	5.6 to 41.1	15.6	1.5	1.6	1.6	0.23	0.25	0.25
Interior Partitions	7.0 to 49.9	19.9	3.9	4.3	4.4	0.78	0.86	0.88
Miscellaneous Items	2.8 to 112.5	19.3	5.2	3.7	9.7	1.00	0.71	1.87
Elevators	2.0 to 20.0	8.9	2.1	1.1	2.2	0.19	0.10	0.20
Sprinklers	2.7 to 20.6	9.1	0.5	—	2.0	0.05	—	0.18
Plumbing	3.0 to 15.9	9.0	4.9	7.2	5.2	0.44	0.65	0.47
Heat., Vent., Air Conditioning	3.9 to 29.2	12.8	13.5	11.0	12.9	1.73	1.41	1.65
Electrical	3.2 to 11.6	7.0	10.1	8.4	11.1	0.71	0.59	0.78
Total	2.0 % to 132.9%	—	100.0%	100.0%	100.0%	18.68%	17.06%	20.91%
	Overall Weighted Average 18.88%							

Workers' Compensation Insurance Rates by States

The table below lists the weighted average Workers' Compensation base rate for each state with a factor comparing this with the national average of 18.3%.

State	Weighted Average	Factor	State	Weighted Average	Factor	State	Weighted Average	Factor
Alabama	30.4%	166	Kentucky	19.8%	108	North Dakota	16.7%	91
Alaska	12.8	70	Louisiana	27.2	149	Ohio	16.1	88
Arizona	17.6	96	Maine	21.8	119	Oklahoma	21.9	120
Arkansas	13.0	71	Maryland	11.9	65	Oregon	19.2	105
California	18.6	102	Massachusetts	26.5	145	Pennsylvania	22.9	125
Colorado	26.4	144	Michigan	21.7	119	Rhode Island	22.3	122
Connecticut	21.1	115	Minnesota	37.6	205	South Carolina	13.9	76
Delaware	12.3	67	Mississippi	23.8	130	South Dakota	17.9	98
District of Columbia	25.2	138	Missouri	15.8	86	Tennessee	14.4	79
Florida	28.0	153	Montana	37.3	204	Texas	24.7	135
Georgia	24.9	136	Nebraska	15.7	86	Utah	12.9	70
Hawaii	16.7	91	Nevada	17.8	97	Vermont	14.9	81
Idaho	11.8	64	New Hampshire	23.5	128	Virginia	11.8	64
Illinois	27.5	150	New Jersey	11.0	60	Washington	12.0	66
Indiana	7.1	39	New Mexico	23.1	126	West Virginia	14.0	77
Iowa	14.6	80	New York	17.0	93	Wisconsin	13.9	76
Kansas	11.0	60	North Carolina	14.0	77	Wyoming	8.9	49
			Weighted Average for U.S. is	18.9% of payroll = 100%				

Rates in the following table are the base or manual costs per $100 of payroll for Workers' Compensation in each state. Rates are usually applied to straight time wages only and not to premium time wages and bonuses.

The weighted average skilled worker rate for 35 trades is 18.3%. For bidding purposes, apply the full value of Workers' Compensation directly to total labor costs, or if labor is 38%, materials 42% and overhead and profit 20% of total cost, carry 38/80 x 18.3% = 8.7% of cost (before overhead and profit) into overhead. Rates vary not only from state to state but also with the experience rating of the contractor.

Rates are the most current available at the time of publication.

From Means Plumbing Cost Data 1999

Figure 8.7

Profit: This percentage is the fee added by the contractor to offer both a return on investment and an allowance to cover the risk involved in the type of construction being bid. The profit percentage may vary from 4% on large, straightforward projects to as much as 25% on smaller, high-risk jobs. Profit percentages are directly affected by economic conditions, the expected number of bidders, and the estimated risk involved in the project. For estimating purposes, *Means Plumbing Cost Data* assume 10% (applied to labor) as a reasonable average profit factor.

Means Order of Magnitude and Square Foot Cost Data

A sample page from Division 17 of *Means Plumbing Cost Data* 1999 (Figure 8.8) indicates order of magnitude costs per rental unit, per apartment, and per bed (for nursing homes). Division 17 also gives square foot costs, cubic foot costs, and percentages of total costs for plumbing, HVAC, and electrical. This division prices 58 building types from apartments through warehouses.

Division 17 has been developed to facilitate the preparation of rapid preliminary budget estimates. The cost figures in this division are derived from more than 10,200 actual building projects contained in the Means data bank of construction costs and include the contractor's overhead and profit. The prices shown *do not* include architectural fees or land costs. The files are updated each year with costs for new projects. In no case are all subdivisions of a project listed.

These projects were located throughout the United States and reflect differences in square foot and cubic foot costs due to both the variations in labor and material costs, and the differences in the owners' requirements. For instance, a bank in a large city would have different features and costs than one in a rural area. This is true of all the different types of buildings analyzed. All individual cost items were computed and tabulated separately. Thus, the sum of the median figures for Plumbing, HVAC, and Electrical will not normally add up to the total Mechanical and Electrical costs arrived at by separate analysis and tabulation of the projects.

The data and prices presented on a Division 17 page (as shown in Figure 8.8) are listed both as square foot or cubic foot costs and as a percentage of total costs. Each category tabulates the data in a similar manner. The median, or middle figure, is listed. This means that 50% of all projects had lower costs, and 50% had higher costs than the median figure. Figures in the "1/4" column indicate that 25% of the projects had lower costs and 75% had higher costs. Similarly, figures in the "3/4" column indicate that 75% had lower costs and 25% of the projects had higher costs.

The costs and figures represent all projects and do not take into account project size. As a rule, larger buildings (of the same type and relative location) will cost less to build per square foot than similar buildings of a smaller size. This cost difference is due to economies of scale as well as a lower exterior envelope-to-floor area ratio. A conversion is necessary to adjust project costs based on size relative to the norm. Figure 8.9 from the Reference pages of *Plumbing Cost Data* 1999 provides instruction in doing size modification calculations.

171 | S.F., C.F. and % of Total Costs

	171 000 | S.F. & C.F. Costs		UNIT	UNIT COSTS 1/4	UNIT COSTS MEDIAN	UNIT COSTS 3/4	% OF TOTAL 1/4	% OF TOTAL MEDIAN	% OF TOTAL 3/4
500	9000	Per apartment, total cost (R171-100)	Apt.	52,600	59,800	75,100			
	9500	Total: Mechanical & Electrical	"	9,600	12,300	14,300			
510	0010	**ICE SKATING RINKS**	S.F.	43.10	74.75	105			
	0020	Total project costs	C.F.	3.01	3.08	3.55			
	2720	Plumbing	S.F.	1.53	2.87	2.93	3.10%	5.60%	6.70%
	2900	Electrical		4.38	6.70	7.10	6.70%	15%	15.80%
	3100	Total: Mechanical & Electrical	↓	7.55	10.90	13.60	9.90%	25.90%	29.80%
520	0010	**JAILS**	S.F.	126	161	208			
	0020	Total project costs	C.F.	11.75	14.40	18.40			
	2720	Plumbing	S.F.	12.70	16.10	21.25	7%	8.90%	13.80%
	2770	Heating, ventilating, air conditioning		11.25	15	29	7.50%	9.40%	17.70%
	2900	Electrical		13.70	17.60	21.80	8.10%	11.40%	12.40%
	3100	Total: Mechanical & Electrical	↓	35	62.10	73.50	29.20%	31.10%	34.10%
530	0010	**LIBRARIES**	S.F.	74.35	94.70	121			
	0020	Total project costs	C.F.	5.20	6.50	8.45			
	2720	Plumbing	S.F.	3.01	4.23	5.75	3.60%	4.90%	5.70%
	2770	Heating, ventilating, air conditioning		6.45	10.90	14.20	8%	11%	14.60%
	2900	Electrical		7.65	10.10	12.50	8.30%	11%	12.10%
	3100	Total: Mechanical & Electrical	↓	22.05	30.15	37.75	18.90%	25.30%	27.60%
550	0010	**MEDICAL CLINICS**	S.F.	73.15	90.60	114			
	0020	Total project costs	C.F.	5.45	7.05	9.40			
	2720	Plumbing	S.F.	4.93	6.95	9.30	6.10%	8.40%	10%
	2770	Heating, ventilating, air conditioning		6.10	7.70	11.30	6.70%	9%	11.30%
	2900	Electrical		6.20	8.85	11.75	8.10%	10%	12.20%
	3100	Total: Mechanical & Electrical	↓	19.55	27.50	38.45	22%	27.60%	34.30%
570	0010	**MEDICAL OFFICES**	S.F.	68.65	85.10	105			
	0020	Total project costs	C.F.	5.10	7	9.60			
	2720	Plumbing	S.F.	3.85	5.95	8.05	5.70%	6.80%	8.60%
	2770	Heating, ventilating, air conditioning		4.66	6.85	8.90	6.20%	8%	9.70%
	2900	Electrical		5.45	7.95	11.05	7.60%	9.80%	11.40%
	3100	Total: Mechanical & Electrical	↓	13.55	19.45	28.90	18.50%	22%	24.90%
590	0010	**MOTELS**	S.F.	44.05	65.20	84.10			
	0020	Total project costs	C.F.	3.84	5.40	8.85			
	2720	Plumbing	S.F.	4.46	5.70	6.80	9.40%	10.60%	12.50%
	2770	Heating, ventilating, air conditioning		2.72	4.05	7.25	5.60%	5.60%	10%
	2900	Electrical		4.16	5.30	6.90	7.10%	8.20%	10.40%
	3100	Total: Mechanical & Electrical	↓	14.15	17.70	30.35	18.50%	21%	24.40%
	9000	Per rental unit, total cost	Unit	22,400	42,600	46,000			
	9500	Total: Mechanical & Electrical	"	4,400	6,600	7,700			
600	0010	**NURSING HOMES**	S.F.	66.15	87.50	107			
	0020	Total project costs	C.F.	5.30	6.95	9.25			
	2720	Plumbing	S.F.	6.25	7.95	11	9.40%	10.70%	14.20%
	2770	Heating, ventilating, air conditioning		6.20	8.60	11	9.30%	11.40%	11.80%
	2900	Electrical		6.85	8.55	11.50	9.70%	11%	13%
	3100	Total: Mechanical & Electrical	↓	16.30	22.80	33.40	26%	29.90%	30.50%
	9000	Per bed or person, total cost	Bed	28,700	35,200	47,000			
610	0010	**OFFICES** Low Rise (1 to 4 story)	S.F.	55.75	71	94.55			
	0020	Total project costs	C.F.	4.04	5.65	7.65			
	2720	Plumbing	S.F.	2.12	3.21	4.55	3.70%	4.50%	6.10%
	2770	Heating, ventilating, air conditioning		4.58	6.35	9.40	7.20%	10.50%	11.90%
	2900	Electrical		4.72	6.55	9.15	7.50%	9.60%	11.10%
	3100	Total: Mechanical & Electrical	↓	11.10	15.40	22.55	18%	21.80%	26.50%
620	0010	**OFFICES** Mid Rise (5 to 10 story)	S.F.	61.50	74.55	101			
	0020	Total project costs	C.F.	4.30	5.45	7.90			
	2720	Plumbing	S.F.	1.86	2.88	4.14	2.80%	3.70%	4.50%
	2770	Heating, ventilating, air conditioning		4.67	6.70	10.65	7.60%	9.40%	11%
	2900	Electrical		4.57	5.85	8.85	6.50%	8.20%	10%
	3100	Total: Mechanical & Electrical	↓	11.65	14.90	29.55	17.90%	22.30%	29.90%

From Means Plumbing Cost Data 1999

Figure 8.8

R171-100 Square Foot Project Size Modifier

One factor that affects the S.F. cost of a particular building is the size. In general, for buildings built to the same specifications in the same locality, the larger building will have the lower S.F. cost. This is due mainly to the decreasing contribution of the exterior walls plus the economy of scale usually achievable in larger buildings. The Area Conversion Scale shown below will give a factor to convert costs for the typical size building to an adjusted cost for the particular project.

The Square Foot Base Size lists the median costs, most typical project size in our accumulated data and the range in size of the projects.

The Size Factor for your project is determined by dividing your project area in S.F. by the typical project size for the particular Building Type. With this factor, enter the Area Conversion Scale at the appropriate Size Factor and determine the appropriate cost multiplier for your building size.

Example: Determine the cost per S.F. for a 100,000 S.F. Mid-rise apartment building.

$$\frac{\text{Proposed building area} = 100{,}000 \text{ S.F.}}{\text{Typical size from below} = 50{,}000 \text{ S.F.}} = 2.00$$

Enter Area Conversion scale at 2.0, intersect curve, read horizontally the appropriate cost multiplier of .94. Size adjusted cost becomes .94 x $66.40 = $62.40 based on national average costs.

Note: For Size Factors less than .50, the Cost Multiplier is 1.1
For Size Factors greater than 3.5, the Cost Multiplier is .90

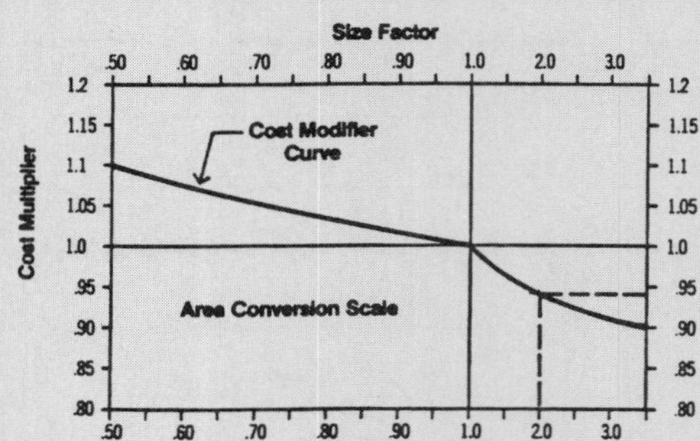

Square Foot Base Size							
Building Type	**Median Cost per S.F.**	**Typical Size Gross S.F.**	**Typical Range Gross S.F.**	**Building Type**	**Median Cost per S.F.**	**Typical Size Gross S.F.**	**Typical Range Gross S.F.**
Apartments, Low Rise	$ 52.60	21,000	9,700.00 - 37,200	Jails	$161.00	13,700	7,500 - 28,000
Apartments, Mid Rise	66.40	50,000	32,000 - 100,000	Libraries	94.70	12,000	7,000 - 31,000
Apartments, High Rise	76.20	310,000	100,000 - 650,000	Medical Clinics	90.60	7,200	4,200 - 15,700
Auditoriums	87.95	25,000	7,600 - 39,000	Medical Offices	85.10	6,000	4,000 - 15,000
Auto Sales	54.40	20,000	10,800 - 28,600	Motels	65.20	27,000	15,800 - 51,000
Banks	118.00	4,200	2,500 - 7,500	Nursing Homes	87.50	23,000	15,000 - 37,000
Churches	79.45	9,000	5,300 - 13,200	Offices, Low Rise	71.00	8,600	4,700 - 19,000
Clubs, Country	79.20	6,500	4,500 - 15,000	Offices, Mid Rise	74.55	52,000	31,300 - 83,100
Clubs, Social	77.05	10,000	6,000 - 13,500	Offices, High Rise	94.50	260,000	151,000 - 468,000
Clubs, YMCA	79.40	28,300	12,800 - 39,400	Police Stations	119.00	10,500	4,000 - 19,000
Colleges (Class)	104.00	50,000	23,500 - 98,500	Post Offices	87.95	12,400	6,800 - 30,000
Colleges (Science Lab)	151.00	45,600	16,600 - 80,000	Power Plants	673.00	7,500	1,000 - 20,000
College (Student Union)	116.00	33,400	16,000 - 85,000	Religious Education	72.85	9,000	6,000 - 12,000
Community Center	82.80	9,400	5,300 - 16,700	Research	124.00	19,000	6,300 - 45,000
Court Houses	112.00	32,400	17,800 - 106,000	Restaurants	107.00	4,400	2,800 - 6,000
Dept. Stores	49.15	90,000	44,000 - 122,000	Retail Stores	52.25	7,200	4,000 - 17,600
Dormitories, Low Rise	84.85	24,500	13,400 - 40,000	Schools, Elementary	76.10	41,000	24,500 - 55,000
Dormitories, Mid Rise	110.00	55,600	36,100 - 90,000	Schools, Jr. High	77.50	92,000	52,000 - 119,000
Factories	47.65	26,400	12,900 - 50,000	Schools, Sr. High	77.50	101,000	50,500 - 175,000
Fire Stations	83.15	5,800	4,000 - 8,700	Schools, Vocational	77.20	37,000	20,500 - 82,000
Fraternity Houses	81.80	12,500	8,200 - 14,800	Sports Arenas	64.70	15,000	5,000 - 40,000
Funeral Homes	91.45	7,800	4,500 - 11,000	Supermarkets	52.45	20,000	12,000 - 30,000
Garages, Commercial	58.10	9,300	5,000 - 13,600	Swimming Pools	121.00	13,000	7,800 - 22,000
Garages, Municipal	74.30	8,300	4,500 - 12,600	Telephone Exchange	141.00	4,500	1,200 - 10,600
Garages, Parking	30.45	163,000	76,400 - 225,300	Theaters	77.60	10,500	8,800 - 17,500
Gymnasiums	76.85	19,200	11,600 - 41,000	Town Halls	85.35	10,800	4,800 - 23,400
Hospitals	145.00	55,000	27,200 - 125,000	Warehouses	35.15	25,000	8,000 - 72,000
House (Elderly)	71.95	37,000	21,000 - 66,000	Warehouse & Office	40.60	25,000	8,000 - 72,000
Housing (Public)	66.60	36,000	14,400 - 74,400				
Ice Rinks	74.75	29,000	27,200 - 33,600				

From Means Plumbing Cost Data 1999

Figure 8.9

There are two stages of project development when square foot cost estimates are most useful. The first is during the conceptual stage when few, if any, details are available. At this time, square foot costs are appropriate for ballpark budget purposes. As soon as details become available in the project design, the square foot approach should be discontinued and the project priced more accurately. After the estimate is completed, square foot costs can be used again—this time for verification and as a check against gross errors.

When using the figures in Division 17, it is recommended that the median cost column be consulted for preliminary figures if no additional information is available. When costs have been converted for location (see City Cost Indexes) the median numbers (as shown in Figure 8.8) should provide a fairly accurate base figure. This figure should then be adjusted according to the estimator's experience, local economic conditions, code requirements, and the owner's particular project requirements. There is no need to factor the percentage figures, as these should remain relatively constant from city to city.

Repair and Remodeling

Cost figures in *Means Plumbing Cost Data* are based on new construction utilizing the most cost effective combination of labor, equipment, and material. The work is scheduled in the proper sequence to allow the various trades to accomplish their tasks in an efficient manner. Figure 8.10 (from Division 010 of *Means Plumbing Cost Data*) shows factors that can be used to adjust figures in other sections of the book for repair and remodeling projects. For expanded coverage, see *Means Repair and Remodeling Cost Data*.

Assemblies Cost Tables

Means' assemblies data are divided into twelve "UniFormat" divisions, which organize the components of construction into logical groupings. The Systems or Assemblies approach was devised to provide quick and easy methods for estimating even when only preliminary design data are available. The groupings, or systems, are presented in such a way so that the estimator can substitute one system for another. This is extremely useful when adapting to budget, design, or other considerations.

Figure 8.11, a representative page from the 1999 edition of *Means Plumbing Cost Data*, shows battery or group mounting of lavatories and the system components. The savings realized by side-by-side or back-to-back installation are indicated. All assemblies prices include the installing (plumbing) contractor's overhead and profit. Figure 8.12 explains how the data is presented.

Each system is illustrated and accompanied by a detailed description. The book lists the components and sizes of each system. Each individual component is found in the Unit Price section.

010 | Overhead & Miscellaneous Data

		010 000 | Overhead	CREW	DAILY OUTPUT	LABOR-HOURS	UNIT	1999 BARE COSTS MAT.	LABOR	EQUIP.	TOTAL	TOTAL INCL O&P	
004	0011	**ARCHITECTURAL FEES**										004
	0020	For new construction										
	0060	Minimum				Project					4.90%	
	0090	Maximum									16%	
	0100	For alteration work, to $500,000, add to fee									50%	
	0150	Over $500,000, add to fee									25%	
012	0010	**CONSTRUCTION COST INDEX** (Reference) over 930 zip code locations in										012
	0020	The U.S. and Canada, total bldg cost, min. (Dalton, GA)				%					66.90%	
	0050	Average									100%	
	0100	Maximum (New York, NY)									133.90%	
016	0010	**CONSTRUCTION MANAGEMENT FEES** $1,000,000 job, minimum				Project					4.50%	016
	0050	Maximum									7.50%	
	0300	$5,000,000 job, minimum									2.50%	
	0350	Maximum									4%	
020	0010	**CONTINGENCIES** Allowance to add at conceptual stage				Project					15%	020
	0050	Schematic stage									10%	
	0100	Preliminary working drawing stage									7%	
	0150	Final working drawing stage									2%	
022	0010	**CONTRACTOR EQUIPMENT** See division 016 (R016-410)										022
024	0010	**CREWS** For building construction, see How To Use This Book										024
028	0010	**ENGINEERING FEES** (R010-030)										028
	0020	Educational planning consultant, minimum				Project					.50%	
	0100	Maximum				"					2.50%	
	0200	Electrical, minimum				Contrct					4.10%	
	0300	Maximum									10.10%	
	0400	Elevator & conveying systems, minimum									2.50%	
	0500	Maximum									5%	
	0600	Food service & kitchen equipment, minimum									8%	
	0700	Maximum									12%	
	0800	Landscaping & site development, minimum									2.50%	
	0900	Maximum									6%	
	1000	Mechanical (plumbing & HVAC), minimum									4.10%	
	1100	Maximum									10.10%	
	1200	Structural, minimum				Project					1%	
	1300	Maximum				"					2.50%	
032	0010	**FACTORS** Cost adjustments (R011-010)										032
	0100	Add to construction costs for particular job requirements										
	0500	Cut & patch to match existing construction, add, minimum				Costs	2%	3%				
	0550	Maximum					5%	9%				
	0800	Dust protection, add, minimum					1%	2%				
	0850	Maximum					4%	11%				
	1100	Equipment usage curtailment, add, minimum					1%	1%				
	1150	Maximum					3%	10%				
	1400	Material handling & storage limitation, add, minimum					1%	1%				
	1450	Maximum					6%	7%				
	1700	Protection of existing work, add, minimum					2%	2%				
	1750	Maximum					5%	7%				
	2000	Shift work requirements, add, minimum						5%				
	2050	Maximum						30%				
	2300	Temporary shoring and bracing, add, minimum					2%	5%				
	2350	Maximum					5%	12%				
	2400	Work inside prisons, add, minimum						30%				
	2450	Maximum						50%				

From Means Plumbing Cost Data 1999

Figure 8.10

PLUMBING | A8.1-580 | Lavatories, Battery Mount

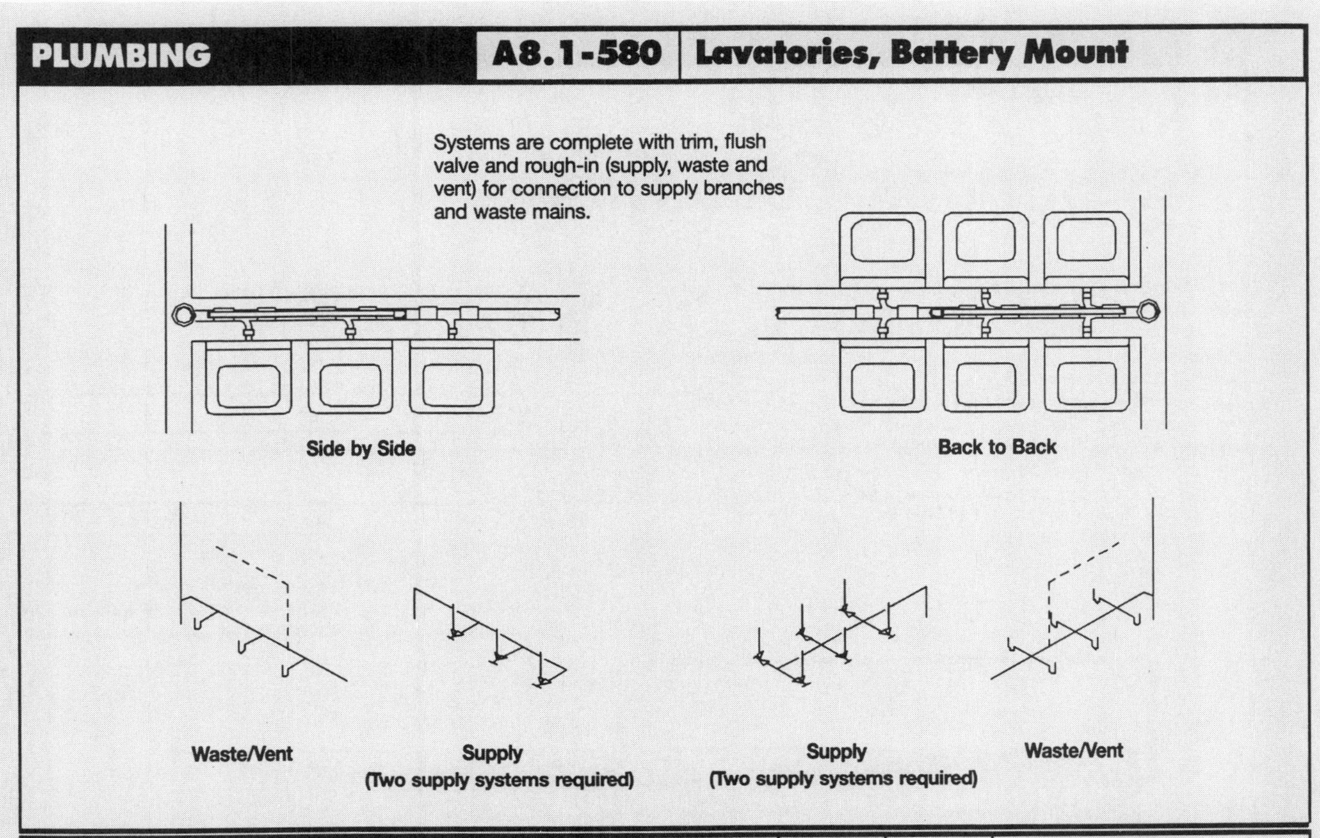

System Components	QUANTITY	UNIT	COST EACH MAT.	INST.	TOTAL
SYSTEM 8.1-580-1760					
LAVATORIES, BATTERY MOUNT, WALL HUNG, SIDE BY SIDE, FIRST LAVATORY					
Lavatory w/trim wall hung PE on CI 20" x 18"	1.000	Ea.	203	89	292
Stop, chrome, angle supply, 3/8" diameter	2.000	Ea.	10.40	32.90	43.30
Concealed arm support	1.000	Ea.	141	66	207
P trap w/cleanout, 20 ga. C.P., 1-1/4" diameter	1.000	Ea.	18.15	22	40.15
Copper tubing, type L, 1/2" diameter	10.000	L.F.	13.90	48.80	62.70
Copper tubing, type DWV, 1-1/4" diameter	4.000	L.F.	11.24	26.40	37.64
Copper 90° elbow, 1/2" diameter	2.000	Ea.	.84	39.50	40.34
Copper tee, 1/2" diameter	2.000	Ea.	1.36	61	62.36
DWV copper sanitary tee, 1-1/4" diameter	2.000	Ea.	14.90	88	102.90
Galvanized steel pipe, 1-1/4" diameter	4.000	L.F.	9.68	32	41.68
Black cast iron 90° elbow, 1-1/4" diameter	1.000	Ea.	3.50	32.50	36
TOTAL			427.97	538.10	966.07

8.1-580	Lavatory Systems, Battery Mount		COST EACH MAT.	INST.	TOTAL
1760	Lavatories, battery mount, side by side, first lavatory		430	540	970
1800	Each additional lavatory, add		400	375	775
2000	Back to back, first pair of lavatories	R151 -410	735	855	1,590
2100	Each additional pair of lavatories, back to back		715	705	1,420

From Means Plumbing Cost Data 1999

Figure 8.11

How to Use the Assemblies Cost Tables

The following is a detailed explanation of a sample Assemblies Cost Table. Most Assembly Tables are separated into three parts: 1) an illustration of the system to be estimated; 2) the components and related costs of a typical system; and 3) the costs for similar systems with dimensional and/or size variations. For costs of the components that comprise these systems or "assemblies" refer to the Unit Price Section. Next to each bold number below is the item being described with the appropriate component of the sample entry following in parenthesis. In most cases, if the work is to be subcontracted, the general contractor will need to add an additional markup (R.S. Means suggests using 10%) to the "Total" figures.

System/Line Numbers (A8.3-151-1760)

Each Assemblies Cost Line has been assigned a unique identification number based on the UniFormat classification system.

UniFormat Division

8.3 151 1760

Means Subdivision
Means Major Classification
Means Individual Line Number

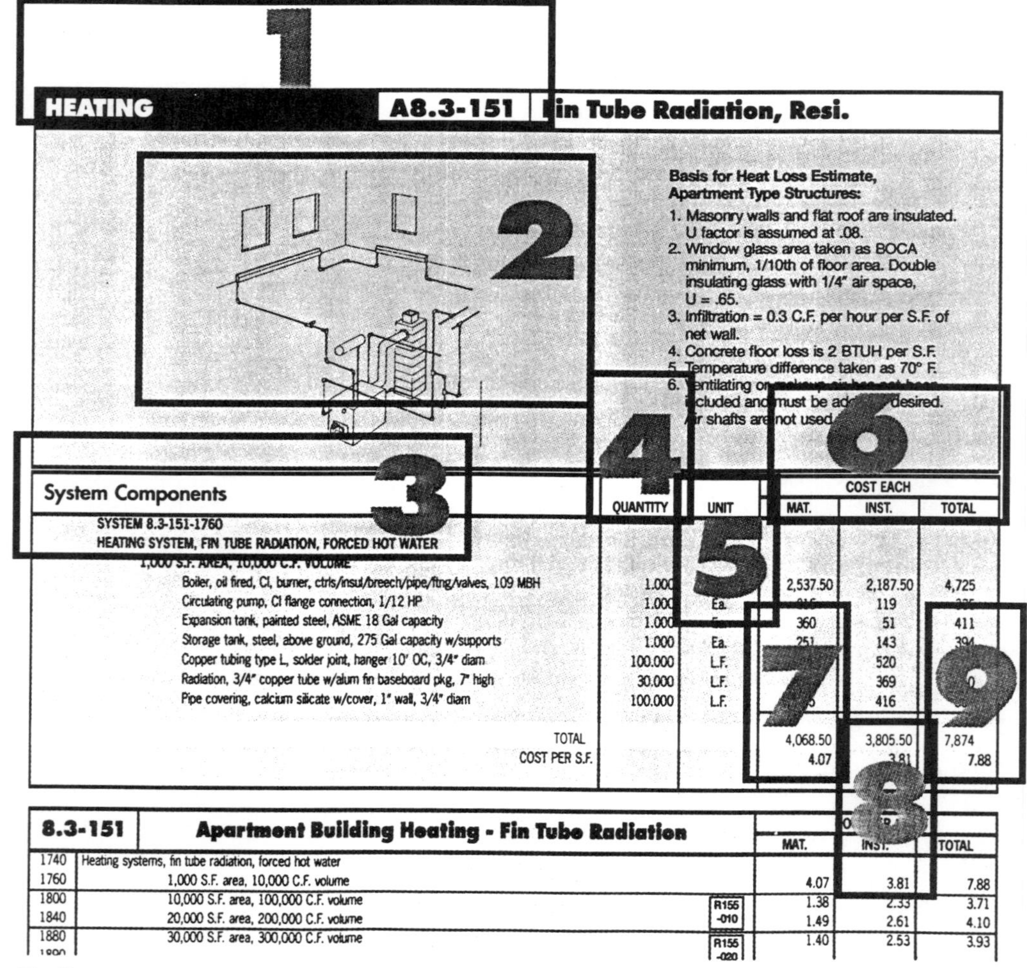

System Components

SYSTEM 8.3-151-1760
HEATING SYSTEM, FIN TUBE RADIATION, FORCED HOT WATER
1,000 S.F. AREA, 10,000 C.F. VOLUME

	QUANTITY	UNIT	COST EACH MAT.	COST EACH INST.	COST EACH TOTAL
Boiler, oil fired, CI, burner, ctrls/insul/breech/pipe/ftng/valves, 109 MBH	1.000	[illegible]	2,537.50	2,187.50	4,725
Circulating pump, CI flange connection, 1/12 HP	1.000	Ea.	[illegible]	119	[illegible]
Expansion tank, painted steel, ASME 18 Gal capacity	1.000	[illegible]	360	51	411
Storage tank, steel, above ground, 275 Gal capacity w/supports	1.000	Ea.	251	143	394
Copper tubing type L, solder joint, hanger 10' OC, 3/4" diam	100.000	L.F.	[illegible]	520	[illegible]
Radiation, 3/4" copper tube w/alum fin baseboard pkg, 7" high	30.000	L.F.	[illegible]	369	[illegible]
Pipe covering, calcium silicate w/cover, 1" wall, 3/4" diam	100.000	L.F.	[illegible]	416	[illegible]
TOTAL			4,068.50	3,805.50	7,874
COST PER S.F.			4.07	3.81	7.88

8.3-151	Apartment Building Heating - Fin Tube Radiation		COST PER S.F. MAT.	INST.	TOTAL
1740	Heating systems, fin tube radiation, forced hot water				
1760	1,000 S.F. area, 10,000 C.F. volume		4.07	3.81	7.88
1800	10,000 S.F. area, 100,000 C.F. volume	R155 -010	1.38	2.33	3.71
1840	20,000 S.F. area, 200,000 C.F. volume		1.49	2.61	4.10
1880	30,000 S.F. area, 300,000 C.F. volume	R155 -020	1.40	2.53	3.93

From *Means Plumbing Cost Data* 1999

Figure 8.12

Illustration

At the top of most assembly pages is an illustration, a brief description, and the design criteria used to develop the cost.

System Components

The components of a typical system are listed separately to show what has been included in the development of the total system price. The table below contains prices for other similar systems with dimensional and/or size variations.

Quantity

This is the number of line item units required for one system unit. For example, we assume that it will take 30 linear feet of radiation for the 1000 S.F. area shown.

Unit of Measure for Each Item

The abbreviated designation indicates the unit of measure, as defined by industry standards, upon which the price of the component is based. For example, baseboard radiation is priced by the linear foot. For a complete listing of abbreviations, see the Reference Section.

Unit of Measure for Each System (Each)

Costs shown in the three right hand columns have been adjusted by the component quantity and unit of measure for the entire system. In this example, "Cost Each" is the unit of measure for this system or "assembly."

Materials (4,068.50)

This column contains the Materials Cost of each component. These cost figures are bare costs plus 10% for profit.

Installation (3,805.50)

Installation includes labor and equipment plus the installing contractor's overhead and profit. Equipment costs are the bare rental costs plus 10% for profit. The labor overhead and profit is defined on the inside back cover of this book.

Total (7,874)

The figure in this column is the sum of the material and installation costs.

Material Cost	+	Installation Cost	=	Total
$4,068.50	+	$3,805.50	=	$7,874

From Means Plumbing Cost Data 1999

Figure 8.12 (*cont'd.*)

Quantity

A unit of measure is established for each assembly. For example, sprinkler systems are measured by the square foot of floor area; plumbing fixture systems are measured by "each;" HVAC systems are measured by the square foot of floor area. Within each system, the components are measured by industry standard, using the same units as in the Unit Price section.

Material

The cost of each component in the Material column is the "Bare Material Cost," plus 10% handling, for the unit and quantity as defined in the "Quantity" column.

Installation

Installation costs as listed in the Assemblies pages contain both labor and equipment costs. The labor rate includes the "Bare Labor Costs" plus the installing contractor's overhead and profit. These rates are shown in Figure 8.4. The equipment rate is the "Bare Equipment Cost," plus 10%.

Estimating References

Throughout the Unit Price and Assemblies sections are reference numbers highlighted with bold squares. These numbers serve as footnotes, referring the reader to illustrations, charts, and estimating tables in the Reference pages, as well as to related information in the Assemblies section. Figure 8.13 shows example reference numbers for plumbing fixtures as they appear on a Unit Price page. Figure 8.14 shows a corresponding reference page from the Assemblies pages. The development of unit costs for many items is explained in the reference tables. Design criteria for many types of mechanical systems are also included to aid the designer/estimator in making appropriate choices. See Figure 8.9 for another example of a reference table.

City Cost Indexes

The unit prices in *Means Plumbing Cost Data* are national averages. When they are to be applied to a particular location, these prices must be adjusted to local conditions. Means has developed the City Cost and Zip Code Indexes for just that purpose. *Means Plumbing Cost Data* contains tables of indexes for 930 U.S. and Canadian cities based on a 30 major city average of 100. The figures are broken down into material and installation for all trades, as shown in Figure 8.15. Please note that for each city there is a weighted average based on total project costs. This average is based on the relative contribution of each division to the construction process as a whole.

In addition to adjusting the figures in *Means Plumbing Cost Data* for particular locations, the City Cost index can also be used to adjust costs from one city to another. For example, the price of the mechanical work for a particular building type is known for City A. In order to budget the costs of the same building type in City B, the following calculation can be made:

$$\frac{\text{City B Index}}{\text{City A Index}} \times \text{City A Cost} = \text{City B Cost}$$

152 | Plumbing Fixtures

	152 100 | Fixtures		Crew	Daily Output	Labor-Hours	Unit	1999 Bare Costs Mat.	Labor	Equip.	Total	Total Incl O&P	
168	0010	**URINALS** A8.1 -450										168
	0100	For automatic flush see 151-141-0972										
	3000	Wall hung, vitreous china, with hanger & self-closing valve										
	3100	Siphon jet type	Q-1	3	5.333	Ea.	271	157		428	535	
	3120	Blowout type		3	5.333		370	157		527	640	
	3300	Rough-in, supply, waste & vent		2.83	5.654		87.50	166		253.50	350	
	5000	Stall type, vitreous china, includes valve		2.50	6.400		645	188		833	995	
	5100	3" seam cover, add		12	1.333		114	39		153	185	
	5200	6" seam cover, add R151 -410		12	1.333		158	39		197	233	
	6980	Rough-in, supply, waste and vent		1.99	8.040		126	236		362	500	
172	0010	**WASH CENTER** Prefabricated,stainless steel, semirecessed										172
	0050	Lavatory, storage cabinet, mirror, light & switch, electric										
	0060	outlet, towel dispenser, waste receptacle & trim										
	0100	Foot water valve, cup & soap dispenser,16" W x 54-3/4" H	Q-1	8	2	Ea.	1,925	58.50		1,983.50	2,200	
	0200	Handicap, wrist blade handles, 17" W x 66-1/2" H		8	2		1,650	58.50		1,708.50	1,925	
	0220	20" W x 67-3/8" H		8	2		2,250	58.50		2,308.50	2,575	
	0300	Push button metering & thermostatic mixing valves										
	0320	Handicap 17" W x 27-1/2" H	Q-1	8	2	Ea.	1,300	58.50		1,358.50	1,525	
	0400	Rough-in, supply, waste and vent	"	2.10	7.619	"	76	224		300	425	
176	0010	**WASH FOUNTAINS** Rigging not included A8.1 -560										176
	1900	Group, foot control										
	2000	Precast terrazzo, circular, 36" diam., 5 or 6 persons	Q-2	3	8	Ea.	2,600	243		2,843	3,250	
	2100	54" diameter for 8 or 10 persons		2.50	9.600		3,250	292		3,542	4,025	
	2400	Semi-circular, 36" diam. for 3 persons		3	8		2,400	243		2,643	3,025	
	2500	54" diam. for 4 or 5 persons		2.50	9.600		2,900	292		3,192	3,625	
	2700	Quarter circle (corner), 54" for 3 persons		3.50	6.857		2,875	209		3,084	3,475	
	3000	Stainless steel, circular, 36" diameter		3.50	6.857		1,425	209		1,634	1,875	
	3100	54" diameter		2.80	8.571		1,650	261		1,911	2,200	
	3400	Semi-circular, 36" diameter		3.50	6.857		1,300	209		1,509	1,750	
	3500	54" diameter		2.80	8.571		2,300	261		2,561	2,925	
	5000	Thermoplastic, pre-assembled, circular, 36" diameter		6	4		2,300	122		2,422	2,700	
	5100	54" diameter		4	6		2,675	183		2,858	3,200	
	5400	Semi-circular, 36" diameter		6	4		1,950	122		2,072	2,325	
	5600	54" diameter		4	6		2,575	183		2,758	3,100	
	5610	Group, infrared control, barrier free										
	5614	Precast terrazzo										
	5620	Semi-circular 36" diam. for 3 persons	Q-2	3	8	Ea.	3,575	243		3,818	4,300	
	5630	46" diam. for 4 persons		2.80	8.571		3,850	261		4,111	4,650	
	5640	Circular, 54" diam. for 8 persons, button control		2.50	9.600		6,000	292		6,292	7,050	
	5700	Rough-in, supply, waste and vent for above wash fountains	Q-1	1.82	8.791		117	258		375	520	
	6200	Duo for small washrooms, stainless steel		2	8		1,975	235		2,210	2,500	
	6400	Bowl with backsplash		2	8		1,625	235		1,860	2,150	
	6500	Rough-in, supply, waste & vent for duo fountains		2.02	7.921		68	232		300	425	
180	0010	**WATER CLOSETS** A8.1 -470										180
	0020	For seats, see 152-164										
	0030	For automatic flush, see 151-141-0972 A8.1 -510										
	0150	Tank type, vitreous china, incl. seat, supply pipe w/stop										
	0200	Wall hung, one piece R151 -410	Q-1	5.30	3.019	Ea.	435	88.50		523.50	615	
	0400	Two piece, close coupled		5.30	3.019		380	88.50		468.50	550	
	0960	For rough-in, supply, waste, vent and carrier		2.73	5.861		254	172		426	540	
	1000	Floor mounted, one piece		5.30	3.019		440	88.50		528.50	615	
	1020	One piece, low profile		5.30	3.019		505	88.50		593.50	690	
	1050	One piece combination		5.30	3.019		545	88.50		633.50	735	
	1100	Two piece, close coupled, water saver		5.30	3.019		133	88.50		221.50	280	
	1150	With wall outlet		5.30	3.019		420	88.50		508.50	595	

Figure 8.13

PLUMBING | A8.1-560 | Group Wash Fountains

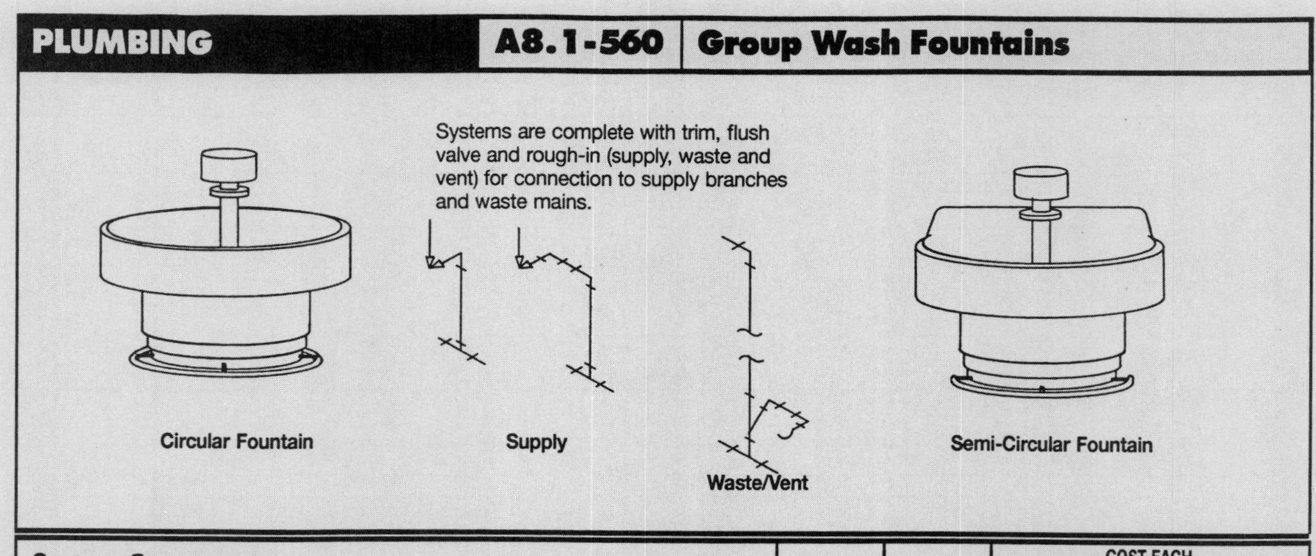

System Components	QUANTITY	UNIT	COST EACH MAT.	COST EACH INST.	COST EACH TOTAL
SYSTEM 8.1-560-1760					
GROUP WASH FOUNTAIN, PRECAST TERRAZZO					
CIRCULAR, 36" DIAMETER					
Wash fountain, group, precast terrazzo, foot control 36" diam	1.000	Ea.	2,875	370	3,245
Copper tubing type DWV, solder joint, hanger 10'OC, 2" diam	10.000	L.F.	46	90	136
P trap, standard, copper, 2" diam	1.000	Ea.	42	26.50	68.50
Wrought copper, Tee, sanitary, 2" diam	1.000	Ea.	11.05	56.50	67.55
Copper tubing type L, solder joint, hanger 10' OC 1/2" diam	20.000	L.F.	27.80	97.60	125.40
Wrought copper 90° elbow for solder joints 1/2" diam	3.000	Ea.	1.26	59.25	60.51
Wrought copper Tee for solder joints, 1/2" diam	2.000	Ea.	1.36	61	62.36
TOTAL			3,004.47	760.85	3,765.32

8.1-560	Group Wash Fountain Systems		COST EACH MAT.	COST EACH INST.	COST EACH TOTAL
1740	Group wash fountain, precast terrazzo				
1760	Circular, 36" diameter		3,000	760	3,760
1800	54" diameter	R151 -410	3,700	835	4,535
1840	Semi-circular, 36" diameter		2,775	760	3,535
1880	54" diameter		3,300	835	4,135
1960	Stainless steel, circular, 36" diameter		1,675	705	2,380
2000	54" diameter		1,925	785	2,710
2040	Semi-circular, 36" diameter		1,550	705	2,255
2080	54" diameter		2,650	785	3,435
2160	Thermoplastic, circular, 36" diameter		2,650	575	3,225
2200	54" diameter		3,050	670	3,720
2240	Semi-circular, 36" diameter		2,275	575	2,850
2280	54" diameter		2,950	670	3,620

Figure 8.14

City Cost Indexes

DIVISION		UNITED STATES 30 CITY AVERAGE			ALABAMA ANNISTON 362			BIRMINGHAM 350 - 352			BUTLER 369			DECATUR 356			DOTHAN 363		
		MAT.	INST.	TOTAL	MAT.	INST.	TOTAL	MAT.	INST.	TOTAL	MAT.	INST.	TOTAL	MAT.	INST.	TOTAL	MAT.	INST.	TOTAL
2	**SITE WORK**	100.0	100.0	100.0	96.6	91.8	92.9	89.7	93.7	92.8	111.6	86.8	92.5	89.1	93.1	92.2	108.8	86.8	91.9
031	CONCRETE FORMWORK	100.0	100.0	100.0	96.9	43.5	51.1	95.4	78.5	81.0	83.1	58.2	61.8	97.0	62.0	67.0	96.2	58.2	63.7
032	CONCRETE REINFORCEMENT	100.0	100.0	100.0	92.7	68.6	79.1	92.7	82.1	86.7	103.5	68.6	83.8	92.7	65.7	77.5	103.5	68.6	83.8
033	CAST IN PLACE CONCRETE	100.0	100.0	100.0	94.0	47.0	74.3	96.2	69.2	84.9	91.7	58.4	77.7	93.5	67.5	82.6	91.7	58.4	77.7
3	**CONCRETE**	100.0	100.0	100.0	92.7	51.6	72.0	89.6	77.1	83.3	93.6	61.9	77.6	88.4	66.2	77.2	93.3	61.9	77.4
4	**MASONRY**	100.0	100.0	100.0	83.0	42.7	58.0	84.1	74.0	77.8	86.2	45.0	60.6	84.2	63.9	71.6	87.2	45.0	61.0
5	**METALS**	100.0	100.0	100.0	96.1	86.9	92.8	98.8	93.6	96.9	95.0	85.9	91.7	98.4	87.3	94.4	95.2	85.9	91.8
6	**WOOD & PLASTICS**	100.0	100.0	100.0	87.7	44.2	65.2	95.4	79.7	87.3	81.6	61.1	71.0	94.4	61.9	77.6	95.8	61.1	77.9
7	**THERMAL & MOISTURE PROTECTION**	100.0	100.0	100.0	97.4	44.8	73.0	97.6	68.8	84.2	97.5	53.9	77.3	97.3	60.7	80.4	97.6	53.9	77.4
8	**DOORS & WINDOWS**	100.0	100.0	100.0	93.3	49.0	82.6	97.0	76.2	91.9	93.3	60.3	85.3	97.0	58.7	87.7	93.4	60.3	85.4
092	LATH, PLASTER & GYPSUM BOARD	100.0	100.0	100.0	106.2	42.9	65.4	113.3	79.6	91.6	105.2	60.4	76.3	109.8	61.2	78.5	110.4	60.4	78.1
095	ACOUSTICAL TREATMENT & WOOD FLOORING	100.0	100.0	100.0	96.0	42.9	61.6	100.2	79.6	86.8	96.0	60.4	72.9	100.2	61.2	74.9	96.0	60.4	72.9
096	FLOORING & CARPET	100.0	100.0	100.0	96.0	43.2	83.2	99.0	60.9	89.7	102.1	34.1	85.6	99.0	63.5	90.3	109.7	34.1	91.3
099	PAINTING & WALL COVERINGS	100.0	100.0	100.0	90.8	37.8	59.7	90.8	57.5	71.2	90.8	64.1	75.1	90.8	59.9	72.7	90.8	64.1	75.1
9	**FINISHES**	100.0	100.0	100.0	96.9	42.9	69.2	99.2	73.3	85.9	100.4	54.4	76.8	98.7	62.0	79.9	103.4	54.4	78.3
10 - 14	**TOTAL DIV. 10 - 14**	100.0	100.0	100.0	100.0	62.7	92.1	100.0	83.2	96.4	100.0	66.7	93.0	100.0	69.5	93.6	100.0	66.7	93.0
15	**MECHANICAL**	100.0	100.0	100.0	97.3	47.1	74.9	100.0	70.7	86.9	98.1	50.8	77.0	100.0	61.7	82.9	98.1	50.8	77.0
16	**ELECTRICAL**	100.0	100.0	100.0	93.2	34.1	53.4	95.5	69.4	77.9	96.4	48.1	63.8	95.9	63.3	73.9	94.5	48.1	63.2
1 - 16	**WEIGHTED AVERAGE**	100.0	100.0	100.0	95.1	53.1	74.8	96.5	77.0	87.1	96.3	59.5	78.6	96.3	68.4	82.8	96.6	59.5	78.7

DIVISION		ALABAMA EVERGREEN 364			GADSDEN 359			HUNTSVILLE 357 - 358			JASPER 355			MOBILE 365 - 366			MONTGOMERY 360 - 361		
		MAT.	INST.	TOTAL	MAT.	INST.	TOTAL	MAT.	INST.	TOTAL	MAT.	INST.	TOTAL	MAT.	INST.	TOTAL	MAT.	INST.	TOTAL
2	**SITE WORK**	112.1	87.1	92.9	95.3	92.9	93.5	88.8	93.1	92.1	94.8	92.6	93.1	100.3	87.3	90.3	100.8	87.1	90.3
031	CONCRETE FORMWORK	78.3	60.4	62.9	92.1	55.8	61.0	97.0	61.5	66.6	99.5	45.6	53.3	97.0	65.4	69.9	95.1	58.7	63.9
032	CONCRETE REINFORCEMENT	104.0	68.6	84.1	101.5	81.5	90.2	92.7	70.7	80.3	92.7	68.8	79.2	95.7	64.2	77.9	95.7	81.1	87.5
033	CAST IN PLACE CONCRETE	91.7	61.5	79.0	93.5	61.8	80.2	91.0	65.0	80.1	103.6	54.9	83.2	96.1	65.5	83.3	97.8	58.7	81.4
3	**CONCRETE**	93.6	63.9	78.6	92.7	64.4	78.5	87.2	66.0	76.5	96.2	55.2	75.5	90.1	66.7	78.3	90.8	64.6	77.6
4	**MASONRY**	86.2	50.7	64.2	82.2	53.4	64.3	84.0	60.8	69.6	79.8	46.6	59.2	84.7	64.3	72.1	85.1	44.7	60.0
5	**METALS**	95.1	85.9	91.8	96.1	92.4	94.8	98.4	88.9	95.0	96.0	86.2	92.5	97.0	86.4	93.2	97.1	91.6	95.1
6	**WOOD & PLASTICS**	76.4	61.1	68.5	82.3	55.7	68.6	94.4	61.1	77.2	90.3	45.3	67.0	94.4	66.7	80.1	92.0	61.1	76.0
7	**THERMAL & MOISTURE PROTECTION**	97.5	56.3	78.4	97.4	59.1	79.6	97.3	62.3	81.0	97.4	49.9	75.4	97.2	64.2	81.9	97.1	56.7	78.4
8	**DOORS & WINDOWS**	93.4	60.3	85.3	93.3	57.5	84.6	97.0	59.4	87.9	93.3	52.6	83.4	97.0	62.9	88.7	97.0	63.1	88.8
092	LATH, PLASTER & GYPSUM BOARD	103.0	60.4	75.5	104.1	54.8	72.3	109.8	60.4	77.9	106.4	44.0	66.2	109.8	66.2	81.6	109.8	60.4	77.9
095	ACOUSTICAL TREATMENT & WOOD FLOORING	96.0	60.4	72.9	96.0	54.8	69.3	100.2	60.4	74.4	94.7	44.0	61.9	100.2	66.2	78.1	100.2	60.4	74.4
096	FLOORING & CARPET	99.5	34.1	83.6	94.0	54.5	84.4	99.0	52.7	87.7	97.0	41.6	83.5	107.3	66.1	97.2	107.3	34.1	89.5
099	PAINTING & WALL COVERINGS	90.8	64.1	75.1	90.8	52.4	68.3	90.8	56.3	70.6	90.8	46.4	64.7	90.8	65.2	75.8	90.8	64.1	75.1
9	**FINISHES**	99.3	55.8	77.0	95.9	54.5	74.7	98.7	58.9	78.3	96.9	44.8	70.2	102.5	65.7	83.6	102.6	54.3	77.9
10 - 14	**TOTAL DIV. 10 - 14**	100.0	69.1	93.5	100.0	75.2	94.8	100.0	77.9	95.3	100.0	63.8	92.4	100.0	77.8	95.3	100.0	75.1	94.7
15	**MECHANICAL**	98.1	53.9	78.4	106.5	54.0	83.1	100.0	56.6	80.6	106.5	40.4	77.0	100.0	60.2	82.2	100.0	50.9	78.1
16	**ELECTRICAL**	92.2	48.1	62.5	94.9	69.4	77.7	95.9	70.8	79.0	95.2	34.6	54.3	95.9	65.8	75.6	95.5	48.1	63.5
1 - 16	**WEIGHTED AVERAGE**	95.9	61.3	79.2	97.0	66.2	82.2	96.1	68.4	82.7	97.5	53.3	76.2	97.0	68.9	83.4	97.1	60.8	79.6

DIVISION		ALABAMA PHENIX CITY 368			SELMA 367			TUSCALOOSA 354			ALASKA ANCHORAGE 995 - 996			FAIRBANKS 997			JUNEAU 998		
		MAT.	INST.	TOTAL	MAT.	INST.	TOTAL	MAT.	INST.	TOTAL	MAT.	INST.	TOTAL	MAT.	INST.	TOTAL	MAT.	INST.	TOTAL
2	**SITE WORK**	116.5	87.2	93.9	108.5	86.8	91.8	89.2	92.6	91.9	127.1	136.7	134.5	113.1	136.7	131.3	124.2	136.7	133.9
031	CONCRETE FORMWORK	88.0	51.6	56.8	84.7	58.2	62.0	97.0	48.1	55.1	129.9	120.0	121.4	131.4	126.1	126.9	131.2	120.0	121.6
032	CONCRETE REINFORCEMENT	102.8	79.9	89.9	103.5	68.6	83.8	92.7	81.5	86.4	143.8	115.1	127.7	120.9	115.2	117.7	107.0	115.1	111.6
033	CAST IN PLACE CONCRETE	91.7	59.4	78.2	91.6	58.4	77.7	94.8	56.0	78.5	178.7	119.1	153.8	151.3	119.7	138.0	179.4	119.1	154.2
3	**CONCRETE**	96.1	61.5	78.6	92.3	61.9	76.9	89.0	59.1	73.9	152.2	117.8	134.9	130.2	120.7	125.4	147.8	117.9	132.7
4	**MASONRY**	86.1	51.0	64.3	91.2	45.0	62.5	84.3	47.2	61.2	174.8	124.1	143.3	167.6	124.1	140.6	155.1	124.1	135.8
5	**METALS**	95.0	91.4	93.7	95.0	85.9	91.7	97.5	92.3	95.6	129.8	102.6	120.0	129.9	102.9	120.2	130.2	102.6	120.2
6	**WOOD & PLASTICS**	87.0	50.9	68.4	83.4	61.1	71.9	94.4	48.4	70.7	123.4	118.5	120.8	123.7	126.4	125.1	123.4	118.5	120.8
7	**THERMAL & MOISTURE PROTECTION**	97.9	57.5	79.2	97.4	53.9	77.2	97.3	55.2	77.8	198.8	112.6	158.8	195.0	114.5	157.7	195.5	112.6	157.1
8	**DOORS & WINDOWS**	93.3	57.2	84.6	93.3	60.3	85.3	97.0	59.3	87.9	132.1	112.3	127.3	129.1	116.6	126.1	129.1	112.3	125.0
092	LATH, PLASTER & GYPSUM BOARD	107.3	49.8	70.2	105.7	60.4	76.4	109.8	47.3	69.5	126.5	119.0	121.7	126.5	127.2	127.0	126.5	119.0	121.7
095	ACOUSTICAL TREATMENT & WOOD FLOORING	96.0	49.8	66.1	96.0	60.4	72.9	100.2	47.3	65.9	133.0	119.0	123.9	133.0	127.2	129.3	133.0	119.0	123.9
096	FLOORING & CARPET	104.9	34.1	87.7	103.0	34.1	86.3	99.0	50.1	87.1	130.2	130.9	130.4	130.4	130.9	130.5	130.2	130.9	130.4
099	PAINTING & WALL COVERINGS	90.8	64.1	75.1	90.8	64.1	75.1	90.8	55.2	69.9	122.9	117.8	119.9	122.9	122.6	122.7	122.9	117.8	119.9
9	**FINISHES**	101.9	48.7	74.6	100.5	54.4	76.9	98.7	48.4	72.9	143.9	122.2	132.8	141.9	127.4	134.5	142.6	122.2	132.1
10 - 14	**TOTAL DIV. 10 - 14**	100.0	74.3	94.6	100.0	66.7	93.0	100.0	71.9	94.1	100.0	116.7	103.5	100.0	117.7	103.7	100.0	116.7	103.5
15	**MECHANICAL**	98.1	51.6	77.4	98.1	50.8	77.0	100.0	44.7	75.3	106.9	109.9	108.2	106.9	118.3	112.0	106.9	111.9	109.1
16	**ELECTRICAL**	95.6	48.1	63.6	94.1	48.1	63.1	95.8	69.4	78.0	158.6	118.6	131.6	161.4	118.6	132.5	161.4	118.6	132.5
1 - 16	**WEIGHTED AVERAGE**	96.9	60.1	79.2	96.2	59.5	78.5	96.2	62.2	79.8	133.1	117.7	125.7	129.3	120.7	125.1	131.2	118.0	124.8

From Means Plumbing Cost Data 1999

Figure 8.15

While City Cost Indexes provide a means to adjust prices for location, the Historical Cost Index, (also included in *Means Plumbing Cost Data* and shown in Figure 8.16) provides a means to adjust for time. Using the same principle as above, a time-adjustment factor can be calculated:

$$\frac{\text{Index for Year X}}{\text{Index for Year Y}} \times \text{Time-adjustment Factor}$$

This time-adjustment factor can be used to determine the budget costs for a particular building type in Year X, based on costs for a similar building type known from Year Y. Used together, the two indexes allow for cost adjustments from one city during a given year to another city in another year (the present or otherwise). For example, an office building built in San Francisco in 1974 originally cost $1,000,000. How much will a similar building cost in Phoenix in 1999? Adjustment factors are developed as shown above using data from Figures 8.15 and 8.16.

$$\frac{\text{Phoenix Index}}{\text{San Francisco Index}} = \frac{90.2}{124.2} = 0.73$$

$$\frac{\text{1999 Index}}{\text{1974 Index}} = \frac{116.4}{41.4} = 2.81$$

Original cost × location adjustment × time adjustment = Proposed new cost.

$$\$\,1{,}000{,}000 \times 0.73 \times 2.81 = \$2{,}051{,}300$$

Historical Cost Indexes

The table below lists both the Means Historical Cost Index based on Jan. 1, 1993 = 100 as well as the computed value of an index based on Jan. 1, 1999 costs. Since the Jan. 1, 1999 figure is estimated, space is left to write in the actual index figures as they become available through either the quarterly "Means Construction Cost Indexes" or as printed in the "Engineering News-Record." To compute the actual index based on Jan. 1, 1999 = 100, divide the Historical Cost Index for a particular year by the actual Jan. 1, 1999 Construction Cost Index. Space has been left to advance the index figures as the year progresses.

Year	Historical Cost Index Jan. 1, 1993 = 100		Current Index Based on Jan. 1, 1999 = 100	
	Est.	Actual	Est.	Actual
Oct 1999				
July 1999				
April 1999				
Jan 1999	116.4		100.0	100.0
July 1998		115.1	98.9	
1997		112.8	96.9	
1996		110.2	94.7	
1995		107.6	92.4	
1994		104.4	89.7	
1993		101.7	87.4	
1992		99.4	85.4	
1991		96.8	83.2	
1990		94.3	81.0	
1989		92.1	79.2	
1988		89.9	77.2	
1987		87.7	75.3	
1986		84.2	72.4	
▼ 1985		82.6	71.0	

Year	Historical Cost Index Jan. 1, 1993 = 100	Current Index Based on Jan. 1, 1999 = 100	
	Actual	Est.	Actual
July 1984	82.0	70.4	
1983	80.2	68.9	
1982	76.1	65.4	
1981	70.0	60.1	
1980	62.9	54.0	
1979	57.8	49.7	
1978	53.5	46.0	
1977	49.5	42.5	
1976	46.9	40.3	
1975	44.8	38.5	
1974	41.4	35.6	
1973	37.7	32.4	
1972	34.8	29.9	
1971	32.1	27.6	
1970	28.7	24.7	
1969	26.9	23.1	
1968	24.9	21.4	
▼ 1967	23.5	20.2	

Year	Historical Cost Index Jan. 1, 1993 = 100	Current Index Based on Jan. 1, 1999 = 100	
	Actual	Est.	Actual
July 1966	22.7	19.5	
1965	21.7	18.6	
1964	21.2	18.2	
1963	20.7	17.8	
1962	20.2	17.4	
1961	19.8	17.0	
1960	19.7	16.9	
1959	19.3	16.6	
1958	18.8	16.2	
1957	18.4	15.8	
1956	17.6	15.1	
1955	16.6	14.3	
1954	16.0	13.7	
1953	15.8	13.6	
1952	15.4	13.2	
1951	15.0	12.9	
1950	13.7	11.8	
▼ 1949	13.3	11.4	

From Means Plumbing Cost Data 1999

Figure 8.16

APPENDICES

APPENDICES

Table of Contents

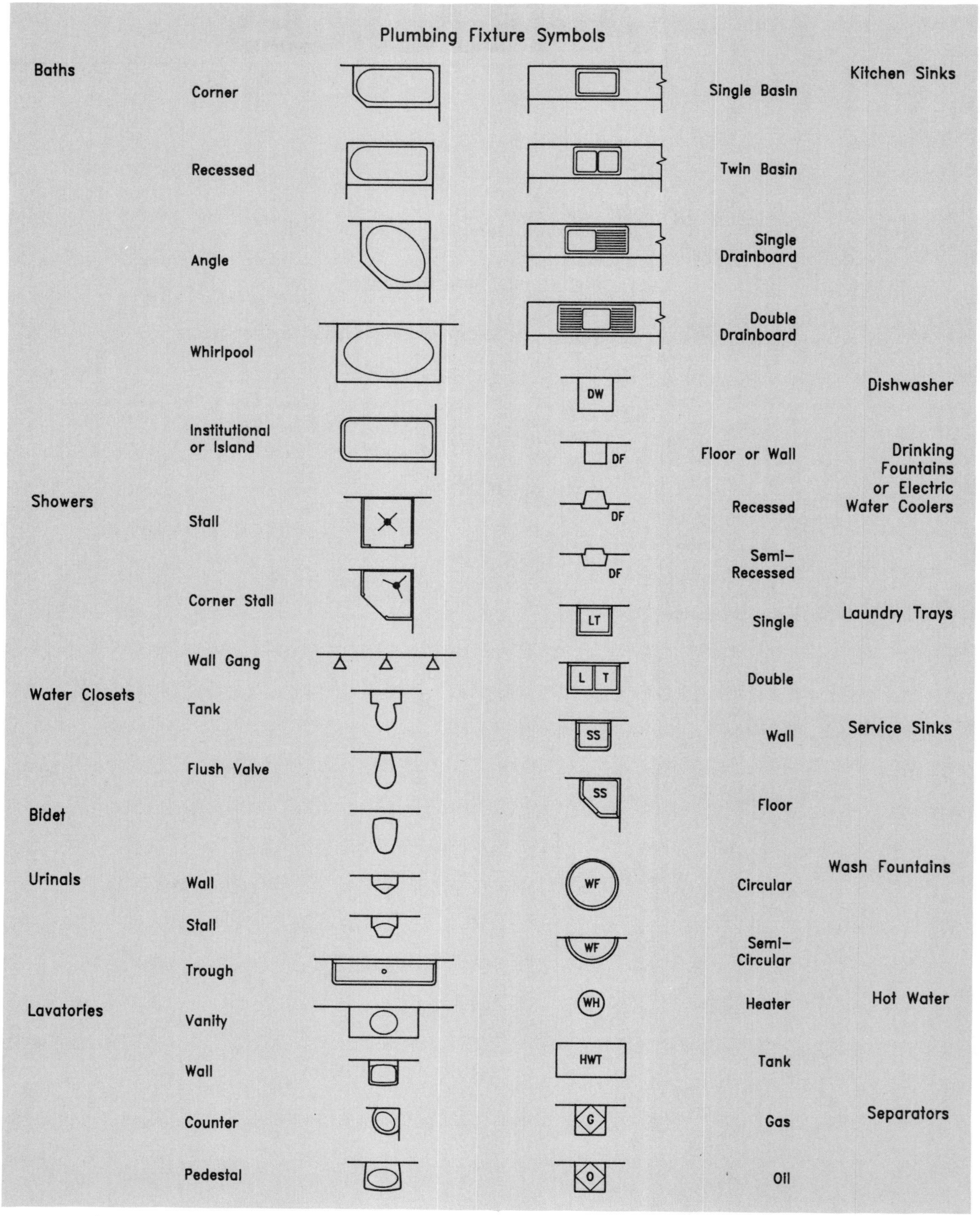

Plumbing Fixture Symbols

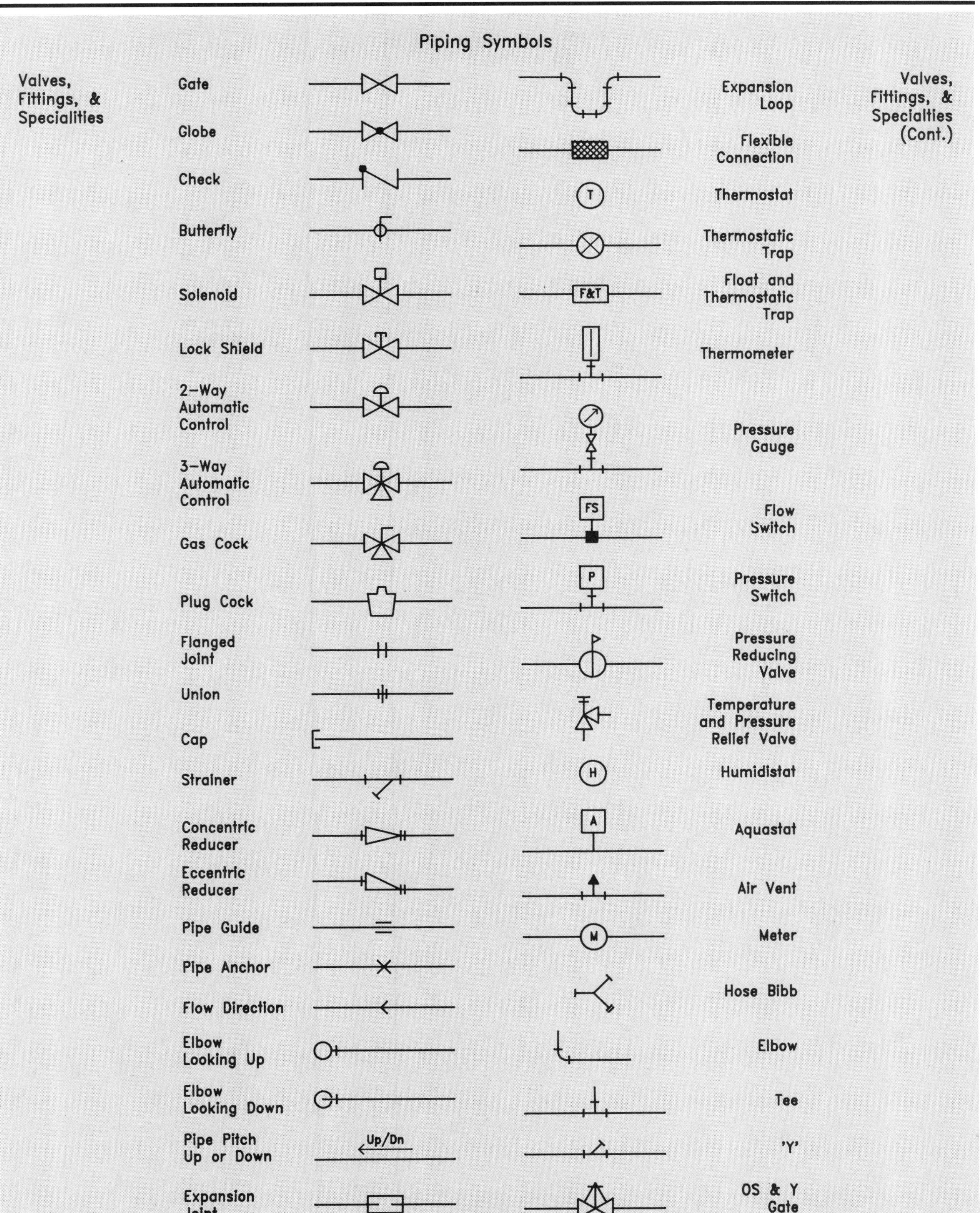
Piping Symbols
Valves, Fittings, & Specialities
Gate
Globe
Check
Butterfly
Solenoid
Lock Shield
2-Way Automatic Control
3-Way Automatic Control
Gas Cock
Plug Cock
Flanged Joint
Union
Cap
Strainer
Concentric Reducer
Eccentric Reducer
Pipe Guide
Pipe Anchor
Flow Direction
Elbow Looking Up
Elbow Looking Down
Pipe Pitch Up or Down
Up/Dn
Expansion Joint
Valves, Fittings, & Specialties (Cont.)
Expansion Loop
Flexible Connection
T
Thermostat
Thermostatic Trap
F&T
Float and Thermostatic Trap
Thermometer
Pressure Gauge
FS
Flow Switch
P
Pressure Switch
Pressure Reducing Valve
Temperature and Pressure Relief Valve
H
Humidistat
A
Aquastat
Air Vent
M
Meter
Hose Bibb
Elbow
Tee
'Y'
OS & Y Gate

Piping Symbols (Cont.)

Valves, Fittings, & Specialties (Cont.)

Description	Symbol	Symbol	Description
Shock Absorber		—— – —— CW	Cold Water
		—— – – —— HW	Hot Water
House Trap		—— – – – —— HWC	Hot Water Circulation
'P' Trap		—— DWS ——	Drinking Water Supply
Floor Drain		—— DWR ——	Drinking Water Return
Indirect Waste	—— IW ——	—— G ——	Gas–Low Pressure
Sanitary Below Grade	– – – S – – –	—— MG ——	Gas–Medium Pressure
Sanitary Above Grade	—— S ——	—— HG ——	Gas–High Pressure
Storm Below Grade	– – – ST – – –	—— CA ——	Compressed Air
Storm Above Grade	—— ST ——	—— V ——	Vacuum
		—— VC ——	Vacuum Cleaning
Vent	– – – – – – – –	—— N ——	Nitrogen
Combination Waste & Vent	—— CWV ——	—— N_2O ——	Nitrous Oxide
Acid Waste Below Grade	– – – AW – – –	—— O ——	Oxygen
Acid Waste Above Grade	—— AW ——	—— LOX ——	Liquid Oxygen
Acid Vent	– – – AV – – –	—— LPG ——	Liquid Petroleum Gas

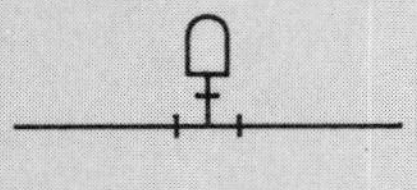

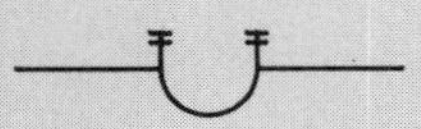

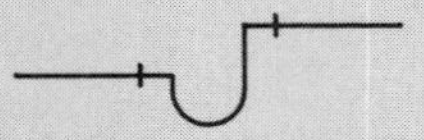

Valves, Fittings, & Specialties (Cont.)

Fire Protection Piping Symbols

Description	Symbol	Symbol	Description
Fire Protection Water Supply	—— F ——		Fire Hydrant
Wet Standpipe	—— WSP ——		Wall Fire Dept. Connection
Dry Standpipe	—— DSP ——		Sidewalk Fire Dept. Connection
Combination Standpipe	—— CSP ——	FHR 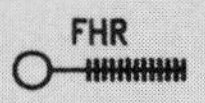	Fire Hose Rack
Automatic Fire Sprinkler	—— SP ——	 FHC	Surface Mounted Fire Hose Cabinet
Upright Fire Sprinkler Heads		 FHC	Recessed Fire Hose Cabinet
Pendent Fire Sprinkler Heads			

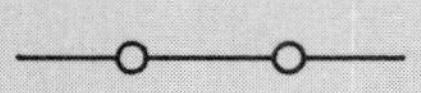

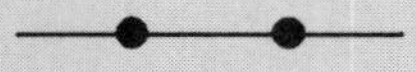

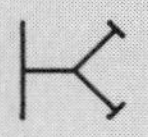

Man-Hours to Install Building Piping Systems

This section contains labor man-hour units for various system installations as well as specialties, fixtures, and equipment. The labor unit man-hours are based on a national average.

The user should evaluate the location and conditions of each individual project and guide their final man-hour allocations accordingly.

PLUMBING FIXTURES

ITEM DESCRIPTION	MAN-HOURS EACH
Water Closet (Flush Valve Floor-Mounted)	2.25
(Flush Valve Wall-Hung)	2.00
(Tank Type Floor-Mounted)	2.25
(Tank Type Wall-Hung)	2.25
Urinal (Flush Valve Wall-Hung)	2.00
Lavatory (Wall-Hung)	1.75
Lavatory (Countertop)	2.00
Wash Fountains (54″ Diameter)	9.00
Bathtub (C.I. Recessed)	3.50
Bathtub (Steel Recessed)	3.00
Shower (Valve Body and Trim Only)	1.00
Shower (Terrazzo Receptor)	2.50
Shower (Stall w/Fiberglass Walls)	4.00
Sink (Service)	3.00
Sink (Countertop) 1 Compartment	2.25
Sink (Countertop) 2 Compartment	2.75
Floor Sink	2.75
Scrub Sink	3.00
Clinical Sink w/Flushometer and Faucet	4.00
Institutional Bathtub w/Base	8.25
Electric Water Cooler (Recessed)	3.25
(Free Standing)	2.25
(Semi-recessed)	3.00
Eye Wash Fountain	2.50
Floor Drain 2″ to 4″	1.00
Area Drain 2″ to 4″	1.00
Roof Drain 2″ to 4″	1.25
Wall Hydrant	.50
Trench Drain (Light Duty, 10 ft. long)	3.00
Emergency Shower	2.50
Support Carriers	
Water Closet Carrier	2.00
Urinal Carrier	1.50
Lavatory Carrier	2.00
Elec. Water Coolers/Drink. Fount. Carrier	2.00

BUILDING EQUIPMENT

ITEM DESCRIPTION	LABOR MAN-HOURS EACH
Constant Pressure Pumps	
1750 R.P.M. 150 G.P.M.	
5 Horsepower (Duplex)	8.00
7½	8.00
10	10.00
15	12.00
20	14.00
25	16.00
5 Horsepower (Triplex)	10.00
7½	10.00
10	12.00
15	15.00
20	18.00
25	20.00

NOTE:
1) Fixture man-hours include distribution, uncrating, trim and connecting to existing piping and testing.
2) Equipment man-hours include distribution, uncrating, set into place and connecting to existing piping, and testing.

EXCLUSIONS
1) All piping, valves, elec. wiring.

BUILDING EQUIPMENT (continued)

ITEM DESCRIPTION		LABOR MAN-HOURS EACH
In-line Circulating Pumps		
1/12 Horsepower (Iron or Bronze Body)		1.25
1/6		1.25
1/4		1.25
1/3		1.25
1/2		1.50
3/4		2.00
1		2.50
Water Meters		
3/4″ Disc Type		0.75
1″		1.00
1½″		1.25
2″		1.50
2″ Compound Type		1.50
3″		2.50
4″		4.00
6″		6.00
Fire Meters		
3″ Detector Type		4.00
4″		6.00
6″		8.00
8″		10.00
Backflow Preventers		
1″ Thread 53 G.P.M.		0.50
1½″	100	1.00
2″	160	1.00
2½″ Flanged 225		2.50
3″	320	2.75
4″	500	4.00
6″	1000	6.00
8″	1600	8.00
Sewage Ejectors		
6 ft. Shaft Cast-Iron Basin		
2 Horsepower 50 G.P.M. (Duplex)		18.00
2	75	18.00
2	100	18.00
3	125	20.00
3	150	20.00
3	200	22.00
5	250	24.00
7½	300	28.00
10	350	30.00
15	450	35.00
20	500	40.00
Sump Pumps		
6 ft. Shaft Cast-Iron Basin		
2 Horsepower 30 G.P.M. (Simplex)		16.00
2	40	16.00

BUILDING EQUIPMENT (continued)

ITEM DESCRIPTION			LABOR MAN-HOURS EACH
2	50		16.00
2	60		16.00
2	75		16.00
2	100		16.00
3	125		18.00
2	30	(Duplex)	18.00
2	40		18.00
2	50		18.00
2	60		18.00
2	75		18.00
2	100		18.00
3	125		20.00
3	150		20.00
3	200		22.00
3	250		24.00
Grease Interceptors			
14 lb. Grease Capacity			3.25
20			3.25
30			3.25
40			4.00
50			4.00
70			5.00
100			5.00
150			6.00
200			6.00
300			7.00
400			7.00
500			8.00
700			8.00
1000			9.00
Oil Interceptors			
10 G.P.M.			3.25
20			3.25
25			3.25
35			4.00
50			4.00
75			5.00
100			5.00
150			6.00
200			6.00
250			7.00
350			7.00
500			8.00

NOTE:
1) Equipment man-hours include distribution, uncrating, set into place, connect to existing piping and testing.

EXCLUSIONS
1) All piping, valves and elec. wiring.

BUILDING EQUIPMENT (continued)	
ITEM DESCRIPTION	LABOR MAN-HOURS EACH
Hot Water Generators (Gas-Fired)	
500 G.P.H. Recovery Rate	14.00
1,000	18.00
1500	20.00
2000	24.00
2500	26.00
3000	28.00
Hot Water Generators (Oil-Fired)	
500 G.P.H. Recovery Rate	16.00
1000	20.00
1500	24.00
2000	26.00
2500	28.00
3000	30.00
Steam Hi-Temp Hot Water Generators	
500 G.P.H. Production Rate	20.00
1000	24.00
1500	28.00
2000	30.00
2500	32.00
3000	35.00
Hot Water Generators (240 Volt Electric)	
500 G.P.H. Production Rate 140 Kilowatts	12.00
1000	14.00
1500	16.00
2000	18.00
2500	20.00
3000	24.00
Electric Water Heaters (Residential)	
8 G.P.H. Recovery Rate (Glass-Lined)	1.00
10	1.00
12	1.25
30	3.00
45	3.00
60	3.50
75	4.00
100	5.00
120	6.00
Gas-Fired Water Heaters (Residential)	
8 G.P.H. Recovery Rate (Glass-Lined)	1.50
10	1.50
12	2.00
30	3.50
45	3.50
60	4.00
75	4.50
100	6.00

BUILDING EQUIPMENT (continued)	
ITEM DESCRIPTION	LABOR MAN-HOURS EACH
120	8.00
Acid Neutralizing Tanks	
5 Gal. Capacity	2.50
15	3.50
30	4.00
55	6.00
100	8.00
150	9.00
200	10.00
250	12.00
350	14.00
500	18.00
Air Compressors w/Dryer	
1 Horsepower w/30 Gal. Receiver (Simplex)	18.00
1½	18.00
2 w/60	20.00
3	26.00
1 (Duplex)	20.00
1½	20.00
2	24.00
2 w/80	26.00
3 w/60	28.00
3 w/80	30.00
5 w/100	32.00
10 w/120	38.00
15 w/120	40.00
Vacuum Pumps (Medical Gas System)	
¾ Horsepower w/30 Gal. Receiver (Simplex)	16.00
1	16.00
1½	16.00
2	18.00
3 w/60	24.00
5 w/80	27.00
7½ w/80	32.00
1 w/60 (Duplex)	18.00
1½	18.00
2 w/80	24.00
3	27.00
5 w/100	30.00
10 w/120	36.00
15	38.00

NOTE:
1) Equipment man-hours include distribution, uncrating, set into place, connect to existing piping and testing.

EXCLUSIONS
1) All piping, valves and elec. wiring.

BUILDING EQUIPMENT (continued)		
ITEM DESCRIPTION	**LABOR MAN-HOURS EACH**	
Fire Pumps (Fire Protection)		
20 Horsepower 500 G.P.M. (Simplex)		16.00
30		18.00
40	750	20.00
50	1000	24.00
Jockey Pump (Fire Protection)		
7½ Horsepower 500 G.P.M.		6.00
10		8.00

MEDICAL GAS SPECIALTIES		
ITEM DESCRIPTION		**MAN-HOURS EACH**
5 Cylinder Manifold		7.00
10		9.00
12		10.00
Single Wall Outlet		1.00
Double		1.50
Triple		2.00
Single Ceiling Outlet		3.00
Double		4.00
Triple		5.00
Single Alarm with Pressure Gauge		2.50
Double		3.00
Single Audio Visual Legend		3.00
Double		3.50
Triple		4.50
Single Zone Valve & Box	½"	2.00
	¾"	2.00
	1"	2.25
	1¼"	2.50
	1½"	2.75
Double	½"	3.00
	¾"	3.00
	1"	3.25
	1¼"	3.50
	1½"	3.75

FIRE PROTECTION DEVICES	
ITEM DESCRIPTION	**MAN-HOURS EACH**
Sprinkler Heads Pendant Type	0.35
Upright	0.35
Sprinkler Alarm Valves	
4" Wet Type	8.00
4" Dry	8.00
6" Wet	10.00
6" Dry	10.00
Fire Hose Cabinets (Recessed 125′ Hose)	3.00
(Semi-recessed 125′ Hose)	3.00
Rack (125′ Hose)	1.50
Siamese Connection 2½" × 2½" × 4"	3.00
2½" × 2½" × 6"	4.00
Roof Manifold 2½" × 4"	2.50
Fire Dept. Valve 2½"	1.00
Fire Extinguishers	1.00
(in Cabinet)	2.00

MISCELLANEOUS ITEMS	
ITEM DESCRIPTION	**MAN-HOURS EACH**
Sheet Lead Flashing 6 S.F. (4 lb.)	1.00
Pressure Gauges	0.24
Thermometers	0.24

NOTE:
1) Man-hours include distribution, uncrating, set in place, connect to existing piping and test.

EXCLUSIONS
1) All piping, valves and elect. wiring.
2) Setting and connecting gas cylinders

VALVES AND CONTROL DEVICES

ITEM DESCRIPTION: BRONZE GATE, GLOBE, ANGLE, CHECK THREADED JOINT, 125, 150 OR 200 LB. RATING.

SIZE	MH EA.	SIZE	MH EA.	SIZE	MH EA.	SIZE	MH EA.	SIZE	MH EA.	SIZE	MH EA.
¼″	0.35	½″	0.43	1″	0.53	1½″	0.66	2½″	1.53	4″	2.55
⅜″	0.43	¾″	0.47	1¼″	0.63	2″	0.78	3″	1.88		

ITEM DESCRIPTION: BRONZE GATE, GLOBE, ANGLE, CHECK BRAZED OR SOLDER JOINT, 125, 150 OR 200 LB. RATING.

SIZE	MH EA.	SIZE	MH EA.	SIZE	MH EA.	SIZE	MH EA.	SIZE	MH EA.	SIZE	MH EA.
¼″	0.22	½″	0.30	1″	0.41	1½″	0.54	2½″	0.77	4″	1.60
⅜″	0.30	¾″	0.34	1¼″	0.47	2″	0.63	3″	0.98		

ITEM DESCRIPTION: BUTTERFLY VALVES—FLANGED, LEVER HANDLE LUG TYPE, 150 LB. RATING.

SIZE	MH EA.	SIZE	MH EA.	SIZE	MH EA.	SIZE	MH EA.	SIZE	MH EA.	SIZE	MH EA.
2″	0.77	3″	1.02	5″	1.53	8″	2.30	12″	3.44	16″	5.10
2½″	0.89	4″	1.28	6″	1.78	10″	2.80	14″	4.34	18″	5.86

ITEM DESCRIPTION: IRON BODY BRONZE MOUNTED THREADED GATE, GLOBE, CHECK, OS & Y VALVES, 125, 150 OR 250 LB. RATING.

SIZE	MH EA.	SIZE	MH EA.	SIZE	MH EA.	SIZE	MH EA.	SIZE	MH EA.	SIZE	MH EA.
1¼″	0.75	1½″	0.82	2″	0.95	2½″	1.75	3″	2.05	4″	2.80

ITEM DESCRIPTION: IRON BODY BRONZE MOUNTED FLANGED GATE, GLOBE, CHECK, OS & Y VALVES, 150 OR 250 LB. RATING.

SIZE	MH EA.	SIZE	MH EA.	SIZE	MH EA.	SIZE	MH EA.	SIZE	MH EA.	SIZE	MH EA.
1½″	0.9	2½″	1.02	4″	1.79	6″	2.30	10″	3.33	14″	5.14
2″	0.92	3″	1.28	5″	2.09	8″	2.72	12″	4.09	16″	6.05

ITEM DESCRIPTION: IRON BODY OR BRONZE GAS COCKS TEE, LEVER HANDLE OR SQUARE HEAD THREADED, 125 LB. RATING.

SIZE	MH EA.	SIZE	MH EA.	SIZE	MH EA.	SIZE	MH EA.	SIZE	MH EA.	SIZE	MH EA.
¼″	0.40	½″	0.45	1″	0.55	1½″	0.75	2½″	1.49	3″	2.13
⅜″	0.45	¾″	0.51	1¼″	0.68	2″	0.80				

MAN-HOURS INCLUDE THE FOLLOWING:

DISTRIBUTION, SET IN PLACE, MAKE UP JOINT & TEST.

VALVES AND CONTROL DEVICES

ITEM DESCRIPTION: WRENCH-OPERATED LUBRICATED PLUG VALVES, FLANGED, 150 LB. RATING.

SIZE	MH EA.	SIZE	MH EA.	SIZE	MH EA.	SIZE	MH EA.	SIZE	MH EA.	SIZE	MH EA.
1¼″	0.87	1½″	0.95	2″	1.10	2½″	1.75	3″	2.13	4″	2.76

ITEM DESCRIPTION: BRONZE BALL VALVES, THREADED, 150 LB. RATING.

SIZE	MH EA.	SIZE	MH EA.	SIZE	MH EA.	SIZE	MH EA.	SIZE	MH EA.	SIZE	MH EA.
½″	0.43	¾″	0.47	1″	0.53	1¼″	0.63	1½″	0.66	2″	0.78

ITEM DESCRIPTION: BRONZE BALL VALVES, SOLDERED JOINT, 150 LB. RATING.

SIZE	MH EA.	SIZE	MH EA.	SIZE	MH EA.	SIZE	MH EA.	SIZE	MH EA.	SIZE	MH EA.
½″	0.30	¾″	0.34	1″	0.41	1¼″	0.47	1½″	0.54	2″	0.63

ITEM DESCRIPTION: ASME RATED BRONZE RELIEF VALVES, THREADED.

SIZE	MH EA.	SIZE	MH EA.	SIZE	MH EA.	SIZE	MH EA.	SIZE	MH EA.	SIZE	MH EA.
½″	0.30	¾″	0.30	1″	0.35	1¼″	0.50	1½″	0.55	2″	0.60

ITEM DESCRIPTION: PRESSURE REDUCING VALVES, FLANGED, 125 LB. RATING—200 PSI.

SIZE	MH EA.	SIZE	MH EA.	SIZE	MH EA.	SIZE	MH EA.	SIZE	MH EA.	SIZE	MH EA.
2″	1.70	2½″	1.91	3″	2.10	4″	2.55	6″	3.61	8″	4.50

ITEM DESCRIPTION: BRONZE YELLOW DRAIN VALVES, THREADED.

SIZE	MH EA.	SIZE	MH EA.	SIZE	MH EA.	SIZE	MH EA.	SIZE	MH EA.	SIZE	MH EA.
½″	0.50	¾″	0.50	1″	0.60	1¼″	0.75	1½″	0.82	2″	0.90

MAN-HOURS INCLUDE THE FOLLOWING:

DISTRIBUTION, SET IN PLACE, MAKE UP JOINT & TEST.

VALVES AND CONTROL DEVICES

ITEM DESCRIPTION: BRONZE BODY "Y" STRAINERS THREADED, 125 LB. RATING.

SIZE	MH EA.	SIZE	MH EA.	SIZE	MH EA.	SIZE	MH EA.	SIZE	MH EA.	SIZE	MH EA.
½"	0.47	1"	0.53	½"	0.66	2½"	1.53	3"	1.88	4"	2.55
¾"	0.47	1¼"	0.63	2"	0.78						

ITEM DESCRIPTION: IRON BODY "Y" STRAINERS FLANGED, 125 LB. RATING.

SIZE	MH EA.	SIZE	MH EA.	SIZE	MH EA.	SIZE	MH EA.	SIZE	MH EA.	SIZE	MH EA.
4"	1.79	5"	2.09	6"	2.30	8"	2.72	10"	3.33	12"	4.09

ITEM DESCRIPTION: VACUUM BREAKERS.

SIZE	MH EA.	SIZE	MH EA.	SIZE	MH EA.	SIZE	MH EA.	SIZE	MH EA.	SIZE	MH EA.
½"	0.47	¾"	0.47	1"	0.53	1¼"	0.63	1½"	0.66	2"	0.78

ITEM DESCRIPTION: EXPANSION JOINTS COPPER BELLOWS TYPE.

SIZE	MH EA.	SIZE	MH EA.	SIZE	MH EA.	SIZE	MH EA.	SIZE	MH EA.	SIZE	MH EA.
½"	0.47	1"	0.53	1½"	0.66	2½"	1.53	4"	2.55		
¾"	0.47	1¼"	0.63	2"	0.78	3"	1.88				

ITEM DESCRIPTION: SHOCK ABSORBERS (PDI)*.*PLUMBING & DRAINAGE INSTITUTE.

SIZE PDI	MH EA.	SIZE PDI	MH EA.	SIZE PDI	MH EA.	SIZE PDI	MH EA.	SIZE PDI	MH EA.	SIZE PDI	MH EA.
A	0.47	B	0.63	C	0.78	D	0.88	E	1.40	F	1.75

ITEM DESCRIPTION: PLASTIC VALVES, SOCKET AND THREADED, 125 LB. RATED.

SIZE	MH EA.	SIZE	MH EA.	SIZE	MH EA.	SIZE	MH EA.	SIZE	MH EA.	SIZE	MH EA.
½"	0.15	¾"	0.18	1"	0.20	1¼"	0.24	1½"	0.31	2"	0.44

MAN-HOURS INCLUDE THE FOLLOWING:

DISTRIBUTION, SET IN PLACE, MAKE UP JOINT & TEST.

PIPE INSULATION, SUPPORTS AND SLEEVES

ITEM DESCRIPTION: ½″ FIBERGLASS PIPE INSULATION.

SIZE	MH/LF	SIZE	MH/LF	SIZE	MH/LF	SIZE	MH/LF	SIZE	MH/LF	SIZE	MH/LF
½″	.045	1″	.050	1½″	.055	2½″	.067	4″	.073	8″	.080
¾″	.045	1¼″	.050	2″	.065	3″	.070	6″	.075	10″	.094

ITEM DESCRIPTION: HANGER ASSEMBLIES (CLEVIS HANGER, 2′-0″ ROD, INSERT W/NUTS & BOLTS).

SIZE	MH EA.	SIZE	MH EA.	SIZE	MH EA.	SIZE	MH EA.	SIZE	MH EA.	SIZE	MH EA.
½″	0.36	1″	0.36	1½″	0.36	2½″	0.36	4″	0.36	8″	0.46
¾″	0.36	1¼″	0.36	2″	.036	3″	0.36	6″	0.41	10″	0.46

ITEM DESCRIPTION: STEEL PIPE SLEEVES.

SIZE	MH EA.	SIZE	MH EA.	SIZE	MH EA.	SIZE	MH EA.	SIZE	MH EA.	SIZE	MH EA.
½″	0.16	1″	0.22	1½″	0.28	2½″	0.40	4″	0.50	8″	0.63
¾″	0.20	1¼″	0.25	2″	0.32	3″	0.45	6″	0.55	10″	0.70

ITEM DESCRIPTION: TOILET AND BATH ACCESSORIES—MAN-HOURS EACH.

GRAB BAR	TOWEL BAR	TOILET PAPER HOLDER	SOAP DISPENSER SURFACE MTD.	MIRROR AND SHELF	MEDICINE CABINET
2.0	1.0	SURFACE 0.50 RECESSED 0.75	1.0	16″ × 20″ 1.0 24″ × 60″ 1.25	SURFACE 1.25 RECESSED 1.50

FACIAL TISSUE HOLDER	SANITARY NAPKIN DISPENSER	TOWEL DISPENSER	PAPER CUP DISPENSER	ELECTRIC HAND DRYER	SOAP DISH
SURFACE .50 RECESSED .75	SURFACE 1.0 RECESSED 1.25	SURFACE .75 RECESSED 1.0	SURFACE 1.0 RECESSED 1.25	1.0	0.50

SHOWER ROD & FLANGES	ASH RECEPTACLE	ASH URN & WASTE RECEPTACLE	TOWEL & ROBE HOOK	JANITORIAL UTILITY SHELF 36″ LONG	UTILITY SHELF 5½″ × 24″
1.0	0.50	1.0	0.50	1.50	1.0

MAN-HOURS INCLUDE THE FOLLOWING:

DISTRIBUTION, SET IN PLACE AND INSTALL.

SITE DRAINAGE AND UTILITIES

ITEM DESCRIPTION: EXTRA STRENGTH VITRIFIED CLAY PIPE AND FITTINGS, RING JOINT (ADD FOR EXCAVATION).

SIZE	MH/LF	SIZE	MH/LF	SIZE	MH/LF	SIZE	MH/LF	SIZE	MH/LF	SIZE	MH/LF
4″	0.10	8″	0.12	12″	0.17	18″	0.26	24″	0.43	36″	0.53
6″	0.11	10″	0.14	15″	0.19	21″	0.34	30″	0.62		

ITEM DESCRIPTION: REINFORCED CONCRETE PIPE, CLASS III, RING JOINT (ADD FOR EXCAVATION).

SIZE	MH/LF	SIZE	MH/LF	SIZE	MH/LF	SIZE	MH/LF	SIZE	MH/LF
12″	0.10	18″	0.14	24″	0.18	30″	0.32	36″	0.39
15″	0.12	21″	0.16	27″	0.22	33″	0.35		

ITEM DESCRIPTION: DUCTILE IRON PRESSURE PIPE & FITTINGS, CLASS 150 CEMENT LINED MECHANICAL JOINT.

SIZE	MH/LF	SIZE	MH/LF	SIZE	MH/LF	SIZE	MH/LF	SIZE	MH/LF	SIZE	MH/LF
4″	0.13	6″	0.17	8″	0.20	10″	0.26	12″	0.31	14″	0.37
										16″	0.51

ITEM DESCRIPTION: DUCTILE IRON PRESSURE PIPE & FITTINGS, CLASS 150 CEMENT LINED NEOPRENE SLIP-ON JOINT.

SIZE	MH/LF	SIZE	MH/LF	SIZE	MH/LF	SIZE	MH/LF	SIZE	MH/LF	SIZE	MH/LF
4″	0.11	6″	0.13	8″	0.16	10″	0.21	12″	0.25	14″	0.32
										16″	0.48

ITEM DESCRIPTION: DUCTILE IRON GATE VALVES WITH BOX MECHANICAL & NEOPRENE SLIP-ON JOINTS.

SIZE	MH/LF	SIZE	MH/LF	SIZE	MH/LF	SIZE	MH/LF	SIZE	MH/LF	ITEM	MH EA.
4″	3.0	6″	3.5	8″	4.0	10″	5.0	12″	7.5	FIRE HYD.	5.0
										WET CONN.	3.0
										WATER TAP	2.0

ITEM DESCRIPTION: SCHEDULE 40 STEEL, THREADED MILLWRAP PIPE & FITTINGS.

SIZE	MH/LF	SIZE	MH/LF	SIZE	MH/LF	SIZE	MH/LF	SIZE	MH/LF	SIZE	MH/LF
¾″	0.04	1¼″	0.05	2″	0.08	3″	0.12	5″	0.22	8″	0.38
1″	0.04	1½″	0.06	2½″	0.10	4″	0.18	6″	0.27		

MAN-HOURS INCLUDE THE FOLLOWING:

DISTRIBUTION, SET IN PLACE AND INSTALL.
1) UP TO 4′ O″ TRENCH DEPTH
2) REQUIRED EQUIPMENT FOR UNLOADING AND PLACING IN TRENCH
   a) VITRIFIED CLAY PIPE 18″ & LARGER
   b) REINFORCED CONCRETE & DUCTILE IRON PIPE—ALL SIZES
3) TESTING
4) CREWS OF THREE MEN ARE ASSUMED

EXCLUSIONS
1) DEWATERING
2) EXCAVATION & BACKFILL

MAN-HOURS TO INSTALL BUILDING PIPING SYSTEMS

ITEM DESCRIPTION:
EXTRA HEAVY CAST IRON PIPE AND FITTINGS
LEAD AND OAKUM JOINT

BELOW GROUND						ABOVE GROUND				
SIZE	PIPE PER L.F.	ONE JOINT FITTING	TWO JOINT FITTING	THREE JOINT FITTING		SIZE	PIPE PER L.F.	ONE JOINT FITTING	TWO JOINT FITTING	THREE JOINT FITTING
2"	.08	.36	.70	1.05		2"	.12	.56	1.10	1.67
3"	.11	.53	1.04	1.57		3"	.17	.83	1.65	2.48
4"	.14	.70	1.38	2.07		4"	.23	1.10	2.19	3.30
5"	.18	.87	1.72	2.58		5"	.28	1.38	2.74	4.11
6"	.21	1.06	2.11	3.17		6"	.33	1.65	3.28	4.93
8"	.32	1.57	3.13	4.70		8"	.49	2.44	4.86	7.30
10"	.41	1.95	3.89	5.85		10"	.61	3.04	6.07	9.11
12"	.56	2.74	5.46	8.19		12"	.82	4.11	8.21	12.32
15"	.70	3.42	6.82	10.23		15"	1.03	5.13	10.25	15.38

MAN-HOURS INCLUDE THE FOLLOWING:

DISTRIBUTION FROM STOCKPILE 100' DISTANCE
MEASURE AND CUT PIPE
INSTALL PIPE AND FITTING IN PLACE
CAULK JOINT WITH OAKUM AND LEAD
NORMAL LOSS TIME
TESTING
UP TO 3'-0" TRENCH DEPTH
UP TO 10'-0" CEILING HEIGHT

EXCLUSIONS

EXCAVATION AND BACKFILL
DEWATERING
HANGERS AND SUPPORTS (BELOW AND ABOVE GROUND)
UNUSUAL JOB CONDITIONS

MAN-HOURS TO INSTALL BUILDING PIPING SYSTEMS (continued)

ITEM DESCRIPTION:
EXTRA HEAVY CAST IRON PIPE AND FITTINGS
NEOPRENE GASKET JOINT

BELOW GROUND						ABOVE GROUND				
SIZE	PIPE PER L.F.	ONE JOINT FITTING	TWO JOINT FITTING	THREE JOINT FITTING		SIZE	PIPE PER L.F.	ONE JOINT FITTING	TWO JOINT FITTING	THREE JOINT FITTING
2″	.06	.29	.56	.83		2″	.09	.43	.85	1.27
3″	.10	.42	.83	1.24		3″	.14	.64	1.26	1.88
4″	.13	.56	1.10	1.65		4″	.18	.85	1.68	2.52
5″	.16	.70	1.38	2.06		5″	.22	1.04	2.06	3.08
6″	.19	.83	1.65	2.46		6″	.26	1.29	2.57	3.84
8″	.26	1.21	2.40	3.59		8″	.36	1.80	3.59	5.37
10″	.33	1.53	3.04	4.56		10″	.46	2.31	4.61	6.90
12″	.43	2.07	4.13	6.19		12″	.65	3.25	6.48	9.71
15″	.53	2.99	5.05	7.56		15″	.81	4.01	8.01	12.00

MAN-HOURS INCLUDE THE FOLLOWING:

DISTRIBUTION FROM STOCKPILE 100′ DISTANCE
MEASURE AND CUT PIPE
INSTALL PIPE AND FITTING IN PLACE
MAKE UP GASKET JOINT
NORMAL LOSS TIME
TESTING
UP TO 3′-0″ TRENCH DEPTH
UP TO 10′-0″ CEILING HEIGHT

EXCLUSIONS

EXCAVATION AND BACKFILL
DEWATERING
HANGERS AND SUPPORTS (BELOW AND ABOVE GROUND)
UNUSUAL JOB CONDITIONS

MAN-HOURS TO INSTALL BUILDING PIPING SYSTEMS (continued)

ITEM DESCRIPTION:
SERVICE WEIGHT CAST IRON PIPE AND FITTINGS
LEAD AND OAKUM JOINT

BELOW GROUND						ABOVE GROUND				
SIZE	PIPE PER L.F.	ONE JOINT FITTING	TWO JOINT FITTING	THREE JOINT FITTING		SIZE	PIPE PER L.F.	ONE JOINT FITTING	TWO JOINT FITTING	THREE JOINT FITTING
2″	.06	.32	.66	1.00		2″	.10	.53	1.07	1.61
3″	.10	.49	1.00	1.51		3″	.15	.80	1.61	2.43
4″	.13	.66	1.34	2.02		4″	.21	1.07	2.16	3.25
5″	.16	.83	1.68	2.53		5″	.26	1.34	2.70	4.06
6″	.19	1.03	2.07	3.12		6″	.31	1.62	3.25	4.88
8″	.30	1.54	3.09	4.65		8″	.48	2.41	4.83	7.25
10″	.37	1.92	3.86	5.80		10″	.59	3.01	6.03	9.06
12″	.53	2.70	5.42	8.14		12″	.81	4.08	8.18	12.27
15″	.67	3.38	6.78	10.18		15″	1.01	5.10	10.22	15.33

MAN-HOURS INCLUDE THE FOLLOWING:

DISTRIBUTION FROM STOCKPILE 100′ DISTANCE
MEASURE AND CUT PIPE
INSTALL PIPE AND FITTING IN PLACE
CAULK JOINT WITH OAKUM AND LEAD
NORMAL LOSS TIME
TESTING
UP TO 3′-0″ TRENCH DEPTH
UP TO 10′-0″ CEILING HEIGHT

EXCLUSIONS

EXCAVATION AND BACKFILL
DEWATERING
HANGERS AND SUPPORTS (BELOW AND ABOVE GROUND)
UNUSUAL JOB CONDITIONS

MAN-HOURS TO INSTALL BUILDING PIPING SYSTEMS (continued)

ITEM DESCRIPTION:
SERVICE WEIGHT CAST IRON PIPE AND FITTINGS
NEOPRENE GASKET JOINT

BELOW GROUND					ABOVE GROUND				
SIZE	PIPE PER L.F.	ONE JOINT FITTING	TWO JOINT FITTING	THREE JOINT FITTING	SIZE	PIPE PER L.F.	ONE JOINT FITTING	TWO JOINT FITTING	THREE JOINT FITTING
2″	.04	.26	.53	.80	2″	.08	.40	.82	1.23
3″	.09	.39	.80	1.21	3″	.13	.60	1.22	1.84
4″	.12	.53	1.07	1.61	4″	.16	.82	1.65	2.48
5″	.14	.66	1.34	2.02	5″	.20	1.00	2.02	3.04
6″	.17	.80	1.61	2.43	6″	.25	1.26	2.53	3.81
8″	.25	1.17	2.36	3.55	8″	.35	1.77	3.55	5.34
10″	.31	1.50	3.01	4.52	10″	.44	2.28	4.57	6.87
12″	.42	2.04	4.10	6.15	12″	.64	3.21	6.44	9.67
15″	.51	2.50	5.01	7.53	15″	.79	3.98	7.97	11.97

MAN-HOURS INCLUDE THE FOLLOWING:

DISTRIBUTION FROM STOCKPILE 100′ DISTANCE
MEASURE AND CUT PIPE
INSTALL PIPE AND FITTING IN PLACE
MAKE UP GASKET JOINT
NORMAL LOSS TIME
TESTING
UP TO 3′-0″ TRENCH DEPTH
UP TO 10′-0″ CEILING HEIGHT

EXCLUSIONS

EXCAVATION AND BACKFILL
DEWATERING
HANGERS AND SUPPORTS (BELOW AND ABOVE GROUND)
UNUSUAL JOB CONDITIONS

MAN-HOURS TO INSTALL BUILDING PIPING SYSTEMS (continued)

ITEM DESCRIPTION:
SERVICE WEIGHT CAST IRON PIPE AND FITTINGS
HUBLESS CLAMP JOINT

BELOW GROUND						ABOVE GROUND				
SIZE	PIPE PER L.F.	TWO JOINT FITTING	THREE JOINT FITTING	FOUR JOINT FITTING		SIZE	PIPE PER L.F.	TWO JOINT FITTING	THREE JOINT FITTING	FOUR JOINT FITTING
1½″	.03	.32	.49	.66		1½″	.04	.41	.62	.83
2″	.03	.39	.60	.80		2″	.07	.49	.75	1.00
3″	.06	.46	.70	.94		3″	.10	.58	.88	1.17
4″	.08	.53	.80	1.07		4″	.14	.66	1.00	1.34
5″	.10	.60	.90	1.21		5″	.17	.75	1.13	1.51
6″	.13	.66	1.00	1.34		6″	.20	.83	1.26	1.68
8″	.21	.87	1.31	1.75		8″	.33	1.09	1.64	2.19
10″	.26	1.07	1.61	2.16		10″	.40	1.34	2.02	2.70

MAN-HOURS INCLUDE THE FOLLOWING:

DISTRIBUTION FROM STOCKPILE 100′ DISTANCE
MEASURE AND CUT PIPE
INSTALL PIPE AND FITTING IN PLACE
MAKE UP CLAMP JOINT
NORMAL LOSS TIME
TESTING
UP TO 3′-0″ TRENCH DEPTH
UP TO 10′-0″ CEILING HEIGHT

EXCLUSIONS

EXCAVATION AND BACKFILL
DEWATERING
HANGERS AND SUPPORTS (BELOW AND ABOVE GROUND)
UNUSUAL JOB CONDITIONS

MAN-HOURS TO INSTALL BUILDING PIPING SYSTEMS (continued)

ITEM DESCRIPTION:
IRON ALLOY (SILICON) PIPE AND FITTINGS
LEAD AND OAKUM JOINT

BELOW GROUND						ABOVE GROUND				
SIZE	PIPE PER L.F.	ONE JOINT FITTING	TWO JOINT FITTING	THREE JOINT FITTING		SIZE	PIPE PER L.F.	ONE JOINT FITTING	TWO JOINT FITTING	THREE JOINT FITTING
2″	.09	.41	.80	1.20		2″	.13	.62	1.22	1.84
3″	.13	.60	1.17	1.76		3″	.19	.93	1.84	2.75
4″	.16	.79	1.56	2.35		4″	.25	1.21	2.40	3.60
6″	.24	1.17	2.33	3.49		6″	.37	1.81	3.60	5.41
8″	.37	1.81	3.60	5.41		8″	.55	2.74	5.46	8.19

MAN-HOURS INCLUDE THE FOLLOWING:

DISTRIBUTION FROM STOCKPILE 100′ DISTANCE
MEASURE AND CUT PIPE
INSTALL PIPE AND FITTING IN PLACE
CAULK JOINT WITH OAKUM AND LEAD
NORMAL LOSS TIME
TESTING
UP TO 3′-0″ TRENCH DEPTH
UP TO 10′-0″ CEILING HEIGHT

EXCLUSIONS

EXCAVATION AND BACKFILL
DEWATERING
HANGERS AND SUPPORTS (BELOW AND ABOVE GROUND)
UNUSUAL JOB CONDITIONS

MAN-HOURS TO INSTALL BUILDING PIPING SYSTEMS (continued)

ITEM DESCRIPTION:
IRON ALLOY (SILICON) PIPE AND FITTINGS
LEAD AND OAKUM JOINT

BELOW GROUND					ABOVE GROUND				
SIZE	PIPE PER L.F.	TWO JOINT FITTING	THREE JOINT FITTING	FOUR JOINT FITTING	SIZE	PIPE PER L.F.	TWO JOINT FITTING	THREE JOINT FITTING	FOUR JOINT FITTING
2″	.06	.49	.73	.97	2″	.09	.61	.91	1.21
3″	.09	.56	.83	1.11	3″	.14	.70	1.04	1.38
4″	.12	.65	.96	1.28	4″	.18	.80	1.19	1.58
6″	.17	.80	1.19	1.58	6″	.26	1.00	1.50	2.00
8″	.26	1.04	1.55	2.06	8″	.40	1.29	1.93	2.57

MAN-HOURS INCLUDE THE FOLLOWING:

DISTRIBUTION FROM STOCKPILE 100′ DISTANCE
MEASURE AND CUT PIPE
INSTALL PIPE AND FITTING IN PLACE
MAKE UP MECHANICAL COUPLING JOINT
NORMAL LOSS TIME
TESTING
UP TO 3′-0″ TRENCH DEPTH
UP TO 10′-0″ CEILING HEIGHT

EXCLUSIONS

EXCAVATION AND BACKFILL
DEWATERING
HANGERS AND SUPPORTS (BELOW AND ABOVE GROUND)
UNUSUAL JOB CONDITIONS

MAN-HOURS TO INSTALL BUILDING PIPING SYSTEMS (continued)

ITEM DESCRIPTION:
DRAIN-WASTE-VENT COPPER TUBE "DWV"
CAST OR WROUGHT FITTINGS—50/50 SOLDER JOINT

SIZE	PIPE PER L.F.	TWO JOINT FITTING	THREE JOINT FITTING	FOUR JOINT FITTING
1¼″	.05	.32	.49	.65
1½″	.06	.36	.54	.71
2″	.06	.41	.62	.82
2½″	.08	.49	.75	1.00
3″	.10	.58	.88	1.16
4″	.12	.83	1.26	1.67
5″	.16	1.26	1.94	2.53
6″	.21	1.68	2.53	3.38

MAN-HOURS INCLUDE THE FOLLOWING:

DISTRIBUTION FROM STOCKPILE 100′ DISTANCE
MEASURE, CUT AND PREPARE TUBING AND FITTING
INSTALL TUBING AND FITTING IN PLACE
SOLDER JOINT WITH TURBO-TORCH
NORMAL LOSS TIME
TESTING
UP TO 10′-0″ CEILING HEIGHT

EXCLUSIONS

HANGERS AND SUPPORTS
UNUSUAL JOB CONDITIONS

MAN-HOURS TO INSTALL BUILDING PIPING SYSTEMS (continued)

ITEM DESCRIPTION:
POLYVINYL CHLORIDE (PVC) PLASTIC PIPE—SCHED. 40
DRAIN-WASTE-VENT (DWV) SOLVENT, SOCKET JOINT FITTINGS

BELOW GROUND						ABOVE GROUND				
SIZE	PIPE PER L.F.	TWO JOINT FITTING	THREE JOINT FITTING	FOUR JOINT FITTING		SIZE	PIPE PER L.F.	TWO JOINT FITTING	THREE JOINT FITTING	FOUR JOINT FITTING
1¼″	.02	.14	.20	.28		1¼″	.03	.18	.27	.37
1½″	.03	.18	.26	.36		1½″	.04	.23	.35	.47
2″	.04	.26	.38	.52		2″	.05	.33	.50	.67
3″	.05	.38	.58	.77		3″	.07	.50	.76	1.01
4″	.06	.46	.70	.93		4″	.08	.60	.91	1.22
6″	.11	.58	.88	1.17		6″	.14	.76	1.14	1.52
8″	.14	.72	1.10	1.47		8″	.19	.95	1.43	1.90
10″	.19	.91	1.38	1.84		10″	.24	1.19	1.78	2.38
12″	.24	1.14	1.73	2.31		12″	.30	1.49	2.24	2.97

MAN-HOURS INCLUDE THE FOLLOWING:

DISTRIBUTION FROM STOCKPILE 100′ DISTANCE
MEASURE, CUT AND PREPARE PIPE
INSTALL PIPE AND FITTING IN PLACE
MAKE UP SOLVENT JOINT
NORMAL LOSS TIME
TESTING
UP TO 3′-0″ TRENCH DEPTH
UP TO 10′-0″ CEILING HEIGHT

EXCLUSIONS

EXCAVATION AND BACKFILL
DEWATERING
HANGERS AND SUPPORTS (BELOW AND ABOVE GROUND)
UNUSUAL JOB CONDITIONS

MAN-HOURS TO INSTALL BUILDING PIPING SYSTEMS (continued)

ITEM DESCRIPTION:
POLYPROPYLENE FUSION JOINT
DRAIN-WASTE-VENT (DWV) SOCKET FUSION TYPE

BELOW GROUND

SIZE	PIPE PER L.F.	TWO JOINT FITTING	THREE JOINT FITTING	FOUR JOINT FITTING
1½″	.06	.30	.44	.59
2″	.07	.37	.54	.72
3″	.09	.50	.75	.99
4″	.10	.65	.98	1.30
6″	.11	.84	1.26	1.67

ABOVE GROUND

SIZE	PIPE PER L.F.	TWO JOINT FITTING	THREE JOINT FITTING	FOUR JOINT FITTING
1½″	.08	.33	.49	.65
2″	.09	.40	.60	.79
3″	.11	.55	.82	1.10
4″	.12	.72	1.08	1.44
6″	.14	.93	1.39	1.84

MAN-HOURS INCLUDE THE FOLLOWING:

DISTRIBUTION FROM STOCKPILE 100′ DISTANCE
MEASURE, CUT AND PREPARE
INSTALL PIPE AND FITTING IN PLACE
FUSE JOINT
NORMAL LOSS TIME
TESTING
UP TO 3′-0″ TRENCH DEPTH
UP TO 10′-0″ CEILING HEIGHT

EXCLUSIONS

EXCAVATION AND BACKFILL
DEWATERING
HANGERS AND SUPPORTS (BELOW AND ABOVE GROUND)
UNUSUAL JOB CONDITIONS

MAN-HOURS TO INSTALL BUILDING
PIPING SYSTEMS (continued)

ITEM DESCRIPTION:
STEEL PIPE—THREADED JOINTS
MALLEABLE OR CAST IRON FITTINGS

SCHEDULE 40—STD.						SCHEDULE 80—EX. HVY				
SIZE	PIPE PER L.F.	TWO JOINT FITTING	THREE JOINT FITTING	FOUR JOINT FITTING		SIZE	PIPE PER L.F.	TWO JOINT FITTING	THREE JOINT FITTING	FOUR JOINT FITTING
½″	.03	.38	.58	.77		½″	.05	.40	.60	.79
¾″	.03	.42	.63	.84		¾″	.05	.43	.65	.86
1″	.04	.47	.71	.94		1″	.07	.50	.75	.99
1¼″	.05	.54	.81	1.08		1¼″	.08	.59	.88	1.16
1½″	.06	.57	.86	1.15		1½″	.09	.62	.93	1.23
2″	.07	.67	1.01	1.35		2″	.10	.72	1.08	1.44
2½″	.10	1.35	2.03	2.71		2½″	.14	1.50	2.25	3.00
3″	.11	1.62	2.44	3.26		3″	.15	1.81	2.71	3.61
4″	.18	2.14	3.20	4.27		4″	.20	2.36	3.54	4.71
5″	.24	2.57	3.84	5.12		5″	.26	2.82	4.22	5.63
6″	.31	3.13	4.68	6.24		6″	.36	3.50	5.24	6.99
8″	.38	3.69	5.52	7.36		8″	.44	4.13	6.18	8.24

MAN-HOURS INCLUDE THE FOLLOWING:

DISTRIBUTION FROM STOCKPILE 100′ DISTANCE
MEASURE, CUT AND THREAD PIPE
INSTALL PIPE AND FITTING IN PLACE
MAKE UP THREADED JOINT
NORMAL LOSS TIME
TESTING
UP TO 10′-0″ CEILING HEIGHT

EXCLUSIONS

HANGERS AND SUPPORTS
UNUSUAL JOB CONDITIONS

MAN-HOURS TO INSTALL BUILDING PIPING SYSTEMS (continued)

ITEM DESCRIPTION:
STEEL PIPE—THREADED
CAST IRON FLANGED FITTINGS

SCHEDULE 40-STD.

SIZE	PIPE PER L.F.	TWO JOINT FITTING	THREE JOINT FITTING	FOUR JOINT FITTING
2″	.08	.77	1.16	1.71
2½″	.12	.94	1.41	2.08
3″	.13	1.15	1.72	2.53
4″	.18	1.51	2.26	3.31
5″	.24	1.92	2.87	4.20
6″	.31	2.28	3.41	4.98
8″	.38	3.04	4.56	6.68

SCHEDULE 80-EX. HVY

SIZE	PIPE PER L.F.	TWO JOINT FITTING	THREE JOINT FITTING	FOUR JOINT FITTING
2″	.09	.90	1.28	1.92
2½″	.14	1.10	1.56	2.35
3″	.15	1.39	1.90	2.86
4″	.20	1.74	2.49	3.84
5″	.26	2.21	3.15	4.78
6″	.36	2.62	3.74	5.67
8″	.44	3.51	5.01	7.58

MAN-HOURS INCLUDE THE FOLLOWING:

DISTRIBUTION FROM STOCKPILE 100′ DISTANCE
MEASURE, CUT AND THREAD PIPE
INSTALL PIPE AND FITTING IN PLACE
MAKE UP THREAD FLANGED JOINT AND BOLT-UP
NORMAL LOSS TIME
TESTING
UP TO 10′-0″ CEILING HEIGHT

EXCLUSIONS

HANGERS AND SUPPORTS
UNUSUAL JOB CONDITIONS

MAN-HOURS TO INSTALL BUILDING PIPING SYSTEMS (continued)

ITEM DESCRIPTION:
COPPER TUBING—95/5 SOLDER JOINT
CAST OR WROUGHT FITTINGS

TYPE "K"

SIZE	PIPE PER L.F.	TWO JOINT FITTING	THREE JOINT FITTING	FOUR JOINT FITTING
½″	.03	.29	.43	.57
¾″	.04	.32	.48	.65
1″	.04	.39	.59	.78
1¼″	.05	.43	.65	.86
1½″	.06	.50	.75	1.00
2″	.06	.57	.86	1.14
2½″	.09	.70	1.05	1.39
3″	.12	.89	1.34	1.71
4″	.14	1.34	2.01	2.68
5″	.18	1.96	2.95	3.93
6″	.24	2.61	3.91	5.21
8″	.36	3.39	5.09	6.78

TYPE "L"

SIZE	PIPE PER L.F.	TWO JOINT FITTING	THREE JOINT FITTING	FOUR JOINT FITTING
½″	.03	.29	.43	.57
¾″	.03	.32	.48	.65
1″	.04	.39	.59	.78
1¼″	.05	.43	.65	.86
1½″	.06	.50	.75	1.00
2″	.06	.57	.86	1.14
2½″	.09	.70	1.05	1.39
3″	.11	.89	1.34	1.71
4″	.14	1.34	2.01	2.68
5″	.17	1.96	2.95	3.93
6″	.23	2.61	3.91	5.21
8″	.34	3.39	5.09	6.78

MAN-HOURS INCLUDE THE FOLLOWING:

DISTRIBUTION FROM STOCKPILE 100′ DISTANCE
MEASURE, CUT AND PREPARE TUBING AND FITTING
INSTALL TUBING AND FITTING IN PLACE
SOLDER JOINT WITH TURBO TORCH
NORMAL LOSS TIME
TESTING
UP TO 10′-0″ CEILING HEIGHT
UP TO 2′-0″ TRENCH DEPTH (TYPE "K" ONLY)

EXCLUSIONS

HANGERS AND SUPPORTS
UNUSUAL JOB CONDITIONS

MAN-HOURS TO INSTALL BUILDING PIPING SYSTEMS (continued)

ITEM DESCRIPTION:
COPPER TUBING—95/5 SOLDER JOINT
CAST OR WROUGHT FITTINGS
TYPE "M"

SIZE	PIPE PER L.F.	TWO JOINT FITTING	THREE JOINT FITTING	FOUR JOINT FITTING
½"	.03	.29	.43	.57
¾"	.03	.32	.48	.65
1"	.04	.39	.59	.78
1¼"	.05	.43	.65	.86
1½"	.06	.50	.75	1.00
2"	.06	.57	.86	1.14
2½"	.08	.70	1.05	1.39
3"	.10	.89	1.34	1.71
4"	.13	1.34	2.01	2.68
5"	.16	1.96	2.95	3.93
6"	.22	2.61	3.91	5.21
8"	.32	3.39	5.09	6.78

MAN-HOURS INCLUDE THE FOLLOWING:

DISTRIBUTION FROM STOCKPILE 100′ DISTANCE
MEASURE, CUT AND PREPARE TUBING AND FITTING
INSTALL TUBING AND FITTING IN PLACE
SOLDER JOINT WITH TURBO TORCH
NORMAL LOSS TIME
TESTING
UP TO 10′-0″ CEILING HEIGHT
UP TO 2′-0″ TRENCH DEPTH (TYPE "K" ONLY)

EXCLUSIONS

HANGERS AND SUPPORTS
UNUSUAL JOB CONDITIONS

MAN-HOURS TO INSTALL BUILDING PIPING SYSTEMS (continued)

ITEM DESCRIPTION:
BRASS PIPE
CAST OR MALLEABLE THREADED FITTINGS

STANDARD—CL. 125 LB.

SIZE	PIPE PER L.F.	TWO JOINT FITTING	THREE JOINT FITTING	FOUR JOINT FITTING
½″	.08	.49	.73	.99
¾″	.08	.53	.78	1.05
1″	.09	.60	.88	1.19
1¼″	.10	.68	1.01	1.36
1½″	.11	.76	1.14	1.53
2″	.12	1.14	1.70	2.28
2½″	.18	1.60	2.39	3.20
3″	.24	2.48	3.71	4.96
4″	.28	2.96	4.43	1.48
5″	.35	3.42	5.12	6.83
6″	.41	3.76	5.63	7.51
8″	.54	4.95	7.41	9.89

EXTRA HEAVY—CL. 250 LB.

SIZE	PIPE PER L.F.	TWO JOINT FITTING	THREE JOINT FITTING	FOUR JOINT FITTING
½″	.08	.49	.73	.99
¾″	.08	.53	.78	1.05
1″	.09	.61	.91	1.22
1¼″	.11	.70	1.04	1.39
1½″	.12	.82	1.22	1.63
2″	.13	1.22	1.83	2.45
2½″	.21	1.75	2.62	3.51
3″	.28	2.74	4.10	5.47
4″	.31	3.30	4.94	6.60
5″	.41	3.83	5.73	7.65
6″	.47	4.32	6.47	8.64
8″	.64	5.70	8.53	11.39

MAN-HOURS INCLUDE THE FOLLOWING:

DISTRIBUTION FROM STOCKPILE 100′ DISTANCE
MEASURE, CUT AND THREAD PIPE
INSTALL PIPE AND FITTING IN PLACE
MAKE UP THREADED JOINT
NORMAL LOSS TIME
TESTING
UP TO 10′-0″ CEILING HEIGHT

EXCLUSIONS

HANGERS AND SUPPORTS
UNUSUAL JOB CONDITIONS

MAN-HOURS TO INSTALL BUILDING PIPING SYSTEMS (continued)

ITEM DESCRIPTION:
POLYVINYL CHLORIDE (PVC) PLASTIC PIPE
PRESSURE FITTINGS—SOLVENT SOCKET JOINTS

SCHEDULE 40						SCHEDULE 80				
SIZE	PIPE PER L.F.	TWO JOINT FITTING	THREE JOINT FITTING	FOUR JOINT FITTING		SIZE	PIPE PER L.F.	TWO JOINT FITTING	THREE JOINT FITTING	FOUR JOINT FITTING
½″	.02	.13	.20	.26		½″	.02	.14	.21	.28
¾″	.02	.13	.20	.26		¾″	.02	.14	.21	.28
1″	.03	.14	.22	.28		1″	.03	.15	.23	.30
1¼″	.03	.18	.27	.36		1¼″	.04	.19	.28	.38
1½″	.04	.23	.35	.46		1½″	.05	.24	.36	.48
2″	.04	.33	.50	.66		2″	.05	.34	.51	.68
2½″	.05	.42	.63	.84		2½″	.08	.50	.74	1.00
3″	.07	50	.76	1.00		3″	.09	.60	.88	1.20
4″	.08	.60	.91	1.20		4″	.11	.71	1.06	1.42
5″	.11	.77	1.16	1.54		5″	.14	.91	1.35	1.82
6″	.15	1.10	1.65	2.20		6″	.19	1.28	1.91	2.56

MAN-HOURS INCLUDE THE FOLLOWING:

DISTRIBUTION FROM STOCKPILE 100′ DISTANCE
MEASURE, CUT AND PREPARE PIPE AND FITTING
INSTALL PIPE AND FITTING IN PLACE
MAKE UP SOLVENT JOINT
NORMAL LOSS TIME
TESTING
UP TO 10′-0″ CEILING HEIGHT

EXCLUSIONS

HANGERS AND SUPPORTS
UNUSUAL JOB CONDITIONS

MAN-HOURS TO INSTALL BUILDING PIPING SYSTEMS (continued)

ITEM DESCRIPTION:
GLASS ACID WASTE AND VENT PIPING
CLAMP JOINT FITTINGS

BELOW GROUND					ABOVE GROUND				
SIZE	PIPE PER L.F.	TWO JOINT FITTING	THREE JOINT FITTING	FOUR JOINT FITTING	SIZE	PIPE PER L.F.	TWO JOINT FITTING	THREE JOINT FITTING	FOUR JOINT FITTING
1½″	.21	.51	.76	1.02	1½″	.24	.54	.82	1.09
2″	.28	.61	.92	1.22	2″	.31	.65	.97	1.29
3″	.32	.82	1.22	1.63	3″	.35	.85	1.27	1.70
4″	.43	.90	1.35	1.80	4″	.45	.94	1.40	1.87
6″	.48	1.31	1.96	2.62	6″	.51	1.36	2.04	2.72

MAN-HOURS INCLUDE THE FOLLOWING:

DISTRIBUTION FROM STOCKPILE 100′ DISTANCE
PIPE ENCASED IN STYROFOAM (BELOW GROUND)
UNPACKING PIPE SECTIONS (BELOW GROUND)
MEASURE AND CUT PIPE
INSTALL PIPE AND FITTING IN PLACE
MAKE UP CLAMP JOINTS
COVER FITTING WITH PLASTIC (BELOW GROUND)
NORMAL LOSS TIME
TESTING
UP TO 3′-0″ TRENCH DEPTH
UP TO 10′-0″ CEILING HEIGHT

EXCLUSIONS

EXCAVATION AND BACKFILL
DEWATERING
HANGERS AND SUPPORTS (BELOW AND ABOVE GROUND)
BREAKAGE
UNUSUAL JOB CONDITIONS

Means City Cost Indexes

The following pages contain examples of several different types of Means construction cost indexes for U.S. and Canadian locations. The Historical Cost Index is used to figure construction cost variations by year. The sample City Cost Index page contains the percentages to be used in adjusting installation and labor costs to any of 305 major city locations. The Installing Contractor's Overhead & Profit pages (union and open shop) show the labor rates for different trades according to an average of 30 major city rates. All of these cost pages represent relative costs as of July 1, 1998. Further information on utilizing these indexes may be found in Chapter 8.

The City Cost Indexes serve as factors that can be used to adjust national average costs to a particular location. If, for example, the estimator is pricing a plumbing job in Tampa, Florida, the material costs as shown in Division 15, Mechanical, are the same as the Means national average. The labor costs for plumbing installations in Tampa are 63.5% of the Means national average. The overall percentage factor (the "Total" column) is 83.7%. (The factor in the "Total" column should be used in instances where the costs are not broken down into Labor and Material, such as in square foot estimates.)

Historical Cost Indexes

The table below lists both the Means Historical Cost Index based on Jan. 1, 1993 = 100 as well as the computed value of an index based on Jan. 1, 1999 costs. Since the Jan. 1, 1999 figure is estimated, space is left to write in the actual index figures as they become available through either the quarterly "Means Construction Cost Indexes" or as printed in the "Engineering News-Record." To compute the actual index based on Jan. 1, 1999 = 100, divide the Historical Cost Index for a particular year by the actual Jan. 1, 1999 Construction Cost Index. Space has been left to advance the index figures as the year progresses.

Year	Historical Cost Index Jan. 1, 1993 = 100		Current Index Based on Jan. 1, 1999 = 100	
	Est.	Actual	Est.	Actual
Oct 1999				
July 1999				
April 1999				
Jan 1999	116.4		100.0	100.0
July 1998		115.1	98.9	
1997		112.8	96.9	
1996		110.2	94.7	
1995		107.6	92.4	
1994		104.4	89.7	
1993		101.7	87.4	
1992		99.4	85.4	
1991		96.8	83.2	
1990		94.3	81.0	
1989		92.1	79.2	
1988		89.9	77.2	
1987		87.7	75.3	
1986		84.2	72.4	
1985		82.6	71.0	

Year	Historical Cost Index Jan. 1, 1993 = 100	Current Index Based on Jan. 1, 1999 = 100	
	Actual	Est.	Actual
July 1984	82.0	70.4	
1983	80.2	68.9	
1982	76.1	65.4	
1981	70.0	60.1	
1980	62.9	54.0	
1979	57.8	49.7	
1978	53.5	46.0	
1977	49.5	42.5	
1976	46.9	40.3	
1975	44.8	38.5	
1974	41.4	35.6	
1973	37.7	32.4	
1972	34.8	29.9	
1971	32.1	27.6	
1970	28.7	24.7	
1969	26.9	23.1	
1968	24.9	21.4	
1967	23.5	20.2	

Year	Historical Cost Index Jan. 1, 1993 = 100	Current Index Based on Jan. 1, 1999 = 100	
	Actual	Est.	Actual
July 1966	22.7	19.5	
1965	21.7	18.6	
1964	21.2	18.2	
1963	20.7	17.8	
1962	20.2	17.4	
1961	19.8	17.0	
1960	19.7	16.9	
1959	19.3	16.6	
1958	18.8	16.2	
1957	18.4	15.8	
1956	17.6	15.1	
1955	16.6	14.3	
1954	16.0	13.7	
1953	15.8	13.6	
1952	15.4	13.2	
1951	15.0	12.9	
1950	13.7	11.8	
1949	13.3	11.4	

City Cost Indexes

	DIVISION	FLORIDA																	
		FORT MYERS			GAINESVILLE			JACKSONVILLE			LAKELAND			MELBOURNE			MIAMI		
		339			326			320,322			338			329			330 - 332,340		
		MAT.	INST.	TOTAL	MAT.	INST.	TOTAL	MAT.	INST.	TOTAL	MAT.	INST.	TOTAL	MAT.	INST.	TOTAL	MAT.	INST.	TOTAL
2	SITE WORK	121.1	87.2	95.0	135.2	86.9	98.0	123.8	88.0	96.2	123.2	86.9	95.3	132.0	87.5	97.8	108.0	73.9	81.8
031	CONCRETE FORMWORK	87.1	58.7	62.8	87.0	61.8	65.4	97.2	62.5	67.5	82.1	58.8	62.1	91.0	69.3	72.4	94.4	66.2	70.2
032	CONCRETE REINFORCEMENT	96.7	73.2	83.5	101.6	64.6	80.8	95.7	65.3	78.6	99.1	73.7	84.8	96.7	79.8	87.2	95.7	84.2	89.3
033	CAST IN PLACE CONCRETE	102.1	65.1	86.6	107.1	55.9	85.7	94.2	61.1	80.3	104.3	66.3	88.4	108.3	73.1	93.5	95.3	71.2	85.2
3	CONCRETE	91.8	65.4	78.5	99.2	61.9	80.4	89.2	64.1	76.6	93.3	65.8	79.5	98.2	73.9	86.0	89.6	72.8	81.1
4	MASONRY	79.1	53.6	63.3	96.5	50.3	67.8	84.3	60.2	69.3	90.1	62.6	73.0	79.8	69.6	73.5	81.1	67.3	72.5
5	METALS	100.8	89.9	96.9	97.0	85.9	93.0	98.9	87.3	94.7	100.5	89.7	96.6	107.2	93.1	102.1	99.2	95.2	97.8
6	WOOD & PLASTICS	86.1	58.8	72.0	87.5	63.2	75.0	95.1	63.2	78.7	80.5	58.8	69.3	88.1	70.0	78.7	89.7	67.6	78.3
7	THERMAL & MOISTURE PROTECTION	97.1	58.7	79.3	97.7	63.5	81.8	97.7	67.1	83.5	97.1	60.9	80.3	97.6	71.8	85.6	100.5	71.6	87.1
8	DOORS & WINDOWS	98.0	59.3	88.7	97.5	58.7	88.1	99.3	59.5	89.6	98.0	56.6	87.9	98.5	67.2	90.9	97.0	67.8	89.9
092	LATH, PLASTER & GYPSUM BOARD	105.7	58.0	74.9	105.9	62.6	77.9	109.8	62.6	79.3	103.3	58.0	74.1	106.2	69.6	82.6	109.3	67.1	82.1
095	ACOUSTICAL TREATMENT & WOOD FLOORING	96.0	58.0	71.4	94.7	62.6	73.9	100.2	62.6	75.8	94.7	58.0	70.9	96.0	69.6	78.9	100.2	67.1	78.7
096	FLOORING & CARPET	108.6	51.4	94.7	109.3	44.1	93.4	112.8	61.5	100.3	105.9	65.2	96.0	109.6	72.0	100.4	121.5	74.8	110.2
099	PAINTING & WALL COVERINGS	106.6	59.0	78.7	106.6	56.8	77.4	106.6	61.0	79.9	106.6	59.0	78.7	106.6	90.4	97.1	103.1	63.3	79.7
9	FINISHES	104.4	56.9	80.1	105.3	57.8	81.0	107.3	61.9	84.0	103.0	59.7	80.8	105.4	72.0	88.3	108.1	67.1	87.1
10 - 14	TOTAL DIV. 10 - 14	100.0	73.9	94.5	100.0	77.0	95.2	100.0	73.7	94.5	100.0	73.9	94.5	100.0	79.1	95.6	100.0	80.0	95.8
15	MECHANICAL	98.2	60.3	81.3	99.7	64.9	84.2	100.0	62.6	83.3	98.2	63.5	82.7	100.0	73.7	88.3	100.0	68.9	86.1
16	ELECTRICAL	99.5	51.9	67.4	96.4	53.8	67.6	95.4	68.8	77.5	96.3	60.2	72.0	95.6	67.4	76.6	96.4	81.5	86.3
1 - 16	WEIGHTED AVERAGE	98.2	64.2	81.8	100.0	64.6	82.9	98.6	68.6	84.1	98.5	67.3	83.5	100.6	75.1	88.3	98.0	74.3	86.6

	DIVISION	FLORIDA																	
		ORLANDO			PANAMA CITY			PENSACOLA			SARASOTA			ST. PETERSBURG			TALLAHASSEE		
		327 - 328,347			324			325			342			337			323		
		MAT.	INST.	TOTAL	MAT.	INST.	TOTAL	MAT.	INST.	TOTAL	MAT.	INST.	TOTAL	MAT.	INST.	TOTAL	MAT.	INST.	TOTAL
2	SITE WORK	124.3	87.2	95.8	139.5	85.0	97.6	136.9	87.3	98.7	125.3	87.0	95.8	124.6	87.0	95.7	125.2	86.7	95.5
031	CONCRETE FORMWORK	97.3	64.9	69.5	96.1	34.4	43.2	85.3	63.2	66.3	97.2	58.7	64.2	94.5	58.7	63.8	97.3	48.1	55.2
032	CONCRETE REINFORCEMENT	95.7	79.7	86.7	99.9	64.0	79.7	102.4	64.3	80.9	95.7	73.6	83.3	99.1	73.6	84.8	95.7	64.6	78.2
033	CAST IN PLACE CONCRETE	101.4	73.4	89.7	98.9	41.1	74.7	98.9	65.2	84.8	106.7	66.2	89.8	105.4	66.2	89.0	97.6	55.4	79.9
3	CONCRETE	92.8	72.1	82.3	97.1	44.1	70.4	95.9	65.7	80.6	95.4	65.8	80.4	95.0	65.8	80.3	90.9	55.8	73.2
4	MASONRY	82.2	70.5	75.0	88.7	35.0	55.4	86.4	63.2	72.0	86.1	62.6	71.5	124.4	62.6	86.0	87.1	49.1	63.5
5	METALS	108.4	92.7	102.8	97.6	72.9	88.7	97.5	86.9	93.7	102.3	89.6	97.7	101.3	89.6	97.1	99.2	85.6	94.3
6	WOOD & PLASTICS	95.1	64.0	79.1	93.7	34.6	63.2	81.9	64.1	72.7	95.1	58.8	76.4	91.9	58.8	74.8	95.1	46.5	70.1
7	THERMAL & MOISTURE PROTECTION	97.7	71.6	85.6	97.9	36.6	69.5	97.6	63.5	81.8	97.4	60.9	80.4	97.3	59.8	79.9	97.8	55.6	78.3
8	DOORS & WINDOWS	99.3	63.1	90.5	97.0	32.4	81.4	97.0	61.0	88.3	99.3	55.9	88.7	98.0	56.4	87.9	99.3	49.7	87.2
092	LATH, PLASTER & GYPSUM BOARD	109.8	63.4	79.9	108.0	33.1	59.6	103.8	63.5	77.8	109.8	58.0	76.4	107.5	58.0	75.6	109.8	45.4	68.2
095	ACOUSTICAL TREATMENT & WOOD FLOORING	100.2	63.4	76.4	94.7	33.1	54.8	94.7	63.5	74.5	100.2	58.0	72.9	94.7	58.0	70.9	100.2	45.4	64.7
096	FLOORING & CARPET	112.8	72.0	102.8	112.1	23.6	90.6	106.6	65.4	96.6	112.8	64.9	101.1	111.3	65.2	100.1	112.8	47.8	97.0
099	PAINTING & WALL COVERINGS	106.6	70.1	85.2	106.6	31.2	62.4	106.6	70.9	85.7	106.6	59.0	78.7	106.6	59.0	78.7	106.6	50.2	73.5
9	FINISHES	107.3	66.5	86.3	106.9	31.5	68.2	104.3	64.4	83.9	107.3	59.7	82.9	105.4	59.7	82.0	107.4	47.5	76.7
10 - 14	TOTAL DIV. 10 - 14	100.0	78.7	95.5	100.0	59.3	91.4	100.0	66.3	92.9	100.0	73.8	94.5	100.0	69.5	93.6	100.0	71.3	94.0
15	MECHANICAL	100.0	65.4	84.5	100.0	32.0	69.7	100.0	63.6	83.8	99.9	61.0	82.5	100.0	63.5	83.7	100.0	50.6	78.0
16	ELECTRICAL	96.5	57.2	70.0	94.1	42.8	59.5	99.5	64.1	75.6	95.9	47.0	62.9	96.3	61.8	73.1	96.5	53.0	67.1
1 - 16	WEIGHTED AVERAGE	100.4	70.6	86.1	99.6	45.6	73.5	99.2	68.5	84.4	100.0	64.6	82.9	101.5	67.5	85.1	99.1	58.6	79.6

	DIVISION	FLORIDA						GEORGIA											
		TAMPA			WEST PALM BEACH			ALBANY			ATHENS			ATLANTA			AUGUSTA		
		335 - 336,346			334,349			317			306			300 - 303,399			308 - 309		
		MAT.	INST.	TOTAL	MAT.	INST.	TOTAL	MAT.	INST.	TOTAL	MAT.	INST.	TOTAL	MAT.	INST.	TOTAL	MAT.	INST.	TOTAL
2	SITE WORK	124.9	87.0	95.8	105.4	74.0	81.2	108.9	75.9	83.5	119.2	91.4	97.8	113.8	93.3	98.0	109.6	91.8	95.9
031	CONCRETE FORMWORK	98.9	58.8	64.6	97.2	65.5	70.1	96.9	52.3	58.7	89.4	46.4	52.5	98.3	75.5	78.8	94.9	63.3	67.8
032	CONCRETE REINFORCEMENT	95.7	73.7	83.3	98.3	65.3	79.7	95.7	88.4	91.6	105.9	84.8	94.0	102.0	89.7	95.1	107.8	73.3	88.3
033	CAST IN PLACE CONCRETE	103.2	66.3	87.7	93.0	67.7	82.4	99.6	49.2	78.5	103.8	51.4	81.9	103.8	71.6	90.3	98.1	57.7	81.2
3	CONCRETE	93.8	65.8	79.7	88.1	67.8	77.9	91.8	59.8	75.6	100.8	56.2	78.3	98.4	76.9	87.6	94.6	63.6	79.0
4	MASONRY	86.0	62.6	71.4	85.0	59.6	69.2	87.2	39.9	57.8	74.0	56.8	63.3	89.5	68.5	76.4	89.6	50.4	65.2
5	METALS	102.2	89.7	97.7	97.5	88.4	94.2	96.6	92.3	95.1	91.9	76.0	86.2	93.6	80.0	88.7	92.3	71.9	84.9
6	WOOD & PLASTICS	96.9	58.8	77.2	94.4	67.6	80.6	94.4	52.9	73.0	93.4	45.4	68.6	98.6	77.7	87.8	95.0	66.3	80.2
7	THERMAL & MOISTURE PROTECTION	97.6	60.9	80.6	97.1	67.2	83.2	97.5	57.8	79.1	94.4	54.2	75.7	94.5	74.4	85.2	93.9	60.1	78.2
8	DOORS & WINDOWS	99.3	55.7	88.7	96.2	62.9	88.1	97.0	57.0	87.3	92.3	52.7	82.7	95.8	75.5	90.9	92.4	61.2	84.8
092	LATH, PLASTER & GYPSUM BOARD	109.8	58.0	76.4	109.9	67.1	82.3	109.8	52.0	72.5	117.9	44.2	70.3	119.5	77.4	92.4	118.4	65.7	84.4
095	ACOUSTICAL TREATMENT & WOOD FLOORING	100.2	58.0	72.9	96.0	67.1	77.3	100.2	52.0	68.9	106.1	44.2	66.0	106.1	77.4	87.5	106.1	65.7	79.9
096	FLOORING & CARPET	112.8	65.2	101.2	115.4	62.6	102.5	112.8	39.9	95.0	84.3	71.9	81.3	85.9	76.1	83.6	84.8	50.8	76.6
099	PAINTING & WALL COVERINGS	106.6	59.0	78.7	103.1	58.5	76.9	103.1	50.3	72.1	93.9	41.9	63.4	93.9	78.2	84.7	93.9	47.8	66.8
9	FINISHES	107.3	59.7	82.9	105.2	64.0	84.1	105.3	48.8	76.4	93.5	49.8	71.1	93.8	76.0	84.7	93.1	59.5	75.9
10 - 14	TOTAL DIV. 10 - 14	100.0	73.9	94.5	100.0	79.9	95.8	100.0	74.8	94.7	100.0	63.1	92.2	100.0	81.7	96.1	100.0	74.0	94.5
15	MECHANICAL	100.0	63.5	83.7	98.2	69.0	85.2	100.0	56.1	80.4	96.8	54.4	77.9	100.1	77.9	90.2	100.1	53.3	79.2
16	ELECTRICAL	95.4	61.8	72.8	95.9	66.8	76.3	90.0	65.9	73.7	94.7	81.4	85.7	93.6	84.2	87.3	95.7	58.3	70.5
1 - 16	WEIGHTED AVERAGE	99.8	67.6	84.2	96.8	69.2	83.5	97.4	61.6	80.1	95.1	64.5	80.3	96.9	79.3	88.4	95.7	62.7	79.8

Installing Contractor's Overhead & Profit (Union Rates)

Below are the **average** installing contractor's percentage mark-ups applied to base labor rates to arrive at typical billing rates.

Column A: Labor rates are based on union wages averaged for 30 major U.S. cities. Base rates including fringe benefits are listed hourly and daily. These figures are the sum of the wage rate and employer-paid fringe benefits such as vacation pay, employer-paid health and welfare costs, pension costs, plus appropriate training and industry advancement funds costs.

Column B: Workers' Compensation rates are the national average of state rates established for each trade.

Column C: Column C lists average fixed overhead figures for all trades. Included are Federal and State Unemployment costs set at 7.0%; Social Security Taxes (FICA) set at 7.65%; Builder's Risk Insurance costs set at 0.34%; and Public Liability costs set at 1.55%. All the percentages except those for Social Security Taxes vary from state to state as well as from company to company.

Columns D and E: Percentages in Columns D and E are based on the presumption that the installing contractor has annual billing of $1,500,000 and up. Overhead percentages may increase with smaller annual billing. The overhead percentages for any given contractor may vary greatly and depend on a number of factors, such as the contractor's annual volume, engineering and logistical support costs, and staff requirements. The figures for overhead and profit will also vary depending on the type of job, the job location, and the prevailing economic conditions. All factors should be examined very carefully for each job.

Column F: Column F lists the total of Columns B, C, D, and E.

Column G: Column G is Column A (hourly base labor rate) multiplied by the percentage in Column F (O&P percentage).

Column H: Column H is the total of Column A (hourly base labor rate) plus Column G (Total O&P).

Column I: Column I is Column H multiplied by eight hours.

		A		B	C	D	E	F	G	H	I
		Base Rate Incl. Fringes		Workers' Comp. Ins.	Average Fixed Overhead	Overhead	Profit	Total Overhead & Profit		Rate with O & P	
Abbr.	Trade	Hourly	Daily					%	Amount	Hourly	Daily
Skwk	Skilled Workers Average (35 trades)	$28.05	$224.40	18.3%	16.5%	13.0%	10%	57.8%	$16.20	$44.25	$354.00
	Helpers Average (5 trades)	20.85	166.80	19.7		11.0		57.2	11.95	32.80	262.40
	Foreman Average, Inside ($.50 over trade)	28.55	228.40	18.3		13.0		57.8	16.50	45.05	360.40
	Foreman Average, Outside ($2.00 over trade)	30.05	240.40	18.3		13.0		57.8	17.35	47.40	379.20
Clab	Common Building Laborers	21.45	171.60	19.9		11.0		57.4	12.30	33.75	270.00
Asbe	Asbestos/Insulation Workers/Pipe Coverers	30.45	243.60	18.9		16.0		61.4	18.70	49.15	393.20
Boil	Boilermakers	32.85	262.80	16.6		16.0		59.1	19.40	52.25	418.00
Bric	Bricklayers	27.60	220.80	18.0		11.0		55.5	15.30	42.90	343.20
Brhe	Bricklayer Helpers	21.60	172.80	18.0		11.0		55.5	12.00	33.60	268.80
Carp	Carpenters	27.30	218.40	19.9		11.0		57.4	15.65	42.95	343.60
Cefi	Cement Finishers	26.15	209.20	11.7		11.0		49.2	12.85	39.00	312.00
Elec	Electricians	31.90	255.20	7.0		16.0		49.5	15.80	47.70	381.60
Elev	Elevator Constructors	33.15	265.20	8.9		16.0		51.4	17.05	50.20	401.60
Eqhv	Equipment Operators, Crane or Shovel	29.35	234.80	11.6		14.0		52.1	15.30	44.65	357.20
Eqmd	Equipment Operators, Medium Equipment	28.40	227.20	11.6		14.0		52.1	14.80	43.20	345.60
Eqlt	Equipment Operators, Light Equipment	27.20	217.60	11.6		14.0		52.1	14.15	41.35	330.80
Eqol	Equipment Operators, Oilers	24.05	192.40	11.6		14.0		52.1	12.55	36.60	292.80
Eqmm	Equipment Operators, Master Mechanics	30.05	240.40	11.6		14.0		52.1	15.65	45.70	365.60
Glaz	Glaziers	26.60	212.80	14.7		11.0		52.2	13.90	40.50	324.00
Lath	Lathers	26.80	214.40	12.4		11.0		49.9	13.35	40.15	321.20
Marb	Marble Setters	27.50	220.00	18.0		11.0		55.5	15.25	42.75	342.00
Mill	Millwrights	28.75	230.00	11.9		11.0		49.4	14.20	42.95	343.60
Mstz	Mosaic & Terrazzo Workers	26.55	212.40	10.3		11.0		47.8	12.70	39.25	314.00
Pord	Painters, Ordinary	24.90	199.20	15.6		11.0		53.1	13.20	38.10	304.80
Psst	Painters, Structural Steel	26.00	208.00	51.6		11.0		89.1	23.15	49.15	393.20
Pape	Paper Hangers	25.10	200.80	15.6		11.0		53.1	13.35	38.45	307.60
Pile	Pile Drivers	27.20	217.60	30.3		16.0		72.8	19.80	47.00	376.00
Plas	Plasterers	25.70	205.60	15.8		11.0		53.3	13.70	39.40	315.20
Plah	Plasterer Helpers	21.60	172.80	15.8		11.0		53.3	11.50	33.10	264.80
Plum	Plumbers	32.60	260.80	9.0		16.0		51.5	16.80	49.40	395.20
Rodm	Rodmen (Reinforcing)	30.40	243.20	32.6		14.0		73.1	22.20	52.60	420.80
Rofc	Roofers, Composition	24.10	192.80	34.6		11.0		72.1	17.40	41.50	332.00
Rots	Roofers, Tile & Slate	24.20	193.60	34.6		11.0		72.1	17.45	41.65	333.20
Rohe	Roofers, Helpers (Composition)	18.10	144.80	34.6		11.0		72.1	13.05	31.15	249.20
Shee	Sheet Metal Workers	31.75	254.00	12.8		16.0		55.3	17.55	49.30	394.40
Spri	Sprinkler Installers	32.50	260.00	9.1		16.0		51.6	16.75	49.25	394.00
Stpi	Steamfitters or Pipefitters	32.75	262.00	9.0		16.0		51.5	16.85	49.60	396.80
Ston	Stone Masons	27.70	221.60	18.0		11.0		55.5	15.35	43.05	344.40
Sswk	Structural Steel Workers	30.60	244.80	42.8		14.0		83.3	25.50	56.10	448.80
Tilf	Tile Layers	26.65	213.20	10.3		11.0		47.8	12.75	39.40	315.20
Tilh	Tile Layers Helpers	21.45	171.60	10.3		11.0		47.8	10.25	31.70	253.60
Trlt	Truck Drivers, Light	21.75	174.00	15.6		11.0		53.1	11.55	33.30	266.40
Trhv	Truck Drivers, Heavy	22.10	176.80	15.6		11.0		53.1	11.75	33.85	270.80
Sswl	Welders, Structural Steel	30.60	244.80	42.8		14.0		83.3	25.50	56.10	448.80
Wrck	*Wrecking	21.45	171.60	42.5		11.0		80.0	17.15	38.60	308.80

* Not included in averages

Installing Contractor's Overhead & Profit (Open Shop Rates)

Below are the **average** installing contractor's percentage mark-ups applied to base labor rates to arrive at typical billing rates.

Column A: Labor rates are based on average open shop wages for 7 major U.S. regions. Base rates including fringe benefits are listed hourly and daily. These figures are the sum of the wage rate and employer-paid fringe benefits such as vacation pay, and employer-paid health costs.

Column B: Workers' Compensation rates are the national average of state rates established for each trade.

Column C: Column C lists average fixed overhead figures for all trades. Included are Federal and State Unemployment costs set at 7.0%; Social Security Taxes (FICA) set at 7.65%; Builder's Risk Insurance costs set at 0.34%; and Public Liability costs set at 1.55%. All the percentages except those for Social Security Taxes vary from state to state as well as from company to company.

Columns D and E: Percentages in Columns D and E are based on the presumption that the installing contractor has annual billing of $1,000,000 and up. Overhead percentages may increase with smaller annual billing. The overhead percentages for any given contractor may vary greatly and depend on a number of factors, such as the contractor's annual volume, engineering and logistical support costs, and staff requirements. The figures for overhead and profit will also vary depending on the type of job, the job location, and the prevailing economic conditions. All factors should be examined very carefully for each job.

Column F: Column F lists the total of Columns B, C, D, and E.

Column G: Column G is Column A (hourly base labor rate) multiplied by the percentage in Column F (O&P percentage).

Column H: Column H is the total of Column A (hourly base labor rate) plus Column G (Total O&P).

Column I: Column I is Column H multiplied by eight hours.

		A		B	C	D	E	F	G	H	I
		Base Rate Incl. Fringes		Workers' Comp. Ins.	Average Fixed Overhead	Overhead	Profit	Total Overhead & Profit		Rate with O & P	
Abbr.	Trade	Hourly	Daily					%	Amount	Hourly	Daily
Skwk	Skilled Workers Average (35 trades)	$19.25	$154.00	18.3%	16.5%	27.0%	10%	71.8%	$13.80	$33.05	$264.40
	Helpers Average (5 trades)	14.35	114.80	19.7		25.0		71.2	10.20	24.55	196.40
	Foreman Average, Inside ($.50 over trade)	19.75	158.00	18.3		27.0		71.8	14.20	33.95	271.60
	Foreman Average, Outside ($2.00 over trade)	21.25	170.00	18.3		27.0		71.8	15.25	36.50	292.00
Clab	Common Building Laborers	13.95	111.60	19.9		25.0		71.4	9.95	23.90	191.20
Asbe	Asbestos/Insulation Workers/Pipe Coverers	20.10	160.80	18.9		30.0		75.4	15.15	35.25	282.00
Boil	Boilermakers	21.70	173.60	16.6		30.0		73.1	15.85	37.55	300.40
Bric	Bricklayers	19.30	154.40	18.0		25.0		69.5	13.40	32.70	261.60
Brhe	Bricklayer Helpers	15.10	120.80	18.0		25.0		69.5	10.50	25.60	204.80
Carp	Carpenters	19.10	152.80	19.9		25.0		71.4	13.65	32.75	262.00
Cefi	Cement Finishers	18.30	146.40	11.7		25.0		63.2	11.55	29.85	238.80
Elec	Electricians	21.35	170.80	7.0		30.0		63.5	13.55	34.90	279.20
Elev	Elevator Constructors	22.20	177.60	8.9		30.0		65.4	14.50	36.70	293.60
Eqhv	Equipment Operators, Crane or Shovel	20.25	162.00	11.6		28.0		66.1	13.40	33.65	269.20
Eqmd	Equipment Operators, Medium Equipment	19.60	156.80	11.6		28.0		66.1	12.95	32.55	260.40
Eqlt	Equipment Operators, Light Equipment	18.75	150.00	11.6		28.0		66.1	12.40	31.15	249.20
Eqol	Equipment Operators, Oilers	16.60	132.80	11.6		28.0		66.1	10.95	27.55	220.40
Eqmm	Equipment Operators, Master Mechanics	20.75	166.00	11.6		28.0		66.1	13.70	34.45	275.60
Glaz	Glaziers	18.90	151.20	14.7		25.0		66.2	12.50	31.40	251.20
Lath	Lathers	18.75	150.00	12.4		25.0		63.9	12.00	30.75	246.00
Marb	Marble Setters	19.25	154.00	18.0		25.0		69.5	13.40	32.65	261.20
Mill	Millwrights	20.15	161.20	11.9		25.0		63.4	12.80	32.95	263.60
Mstz	Mosaic & Terrazzo Workers	18.60	148.80	10.3		25.0		61.8	11.50	30.10	240.80
Pord	Painters, Ordinary	17.70	141.60	15.6		25.0		67.1	11.90	29.60	236.80
Psst	Painters, Structural Steel	18.45	147.60	51.6		25.0		103.1	19.00	37.45	299.60
Pape	Paper Hangers	17.80	142.40	15.6		25.0		67.1	11.95	29.75	238.00
Pile	Pile Drivers	19.05	152.40	30.3		30.0		86.8	16.55	35.60	284.80
Plas	Plasterers	18.00	144.00	15.8		25.0		67.3	12.10	30.10	240.80
Plah	Plasterer Helpers	15.10	120.80	15.8		25.0		67.3	10.15	25.25	202.00
Plum	Plumbers	21.50	172.00	9.0		30.0		65.5	14.10	35.60	284.80
Rodm	Rodmen (Reinforcing)	20.35	162.80	32.6		28.0		87.1	17.70	38.05	304.40
Rofc	Roofers, Composition	16.65	133.20	34.6		25.0		86.1	14.35	31.00	248.00
Rots	Roofers, Tile & Slate	16.70	133.60	34.6		25.0		86.1	14.40	31.10	248.80
Rohe	Roofers, Helpers (Composition)	12.50	100.00	34.6		25.0		86.1	10.75	23.25	186.00
Shee	Sheet Metal Workers	20.95	167.60	12.8		30.0		69.3	14.50	35.45	283.60
Spri	Sprinkler Installers	21.45	171.60	9.1		30.0		65.6	14.05	35.50	284.00
Stpi	Steamfitters or Pipefitters	21.60	172.80	9.0		30.0		65.5	14.15	35.75	286.00
Ston	Stone Masons	18.85	150.80	18.0		25.0		69.5	13.10	31.95	255.60
Sswk	Structural Steel Workers	20.50	164.00	42.8		28.0		97.3	19.95	40.45	323.60
Tilf	Tile Layers	18.65	149.20	10.3		25.0		61.8	11.55	30.20	241.60
Tilh	Tile Layers Helpers	15.00	120.00	10.3		25.0		61.8	9.25	24.25	194.00
Trlt	Truck Drivers, Light	15.45	123.60	15.6		25.0		67.1	10.35	25.80	206.40
Trhv	Truck Drivers, Heavy	15.70	125.60	15.6		25.0		67.1	10.55	26.25	210.00
Sswl	Welders, Structural Steel	20.50	164.00	42.8		28.0		97.3	19.95	40.45	323.60
Wrck	*Wrecking	14.35	114.80	42.5		25.0		94.0	13.50	27.85	222.80

* Not included in averages

Means Open Shop Cost Data

Codes and Standards

AMERICAN NATIONAL STANDARDS INSTITUTE (ANSI)
11 West 42nd Street
New York, NY 10036
Telephone: (212) 642-4900
www.ansi.org

BUILDING OFFICIALS AND CODE ADMINISTRATORS
INTERNATIONAL INC. (BOCA)
4051 WEST FLOSSMOOR ROAD
Country Club Hills, IL 60478
Telephone: (708) 799-2300
www.bocai.org

INTERNATIONAL ASSOCIATION OF PLUMBING AND
MECHANICAL OFFICIALS (IAPMO)
2001 East Walnut Drive South
Walnut, CA 91789
Telephone: (909) 595-8449
www.iapmo.org

INTERNATIONAL CONFERENCE OF BUILDING OFFICIALS (ICBO)
5360 Workman Mill Road
Whittier, CA 90601
Telephone: (562) 699-0541
www.icbo.org

PLUMBING - HEATING - COOLING - CONTRACTORS ASSOCIATION (PHCC)
180 S. Washington Street
P.O. Box 6808
Falls Church, VA 22040-6808
Telephone: (800) 533-7694
www.naphcc.org

NATIONAL FIRE PROTECTION ASSOCIATION (NFPA)
1 Batterymarch Park
P.O. Box 9101
Quincy, MA 02269-9101
Telephone: (617) 770-3000
www.nfpa.org

AMERICAN SOCIETY OF MECHANICAL ENGINEERS (ASME)
Three Park Avenue
New York, NY 10016-5990
Telephone: (212) 591-7722
www.asme.org

SOUTHERN BUILDING CODE CONGRESS INTERNATIONAL, INC. (SBCCI)
900 Montclair Road
Birmingham, AL 35213-1206
Telephone: (205) 591-1853
www.sbcci.org

Price Guides

MEANS PLUMBING COST DATA
R. S. Means Company, Inc.
Construction Plaza
P.O. Box 800
Kingston, MA 02364
Telephone: 800-334-3509
www.rsmeans.com

THE BRADFORD PRICE BOOK
for the Plumbing and Heating Trades
Harrison Publishing House Incorporated
P.O. Box 320
995 Industrial Park Road
Littleton, NH 03561-0320
Telephone: 800-890-0820
www.hphguide.com

NATIONAL MECHANICAL CONTRACTOR ESTIMATOR
Harrison Publishing House Incorporated
P.O. Box 320
995 Industrial Park Road
Littleton, NH 03561-0320
Telephone: 800-890-0820
www.hphguide.com

NATIONAL PLUMBING & HVAC ESTIMATOR
Craftsman Book Company
6058 Corte del Cedro
Carlsbad, CA 92009
Telephone: 800-829-8123
www.craftsman-book.com

Abbreviations

A
Area

Ab
Above

Abs
Absolute

ACP
Asbestos cement pipe

AD
Area drain

AFF
Above finished floor

AGA
American Gas Association

AISI
American Iron and Steel Institute

Al
Aluminum

ANSI
American National Standards Institute

API
American Petroleum Institute

ASA
American Standard Association

ASCE
American Society of Civil Engineering

ASHRAE
American Society of Heating, Refrigerating and Air Conditioning Engineers

ASME
American Society of Mechanical Engineers

ASPE
American Society of Plumbing Engineers

ASSE
American Society of Sanitary Engineers

ASTM
American Society for Testing and Materials

AV
Acid vent

Avg
Average

AW
Acid waste

AWWA
American Water Works Association

B&S
Bell and spigot

Bbl
Barrel

BCF
Backfill

BOCA
Building Officials and Code Administrators

BOD
Biochemical oxygen demand

Br
Branch

BT
Bathtub

BTU
British thermal unit

BV
Balancing valve

C
Centigrade

°C
Degrees centigrade

C to C
Center to center

CA
Compressed air

CB
Catch basin

CF
Cubic feet

Cfm
Cubic feet per minute

Chk. V.
Check valve

CI
Cast iron or cubic inches

Circ.
Circulator/Circulation

CISP
Cast iron soil pipe

CISPI
Cast Iron Soil Pipe Institute

CIWP
Cast iron water pipe

Cl
Chlorine

CL el
Centerline elevation

Clg
Ceiling

CO
Cleanout

CODP
Cleanout deck plate

CS
Cast steel (or commercial standard)

CTE
Connection to existing

Cu
Copper

CW
Cold water

CY
Cubic yard

D
Drain

Deg or °
Degrees

DF
Drinking fountain

DI
Ductile iron/drain inlet

Dn
Down

Dp
Deep

Drg
Drainage

Dwg
Drawing

DWV
Drainage waste and vent

ED
Sewage ejector discharge

Elev.
Elevation

Ell
Elbow

EWC
Electric water cooler

EWF
Eye wash fountain

ES
Emergency shower

Exc
Excavation

F
Fahrenheit

°F
Degrees Fahrenheit

FAI
Fresh air intake

FD
Floor drain

FDV
Fire department valve

Fe
Iron

Fed Spec
Federal specification

FF
Finish floor

FG
Finish grade

FH
Fire hydrant

FHC
Fire hose cabinet

FHR
Fire hose rack

Fig
Figure

Fixt
Fixture

Flr
Floor

FP
Fire plug

FS
Floor sink

FSP
Fire standpipe

FU
Fixture unit

G
Gas

Ga
Gauge

Gal
Gallon (231 CI)

Galv
Galvanized

Gas
Gallons

GC
Gas cock

Gl V
Globe valve

GPD
Gallons per day

GPH
Gallons per hour

GPM
Gallons per minute

GT
Grease trap

GV
Gate valve

H
Hydrogen or handicapped

HB
Hose bibb

HClg
Hung ceiling

Hd
Head

HD
House drain

Hgr
Hanger

HP
Horsepower

Hr
Hour

HT
House trap

Htr
Heater

HW
Hot water

IAPMO
International Association of Plumbing and Mechanical Officials

IB
Iron body

ICBO
International Conference of Building Officials

ID
Inside diameter

IE
Invert elevation

In
Inch

IPS
Iron pipe size

Jt
Joint

kW
Kilowatt

L or Ldr
Leader

L or Lth
Length

Lav
Lavatory

Lb
Pound

LF
Linear feet

Mal
Malleable

Mat
Material

Max
Maximum

MCAA
Mechanical Contractors Association of America

Mech
Mechanical

MER
Mechanical equipment room

Mfr
Manufacturer

MGD
Million gallons per day

MH
Manhole

MI
Malleable iron

Min
Minimum (or minute)

MS
Milled steel

N^2
Nitrogen

N^2O
Nitrous oxide

NAPHCC
National Association of Plumbing, Heating and Cooling Contractors

NBFU
National Board of Fire Underwriters

NBS
National Bureau of Standards

NFPA
National Fire Protection Association

NH
No hub

NPS
Nominal pipe size (Also called IPS)

NTS
Not to scale

O^2
Oxygen

OD
Outside diameter

Oz
Ounce

P
Pump

P&T
Pressure and temperature

Pb
Lead

PD
Pump discharge

PDI
Plumbing and Drainage Institute

PG
Pressure gauge

pH
Hydrogen concentration

PIV
Post indicator valve

PO
Plugged outlet

Ppm
Parts per million

Press
Pressure

PRV
Pressure reducing valve

PSI
Pounds per square inch

PVC
Polyvinylchloride

Qt
Quart

Qty
Quantity

R
Hydraulic radius

Rad
Radius

RCP
Reinforced concrete pipe

RD
Rate of demand (or roof drain)

Red
Reducer

RT
Running trap

RV
Relief valve

S
Soil

S&W
Soil and waste

SA
Shock absorber

San
Sanitary

Sb
Antimony

SBCC
Southern Building Code Congress

SC
Sillcock

SE
Sewage ejector

Sec
Second

SF
Square foot

Shwr
Shower

SI
Square inches

Siam. Conn.
Siamese Connection

Sk
Sink

Sn
Tin

Sol
Solder/Solenoid

Sp
Sprinkler

SP
Sump Pump

Spec
Specification

SS
Service sink (slop sink)

St
Storm

Std
Standard

Str
Strainer

Sv
Service

SW
Service weight

T
Temperature (or time)

TD
Trench drain

Therm
Thermometer

Thrd
Threaded

TP
Threadless pipe

UL
Underwriters' Laboratories, Inc.

Ur
Urinal

USASI
USA Standards Institute

V
Vent

Vac
Vacuum

Val
Valve

VB
Vacuum breaker

VCP
Vitrified clay pipe

Vel
Velocity

VIV
Valve in vertical

Vol
Volume

VTR
Vent through roof

W
Waste

WC
Water closet

WClr
Water cooler

Wgt
Weight

WH
Wall hydrant

WL
Water level

WPOA
Western Plumbing Officials Association

XH
Extra heavy

XHCI
Extra heavy cast iron

GLOSSARY

GLOSSARY

Absorption
This term applies to immersion in a fluid for a definite period of time. It is usually expressed as a percent of the weight of the dry pipe.

Addendum
Any change in the drawings or specifications made by the architect or engineer, prior to bid.

Air break
A piping arrangement in which a drain from a fixture appliance or device discharges through an open connection into a receptacle or interceptor at a point above the flood level rim of the receptacle. Also known as an air gap.

Air compressor
The manufactured item of equipment which compresses air so that its expansion may be utilized as a source of power.

Anaerobic
Bacteria living without air.

Anchor
An anchor is usually pieces of metal used to fasten or secure pipes to the building or structure.

Area of circle
To find the area of a circle, multiply the square of the radius by pi. Area $= \pi r^2$

Backfill
That portion of the trench excavation which is replaced after the sewer line has been laid is called the backfill. It is the material above the pipe up to the original earth line.

Backflow
The flow of water or other liquids, mixtures or substances into the distributing pipes of a potable supply of water from any source or sources other than its intended source. Reversal of flow.

Backflow preventer
This is a device or assembly designed to prevent backflow into the potable water system.

Back-siphonage
The flowing back of used, contaminated or polluted water from a plumbing fixture or vessel into a water supply system due to a negative pressure in such pipe.

Back vent
An individual vent pipe connected directly into the back of the fixture waste fittings.

Base
The lowest portion or lowest point of a stack of vertical pipe.

Battery of fixtures
Any group of two or more similar adjacent fixtures that discharge into a common horizontal waste or soil branch.

Bell and spigot
A particular type of pipe joint where the spigot or straight end fits into the bell or flared end and is made tight with lead or rubber gaskets.

Below grade
Work below ground level.

Bid
A proposal by a contractor to perform work for a given sum of money.

Branch
The part of a piping system other than the main riser or stack that extends to fixtures on one or two consecutive floors.

Branch vent
A vent connecting one or more individual vents with a vent stack or stack vent.

Building gravity drainage system
A drainage system that drains by gravity into the building house sewer.

Carrier fitting
A manufactured support for a plumbing fixture that is also an integral part of the soil piping system.

Caulking
Caulking is the operation or method of rendering a joint tight against water or gas by means of plastic substances such as lead and oakum.

Circuit vent
A vent containing a separate vent stack which may or may not extend through the roof independently of the stack vent.

Circumference of a circle
To find the perimeter or circumference of a circle, multiply the diameter of the circle by pi. Circumference = πD

Cleanout
A manufactured fitting with a plug end which can be opened to service soil lines that have become clogged.

Color code
The color choices made by an estimator to readily identify piping systems on drawings.

Common vent
A vent connecting at the junction of two fixtures and drains and serving as a vent for both fixtures and drains.

Compression
Stress which resists the tendency of two forces acting toward each other.

Conductor
A conductor is that part of the vertical piping which carries the water from the roof to the storm drain, which starts either 6" above grade if outside the building, or at the roof sump or gutter if inside the building.

Continuous vent
A vertical vent that is a continuation of the drain to which it connects.

Cross connection
A cross connection or inter-connection is any physical connection between a city water supply and any waste pipe, soil pipe, sewer, drain, or any private or uncertified water supply. Furthermore, it is any potable water supply outlet which is submerged or can be submerged in waste water and/or any other source of contamination.

Crude or raw sewage
The terminology applies to untreated sewage.

Dead end
A dead end is a branch leading from any soil, waste or vent pipe, building drain, or building sewer, which is terminated at a developed distance of two (2) feet or more by means of a cap, plug or other fitting not used for admitting water or air to the pipe, except branches serving as cleanout extensions.

Developed length
The length along the center line of pipe and fittings, both horizontal and vertical.

Diameter
Unless specifically stated, the term diameter is the nominal diameter as designed commercially.

Direct cost
The cost of a project prior to the addition of any supplementary costs, such as overhead and profit.

Discount
The percentage deduction from a material's list price afforded the contractor.

Drain
Any pipe that carries waste water or water-borne wastes in a building drainage system.

Drains, combined
The combined drain is that portion of the drainage system within a building which carries storm water and sanitary sewage.

Drains, storm
Storm drains are part of the horizontal piping and its branches which convert subsoil and/or surface drainage from areas, courts, roof, or yards to the building or storm sewer.

Drains, subsoil
The subsoil drain is that part of the drainage system which conveys the subsoil, ground or seepage water from the footings of walls, or from under buildings, to the building drain, storm water drain, or building sewer.

Drainage system
Includes all the piping within public or private premises which conveys sewage, rain water, or other liquid wastes to a legal point of disposal.

Dry well
A covered pit constructed to allow the liquid contents to seep into the ground.

Ejector
A mechanical device used to eject or pump sewage.

Erosion
The gradual destruction of metal or other material by the abrasive action of liquids, gases, solids, or mixtures of these materials.

Escutcheon
Chrome-plated ring used to cover a penetration in a wall where pipe is passing through it.

Estimate
An approximate judgement regarding the dollar value of a project.

Estimate form
The form on which all quantities are entered in order that they may be priced.

Excavation
The operation of removing earth for the purpose of installing underground piping.

Fire hose cabinet
The cabinet containing fire hose and a fire department valve, connected to the fire standpipe system.

Fire hydrant
The water supply device on a site used for fire fighting purposes.

Fire line
A system of pipes used exclusively to supply water for extinguishing fires.

Fitting
A manufactured device used to connect pipe.

Fixture branch
A water supply pipe connecting one or more fixtures to the main water supply header or riser.

Fixture unit
A fixture unit is that amount of fixture discharge equivalent to seven and one-half (7-1/2) gallons or more, one (1) cubic foot of water per minute.

Fixtures, battery of
A battery of fixtures is an integral unit such as a kitchen sink and a laundry unit.

Fixtures, plumbing
Plumbing fixtures are installed receptacles, devices or appliances which are supplied with water, or which receive liquids and/or discharge liquids, or liquid-borne wastes, either directly or indirectly into the drainage system.

Flood level rim
The flood level rim is the top edge of the receptacle from which water overflows.

Floor drain
A device installed to receive liquid wastes collecting on a floor and to discharge them into the sanitary system.

Fixture supply
A water supply pipe connecting the fixture with the fixture branch.

Flush valve
A device that discharges a predetermined quantity of water to fixtures for flushing purposes and is activated by direct water pressure.

Fresh air inlet pipe
A pipe connected to the building house drain immediately upstream from the house trap to prevent air lock between the fixture trap and the main trap. It also supplies the whole building drainage system with a circulation of fresh air.

Gas meter
The device used to measure gas consumption in a building.

Gas regulator
The device used to regulate gas pressure in a building.

Hubless joint
A type of pipe joint used on no hub cast-iron soil pipe, requiring clamps.

Indirect waste
A drain pipe used to convey liquid wastes that does not connect directly to the drainage system but which discharges into the house drainage system through an air break into a trap, fixture, receptacle, or interceptor.

Interceptor
A device designed to separate and retain harmful, hazardous, or undesirable matter from normal wastes and permit normal sewage or liquid wastes to discharge into the disposal terminal by gravity.

Labor
The physical operation of installing items.

Labor wage rate
The prevailing hourly pay for a worker.

Leader
A vertical drainage pipe for conveying storm water from roof or gutter drains to the building storm drain.

Low bid
The lowest dollar proposal by a contractor to perform work.

Main
The principal artery or arteries of a piping system to which all branches, risers, and runouts are connected.

Manhole
A device constructed of brick or pre-cast concrete used to service site sewer lines and additionally used as a junction point between two sewer lines.

Man-hour
The unit of time required to install an item.

Master plumber
The master plumber's license grants him the authority to install and to assume responsibility for contractual agreements pertaining to plumbing and to secure any required permits. The journeyman plumber properly licensed is allowed to stall plumbing only under the supervision of a master plumber.

Material
The item or items on a project requiring installation.

Medical gas outlet
The device used to gain access to medical gases.

Neutralizing basin
The device used to neutralize acid-bearing wastes before their entry into the building drainage system.

Offset
An offset in a line of piping is a combination of pipe, pipes and/or fittings which join two approximately parallel sections of the line of pipe.

Outfall sewers
Are those receiving the sewage from the collection system and carrying it to the point of final discharge or treatment. It is usually the largest sewer of the entire system.

Overhead
Business operating expenses of a contractor.

Pipe, horizontal
This is any pipe or part thereof which is installed in a horizontal position or which makes an angle of less than 45° with the horizontal.

Pipe supports
The manufactured devices used to support piping from ceilings, walls, floors, or other structural members.

Pipes, water service
The water service pipe is that portion of the water piping which supplies one or more structures or premises and which extends from the public or private main in the street, alley, or easement to the meter or, if no meter is to be provided, to the first stop cock or valve inside the premises.

Pitch
The item pitch is used to indicate the amount of slope or grade given to horizontal piping and is expressed in inches of vertically projected drop per foot on a horizontally projected run of pipe.

Plumbing code
The minimum legal standards set forth by municipalities for the installation of plumbing work.

Plumbing inspector
A plumbing inspector is any person who, under the supervision of the authority having jurisdiction, is authorized to inspect plumbing and drainage as defined in the code for the municipality, and complying with the laws of licensing and/or registration of the state, city, or county.

Potable water
Water free from impurities present in amounts sufficient to cause disease or harmful physiological effects.

Pricing
The physical operation of costing out an estimate.

Profit
Amount of money due the contractor directly for performing work.

Revent
A revent pipe is that part of a vent pipe line which connects directly with any individual waste or group of wastes, underneath or back of the fixture, and extends either to the main or branch vent pipe.

Riser
A pipe extending floor to floor.

Roof drain
A device installed to receive water collecting on the surface of a roof and to discharge it into the leader.

Roughing
The soil, waste, vent, and water piping immediately behind the fixtures and connected to either the waste and vent stacks or branches, or water risers or branches.

Sanitary sewer
A pipe that carries sewage and excludes storm, surface and ground water.

Scale
A device used to measure scaled drawings. The appropriate reduced dimensions on a drawing.

Septic tank
A receptacle which receives the discharge of a drainage system or part thereof, and is designed and so constructed to separate the solids from the liquid, digest the organic matter through a period of detention, and allow the liquids to discharge into the soil outside of the tank through a system of open-joint or perforated piping, or into a disposal pit.

Sewage
Any liquid waste containing animal or vegetable matter in suspension or solution.

Sewer connection
The physical operation of connecting a sewer on the site.

Sheeting and shoring
The physical operation of bracing earth on trench walls with planks to prevent cave-in.

Sitework
That portion of outside work beginning from a point five feet past the building wall.

Sludge
The accumulated suspended solids of sewage deposited in tanks, beds or basins, mixed with more or less water to form a semi-liquid mass.

Soil pipe
A pipe that conveys sewage containing fecal matter.

Sovent
A special copper D.W.V. fitting that eliminates the need for a vent stack, through a process of aeration and de-aeration.

Specifications
The standards set forth by the design engineer regarding quality of materials and nature of workmanship for a project.

Stack
Any vertical line of soil, waste, vent or inside leader piping.

Stack venting
A method of venting a fixture or fixtures through the soil or waste stack.

Storm sewer
A sewer used for conveying rain water, surface water, condensate, cooling water, or similar clear liquid wastes.

Strain
Change of shape or size of a body produced by the action of stress.

Stress
When external forces act on a body they are resisted by reactions within the body which are called stresses.

Subsoil drain
A drain which receives only subsurface or seepage water and conveys it to a place of disposal.

Summary sheet
The form an estimator uses to summarize a project, indicating all supplementary costs such as overhead and profit.

Sump pump
A mechanical device used to eject liquid waste from a sump pit into the gravity drainage system.

Takeoff
To physically measure and list items shown on drawings.

Takeoff sheets
The sheets used to record quantities while a project is being taken off.

Tension
That stress which resists the tendency of two forces acting away from each other to pull apart two adjoining planes of a body.

Trade price sheet
The published price sheet issued to contractors by manufacturers.

Trap
A waste fitting which provides a liquid seal.

Trap seal
The maximum vertical depth of liquid that a trap will retain, measured between the crown weir and the top of the dip of the trap.

Turbulence
Any deviation from parallel flow in a pipe due to rough inner wall surfaces, obstructions or directional changes.

Vacuum
Vacuum is any pressure less than that exerted by the atmosphere and may be termed a negative pressure.

Vacuum pump
The item of equipment in which a partial vacuum can be produced; used on hospital vacuum systems.

Valve
A device used to control the flow of liquids and gases.

Velocity
Time rate of motion in a given direction and sense.

Vent, loop
A loop vent is a vent from a single fixture or battery of fixtures which is connected into the same stack into which the fixtures discharge. If the loop vent serves more than one fixture, it is one type of circuit vent.

Vent, wet
A wet vent is a vent which receives the discharge of wastes other than from water closets.

Vent, yoke
This is a pipe connecting upward from a soil or waste stack to a vent stack for the purpose of preventing pressure changes in the stacks.

Vent stack
A vent stack is a vertical vent pipe installed primarily for the purpose of providing circulation of air to and from any part of the drainage system. A vent stack or main vent is that part of a venting system to which circuit vents are connected. Branch vents, revents or individual vents may be lead to and connected with a vent stack. The foot of the vent stack may be connected either into a horizontal drainage branch or into a soil or waste stack.

Vent system
Pipe or piping installed to provide a flow of air to or from a drainage system.

Waste pipe
A pipe that conveys only liquid wastes, free of fecal matter.

Water heater
The manufactured item of equipment which generates hot water.

Water meter
The device used to measure water consumption in a building.

Water pipe
Piping that conveys water to the plumbing fixtures and other water outlets.

INDEX

D

E

F

G

Q

R

S

Z